Philosophies of Transformative Practice

Philosophies of Transformative Practice

Social Movements in India

Papers Presented at the 43rd Annual Research Seminar of ACPI held at the Socio-Religious Centre (SRC), Kozhikode, Kerala 20-23 October, 2018

Edited by

Jose D. Maliekal

Association of Christian Philosophers of India

&

Christian World Imprints

ACPI Annual Philosophy Series No. 20

Series Editors: Keith D'Souza, Sekar Sebastian & Kurian Alumkal

First Published in 2019 by

Association of Christian Philosophers of India
through The Secretary, ACPI
Vijnananilayam, Janampet, Vijayarai PO
Eluru-534475, West Godavari Dt., A.P.
sekarsebastin@gmail.com
Ph: +91 9952327856
&
Christian World Imprints
Christian Publishing & Books from India
C-3, Shop No. 14, Ground Floor
Wazirpur Industrial Area, **Delhi-110052**
cwidelhi2017@gmail.com
www.ChristianWorldImprints.com
Phone: +91 11 41526079

ISBN: 978-93-5148-389-2 (HB)
ISBN: 978-93-5148-390-8 (PB)

Printed in India.

Contents

Editorial

Recently, the World Bank has decided to pull out of the $300 million lending to the Amaravati Capital City project in Andhra Pradesh. The Working Group on International Financial Institutions (WGonIFIs) and the affected communities of the Amaravati Capital City Project have welcomed the decision, saying the project was being implemented without taking into account, the threat to people's livelihood. The Bank arrived at this decision after a series of representations it received from many people's movements and civil society organizations over the past years, and a complaint to its accountability mechanism, Inspection Panel, by the affected communities. Medha Patkar, the senior activist of *Narmada Bachao Andolan* (NBA) and the National Alliance of People's Movements (NAPM), India's top human rights network expressed her view over this development. "We are happy that the World Bank took cognisance of the gross violations involved in the Amaravati Capital City project, threatening the livelihood of people and fragile environment. After Narmada and Tata Mundra, this is the third major victory against the World Bank Group... While we celebrate this victory of the people, who stood up to the intimidation and terror of the state, we warn the government and financial institutions not to push their agenda without the consent of the people."[1]

Travesty of justice happens where there is lack of solidarity between human beings. Solidarity is the new name for justice. The culture of globalisation and liberalisation function by turning individuals, into monads. By depoliticising, globalisation tries to break the solidarity among the people, from which new avatars of injustice proceed. In this scenario, the fostering of solidarity assumes greater importance. To create this solidarity among the peoples and to create social transformations, Gustavo Esteva rightly suggests

---

1 Rajkaran Bureau, "World Bank pulls out of Amaravati Capital City Project: Major Victory to People, activists say," *Rajkaran* (July 20, 2019), accessed July 22, 2019, https://rajkaran.com/world-bank-pulls-out-of-amaravati-capital-city-project-major-victory-to-people-activists-say/.

that one need to "*regenerate people's space.*"[2] Regenerating people's space means building up participation and democracy from bottom up, by activating the public realm, through social movements and civil society, and by creating public opinion, through which one can dream of a transformative society, relived with justice and solidarity.

In this context, the challenge posed by Meda Patkar, against intimidation and terror of the state, and the warning to the financial institutions against pushing their agenda without the consent of the people is a strong expression of solidarity with the people. It is this spirit of solidarity, and the fearlessness to speak truth to power, which should be the hallmark of a social movement. So also of the philosophers, who wish to journey with the people. As Johnson Puthenpurackal, one of the contributors, to this volume succinctly puts it, in his article, entitled, "*From the Ideal to the Real: A Shift in Philosophizing,*" 'In the twentieth century, more than before, humans were confronted with the concrete experience of their unique life situations, which were not considered to be worthy of philosophical reflections, in the traditional philosophy of the ideal realm. As humans were caught up in the trap of their naked existence, and found no way to escape from their concrete naked life situations, a shift in philosophizing was necessitated—a shift from the ideal to the real! Such a shift took place not by chance, but by necessity! This change is concretely seen in many areas, such as in philosophical themes, in philosophizing style, in the label of being philosophers, in the mode of philosophical communication, etc. Philosophizing has become more earthly and contextual!' Philosophy's turn to practice has made it a more credible and useful exercise.

The desire of the members of the Association of the Christian Philosophers of India (ACPI), to become catalysts in the process of developing **Indian Christian Philosophies of Liberation**, with concrete historical contents and impacts, arose as a response to this shift in philosophizing. Philosophy of Liberation,[3] as it is widely known to us today, emerged first in Argentina in 1960s, and later spread to the other parts of the world. "Philosophy of Liberation" stands for a movement and method of philosophizing, in view of responding to limiting and dehumanizing factors and situations in the socio-economic, cultural, political and religious realms of human life. "Philosophy, when it is philosophy and not sophistry or ideology, does not ponder philosophy. [...] Philosophy ponders the nonphilosophical; the reality."[4]

During the Annual Research Seminar held at Socio-Religious Centre (SRC), Kozhikode, between 20-23 October, 2018, many of the participants

---

2 Gustavo Esteva, "Regenerating People's Space," *Alternatives*, 12, no. 1 (1987), 125-152.

3 Enrique Dussel, *Philosophy of Liberation* (Maryknoll, New York: ORBIS Books, 1985).

4 Dussel, *Philosophy of Liberation,* 3.

presented their philosophical reflections, around the theme, "**Philosophies of Transformative Practice: Social Movements in India**". Social Movements, in their liberative and practical thrust, were the *loci* of the discussions, the interlocutors and conversation partners, during the seminar.

A social movement is a collective, loosely organized, and yet sustained campaign and activity to achieve a tangible social change. There is no single, standard typology of social movements. Scholars have classified social movements in reference to their different dimensions. In reference to the nature of the desired change, social movements are generally classified as revolutionary, reformist, reactionary, conservative, etc. It can be argued that some of the most important political changes in the 19th and 20th centuries were brought about by the actions of social movements. Powerful examples are the Civil Rights Movement in the United States, the Green Movement, and the Women's Movements, but one could also think about organizations aimed at promoting Gay rights or the protest against authoritarian regimes in Central and Eastern Europe in the 1980s. Social Movements, therefore, are usually identified with contentious politics: They try to bring about political change by challenging the political elite. As such, they give voice to those who have been excluded from the political system.[5] As Dr Babu Thomas rightly reminded us, during his keynote address at the seminar, people's Movements resist all tendencies to fundamentalism and fascism, and make the Indian Constitution, a living constitution, constituting the Constitution, an ongoing task, in action, giving it ever new life.

The Papers presented in this seminar have been gathered under three clusters. The first cluster is titled as, "Towards an Archaeology of Social Movements." Under it, we have all the contributions, of a Foundational nature, not of course, in the static sense, but in the Foucauldian sense of archaeology. The second cluster is titled as "Towards a Genealogy of the Social Movements," and is genealogical in nature, enquiring into the dialectical factors, which lie beneath the events/the insurrection of knowledge(s), which trigger the origin and the trajectory of social movements. Following these two clusters, which, more or less, deal with the theoretical part, we have the third cluster, entitled "Praxis: Programmatic and Pragmatic." It is programmatic and pragmatic, in thrust and orientation. The contributions in it, critically assess the significant social movements in India, bringing into relief, their vision(s) and strategies, with an eye, to the future, yet, grounded in the emerging socio-economic, cultural and political scenario, at the national and the global level.

---

5 Cfr Marc Hooghe, "Social Movements," in *21st Century Political Science. A Reference Handbook, Vol. I.*, eds, John Ishiyama and Marijke Breuning (Thousand Oaks: Sage, 2011), 225-232.

Towards an Archaeology of Social Movements

Johnson Puthenpurackal's, "From the Ideal to the Real: A Shift in Philosophizing," the first of the articles, appearing under the archaeological cluster, plays the role of being a philosophical launching pad, for the task. The author makes a methodological and operative distinction between Philosophy and Philosophizing, as a dynamic and dialectical process, and deploys it as a hermeneutical tool, to engage himself in a *tour de force* of Western Philosophy. He reaches the conclusion that after the not so rigorous approach of the Presocratics, the trio of Socrates, Plato and Aristotle, led the art of Philosophizing to realms of rigour, but as a tryst with the *Ideal*. A shift happened with the daring pioneers, in the persons of Nietzsche and Heidegger, who brought down the art of philosophizing, from the realm of the *ideal*, to the *real*. **Keith D'Souza,** in the next article, entitled, "Liberation Philosophy: Wisdom, Power and Care Within Transformative Social Practice," in his characteristic, gentle style of philosophizing, calls for a Liberative Philosophy. According to D'Souza, "liberation philosophy" needs to be governed by three primary values: wisdom, power and care, all of them, in mutual interaction and complementarity. Beyond the dystopian, utopian and the myopic, which are limited in scope, and at times, even harmful, and selective, in the target group, D'Souza outlines the kaleidoscopic form of social practice, deemed salutary, with features like simplicity, practicality, creativity, flexibility, dynamism, and joy.

Kuruvilla Pandikattu, in his article, "The Rise and Fall of Social Movements" approaches the Life Cycle of the social movements, with the heuristic key from the historian Arnold Toynbee, that "Civilizations die from suicide, not by murder." Deploying this heuristic insight, Pandikattu after analyzing the significant role of Social Movements, explores their life cycle, in their four stages: Emergence, Coalescence, Formalisation and Decline. It is the author's view that Arnold Toynbee's analysis of the decline of civilizations can only be partially applied to social movements. An insider's view of the social movements is communicated to us, by **Anthony Dias**, through his contribution, entitled, "Nature and Scope of Social Movements in Democratic Societies," through a grounded analysis of the three renowned Social Movements of India, namely, *Narmada Bachao Andolan* (NBA), the *Bandhua Mukti Morcha* (BMM) and the *Mazdoor Kisan Shakti Sangathan* (MKSS). He highlights the way, NBA challenged the reigning Development models, BMM, through advocacy and Public Interest Litigation (PIL) attempted eradicating bonded labour, and led the campaign for the National Minimum Wage, and how the MKKSS intervened towards People Empowerment, via 'non-party politics.' **Ashley Miranda**, in "Building Capacities and Enhancing Freedoms: Movements that foster Social Development," engages himself in a perceptive analysis of the inner workings of the social movements, in their trajectories of growth and evolution, and reaches the sage conclusion that the goal of every social movement must always be to create a culture, where people are empowered to believe in their own potential to be agents of the change they want to see in their lives. Through his finely argued paper, entitled, "Towards a Biblical Philosophy of Liberation," **Martin Kallungal**, establishes that a philosophy that prefers periphery to the centre, a philosophy that has liberated itself from various ideological dominations and the idolatry of the text, will be a philosophy of liberation. And the Bible should drive its readers to the peripheries.

Towards a Genealogy of Social Movements

The first among the genealogical cluster of papers is **Victor Ferrao's,** "Productive Semiotics of Social Movements." True to its title and the dynamic communicative style of the author, the paper challenges us to a new semiotics, in our case, of social movements. The study attempts to seek a relation of transpositions between the film theory of Deleuze and the social movements, and thus opens the doors for a productive semiotics. In the next article, "Religious Beliefs and Practice: The Philosophical Treatment after Wittgenstein," **Jose Nandhikkara** claims that philosophical investigations took a decisive 'linguistic turn' in twentieth century, examining the nature of human languages and its relation to human existence and nature. Nandhikkara suggests that this linguistic turn, was in fact a 'praxis turn'. **Nishant A. Irudayadason**, through his timely, analytical and programmatic contribution, entitled, "Critical Theory and the Youth Movements of the Sixties: A privileged and Complex Relationship" delves into the genealogical relationship between theory and practice, between intellectual development and social movements, enquiring into the chequered history of the difficult and complex relationship between Critical Theory of Frankfurt School and the Youth Movements of the 1960s. The paper ends on a programmatic note, calling upon the intellectuals, to sustain the Youth Movements of India, in today's context, by working out theories of social revolution, braving the present political climate.

Jojo Varakukalayil's article, "'Not without Difference': Re-visiting Emmanuel Levinas on Racism," once again, has strong programmatic overtones. The core-argument of the work is that the ordinary understanding of race and the development of its meaning, through a racialist's appropriation of it is malevolent. The author attempts at a deconstruction of the essentialist logic of race, a-la Emmanuel Levinas, to assert with him, that racism is a denial of the otherness of the other. The author concludes that the global situation of migration of people to different countries in search of work and living, make the earth one of living, beyond the borders, but not without differences.

This has implications for India, which is a multicultural and multi-religious nation. In "Royce's Beloved Community: An Antidote to Globalizing India," **Francis Aykaraparampil** presents the vision of the Beloved Community, as enshrined in the philosophical thought of Josiah Royce. The ideal of the Beloved Community, according to Aykkaraparampil, is a "Philosophy of Transformative Practice," challenging the philosophers, to live up to their serious responsibility of being catalysts of transformation, and inviting them to be members of the Beloved Community in this globalized and globalizing world, and globalizing India.

Praxis: Programmatic and Pragmatic

First in this cluster, is the contribution of **Ivan D'Souza**, entitled, "*Śaraṇa* Movement: A Revolution for the New Society." The study is historical in nature, delving into the countercultural origin and the egalitarian impact of the *Śaraṇa* Movement. Ivan has dynamically portrayed the vicissitudes of the *Liṅgāyatis* and indicated the historical justification, why they should be considered a separate religion, different from the mainline Hinduism, as well as *Vīraśaivism,* both of which are attempting to subsume it, to serve their vested interests. **Biju Pallipadan's** panoramic presentation, entitled "*Bhakti* Movements in Contemporary Religions," ventures into giving us a bird's-eye view of the numerous *Bhakti* Movements, which had emerged in Medieval India, from Vaishnavism, Sufism, to the Movements initiated by Kabir and Guru Nanak, as well as the world of contemporary Gurus and the Christian Movements. Pallipadan explores the subversive origin of the *Bhakti* Movements and their contribution to vernacular cultures and languages. **Lawrence Pius**, a Gandhian Scholar, through his well-researched article, "Gandhian Movement for Liberation in India," presents us with new insights into the unique way in which Gandhi empowered women, respecting their agency, primarily, and giving space for it, in his own Movements. In the concluding section, Pius also hints at some ambiguities, in Gandhi's approach to women, from a feminist perspective.

Gregory Malayil's "The Chipko Movement and its Aftermath: A Few Reflections Based on Environmental Philosophy" is a window to the genealogy of the emergence of the Chipko Movement, and its evolution as an icon of national conscience and consciousness, in the area of environmental consciousness. It also presents the movement as an experiment in women's participation and partnership in the development process. The paper also interrogates the anthropocentrism, prevalent in Environmental Philosophy, and throws light on our moral obligation, as ecological/environmental citizens and the need of ecological conversion. "Alternative Media Movement" penned by **Francis Arackal Thummy** is enlightening in more ways than one. The author, who is both a philosopher and a media expert, presents the philosophy of social movements, and how the New Social Movements have made use of the Alternative Media, especially after the arrival of the Internet, as the world witnessed in the case of Arab Spring, protest against the WTO and the mobilization of logistics and aid, during the recent floods in Kerala. "From Sudra to Servanthood: Reimagining Education in India" by **Jose D. Maliekal** is an attempt at interrogating the process of the educative imagination of the nation, under the throes of Neo-Liberalization, as to its "Social Movement" orientation. Concretely, the task is undertaken through a socio-political audit of the Christian engagement in the ministry of education, calling for a shift of keys in this engagement, from being a *Sudra* (traditional service-providing caste), to *Servanthood* (capable of evoking a consciousness and praxis of service for the downtrodden). The audit weaves itself into a counter-narrative and a reimagination of education as a common good, socially and politically conscious, capable of building a culture of partnership, constitutional morality and dissent, and valorization of indigenous knowledge(s).

James Ponniah, in his research, "The Emerging Phenomena of Contemporary Inter-Faith Harmony Movements in Urban India" undertakes an empirically grounded study of the three religious organizations, namely, Sri Vishnu Mohan Foundation - SVMF (Hindu), Islamic Foundation Trust Chennai - IFT (Muslim) and Institute of Dialogue with Cultures and Religions - IDCR (Christian), to explore how inter-religious harmony in the city of Chennai is promoted by these organizations. His discovery is that moving beyond the idea of cultivating religious tolerance through formal inter-religious dialogue, inter-faith peace Movements in Urban Chennai focus on celebrating religious differences that are already present and deeply rooted in Indian societies, braving the growing campaigns of religious bigotry and religious fundamentalism. What is novel about the study is that it deploys two theoretical tools, namely social capital and religious capital. **Jose Pennaparambil** in "The Pro-Life Movement-A Transformative Movement of Society" presents the Pro-Life Movement as a movement for life, challenging whatever is opposed to life and the integrity of the human person. The author attempts at a philosophical analysis of "Culture of Life" Vs " Culture of Death," especially bringing into relief, the powerful cultural, economic and political currents, which support the culture of death, for their own vested interests. "Science-Religion Dialogue as a Movement: The Need of the Hour to Transform Society" is a lucidly written essay by **S. Stephen Jayard**, exploring the possibilities of making the dialogue between science and religion, into a popular social movement, beyond the academia. Science and Religion are two powerful enterprises of humanity. When we bring them together for healthy interaction and integration, not only science and religion get enriched but also humanity grows to be holistic. Among several common platforms between science and religion, the author focuses on just one important notion of 'life.'

George Panthanmackel, in his well-documented paper, entitled, "*Agapocracy*: A New Response to the Ideological Foundation of the RSS Movement," traces the trajectory of the growth of RSS, as a movement, in three phases, from 1925 to 1940, 1940 to 1973, and 1973 to 1994. Following upon this, he examines the ideology of Hindutva and Nationalism, of various hues, which have nurtured the RSS. In his critique of the RSS ideology, Panthanmackel is of the view that it is not an inclusive ideology, rather the opposite, which will not be able to hold India together. Rather, it will lead to the destruction of the greatness of Hinduism, and in turn, of India itself. He proposes *Agapocracy*, an inclusive transcendence of democracy, which will enhance the fundamental values of the Indian constitution, as an alternative to the exclusive and destructive ideology of the RSS. **Sujan Amurutham**, in his paper, "Communist Movement in India: Democracy Implications," undertakes a social-movement audit of the Left Movement in India. According to Amurutham, Left Political parties, as a movement, became very much like any other political party, after Independence. The paper evaluates, how the Left Parties were struggling to cope up with running their governments within the framework of a democratic country. It also analyzes how they lagged behind in meeting the new challenges put forward by new social and cultural Movements in the country, lacking a progressive and inclusive approach. A critique of their errors in praxis, as well as theorizing, is attempted, with the framework of insights from Amartya Sen, as a toolkit.

Towards a Forward Thrust

Holistic philosophizing of 'Transformative Practice' will necessarily give rise to 'Social Movements'(with *hand*), that are the concrete expressions of what one knows (with *head*) and what one is convinced of (with *heart*), of a kaleidoscopic nature, beyond the myopic, dystopic and the merely utopian, refusing to be co-opted. A social movement, which addresses the real issues of people, will be striving for deepening the grassroots democracy and overcoming democratic deficit, especially during these times of rising majoritarian, cultural and religious nationalism, with overtones of fascism. Human development is about adding value to human life rather than seeking to just further economic growth under the mistaken assumption that this will automatically translate into greater well-being for all. Any movement towards the Other, to the periphery, is not a contamination, but a virtue, a celebration of community, of identities, with differences, an *Agapocracy*, where science and religion, join hands to empower peoples. We have to reorient the educative processes of our nation, towards a critical, political consciousness for democracy, dissent and partnership.

As Karl Marx, famously and programmatically stated in his *Eleventh Thesis on Feurbach*, "Hitherto, the philosophers have been interpreting the world, the task, however, is to change it." This engaging ourselves, as memebrs of the ACPI, in the task of elabourating the Philosophies of Transformative Practice, in dialogue with the Social Movements of different hues and shades and praxis-horizons, have surely placed us in the Deleuzean Desire/Movement mode, towards action, towards networking with religions and all the agencies, in a praxis-turn. The process urges us towards working for peace and transformation. It also facilitates the emergence of non-NGOized social movements, as Arundhati Roy called for, while commenting on the massive victory of Bharatiya Janata Party, on May 23, 2019. She stated, that the victory was the predictable outcome of the power-money-clinically precise and organized propaganda machine of the Sangh Parivar. Instead, she dreams of the emergence of non-NGOized social movements that, will have the new energy and the new kind of opposition that cannot be tamed.[6]

In a similar vein, Yogendra Yadav, genealogically analyzed the intentions and the reasons of the people, by which they voted BJP back to power, as well as the causes, at the macro-level, which enabled BJP to win the elections. His insightful analysis was that there is still space and need for politics, even in the seemingly monolithic majoritarian and seemingly invincible space, occupied by the *Sanghparivar*, to the near-exclusion of all the other political parties. Mr Yadav's rationale for a New Politics, Post-May 23, 2019, is our need to get back to the people, not in an elitist vein, but in a listening and participatory-movement mood and mode of mutuality. If the *Sanghparivar* juggernaut has money, muscle and media, the alternative democratic movement of the people, has the Kabir-Guru Nanak dialogical religious tradition, egalitarian, empowering, republican impulse of Ambedkar, and the bottom-up democratic inspiration of Mahatma Gandhi.[7]

It is hoped that this volume, which has gathered the liberative dreams and the aspirations of the ACPI, will be a catalytic, symbolic and organic contribution, towards, this Post May 23, 2019 New Political Movement of the Peoples of India. It will be towards their idea of India, where differences are

---

6 Arundhati Roy in Interview with Samuel Earle, "Arundhati Roy on India's Elections: "A Mockery of What Democracy Is Supposed to Be," *The New Republic*, May 28, 2019, accessed June 21, 2019, https://newrepublic.com/article/154011/arundhati-roy-indias-elections-a-mockery-democracy-supposed-be.

7 Yogendra Yadav, "How India Voted: Making Sense of the 2019 General Election - Yogendra Yadav," *The Print*, accessed June 21, 2019, https://youtu.be/dQPgoW6sdHc.

celebrated, and where, as for Nehru, democracy is akin to a political culture, where a hundred opinions could bloom.[8]

Thanks...

As I conclude, I would like to express my deep-seated gratitude to all the contributors to this volume, interactions with whom, have been an enriching experience, apart from the intellectual stimulation and inspiration, I received, by reading through and editing their thought-provoking contributions. Thanks also for their immense and admirable patience, in reshaping and fine-tuning their papers several times over. My special thanks are due to the executive committee of the ACPI, for having entrusted me with the task of editing this volume on philosophizing on the social movements. I am especially indebted to Dr Keith D'Souza, the President of the ACPI, for his solicitude and fraternal guidance, able assistance, and his judicious facilitations, through the entire process of editing, till this volume saw the light of day. The timely help of Bro P.V. Joseph, the Assistant of St John's Regional Seminary, Kondadaba and his team of seminarians, E. Pavan, P. Obez and K. Bala, whose meticulous team work, in rationalizing and streamlining the methodological style of this volume, did indeed lighten my burden. The typographical assistance by Mr. Ch. Sairam is acknowledged, with friendly gratitude. We are specially thankful to John Sylvester, for his imaginative and symbolically rich cover design. Finally, I thank Mr. Sudhanshu Kanda and his publishing team at the Christian World Imprints, our co-publishers, for their touch of professionalism, displayed in bringing out this volume.

May this volume inspire its readers, towards networking with others in social movements and civil society, along the trajectory of a New Politics, in the times ahead, and may it provoke us into the task of ever questioning the majoritarian agendas, which domesticate the democratic and the transformative impulses.

8 Manash Firaq Bhattacharjee, "The Danger of Territorial Nationalism," *The Hindu*, June 18, 2019, 8.

Chief Guest's Address

Rt Rev. Dr Varghese Chakkalakal
(Bishop of Calicut)

First and foremost, I extend to all of you the members of the Association of Christian Philosophers of India (ACPI) a warm welcome to Calicut. This is the Malabar coastal region and the third largest city in Kerala. Having great cultural traditions and jargon of its own, the city is a major trading center for spices and tiles and sometimes known as the 'land of spices'. The city found its place in world history when Portuguese navigator Vasco Da Gama discovered this as a sea route to India in 1498. Calicut is considered as the paradise of tasty foods and Biriyanis. Have a good stay and I wish that your visit may remain as a memorable one.

I appreciate the organizers for selecting a very relevant theme for the 43rd Annual Research Seminar of ACPI: "Philosophies of Transformative Practice: Social Movements in India." Congratulations to you. It is relevant because we are in the season of Movements and we hear the echo of its consequences either positive or negative. '# Me too' is the most recent one culminating in the list of several religious, social, tribal and secular Movements. The time has come to explore into these transformations philosophically. I am sure that such a move will enrich us with convincing answers to many questions regarding social, religious, political and cultural life in this Postmodern world. Awareness is a key ingredient in success. Quoting the words of Joybell (She is an author of several philosophical books) "I think we are like stars. Something happens to burst us open; but when we burst open and think we are dying; we are actually turning into a supernova. And then when we look at ourselves again, we see that we are suddenly more beautiful than we ever were before." My wish for you is that you may experience this beauty of life in these days through an intellectual movement of analyzing the social movements in India in three levels.

1. A Move Towards a Comprehensive Approach

The first move is towards a comprehensive approach. Who does not like a panoramic view of the realities? People have certain ways of focusing on things and some arrange their lens to a pinhole in order to focus only on their goal but a philosopher tries to use a giant lens because he aims at a comprehensive and panoramic view of all the components of the reality. As we analyse the social movements of India through a philosophical eye of the transformative practices, let us aim at this comprehensive approach. Many try to define the term *Transformative Practice* through their ideologies and experiences. Some define "transformative practice" as an approach in organizing and movement building strategies that provide a daily way to embody the change we hope to see within ourselves, our organizations and our society. At the root, transformative practices are a doorway to creating the kind of world we all want to live in. Such a definition focuses on a comprehensive approach. Wide-ranging transformation can only happen simultaneously through the body and the mind, particularly in fight for justice. Transformation itself implies a depth and fundamental shift in thinking, form or being that is different than "change". Because, of this there is an "undoing" that needs to happen in order to make room for something new to emerge. This undoing can happen in crisis, but it can also be facilitated by an intentionally transformative practice. Hence, our thirst to know the ideal and the real must be oriented towards the comprehensive and integrated view of all the transformative practices because they are exercises designed to create, through repetition, intentional shifts in awareness, patterns of thinking, and habits of action. A comprehensive approach makes us rich for we understand ourselves. Jiddu Krishnamurthy said that "if you begin to understand what you are without trying to change it, then what you are undergoes a transformation." Hence philosophy of Transformative Practice actually transforms the philosopher, the lover of wisdom.

2. A Move towards Scrutinization

The second move is towards an act of Scrutinization, a critical examining. Though Scrutinization looks to be negatively shaped, it really aims at the good result and best output. It is an art of examining. 'The unexamined life is not worth living' is a famous dictum apparently uttered by Socrates at his trial for impiety and corrupting youth. A critical approach towards the social movements is the need of the hour.

Studying social movements means focusing on at least some of the dimensions, most importantly, on how ideas, individuals, events, and organizations are linked to each other in broader processes of collective action, with some continuity over time. Given their complex, multidimensional nature, it is no surprise that social movements may be approached in reference to very diverse intellectual questions. Every philosopher is called to scrutinize the reality. Investigative mind is the treasure of a philosopher. In the words of the Angelic doctor St Thomas Aquinas, "Three things are necessary for the salvation of man: to know what he ought to believe; to know what he ought to desire; and to know what he ought to do." The intellectual searches into the dominating forces behind the social movements are to be scrutinized because that would make the life of humanity better. We are in the opportune time to analyze the philosophies behind the transformative practice for better tomorrow. The papers that are going to be presented here surely will scrutinize the ideologies behind every social movement and help us in adapting the right ones matching with the integrated growth of each individual and society intended by Christ and his Gospel.

3. A Move towards a Truth-Oriented Culture

The third way is a move towards the truth oriented culture. Aristotle highlighted the importance of truth in his life by saying "Plato is dear to me but dearer still is the truth." All of us are called to embrace the truth but for such an act we need to be genuine within. Social Movements are originated in a space to speak the truth in public without the fear of oppressive power of the external. But, the questions arise from the facts we see in and around. Are the social movements of India formed to aim at the truth? Do they hold on to the strategies and ideologies that uphold truth? Today, the study of social movements is solidly established, with specialized journals, book series, and professional associations. They analyze the relationship between structural change and transformations in patterns of social conflict. These studies examine the process through which values, interests, and ideas get turned into collective action. The practical life experiences report to us about the sad picture of missing the truth oriented culture in many of these Movements. Hidden agendas, false ideologies and selfish motives dominate the planning and formation of many social movements. Such facts should never make us discouraged and disappointed. A social movement is a combination of shared ideas and activities that are concerned with changing the patterns of social life. The world is undergoing deep, dramatic transformations - even a revolution. A question needs to be reflected in such researches. Can we be the harbingers of truth in life? As true Christians we need to proclaim Jesus Christ who said that 'I am the Way, the Truth and the Life (John 14:6). It is a hard and narrow way. Archbishop Fulton J. Sheen says, "It is easy to find the truth, though it is hard to face it and harder still to follow it." I am sure that the philosophers are formed or trained to take such an adventurous move even though the road is narrow and hard. All the wishes and prayers for you.

Let me conclude, I wish and pray that you may hold on to a comprehensive approach, scrutinize all the social movements and promote truth oriented culture in this annual research seminar. As Paulo Coelho says, "the secret of life, though, is to fall seven times and to get up eight times." A philosopher can get up not only eight times but more than that. May you come out with much success and satisfaction in all your discussions and presentations. I take this auspicious opportunity to thank you very sincerely for having invited me. With the sentiments of esteem and joy, I declare this 43rd Annual Research Seminar of the ACPI as officially inaugurated. May God bless you. Thank you.

Part 1

Towards an Archaeology of Social Movements

1

From the Ideal to the Real: A Shift in Philosophizing

Johnson J. Puthenpurackal, OFMCap
Vijnananilayam, Institute of Philosophy and Religion, Janampeta, Eluru

Abstract: This paper is intended to give a philosophical basis to the main theme of the ACPI Research Seminar "Philosophies of Transformative Practice: Social Movements in India." After giving an introductory clarification of the key-terms, the paper looks at the way in which philosophizing has been confined to the realm of the ideal for the last two millennia. The Pre-Socratic thought was found to be lacking in philosophical rigour, and hence philosophy was made to be logically clear and conceptually precise, dealing with the abstract realm. The victorious march of philosophy with the ideal realm slowly came to a stop in the twentieth century through the instrumentality of mainly Nietzsche and Heidegger. The need was generally felt that philosophy should start dealing with the *real world.* It showed itself in making philosophy accessible to the ordinary man, and in dealing with existential questions of relevance. Philosophizing thus became not exclusively of the 'head,' but of the 'heart' and of the 'hands.'

Keywords: Philosophizing, Ideal, Real, Earthly, Abstract, Plato, Nietzsche, Heidegger, Nihilism, Spatio-temporal.

Introduction

Without quite knowing the depth and the width of the question to be discussed in this study, "From the Ideal to the Real: A Shift in Philosophizing," we are delving into it, knowing that as we swim through the stream we will have better clarity regarding areas to be covered and the depth to be reached. We begin the paper with an introductory clarification of the key-notions in the title of this paper. It will be followed by the main body of this study, namely, looking both at the way philosophizing has been confined to the realm of the ideal, and at the ways in which attempts have been made to bring it down from the ideal to the real. The concluding part will make a reference as to how 'philosophizing with the real realm' shows itself in social praxis.

1. Notional Clarifications

In the title as well as in the text, the term 'philosophizing' occupies a prominent place. The notion 'philosophizing' has become in recent times more widespread in its being used in philosophical circles, in comparison to the more popular term 'philosophy.' This change is not a mere terminological change of one term (philosophizing) replacing another term (philosophy). There is a basic difference between 'philosophy' and 'philosophizing' in their meaning and content. The term 'philosophy' is nominal in its structure, static and dead in its meaning, and refers to the finished product of thought, while the term 'philosophizing' is verbal in its structure, dynamic and alive in its meaning, and refers to the process of thinking. 'Philosophy' presupposes a truth—at least it has been so—characterized by perenniality and universality, untouched by time and space. Contemporary thought pattern has destroyed such a myth,[1] and has opted for a more humble attitude. 'Philosophizing' reflects such a philosophical humility of being constantly in search, taking serious consideration of the elements of time and space.[2] Thus *philosophizing* is and has to be different according to the different places, times and perspectives.

The terms, 'ideal' and 'real', are very commonly used in our day-to-day language; still we need to clarify them by specifying the meaning in which we use them in this paper. 'Ideal' can be taken in two senses, both of which are closely related. First of all, it means: the best, the most suitable, etc.[3] For instance, 'an *ideal* teacher' is a model teacher in all respects, and thus the best teacher; 'an *ideal* climate for plantation' refers to the climate best suited for plantation. 'Ideal' can also be taken as the adjectival form of *idea*, and thus it means: 'related to an idea', 'existing only in an idea', etc.[4] Plato's '*ideal* world' refers to a world that consists of ideas, and that exists only as an idea. It

---

1 In postmodern thought the myth of dogmatism and absolute certainty got crumbled, as a result of which philosophy today is less presumptuous and more humble. For a concise consideration of 'postmodernism,' see: *The Postmodern...A Siege of the Citadel of Reason*, ed., Johnson J. Puthenpurackal (Delhi: Media House, 2002).

2 Johnson J. Puthenpurackal, "Editorial," *Vijnanadipti* 6, no. 2 (June 2004), 123.

3 https://dictionary.cambridge.org/dictionary/english/perfect, accessed September 30, 2018.

4 *The Concise Oxford Dictionary*, 7th edition (Oxford: Clarendon Press, 1982), s.v., "ideal."

is primarily in this sense that we use the expression 'ideal' in this paper.[5] The Dictionaries[6] give the meaning for 'real' as follows: actually existing, occurring in fact and not imagined, genuine or authentic, and relating to something as it is. In this paper we are contrasting the ideal (existing as an idea) and the real (existing in reality).

Finally a word of clarification is to be given for the term 'shift' in the expression 'A shift in philosophizing'. From the various meanings of 'shift' in the Dictionaries we use it in this paper in the sense of 'change of position or form' and 'substitution of one thing for another.'[7] This study is intended to show that a change is taking place in the mode of philosophizing, not by chance, but by necessity. This change is not a sudden shift, but a process of change that has been gradually showing itself in the different periods of history, but more intensely during the contemporary period. Hence by 'shift in philosophizing' we refer both to what has been gradually taking place in the past and what is yet to take place in the future.

Enlightened by the above-given notional clarification, we take a cursory look at 'philosophizing with the ideal'. Since the main thesis of the paper is to highlight the need of philosophy coming down from the ideal to the real, we shall place greater emphasis in clarifying 'philosophizing with the real'.

2. Philosophizing with the Ideal

Philosophizing as dealing with 'the ideal' was formally started with Plato, and it continued to remain in the 'ideal realm' for around two millennia until the contemporary period.[8]

Western Philosophy formally began with the great masters of Western thought, namely, Socrates, Plato and Aristotle, according to whom the Pre-Socratic thought did not have the philosophical rigour as it was socio-religious in its content and mythico-poetic in the style of expression. Hence these three great masters, each of them in their specific styles, contributed towards making philosophy logically clear and conceptually precise. Socrates through his dialogical method highlighted that human life and thought must be based on what is logically *true* and morally *right*;[9] he thus started the philosophical

5 It must be said that although we make a distinction between two meanings of 'ideal,' they are related. The ideal of beauty is based on the idea of beauty, and thus both the meanings are closely related.

6 *Cambridge English Dictionary; Oxford Dictionary; Collins English Dictionary*, etc.

7 *The Concise Oxford Dictionary*, s.v., "shift."

8 It is quite rightly said that the Western Philosophy of last two millennia has been nothing but a series of footnotes to Plato.

9 "He was…a religious figure of reason incarnate, and the world's first martyr to the truth." James K. Feibleman, *Understanding Philosophy: A Popular History of Ideas* (Mumbai: Jaico Publishing House, 1999), 43-44.

journey to the *ideal*. It was Plato who firmly and definitively established philosophy in and with the ideal world. Socrates' pursuit of the truth was taken up by Plato and elabourated; the Socratic rhetoric was overcome and replaced with the Platonic idea. He refers to two worlds or realms: the spatio-temporal 'real world' (the world of the 'sensible') and the trans-spatio-temporal 'ideal world' (the world of the 'intelligible'). The ideal world of Plato consists of 'ideas' (*Eidos*);[10] world of ideas is immaterial and permanent. Aristotle called Plato's ideas 'forms,' and in the middle ages they came to be known as 'universals.'[11] Philosophizing for Plato consists in having direct access to the 'true Reality', as distinct from the ordinary world of ever-changing things. Philosophy concerns itself with the relationship between the eternal and unchanging reality of the ideal world, the realm of ideas grasped by reason. Thus, Plato has taken philosophizing to the ideal realm.

Unlike Plato, Aristotle had an intense interest in the sensible world. He rejected the existence of a separate world of ideas or forms. He declared that forms exist *in* things; there is no matter-less form, or form-less matter. Although, Aristotle situated the *intelligible* (ideas, concepts, forms) in the *sensible* (material reality of time and space), which was separated by Plato, his philosophizing was not in any way brought down to the concrete realm of time and space. According to Aristotle, in philosophy, we proceed from the particular to the universal, from the concrete to the abstract, from the image to the concept. Thus philosophy for Aristotle was a rational enterprise, dealing with the abstract realm.[12]

What the great three masters of Greek philosophy started was faithfully carried further by the later philosophers in their own style, keeping it as *meta-physical* in the abstract realm. With the arrival of Christianity and especially with the development of a Western Christian theology in the medieval period and the translation of Greek thought into Latin, philosophy became conceptually and logically more rigorous. With the advent of modern philosophy, the metaphysical tradition became epistemological, with Descartes' *Cogito*, exalting the subjectivity. In the absolute idealism of Hegel, philosophizing with the ideal realm reaches its climax.[13] Western Philosophy has been rightly characterized as a conceptual enterprise, which has its merit of having

---

10 It should be noted that *idea* in English according to the popular understanding stands for the 'mental picture,' which is not the case in Plato's *eidos*.

11 Feibleman, *Understanding Philosophy*, 49.

12 In conceptual and logical philosophy, according to Aristotle one reaches the third degree of abstraction, whereas empirical sciences employ the first degree and mathematics, the second degree of abstraction.

13 Although it was Heidegger who has highlighted it in his critique of metaphysics, this assessment is shared by many of the contemporary thinkers.

mathematical precision and analytical clarity. Thus, Western Philosophy has been journeying comfortably in the ideal realm for more than two millennia.

3. Philosophizing with the Real

In the twentieth century, more than before, humans were confronted with the concrete experience of their unique life situations, which were not considered to be worthy of philosophical reflections in the traditional philosophy of the ideal realm. As humans were caught up in the trap of their naked existence, and found no way to escape from their concrete naked life situations, a shift in philosophizing was necessitated—a shift from the ideal to the real! Such a shift took place not by chance, but by necessity! This change is concretely seen in many areas, such as in philosophical themes, in philosophizing style, in the label of being philosophers, in the mode of philosophical communication, etc. Philosophizing has become more earthly and contextual! We shall consider it step by step.

3.1. From the Ideal to the Real: The Daring Pioneers

The above-given rough picture of the shift in the mode and content of contemporary philosophizing was the result of a few daring and creative thinkers, who were courageous enough to think 'otherwise', the prominent being Nietzsche and Heidegger, who are rightly considered to have brought about the 'transition' from modernity to post-modernity, from the ideal to the real. The transition was made possible by the critical stance they took to the traditional philosophy.

Nietzsche carries out the critique by his twofold proclamation: 'death of God', and 'decadence of reason'. Proclamation of 'death of God' is not a profession of atheism, but an announcing the irrelevance and impossibility of holding to anything that transcends time and space. He also makes another proclamation: reason, exalted in the modern philosophy, has decayed. 'Death of God' and 'decadence of reason': with these two phrases Nietzsche does not refer to two different phenomena, but rather he shouts aloud the same fact: the announcement of *nihilism*. What has been held as sacrosanct in the West for centuries—metaphysics, theology, culture, morality—has begun to lose its ground, and has become meaningless and irrelevant. Thus, the long period of decadence—reign of eternality and rationality—was terminated with the advent of *nihilism*.[14] According to Nietzsche the origins of nihilism can be traced back to the twin sources of Western civilization, Socrates and Christ—rationality and eternality. Socrates is presented as the embodiment of rationalism, as responsible for the birth of reason (knowledge) and the death of

14 For more on 'nihilism', see: Arthur Danto, *Nietzsche as Philosopher* (New York: Columbia University Press, 1980), 19-35.

art (Greek tragedy). In giving precedence to being over becoming, Christianity, like Platonism, transfers the *locus* of eternity from this world. By his critical stance against Socrates and Christ, Nietzsche symbolically closes the reign of decadence, and inaugurates the advent of nihilism.

Heidegger has, unlike Nietzsche,[15] more systematically and historically worked out his critique of Western Philosophy. Western metaphysics, according to him, was started by Plato and Aristotle by transforming the Pre-Socratic poetic insights and artistic intuitions into logically precise metaphysical concepts—a shift from *mythos* to *logos*! Reason started its reign with the great masters of Greek thought. Heidegger finds the whole structure of Western thought as onto-theo-logical, in sofar as Being has been identified with '*beingness*' (ontology) and/or '*highest being,* God (theology).'[16] Gradually Western Philosophy is changed into epistemology with emphasis on the subject-object polarity. The subject becomes the arbiter of truth; the world becomes the 'object' (*Gegenstand*)—something that is made to stand over against the representing subject.[17] Even God is not spared by the domineering reason, as He is reduced to an object of human estimation! The conceptual object is kept in a trans-spatio-temporal (ideal) realm far away from the realm of the spatio-temporal subject.

The critique of philosophizing with the ideal realm made by Nietzsche and Heidegger was born from a collective experience of 'suffocation' in the wake of the 'logico-conceptual' approach of Western Philosophy. 'Philosophy' was born with the enforced death of what has been considered to be the vague and imprecise poetico-mythical thinking of the Pre-Socratics. When we give precision to a notion by defining it, we are placing it within a boundary, untouched by time and space, making it universal and perennial. Nietzsche and Heidegger, with their critique of such a monolithic structure of Western Philosophy, have initiated a move to work out a shift in philosophizing from the ideal to the real.

The merit of Nietzsche and Heidegger consists not merely in having laid bare the picture of traditional Western Philosophy, but mainly in having lit the torch and begun to move away from the ideal to the real realm. The 'movers' of such daring movement are branded as 'mad' (*verrückt*)—displaced and untimely. Nietzsche gives some poetic indications of the new vision of philosophizing with the real.

---

15 Nietzsche's critique of Western thought is expressed in his typically powerful and sharp language, pregnant with metaphors and symbols; whereas Heidegger's style of expression and language is more systematic and less symbolic in comparison to that of Nietzsche.

16 Martin Heidegger, *Identität und Differenz* (Pfullingen: Neske, 1978), *Identity and Difference*, trans., J. Stambaugh, (New York: Harper Torchbook Edition, 1974), 58.

17 In his *Der Satz vom Grund* (Pfullingen: Neske, 1978), Heidegger brings to light the representational character of metaphysical thinking.

In his *Thus Spoke Zarathustra* Nietzsche reflects on as to how to accomplish a transition from what has been to what could be, from the *ultimate man* (man of *decadence*) to *superman* (the this-worldly ideal). Zarathustra comes from the forest to the crowd of the market place where people are watching a tight-rope walker, and presents superman as the meaning of the earth. He asks them "to remain faithful to the earth,"[18] and tells them, "Man is a rope, tied between animal and superman—a rope over an abyss."[19] He teaches that the human is a 'dynamic between' and that one needs to get away from the crowd of stagnant suffocation to the freedom of 'becoming' (moving towards) the superman: a call to transition! But, his message fell on deaf ears; the people asked for the *ultimate man* of decadence.[20] Zarathustra attempts again to foster a transition to the future with the help of an allegory, *The Three Metamorphoses*: 'camel' (bearing the burden of decadence), 'lion' (a defiant 'no' in nihilism) and 'child' (new vision of spontaneity and freedom). Disappointed at the people's lack of desire for change, Zarathustra leaves the market place and falls into a 'tomb of nausea'. But Nietzsche observes, "only where there are tombs are there resurrections." Only by passing into and through this great night of tomb can one rise again.[21] Finally Zarathustra makes a plea not to run away from the *temporal* existence (as in Platonism and Christianity), but to accept the eternal flux of becoming. After trying in futile to advocate the message of life and becoming, Zarathustra returns to his mountain in the company of his animals, indicating thereby the need to be *rooted* in one's own and to be *at home* with the earth of time and space.[22]

Although, Nietzsche prepared the transition from the ideal to the real, he did not philosophically work it out, as was done by Heidegger. But, the transitional possibilities suggested by Heidegger are far less concrete than what Nietzsche has proposed.[23] Heidegger developed a thought centred on both *Verwindung* (an overcoming, a *thinking ahead*) and *Andenken* (a recollection, a *thinking back*). "The most thought-provoking is that we are still

---

18 *Thus Spoke Zarathustra*, trans., R.J. Hollingdale (Middlesex: Penguin Books, 1978), 42.

19 Ibid., 43.

20 Ibid., 47.

21 G. B. Smith, *Op. Cit.*, 113.

22 After having sketched the dynamics of a transition from the past to the future in *Thus Spoke Zarathustra*, Nietzsche gives a more concrete glimpse of the future mainly in his *Beyond Good and Evil*, referring to a philosophy of the Free Spirits, creativity, earthly religion, the rule of the contingent, the unpredictable, instinct, appearance, the hegemony of the surface.

23 Just as Nietzsche, Heidegger too refers to humans' ecological and religious dimensions, as transitional possibilities. Towards the fag end of his philosophical itinerary in the company of Hölderlin we clearly note the religious tinge in his thought and language. The Post-metaphysical future reality will have to be seen as 'holy' beyond the 'death of God'.

not thinking," declares Heidegger repeatedly.[24] His philosophy is eminently transitional, as it enables the very 'thoughtlessness' to evoke 'thought'. His thought involves a *thinking-back* to the metaphysical past and a *thinking-ahead* into the presencing (*Anwesen*) of the present—a new *Ereignis* (e-venting) in the post-metaphysical future.

The philosophical revolution that brought philosophy to the real realm consisted in Heidegger's thinking that brought 'Being' and 'Time' together. Plato took 'Being' as an idea or conceptual notion, untouched by the limiting elements of space and time, and confined in the ideal realm. Down through the centuries Being has been considered as an abstract concept that is perennial and universal. Inspired by Nietzsche's proclamation of *nihilism*, and the driving away of the long reign of eternality and rationality, Heidegger considers the question of 'Being and Time' together. Thus, the question of Being, locked up for two millennia in the ideal realm, was released and brought down to the *real world* of time and space. Heidegger has, thus, definitively brought about a shift in philosophizing from the *ideal* to the *real*.

3.2. The Shift to the Real, Concretely Shown

Now that the philosophical basis for the shift from the ideal to the real in philosophizing is put forward, we can refer to a few areas in which the change is concretely manifested.

The very term 'philosophy' has been creating in most of the people a kind of alarm and aversion, since it neither 'speaks' their language, nor 'deals' with their questions; this fear is not totally without any reason. Traditionally philosophizing was limited to the strange themes from classical thought, such as being, substance, accidents, causality, cause vs. effect, matter vs. form, essence vs. existence, definition, division, syllogism, fallacies, dilemma, etc. Such themes, though philosophically important and significant, are not questions that the ordinary humans have hardly anything to do with. But, themes like finitude, death, anxiety, fear, despair, hope, love, body, sexuality, work, violence, hatred, indifference, culture, ecology, technology, etc., resonate with an existential flavour;[25] these are *our* questions with which we grapple in our day-to-day life. Contemporary philosophy has begun to consider such questions with passionate involvement: an indication of the shift in philosophizing from the ideal to the real.

Along with the change from the ideal to the real, there took place a marked difference in the style of philosophizing. In the traditional philosophizing the

---

24 "Das bedenklichste ist, daß wir noch nicht denken." *Was heißt Denken?* 2, 3, 11; *What Is Called Thinking?* 4, 6, 28.

25 In fact, such existential questions began to be considered in philosophy with the birth of Existentialism that deals with the question of the human in its various dimensions.

subject-object dichotomy was strictly maintained—the spatio-temporal subject epistemologically considers the meta-spatio-temporal conceptual object in the abstract realm. As the object is brought down to the real realm, the distance between the subject and the object began to be narrowed down to the extent of one being identified with the other—identity taken in the sense of 'belonging together' (*Zusammengehörigkeit*). The process of reconciling the subject and the object was worked out in the phenomenological method of Husserl through the notion of 'intentionality', according to which the subjective act and the objective content belong together—it is in the act of one's getting frightened (subjective act) that something is constituted as frightening (objective content). The existentialists, by their philosophizing from the stand-point of 'actor', consider philosophical questions, not as problems to be dispassionately solved, but as 'mystery' in which the subject is passionately involved. Even the question of God is considered as existentially close to the humans. Such passionate involvement is intensely felt by the subject since the questions to be reflected emerge from one's personal experiences.[26] Rightly does Marcel refer to his thought as a spiritual itinerary.

Philosophy today is not a strange discipline accessible only to a few arm-chair philosophers, since it can easily be reached by anyone because of the easily accessible means of communication. Formerly philosophical thought was conveyed through the abstruse philosophical treatises that were neither available to nor understandable for the ordinary folk. Today it is not the case; philosophy is expressed and conveyed through the easily accessible and understandable means such as novels, stories, poems, plays, anecdotes, etc. Besides, the thoughts of various philosophers are the inspiration for many of the novelists and play-wrights, making the philosophical thoughts and insights accessible to the ordinary people in a digested form. As philosophy came down to the earthly realm, philosophizing is no more the monopoly of a few formally acknowledged 'philosophers', rather philosophizing is carried out by every thinking person.

The concrete manifestation and application of philosophy in the real realm of humans can be seen in different philosophers in the contemporary period. Special mention must be made of Marxian thought, which got shaped as a philosophy in support of the emancipation of the impoverished and alienated working class of people. It was a great socio-philosophical movement that disturbed the established political and religious structures all over the world.

---

26 Most of the existentialist thinkers' biography and philosophy were closely related. Their philosophical themes had the rootedness in their existential experience. Special mention must be made of Marcel and Kierkegaard.

We have come to notice that the shift in philosophizing shows itself, not merely as a theoretical change, but rather it shows itself concretely in various ways and through various means.

3.3. Philosophizing with the Real: Practical Implications

Insofar as philosophizing is carried out from within us, philosophical themes are emerging from our existential experiences, and philosophers are we ourselves, philosophy cannot but be embracing every dimension of the human, which we express with a phrase of ours: 'philosophizing with head, heart, hands.'[27]

The total person includes the dimensions of head, heart and hands, understood in their intentional meaning. 'Head' stands for that dimension of the human by which one understands reality with conceptual clarity and precision. The great edifice of Western thought built on human reason has been reigning supreme in the world of philosophy. Because of its conceptual clarity, mathematical precision and logical order, Western thought largely contributed towards human progress and development. Thus the dimension of accurate knowledge is referred to by the term 'head'.

'Heart' stands for the core and the inner of one's being. One may present a conceptually precise thought in an elegant language; but it will remain merely shallow if it does not emerge from one's inner being—from one's conviction and decision, from one's 'heart'. When 'heart' becomes the centre of our thinking, speaking and doing, it does away with the philosophy of abstract thinking. What is carried out by the 'head' has to be founded on the 'heart'.

As different from 'heart' that stands for the 'within' of the person, the 'hands' are the extensions of the 'within', and these extensions are meant to receive and to give out. They function as the antennae by which we experience reality, and through which we express ourselves. It is *through the hands* that the humans get an existential touch from the earth; it is *with the hands* that the humans give an existential touch to the earth. Hence, philosophizing has to be well-grounded on one's existential experience, and it expresses itself through one's actions (*with the hands*). If our philosophizing does not contain any of these dimensions, it will be a mutilated philosophizing.

Holistic philosophizing of 'Transformative Practice' will necessarily give rise to 'Social Movements', (with *hand*) that are the concrete expressions of what one knows (with *head*) and what one is convinced of (with *heart*).

---

27 The present author has carried out the following reflective study on this question. "Towards an Authentic philosophizing with Head, Heart, Hands: Philosophical Reflection and Autobiography," in *Authentic Existence: A Philosophical Probe,* Festschrift in Honour of Dr Johnson J. Puthenpurackal, OFM Cap, ed., George Panthanmackel, MSFS (Bangalore: Asian Trading Corporation, 2012), 495-519.

"Philosophy is an adventure,"[28] and philosophers are adventurous and creative insofar as they give the lead in being 'daring pioneers' by stepping ahead from the 'safety' and 'comfort' of philosophizing in the abstract with mediocrity in thought and life. "Philosophy has no weight and no interest whatever unless it sounds an 'echo' in our life,…."[29] An 'earthly' philosophizing with the real will be vibrating as a persisting 'echo' in human life. In this respect philosophers are to be not 'teachers' but 'awakeners' who awaken people to thought, disturb them from their slumber of conventionality and mediocrity, spur them to creative action and motivate them to Movements of social relevance; it calls for a shift in philosophizing from the ideal to the real.

28 G. Marcel, *Tragic Wisdom and Beyond*, trans., S. Jolin and P. Mc Cormick, (Evanston: North Western University Press, 1973), 11.

29 Ibid., 17.

2

Liberation Philosophy: Wisdom, Power and Care Within Transformative Social Practice

Keith D'Souza
St Xavier's College, Mumbai

Abstract: The paper outlines the general contours of a liberation philosophy, which is similar to the liberation theologies articulated since about half a century ago. Unlike liberation theology, though, the depth and breadth of the canvas of liberation philosophy promises to be deeper and wider, as the nature and scope of the discipline of philosophy in general is broader in its embrace of issues and perspectives than that of theology—liberation or otherwise.

The paper advocates three main components of liberation philosophy, namely, wisdom at the cognitive level, power at the volitional or conative level and care at the affective level. Any attempt at transformative social action needs to include these cognitive, conative and affective dimensions. Each of these primary components is further subdivided, so that what we have is a highlighting of the core dimensions of a comprehensive philosophy of liberation.

Four primary forms of transformative social practice are then presented, namely, dystopic, utopian, myopic and kaleidoscopic: forming a hierarchical typology, from the most dysfunctional to the most salubrious. The paper concludes by indicating various nuances connected with this typology, demonstrating that instead of an easy demarcation or location of different types of social transformation within this typology, what we find in reality are often complex and flexible narratives of transformative social practice.

Keywords: Liberation, Wisdom, Power, Care, Discernment, Dystopic, Myopic, Utopian, Kaleidoscopic

Introduction

In the famous words of Jean-Jacques Rousseau, "man was born free, and everywhere he is in chains. Many a one believes himself the master of others, and yet he is a greater slave than they."[1] The social and structural reasons for these master-slave dynamics were eloquently articulated by Karl Marx, whose methodological analysis of social ills had a vast impact on liberation theology. While liberation theology does not share in the atheistic—and in many cases even the spontaneous revolutionary—presuppositions of Marx, it highlights the nature and dynamics of unjust economic and political relations which generally hamper authentic spiritual and religious experience and expression.[2] Liberation theology proposes structural or socially systemic changes at various levels—economic, political and cultural—in order to offset and mitigate these unjust relations.

The aim of this article is to lay down the foundations for a liberation philosophy which will be in congruence with liberation theology in terms of bringing about relevant social transformation as a significant—if not a necessary—condition for wholesome human life, labour and relationships to flourish. However, liberation philosophy is in a sense freer than liberation theology, as it is not limited to specific theological presuppositions. There may also be various liberation philosophies—much wider in nature and scope as compared to similarly different liberation theologies—depending on the specific philosophical influence, focus and strategies adopted as most wholesome for liberation.[3]

1. The need for a "Liberation Philosophy"

The term "liberation" as a prefix to philosophy may have two quite distinct meanings. One meaning is associated with liberalism, or the freedom to think, express oneself and behave with limited constraints, with libertarians favouring uninhibited conditions for such freedom of expression. Liberalism

1 Jean-Jacques Rousseau, *The Social Contract and The First and Second Discourses* (New Haven: Yale University Press, 2002), 156.

2 For a scholarly overview of liberation theology, see: Christopher Rowland, ed., *The Cambridge Companion to Liberation Theology* (Cambridge: Cambridge University Press, 1999).

3 Some of the works of Enrique Dussel come closest to this project of developing a "liberation philosophy." See: *Philosophy of Liberation*, trans., Aquilina Martinez and Chrisine Morkovsky (Maryknoll, NY: Orbis Books, 1985) and *The Underside of Modernity: Apel, Ricoeur, Rorty, Taylor, and the Philosophy of Liberation*, trans., and ed., Eduardo Mendieta (Atlantic Heights, NJ: Humanities Press, 1996).

has come into short shrift over recent times, especially when the prognosticated project of secularism seems to have failed in most parts of the globe. Instead of the preponderance of secularism, what we are seeing the world over is a reinstatement of the assertion of cultural, religious and national identities. Liberal thinkers have come to be disparagingly called "libertards" in India—to rhyme with the common term for illegitimate children—just as objective and progressive journalists are labelled with the name "presstitutes"—along the lines of the oldest profession in the world.[4]

Yet another meaning associated with the term "liberation" exists at the other end of the economic and cultural spectrum. This understanding of liberation is applied to societies and communities as a whole which need to be set free from various social ills and unhealthy habits and presuppositions. Social theorists and activists who favour structural reform towards this end may be termed "liberationists"—as opposed to "liberalists" who favour individual freedoms.

In this paper, by the term "liberation philosophy," what is primarily intended is this second use of the term, that is, the cognitive support for any process which seeks to create freer and fairer conditions for equality of social status and opportunity. However, along with basic egalitarianism, cultural conditions and social laws need to also ensure liberty, and preferably the experience of fraternity or a sense of community—these being three perennial values emphasized in various forms—albeit unequally—in human history, though made popular since the time of the French Revolution. A truly free society is one which would offer its members a lived experience of liberty, equality and fraternity. While the term "liberation" seems to be more closely related to the value of liberty in this triad, a wholesome and comprehensive understanding of liberation would entail the operative presence of all three values in any given society.

How may the theme of liberation and the discipline of philosophy be related? I suggest that both of these need to be viewed in a mutually influential manner. There is, on the one hand, a need for liberation thinking to be philosophical in process and orientation, that is, to be deliberative at the rational or cognitive level and to be discerning at a deeper level of human decision making. These features of rationality and discernment, for example, would lead us away from easy attractions towards violent revolutions as a means to solve distressing social situations. These means towards social change are pragmatically counter productive, morally unethical and socially

4 Chahat Rana, "Social Media and the Vocabulary of Hate," *thecitizen.in*, accessed December 15, 2019, https://www.thecitizen.in/index.php/en/NewsDetail/index/2/11061/Social-Media-and-the-Vocabulary-of-Hate, for the worrisome rise of derogatory terms such as "*sickulars, libertards, anti-nationals, the most recently and ingeniously coined liberandu, and of course the highly misogynistic presstitute*" (original italics).

insensitive, on account of the amount of human suffering intentionally or collaterally engendered.

Just as liberative thinking needs to be philosophical, so also the discipline of philosophy needs to be perceived and engaged in as a liberative exercise of some form or the other. This applicative focus of philosophy in the direction of liberation is more evident in Eastern—and especially Indian—philosophical history, even though the "liberation" understood in these traditions has been more oriented towards transcendent and spiritual concerns. This perception of philosophy as an exercise in liberation will enhance its stature as a contemporary academic discipline and restore the primacy which philosophy had in earlier times in various cultures and traditions across the globe as a significant cultural and intellectual resource.

2. Features of Liberation Philosophy

Any philosophy of liberation needs to integrate several aspects of human experience, involving or engaging the body, mind, heart, spirit, community, and the larger world of nature. Integral liberation thus includes the whole person, the whole community, the whole human family and the whole of nature. There are three primary components of liberation: the cognitive component, which is symbolically represented by "wisdom" as a cluster concept, the action oriented or volitional component, which is represented by "power" and the affective or emotional component, which is represented by "care."

2.1. Wisdom

The etymology of the term "transformation" entails a movement from operative or regulative "forms" towards newer and more desirable "forms". At least from the time of Plato in the Western tradition and the Vedic *Rshis* in the Indian tradition, there has been a recognition of the need for authentic meditative knowledge regarding true forms or ideas. This capacity to acquaint oneself with this type of knowledge and to be able to subsequently articulate it has always been rated highly, in different traditions and in different ways.

In the wake of hermeneutics and postmodern critique this desire to attain truth has taken on new dimensions. The seeking for "forms" has itself undergone trans-"form"-ation. This is why the generative as well as applicative use of knowledge requires an even higher and finer skill, namely, that of the cultivation of wisdom. Especially when it comes to the important area of social transformation, wisdom needs to be given a very high priority, in terms of reflective, communicative and practical action. I will highlight only a few important aspects of the feature of wisdom, as applied to socially transformative practice.

2.1.1. Vision

A primary component of wisdom is the ability to identify and articulate a vision of what type of society is desirable. Wisdom may be the work of an extraordinarily gifted individual—when accepted on a mass scale, these persons subsequently attain the status of social, cultural or religious reformers. But, vision could also be formulated by an enlightened group of leaders within a community—a good example is the composition of Constitutions of various nations. In today's more democratically oriented societies, the wider the consultation in the formulation of the vision, the more motivation it will generate and the more likely it will be followed through by way of actualization.

2.1.2. Breadth and Depth

Vision needs to have both breadth and depth. Breadth entails a wide general knowledge about human history and about the stories of several human communities and their achievements in various fields. Breadth also entails an attitude of broad mindedness, which transcends the operative influence of fear and constraints generated by narrow concerns and interests. Breadth is related to wide circles of human interaction and relationship—the more one has interacted with, and learned from persons from different communities, the wider will be one's understanding of the human situation.

Complementary to breadth is the feature of depth. Depth entails the dimension of multilateral considerations, including diverse aspects of human life: the spiritual, cultural, religious, relational, political and economic. Depth also entails the ability to engage in sound and wholesome social analysis, so that the structural or systemic causes of healthy and dysfunctional social phenomena are identified. There may often arise the need for a productive "hermeneutics of suspicion" as part of this social analysis, with a view to ameliorate unhealthy social customs and circumstances.[5] Finally, depth solutions avoid the generation of *ad hoc*, knee jerk responses to social problems, and instead seek to address and resolve problems at causal or fundamental levels.

2.1.3. Discernment

Perhaps the most important aspect of wisdom is the skill of discernment, not only in the formulation of a social vision but especially in terms of its productive

---

5 The term "hermeneutics of suspicion" was made famous by Paul Ricoeur. See Ricoeur, *Freud and Philosophy: An Essay in Interpretation*, trans., Denis Savage (New Haven, CT: Yale University Press, 1970), 32-36. This aspect of interpretation theory pays attention to hidden power features, relations and conflicts, which may otherwise escape the normal route of argumentative representation and discussion. Ricoeur had three main thinkers or intellectual protagonists in mind when he coined this term: Marx, Nietzsche and Freud.

or constructive implementation.[6] Discernment enables us to judge which strategies work in which type of social situations, and which strategies may comparatively prove to be counter-productive. The most important ingredient of discernment is the objective and thorough collection of initial data in which situations are assessed, as well as the relatively impartial dispositions people adopt while evaluating and articulating a response to specific social situations. If these initial conditions are not met, it is unlikely that what follows will be wise in intention or articulation, or fruitful in practice.

2.2. Power

In contemporary philosophical thought, power for the most part has come to be looked upon as a suspicious means or instrument to bring about change.[7] However, an important aspect of social transformation is the ability to influence individual and collective behaviour towards desirable directions and ends. When combined with wisdom—and care—this influence will normally be channelled into productive and collabourative avenues—rather than destructive and competitive ones. I have highlighted some of the more important aspects of human dynamism which would facilitate this drive towards positive ends.

2.2.1. Passion

Perhaps the most important ingredient for any form of social action is motivation, determination, perseverance. This entails the ability of doggedness or a "never say die" attitude. One needs to be driven by fearlessness or courage, the tenacity or holy stubbornness of sticking to well-thought out convictions and desirous plans. Passion enables one to be adequately and optimally driven to action. Even though one may face adversity and opposition—and the scepticism of one's critics—passion enables one to move ahead doggedly. However, passion needs to be complemented by adequate wisdom and care, else it will likely become obdurate, violent and counterproductive. Wisdom prunes passion of its potential excesses and care orients it towards the wellbeing of persons and communities.

---

6 Discernment is generally associated with a process of spiritual decision making, which attempts to be deeper than that employed by merely pragmatic and instrumental methods of decision making. See Thomas Green, *Weeds Among the Wheat: Discernment—Where Prayer and Action Meet* (Notre Dame, IN: Ave Maria Press, 1984), for a popular yet comprehensive treatment of the theme of spiritual discernment.

7 See: Michel Foucault, *Power/Knowledge*, ed., Colon Gordon (NY: Pantheon Books, 1980), 52, in which the author states, "it is not possible for power to be exercised without knowledge, it is impossible for knowledge not to engender power." Foucault and other postmodern thinkers wish to foreground the intrinsic relationship between the forms, possession and dissemination of knowledge on the one hand, and often unequal power relations on the other.

2.2.2. Dynamic Action, Reflection, Action Model

A common idiom states that vision without action is only a dream, whereas action without vision could be a nightmare. Both indeed are necessary. However, they need to be viewed not in isolation, but instead as symbiotically influencing one another. A dynamic interplay between vision and action serves to modify or correct the inadequacies or excesses of the other. Simply articulating a vision and hoping that action will adequately follow through—without any strategic plan—is chimeric. Similarly, engagement in some form of dynamic action without taking recourse to the vision that undergirds action may lead to unproductive—or in some cases counterproductive—outcomes. There is a need to go back to the visionary drawing board when necessary, in order to take stock of new circumstances which may demand new plans and strategies. This requires humility to accept that one's well thought out plans did not work out as expected, creativity to think of new approaches and patience and perseverance to try out something new, hoping for better outcomes.[8]

2.2.3. Collabouration and Networking

Power may be dangerous when placed in the hands of one or a few, but when diffused in a discerned and deliberative manner among many able, wise and caring persons, power becomes an optimal force. Today what needs to be cultivated and celebrated is not the power of one, nor even the power of a few, but the power of many—not necessarily in a blindly procedural or democratic manner which may be easily manipulated by powerful and vested forces, but in an enlightened and participatory process. Given the tremendous opportunities provided by information technology and developed means of social media, possibilities of collabouration and networking have never been as easy at the technical level.

2.2.4. Checks and Balances

Unbridled power is obviously a source of threat to stable social systems and relationships. But, even more subtle forms of power differentials which are inbuilt into social systems pose a serious threat to social health and stability. There is thus a need for multilateral and "polylogical"—not just dialogical—forms of discourse and action. Such multilateral approaches ensure that power does not run amok, and that feedback mechanisms from divergent stakeholders become part of the procedural systems which are created to facilitate social development.

---

8 The Ignatian Pedagogical Paradigm (IPP) is a method which attempts to link action and reflection with one's context, experience and evaluation of what has been learned. See: "Ignatian Pedagogy," accessed January 20, 2019, https://commons.georgetown.edu/teaching/design/ignatian-pedagogy/.

2.3. Care

While wisdom is an important cognitive skill or virtue to cultivate and salubrious aspects of power are necessary at the level of the will, it is important to foreground the *affective* aspect of care, so that attempts at social transformation do not degenerate into violent exercises of social engineering. What follows are a few important principles and values which are central to the element of care in transformative social practice.

2.3.1. Means cannot Justify Ends

One of the most striking of Kant's categorical imperatives is that persons ought never to be used as means, but always as ends in themselves.[9] This aphorism is important to bear in mind, especially in our age, when vast numbers of people are brainwashed into adopting religious, cultural and national ideologies, at the expense of the wellbeing of those who suffer on account of these ideological positions and plans. It is not uncommon to find agents of social transformation who espouse strong ideological theories, but who are unable to relate easily and sensitively with those around them. Speaking volumes about the virtues of universal peace and justice—and numerous other values—is easy, but ensuring that these values are emphasized within the means used is both demanding and necessary.

2.3.2. Inclusiveness

At the social or communitarian level, care entails the inclusion of interests and needs of other communities and persons who live outside the folds or boundaries of one's communitarian concerns. This is more imperative in our globalized and interconnected world, in which the "other" may no more be considered to be too distant or insignificant. Too often ideology excludes the obvious sentiments of the other, as if they did not matter. This may arise at best from ignorance of the other, but quite often social discourse in many communities reveals a tangible sense of superiority towards others, and a systemic neglect of others in the larger scheme of things.

2.3.3. Recognition

Perhaps more than the need to receive economic justice and to live stable political lives is the need to have one's status as a person and as a member of a group recognized by those with whom one lives and works. Human beings are not just economic or political animals, but more so cultural animals, with distinct

9 The second formulation of the categorical imperative states: "Act in such a way that you treat humanity, whether in your own person or in the person of another, always at the same time as an end and never simply as a means." From; Immanuel Kant, *Grounding for the Metaphysics of Morals*, trans., James Ellington, 3rd ed. (Hackett, 1993), 36 (Ak. 429).

personal and social characteristics and needs. Recognition takes inclusiveness to a more refined height, as it consciously factors into any programme of development the presence and uniqueness of others who are encountered along the way of progress.[10] When recognition of persons and communities finds its ways into legal frameworks, care becomes institutionalized and operationalized. Care thus goes beyond the interpersonal realm, to include the structural and legal realm as well.

2.3.4. Non-Violence

It is unjustifiable and unacceptable to consciously plan to engage in any form of violence towards others while articulating one's vision, plans and strategies. Beyond this, any social movement will also need to factor in the extent of collateral damage possibly caused by the social forces released as part of the movement. One cannot simply dismiss such violent consequences on the lives of others as being insignificant, as compared to the grand vision of goals to be attained. Instrumental violence very seldom begets lasting peace. It instead builds up resistance and instability for generations to come, when narratives of loss and the desire for vengeance are remembered and re-enacted by parties who have inherited embittered relationships.

3. Types of Social Practice

There are numerous types of transformative social practice. Some of these seem promising in terms of vision and method, but may eventually bring about more harm than good. It is important to distinguish between various types of social practice, in order to identify which are more promising in terms of integral social liberation and which are less so. What follows is a hierarchy or taxonomy of types of transformative practice, from the most limited to the most promising.

3.1. Dystopic Social Practice

As the name suggests (from Greek *dys* meaning "bad" and *topos* meaning "place"), the vision, goals and objectives envisioned by such social movements are not healthy places either for the ones who wish to inhabit it, or for others, and in many cases for both. The reason why such visions are dysfunctional are several: the imaginative texture of the vision itself may be somewhat gross and rough, the horizon of social considerations may be too limited or exclusive, the means proposed to realize the vision may be too violent, there may be a lack of concern for individual persons or communities who fall within the ambit of the end or the means, the stakeholders considered may be too few or select or

10 See: Axel Honneth, the third-generation critical theorist, for several works on the theme of recognition. His seminal work is *The Struggle for Recognition: The Moral Grammar of Social Conflicts*, trans., Joel Anderson (Cambridge, MA: The MIT Press, 1996).

privileged, etc. Several Movements at both ends of the ideological spectrum—right and left—manifest such features. The efforts of such Movements often prove to be counterproductive, and their successes short-lived.

3.2. Utopian Social Practice

While the 'topos' of dystopian thinking is not perceived to be socially healthy—often by external stakeholders—utopian thinking is usually characterized by an over idealistic or "pie in the sky" approach. While the intentions of those who propose such an ideology or futuristic approach may be genuine or even noble, such thinking is not sufficiently realistic. Either the goal imagined is too unreasonable or farfetched, or the means expressed to arrive at such goals are not adequate. It will be difficult to persuade a wider scope of stakeholders to own such visions and strategies, if they are found to be too lofty and unreachable. Radical socialist Movements on the left and culturally reactionary Movements on the right are examples of such Movements which struggle to be socially productive, as they fail the test of realism and the challenge to meet the ordinary needs and aspirations of people. They also often succumb to the temptation to take recourse to violent means towards their ends. When this happens, they become dystopic, especially for others.

3.3. Myopic Social Practice

Some attempts at social reform are not only warranted and necessary—they are also realistic and based on the realization of present and achievable goals. However, if these positive and necessary social contributions or changes are limited in terms of the scope of people whom they will specifically benefit, such Movements may suffer from a form of visionary myopia. Many successful—and often worthy—socially transformative Movements are indeed myopic. They focus on a marginal group which needs some form of redemption from oppression and suffering. However, in focusing upon the emancipatory needs of narrow stakeholders, such transformative practice often runs the risk of excluding the sentiments, critique and concerns of others. To give a contemporary example: Western feminist Movements often ignore the context and aspirations of women in other parts of the globe who do not share their otherwise privileged conditions in terms of nationality, class, race and educational capital.[11] Also, while solving one social problem, myopic Movements ignore others which are related, or worse, collaterally cause other social problems to emerge or to be accentuated. While the solutions offered in the utopian variety of social transformation may be judged to be too unrealistic, those stemming from myopic perspectives may be found to be too simplistic,

11 See: Kanchana Mahadevan, *Between Feminity and Feminism: Colonial and Postcolonial Perspectives on Care* (Delhi: D.K. Print World, 1914), especially the last chapter, which highlights this problem.

as they gloss over the nuances which are part of the problems they wish to resolve, and in many cases exaggerate aspects relevant to their cause beyond due proportion.

3.4. Kaleidoscopic Social Practice

The first two forms of social practice were based on a spatial metaphor (*topos*). The third was based on a visual ability—or rather, disability. I would like to propose a more salubrious form of social practice by using the representative metaphor of the "kaleidoscope". David Brewster is credited with the invention of the kaleidoscope,[12] whose name he derived from the Greek "kalos", meaning beautiful, combined with "eidos", which means form or shape, and "skopeo", which means to perceive or examine. In our modern parlance, "kaleidoscopic" would mean "the perception of beautiful forms or shapes."

A kaleidoscope is an optical instrument which typically has a few sparkling glass crystals or particles of different colours placed in a cell at the end of a tube, which has two or more mirrors aligning the walls of the tube. One who looks through the kaleidoscope at the other end of the cell sees a symmetrical pattern of configuration of these crystals. When the kaleidoscope is shaken, the glass crystals get reconfigured, and one is able to see a new design. There are numerous such designs which may be configured within the kaleidoscope.

In what ways does the kaleidoscope represent or symbolize wholesome transformative practice? First of all, the kaleidoscope is simple and practical. It is extremely simple in design, containing a few shining particles and glass surfaces. Effective vision-mission statements are often those that are simple and not too convoluted or unrealistic. The kaleidoscope is extremely practical, and even a child can put it to good use. Good visions need to have doable plans and strategies, else they will not bear fruit. The simplicity of a vision enables more cognitive clarity, volitional motivation and affective resonance. The communicative style of Pope Francis is a good example of simple yet effective use of metaphors and word pictures in order to motivate people to action.

Secondly, the kaleidoscope represents creativity and flexibility. It consists of a limited number of shining particles which could be transformed into a multitude of several shapes, depending on the effort put in to change the configuration from time to time. The kaleidoscope demonstrates the power to bring about marvellous results with limited resources and capacities. This is similar to social transformation, which depends to a large extent on the creativity and flexibility of human agency, given the often-limited human and social capital with which one has to work. Social transformation does not

12 See: "Inventor of the Kaleidoscope," accessed February 25, 2019, https://brewstersociety.com/kaleidoscope-university/sir-david-brewster/.

need the power of wealth and social position to bring about change. It needs the commitment of a critical mass of people who can do wonders with even meagre resources. Numerous social movements have played a significant role in transitional moments—such as national freedom struggles against colonial powers—in spite of opposition and the lack of material resources.

Thirdly, the kaleidoscope is a dynamic, not a static instrument. Left to itself, it will demonstrate or reveal only one pattern. Similarly, any movement needs to be able to change and modify or reinterpret itself with time. Static Movements will develop rigidity and intolerance, and will find it difficult to survive when circumstances change. Here the importance of reinterpretation of old motivational teachings and practices comes into play. The effectiveness of a transformative movement is directly proportional to the ability of the movement to respond to the signs of the times in a creative, attractive and productive manner. It is important to transcend narrow obsequiousness to any ideological position and obstinacy in its execution. Healthy transformative practice puts context and persons first, and relativizes ideological fixation.

Fourthly, the kaleidoscope is a source of much joy and delight. It brings about a brilliant and enjoyable outcome—something beautiful from something plain. The membership of, and work within social movements does not necessarily have to be an experience which is dreary and fraught with gravity and a spirit of seriousness. The task of social transformation—of future-oriented social creativity—could as well reflect the lightness, beauty and joy capable of the human spirit. Often, what is required is a sense of humour, and a relativisation of personal ego. This manifestation of joy also serves to motivate others to join such Movements.

In the hands of a wise, influential (powerful) and caring person or community, the building blocks of socially transformative Movements—like the elements of the kaleidoscope—serve as invaluable—if not necessary—social capital to bring about positive change.

4. Nuances of Socially Transformative Practices and Movements

It may not be easy to simply reduce a movement to one or another of these four types. This may be because over time different features may be expressed or focused upon, depending on the context and the nature of the leadership of any given movement. But, more fundamentally, the foundational philosophy of a movement may by itself bear sufficient nuance to escape these easy categorizations.

Beyond the fuzziness or ambiguity of the vision, goals and strategies of any movement, it is quite possible for a movement to consciously change its focus over time and in different social and temporal spaces. For example, the Second Vatican Council is a good example of a tangible sea change brought about in various aspects of the transnational and two millennium old Christian faith movement. Some examples of this paradigm shift are the understanding of faith itself as being more inclusive of the contribution of lay faithful, internal relationships within the organization which are more participative and less directive, and relationships with other communities and Movements which are more dialogical rather than apologetic or conflictual. To give a local example, recently the leader of the RSS seems to have attested to a major change of policy of the movement, in terms of allowing for reservations and being more accepting of Muslims. Some have called this a *Perestroika*—to mention yet another powerful movement which strove for social change within the erstwhile USSR. Others are more sceptical, and are waiting to see if this is only a political strategy.[13] Time will tell if there is a serious transition of thought within the RSS, in terms of being more positive and inclusive towards other communities.

Interaction with other social movements—collabourative, competitive or conflictual—often brings about a new awareness of the presuppositions and assumptions of one's social movement. This takes the form of an opportunity—or in some cases a crisis—to reform or transform one's vision and strategies, in the light of this new data. For those who are more secure and seek feedback from others, actual engagement with those who live beyond the scope of the movement provides a more systematic approach towards revisioning and reformulation of one's attested goals and objectives. It may be surprising to many people engaged in social change to learn that their efforts may be based on narrow and sometimes unhealthy presuppositions. One's noble intentions—and those of one's community or leaders engaged in social change—may be tainted with subconscious desires or interests which are not so salubrious at the objective level.

Conclusion

There is a need for philosophy to take on a liberative nature and for liberation Movements to factor in philosophical reflection as part of their way of proceeding. This paper is an exercise in producing a "liberation philosophy" which will help support transformational social practice and the development of social movements. I have argued that "liberation philosophy" needs to be governed by three primary values: wisdom, power and care. Each of these by themselves already bears some positive contribution towards social wellbeing and progress, but needs to be complemented by the other two, else it may run the risk of violence, or at best, impotence in bringing about necessary and wholesome change. Wisdom without power and care is chimerical and even

13 See: Rahul Kumar, "Mohan Bhagwat's New Avatar: Is it Really a Change of Heart or a New Wicked Strategy?" *countercurrents.org*, accessed November 17, 2019, https://countercurrents.org/2018/09/24/mohan-bhagvats-new-avatar-is-it-really-a-change-of-heart-or-a-new-wicked-strategy/.

potentially violent, power without wisdom and care is obviously dysfunctional and potentially catastrophic, and care without wisdom and power will not likely bring about desired social transformation.

There are different types of transformative social practices, some more limited in their scope and extent of influence, and some more fruitful. Among the clearly more limited—and even harmful—types of social practice outlined above are the dystopian and utopian varieties. While the myopic type of social practice may bring about necessary social change for a specific target group, what is more desirable is one which has a wider scope of influence and impact, and takes more people along the pathway of social progress. The kaleidoscopic form of social practice outlined above possesses features which are more desirable: simplicity, practicality, creativity, flexibility, dynamism and joy.

While it may not be easy to locate specific social movements within the typology presented above—as possibilities for a change of focus in intent and strategy always exist—what is required for the positive development of such Movements is collabouration and networking with others involved in social change, and wherever possible, feedback from other stakeholders about the influence and impact of any given social movement. When these conditions are met, it becomes easier for social movements to be positively and productively transformative.

3

The Rise and Fall of Social Movements

Kuruvilla Pandikattu
Jnana-Deepa Vidyapeeth, Pune

Abstract: This article, first, tries to see the significant role of social movements. Then it tries to explore the life cycle of it. This helps us to understand the four stages of social movements as the initial state of emergence, which social movements responds to a concrete challenge in the society then it grows and to coalescence state. Also known as the "popular stage", it is characterized by a more clearly defined sense of discontent. It is no longer just a general sense of unease, but now a sense of what the unease is about and who or what is responsible. The third stage is that of formalization or bureaucratization. This stage is characterized by higher levels of organization and coalition-based strategies. In this stage, social movements have had some success in that they have raised awareness to a degree that a co-ordinated strategy is necessary. Then the final stage of decline, which may be due to the following five reasons; repression, co-optation, success, failure and being absorbed by the mainstream. Then move to explore some philosophical reflections on the phenomena and dynamics of social movements, which are absolutely necessary in the civil society, to make it liberative, humanizing and constructive.

Keywords: Social Movements, Dynamics of Social Movements, Decline, Co-optation.

Introduction

In his 12-volume *A Study of History,*[1] *the British historian Arnold* Toynbee (1889-1975) examined the rise and fall of 26 civilizations in the course of

1 Arnold Toynbee, *A Study of History,* (London: Oxford University Press, 1961). The 12 volumes were published between 1934 and 1961.

human history, and he concluded that they rose by responding successfully to challenges under the leadership of creative minorities composed of elite leaders.

Civilizations declined when their leaders stopped responding creatively, and the civilizations then sank owing to the sins of nationalism, militarism, and the tyranny of a despotic minority. Unlike Spengler in his *The Decline of the West,*[2] Toynbee did not regard the death of a civilization as inevitable, for it may or may not continue to respond to successive challenges. Unlike Karl Marx, he saw history as shaped by spiritual, not economic forces. His basic insight is that "Civilizations die from suicide, not by murder."

In this article, I draw this insight from Toynbee's study of civilizations and apply to social movements. I attempt to show the life cycle of social movement and try to articulate its philosophical implications.

1. What and Why of Social Movements

Understanding precisely what a social movement is can be difficult. It is not a political party or interest group, which are stable political entities that have regular access to political power and political elites; nor is it a mass fad or trend, which are unorganized, fleeting and without goals. Instead they are somewhere in between.[3] Some characteristics of social movements are that they are "involved in conflictual relations with clearly identified opponents; are linked by dense informal networks; [and they] share a 4 collective identity."[4] Social Movements, then, can be thought of as organized yet informal social entities that are engaged in extra-institutional conflict that is oriented towards a goal. These goals can be either aimed at a specific and narrow policy or be more broadly aimed at cultural change.[5]

We know that social movements can occur on the local, national, or even global stage. There is no single, standard typology of social movements. Sociologist David Aberlle[6] classifies social movements based on what they want to change and how much change they want. Reform Movements seek to change something specific about the social structure. Some of the examples are *Narmada Bachao Andolan*, advocacy for Marriage Equality, etc. Revolutionary Movements seek to completely change every aspect of society. These include the 1960s counterculture movement, JP Movement, etc. Religious/Redemptive Movements are "meaning seeking", and their goal is to provoke inner change

2 Oswald Spengler, *The Decline of the West*, (London: Windham Press, 2013).

3 J. Freeman & V. Johnson, *The COINTELPRO Papers: Documents from the FBI's Secret Wars Against Domestic Dissent* (Boston: South End Press, 1990).

4 D. De la Porta & M. Diani, *Social Movements: An Introduction*, 2nd ed, (Malden MA: Blackwell Publishing, 2006), 20.

5 Jonathan Christiansen, "Four Stages of Social Movements," *Ebscohost*, accessed Sept. 12, 2018, https://www.ebscohost.com/uploads/imported/thisTopic-dbTopic-1248.pdf.

6 David F. Aberelle, *The Peyote Religion among the Navaho* (Chicago: Aldine, 1966).

or spiritual growth in individuals. Charismatic movement is a typical example. Alternative Movements are focused on self-improvement and limited, specific changes to individual beliefs and behaviour. These include trends like transcendental meditation and Yoga meditation, etc. Resistance Movements seek to prevent or undo change to the social structure. Contemporary Hindutva could be considered an example for this.[7]

2. Life Cycle of Social Movements

Later sociologists studied the life cycle of social movements—how they emerge, grow, and in some cases, perish. As indicated by Blumer (1969) and Tilly (1978) in the *preliminary stage*, people become aware of an issue, and leaders emerge. This is followed by the *coalescence stage* when people join together and organize in order to publicize the issue and raise awareness. In the *institutionalization stage*, the movement no longer requires grassroots volunteerism: it is an established organization, typically with a paid staff. When people fall away and adopt a new movement, the movement successfully brings about the change it sought, or when people no longer take the issue seriously, the movement falls into the *decline stage.*

As an enduring, sustained collectivity a social movement undergoes significant changes during its existence. This has led some scholars to formulate a theory of a "life cycle" or "natural history" common to all social movements. It can surely be said that a social movement has a career; for as it endures it always undergoes changes in many of its characteristics, though the sequence of these changes may vary from movement to movement.[8]

One of the most apparent changes is a shift in leadership. In its earliest stages the strongest influence on a movement is likely to be the charismatic leader or founder who personally symbolizes its values. At some point intellectuals play a leadership role by contributing to the developing ideology of the movement. And if a movement endures and grows for any length of time, administrative leaders arise who are concerned with the practical matters of organization and strategy.

Usually the membership of a movement grows during its initial period, which introduces an element of greater heterogeneity. In the early stages the followers typically are deeply committed with an almost fanatical dedication to the movement's values. If the movement gains a measure of respectability in some segment of society, members may be acquired who

---

7 "Reading: Types and Stages of Social Movements," *lumenlearning.com*, accessed September 3, 2018, https://courses.lumenlearning.com/alamo-sociology/chapter/reading-types-and-stages-of-social-movements/.

8 The Editors of Encyclopedia Britannica, "The Consequences Of Social Movements," accessed September 14, 2018, https://www.britannica.com/topic/social-movement/The-consequences-of-social-movements.

are not deeply committed. They are likely to have significant reservations about the movement, and their participation may be only infrequent. This heterogeneity also can be the basis for internal conflict in a movement. On the other hand, if a movement is publicly defined as revolutionary and subjected to harsh oppression, the membership is likely to be reduced mainly to deeply committed converts or to fanatics who derive some satisfaction from the feeling of being persecuted.

The movement is then transformed into a bureaucratic association, as happened, for example, with Aam Aadmi Party Movement and the Congress Party of India after British rule ended.[9]

3. Four Stages of Social Movements

So Blumer[10] and Tilly[11] provide a four-stage process for social movements. They are created (stage 1: emergence), they grow (stage 2: coalescence), they achieve successes or failures (stage 3: bureaucratization), and eventually, they dissolve and cease to exist (stage 4: decline).[12]

One of the earliest scholars to study social movement processes was Herbert Blumer, who identified four stages of social movements' lifecycles. The four stages he described were: "social ferment," "popular excitement," "formalization," and "institutionalization."[13] Since his early work, scholars have refined and renamed these stages but the underlying themes have remained relatively constant. Today, the four social movement stages may be summed up as:

1. Emergence
2. Coalescence
3. Bureaucratization and
4. Decline.

Although the term decline may sound negative, it should not necessarily be understood in negative terms. Some scholars have noted that social movements may decline for several reasons and have identified five ways they do decline, all of them may not be necessarily negative. These are

- Success
- Organizational failure

9 The Editors of Encyclopedia Britannica, "The Consequences of Social Movements," accessed September 14, 2018, https://www.britannica.com/topic/social-movement/The-consequences-of-social movements.

10 Herbert Blumer, *Symbolic Interactionism: Perspective and Method* (Berkeley, California: University of California Press, 2005).

11 Charles Tilly, *From Mobilization to Revolution* (New York: London: McGraw-Hill, 1998).

12 Ibid.

13 D. & M. Diani, *Social Movements: An Introduction*, 150.

- Co-optation by the mainstream
- Repression or
- Establishment within mainstream society[14]

Stage 1: Emergence

The first stage of the social movement life cycle is known as the emergence, or, as described by Blumer, the "social ferment" stage.[15] Within this stage, social movements are very preliminary and there is little to no organization. Instead this stage can be thought of as widespread discontent.[16] Potential movement participants may be unhappy with some policy or some social condition, but they have not taken any action in order to redress their grievances, or if they have it is most likely individual action rather than collective action. A person may comment to friends and family that he or she is dissatisfied with conditions or may write a letter to the local newspaper or representative, but these actions are not strategic and not collective. Further, there may be an increase in media coverage of negative conditions or unpopular policies which contributes to the general sense of discontent.[17]

This early stage can also be considered within a specific social movement organization. A social movement organization is an organization that is or has been associated with a social movement and which carries out the tasks that are necessary for any social movement to survive and be successful. An example of a social movement organization is the *Chipko* Movement of the 1970's. Within the emergence stage, its members serve as agitators. Agitators raise consciousness around issues and help to develop the sense of discontent and raise their consciousness.

Stage 2: Coalescence

Next stage in the life cycle, social movements overcome some obstacles which many never overcome. Often, social unrest or discontent passes without any organizing or widespread mobilization. For example, people in a community may complain to each other about a general injustice, but they do not come together to act on those complaints and the social movement does not progress to the next level. Stage two, known as coalescence, or the "popular stage", is

---

14 F. D. Miller, "The End of SDS and the Emergence of Weatherman: Demise through Success," in *Waves of Protest: Social Movements since the Sixties*, eds, J. Freeman & V. Johnson, (Lanham, Maryland: Rowman & Littlefield Publishers, 1999), 303-324., See also: J. J. Macionis, *Sociology*, 8th ed. (New Jersey: Prentice Hall, 2001).

15 D. & M. Diani, *Social Movements: An Introduction*.

16 J. J. Macionis, *Sociology*, 8th ed. (New Jersey: Prentice Hall, 2001)., See also: R. D. Hopper, "The Revolutionary Process: A Frame of Reference for the study of Revolutionary Movements," *Social Forces* 28, no. 3 (1950), 270-280.

17 Ibid.

characterized by a more clearly defined sense of discontent. It is no longer just a general sense of unease, but now a sense of what the unease is about and who or what is responsible. Rex D. Hopper (1950), in examining revolutionary processes, states that at this stage "unrest is no longer covert, endemic, and esoteric; it becomes overt, epidemic, and exoteric. Discontent is no longer uncoordinated and individual; it tends to become focalized and collective."[18] Further he states "this is the stage when individuals participating in the mass behaviour of the preceding stage become aware of each other."[19] At this point leadership emerges and strategies for success are worked out. Also, at this stage mass demonstrations may occur in order to display the social movement's power and to make clear demands. Most importantly this is the stage at which the movement becomes more than just random upset individuals; at this point they are now organized and strategic in their outlook.

The emergence of Congress Party provides a good example. After the initial emergence, the movement began a series of high profile campaigns, which sought to highlight the suffering and non-freedom of the Indians. After many years of successful, but hard fought campaigns and strong leadership, it achieved its purpose. Then the movement took on a political dimension and become a political party.

Stage 3: Bureaucratization

The third stage is known as bureaucratization. This stage, defined by Blumer as "formalization,"[20] is characterized by higher levels of organization and coalition-based strategies. In this stage, social movements have had some success in that they have raised awareness to a degree that a coordinated strategy is necessary across all of the SMOs. Similarly, SMOs will come to rely on staff persons with specialized knowledge that can run the day-to-day operations of the organization and carry out movement goals. Social Movements in this stage can no longer just rely on mass rallies or inspirational leaders to progress towards their goals and build constituencies; they must rely on trained staff to carry out the functions of organizations.[21] In this phase their political power is greater than in the previous stages in that they may have more regular access to political elites. Many social movements fail to bureaucratize in this way and end up fizzling out because it is difficult for members to sustain the emotional excitement necessary and because continued mobilization becomes

18 Rex D. Hopper, "The Revolutionary Process: A Frame of Reference for the Study of Revolutionary Movements," *Social Forces* 28, no. 3 (1950), 273.

19 Ibid., 273.

20 D. & M. Diani, *Social Movements: An Introduction.*

21 Ibid.

too demanding for participants. Formalization often means that paid staff can fill in when highly enthusiastic volunteers are not readily available.[22]

Here we may recall Max Weber's dilemma of institutionalization. For any movement to continue, it needs institution. But, by its very nature institution of the charism, saps the energy to itself and in the process the priority goes to the institutional elements at the expense of the process or goal of the movement.

Stage 4: Decline

Finally, the last stage in the social movement life cycle is decline, or "institutionalization." Decline does not necessarily mean failure for social movements though. Instead, Miller argues, there are four or five ways in which social movements can decline.[23] The decline need not be a natural process. Some of the reasons for the decline are discussed in the next section.

4. Reasons for Decline

In general, we can find the following reasons for the reasons for the decline and possible death of these Movements.

a. Repression

The first way social movements can decline is through repression. Repression occurs when authorities, or agents acting on behalf of the authorities, use measures (sometimes violent) to control or destroy a social movement. Further, Miller states "repressive actions may be defined as legitimate by the state…but they are never legitimate from the perspective of the movement."[24] This means that governments will often pass laws outlawing specific movement activities or organizations, or justify attacks on them by declaring them somehow dangerous to public order. This type of repression makes it exceedingly difficult for social movements to carry out their activities and recruit new members. Some of the examples are the political Movements like Tamil Tigers, Khalistan movement, etc.

b. Co-optation

Movements can also decline, if their organizations are highly dependent on centralized authority or on charismatic leadership, through co-optation. Co-optation occurs when movement leaders come to associate with authorities

---

22 J. J. Macionis, *Sociology*, 8th ed. (New Jersey: Prentice Hall, 2001)., See also: R. D. Hopper, "The Revolutionary Process: A Frame of Reference for the study of Revolutionary Movements," *Social Forces* 28, no. 3 (1950), 270-280.

23 J. J. Macionis, *Sociology*, 8th ed. (New Jersey: Prentice Hall, 2001).

24 F. D. Miller, "The End of SDS and the Emergence of Weatherman: Demise through Success." In *Waves of Protest: Social Movements since the Sixties*, eds, J. Freeman & V. Johnson (Lanham, Maryland: Rowman & Littlefield Publishers, 1999), 303-324.

or movement targets more than with the social movement constituents. For example, a leader could be asked to work for the organization that is the target of a movement with offers of being able to change things from the inside. Instead they themselves become integrated into the organization and take on its values, rather than the social movement's values. Leaders could also be paid off by authorities or target groups who ask them to redirect their activities in exchange.

c. Success

Of course, not all social movements end in defeat through repression or co-optation; some decline because they are successful. Smaller, localized Movements with very specific goals often have a better chance at outright success. Miller uses the example of an area that mobilizes to halt the construction of an airport. He also mentions that the women's suffrage movement was a national organization that achieved its goals and thus declined. Both of these examples point to Movements with very specific goals. Many social movements have goals that are much less clearly defined and many organize new campaigns once others are wrapping up either through success or compromise.

We may consider the view of Gandhi that Congress Party should be disbanded after regaining the freedom of India could be seen as an example. Though it did not factually happen, once the explicit aim of a movement is achieved, it does not have *locus standi* to exist, unless the movement changes its direction. That is what happened to the Congress Party, which was originally formed for India's independence, after its success changed the direction and retained its changed identity.

d. Failure

At times, Movements die out if they are not able to handle the rapid expansion that occur because of their success and due to organizational strain. They collapse into different factions. Failure of social movements due to organizational or strategic failings is common for many organizations. When failure occurs at the organizational level, Miller argues, it is usually for two reasons: factionalism and encapsulation.

As the factionalism grows worse and repression continues, Miller argues that groups became increasingly insular, leading to encapsulation. This is the process wherein a cadre of activists become isolated from the broader movement because they come to share many of the same habits and culture and their ideology becomes more similar to one another's and at the same time more rigid. They become so dedicated to the movement that they fail to sympathize with those who do not make the movement the dominant aspect of their life. Likewise, potential recruits find it hard to penetrate the close knit group.[25]

e. Establishment with Mainstream

Others have noted that a fifth reason for decline exists; mainly, that an organization becomes part of the established mainstream. That is, their goals or ideologies are adopted by the mainstream and there is no longer any need for a movement. An example of this would be the labour movement in the United States. For many years the labour movement was brutally repressed by authorities, but today the U.S. labour movement is well integrated into the political and economic system. Collective bargaining rights are guaranteed by the federal government (in most cases) and the labour movement is well established within the political system.[26]

Coming back to the insight of Toynbee, it may be said that many civilizations decline and die due to internal struggles and conflicts. Also lethargy and indifference may cause the gradual decline of civilizations. But, when it comes to social movements it is not always true that "civilizations die from suicide and not from murder."

Among the reasons proposed above, co-optation and failure may be said to favour the suicide theory, but not the other three. Thus according to the views proposed by us, death by suicide may be only one of the reasons for the downfall of social movements.

5. Philosophical Reflections

Social Movements continue to be a major force in the world. Sociologists provide important analysis of social movements that helps us to understand both past and present societies, as well as to anticipate changes and trends that may play out in the future. As new Movements develop, they can learn from the investigation of prior Movements' experience to better prepare for future possibilities. The model of analysis provided by the theory of the four stages of social movements is an important aspect in the development of knowledge about collective action. As social movements continue to change, so too do the methods sociologists use in analyzing them. Examining the four stages of social movements is one way of understanding how social movements form, develop, solidify, and decline. The model can be seen as one of many tools that sociologists use in examining our world.

From a philosophical point of view, we need to recognise that most of the social movements begin with a lot of enthusiasm for a change, involving

---

25 F. D. Miller, "The End of SDS and the Emergence of Weatherman: Demise through Success." In *Waves of Protest: Social Movements since the Sixties*, eds, J. Freeman & V. Johnson (Lanham, Maryland: Rowman & Littlefield Publishers, 1999), 303-324.

26 J. J. Macionis, *Sociology*, 8th ed. (New Jersey: Prentice Hall, 2001).

self-sacrifice, good will and commitment. The change demanded is normally against the larger society. But, gradually as the social movements develop, some of the characteristics which the social movements oppose in the larger society slowly creeps in, like inertia and selfishness. The initial goodness which was prevalent among the volunteers and leaders of the movement gradually disappears and the movement itself takes on the values of the larger society.

It is here that we need to recognise that majority of us do not want to leave the "comfort zones" of settled foundations. It is not proper to say that the initiators of the social movement are prophetic and can protest and the others are oppressive and stands for *status quo*. The same persons, as they grow up, exhibits both these characteristics of being prophetic and being oppressive, in a broader sense.

Further we need to recognize that the dynamics in the beginning of any social movements, where only a few people are involved is very different from the stage when a successful social movement may include thousands of people. From the initial level of say 15 people, when the social movements attempt to involve themselves into the larger sections of the society, if the social movements goes beyond, say 50 members, very different social, emotional and political dynamics takes on. This makes the possibility of the continuance of the social movement very different from their initial stages.

It is here that we need to understand that sometimes "revolution can eat its own children." Unless we are very careful, the normally liberative social movements, in the course of its development, can become oppressive. Thus eternal vigilance is the prize we pay to keep the social movements liberative, humanizing and constructive.

Conclusion

We first tried to see the significant role of social movements. Then we tried to explore the life cycle of it. This helps us to understand the four stages of social movements as the initial state of emergence, which social movements responds to a concrete challenge in the society Then it grows and to coalescence stage. Also known as the "popular stage", it is characterized by a more clearly defined sense of discontent. It is no longer just a general sense of unease, but now a sense of what the unease is about and who or what is responsible. The third stage is that of formalization or bureaucratization. This stage is characterized by higher levels of organization and coalition-based strategies. In this stage, social movements have had some success in that they have raised awareness to a degree that a coordinated strategy is necessary. Then the final stage of decline, which may be due to the following five reasons; repression, co-optation, success, failure and being absorbed by the mainstream. Here we understand that Arnold Toynbee's analysis of the decline of civilizations can only be partially applied to social movements. Then we have dealt briefly with some philosophical reflections on the phenomena and dynamics of social movements, which are absolutely necessary in the civil society, to make it liberative, humanising and constructive. So, eternal vigilance is the price we have to pay to make the social movement relevant to the larger civil society.

4

Nature and Scope of Social Movements in Democratic Societies

Dr Anthony Dias SJ
Xavier Institute of Social Research, Nashik

Abstract: In avowedly democratic societies such as India, with various rights and freedoms enshrined in written constitutions, many public-spirited individuals, voluntary organizations and social movements emerge. The scope for them, in principle, is unbounded. The first section of this paper outlines the nature of these Movements. The second deals with some Movements that have contributed to society in terms of improving the life of citizens, especially the more vulnerable ones such as the displaced; in freeing people from bonded labour; making efforts to improve the environment and combating climate change; helping labourers obtain minimum wages and better conditions of living; and so on. The third section deals with the situation where there are democracy-deficits and entrenched majoritarianism within democratic societies, the consequences of the same for social movements and how the latter strategize and negotiate with the state, including the Judiciary, and other institutions and actors, to protect their shrinking and threatened spaces. The concluding section dwells on the future of these Movements and points out to some hope on the horizon.

Keywords: Nature of Social Movements, Liberatory Praxis; Dussel, Enrique, The *Narmada Bachao Andolan*; The Narmada movement; Development; Gandhian Ethics; Gandhi's Talisman; Rehabilitation, *Bandhua Mukti Morcha*; Swami Agnivesh; bonded labourers; child labour; human rights jurisprudence, *Mazdoor Kisan Shakti Sangathan*; non-Party Political Movement; Alternative Politics; RTI; MNREGA; minimum wages; public hearing, Emergency; Democracy-deficit; Majoritarianism,

Award *Wapsi*, *Caravan-e-Mohabbat*; *Mere Ghar me Aake toh Dekho*; citizens against hate; *Padayatras*, Genocidal Majoritarianism; lynching; De-notified tribes; Dissent;.

Introduction

Social Movements have heralded major changes in society. Much before 'Occupy Wall Street' and the 'Arab Spring' Movements caught the attention of the world. There were Movements such as the women's right to vote led by Brit Emmeline Pankhurst in England; the civil rights movement led by Martin Luther King Jr; the LGBT movement; resistance to apartheid led by Nelson Mandela; the environmental movement; and so on. Pre-independent India witnessed a significant movement in the mid-nineteenth century (1857), which shook the British Raj. It was directed against an oppressive occupier regime that sought to foist its will on the people and exploited them and their natural resources. The first major mobilization of the Indian people was before Independence. Known as the 'freedom movement,'[1] it was led by Mahatma Gandhi and saw the end of the British rule in India.

Nature of Social Movements

A social movement may be described in several ways. Objectives of the movement can guide some classification. The social institution in or through which social change is to be brought about provides one basis for categorizing social movements as political, religious, economic, environmental, educational, cultural, and so on. There are reform and revolutionary Movements. A reform movement advocates a change that will preserve the existing values but will provide better means of of implementing them. The revolutionary movement, on the other hand, is regarded as advocating replacement of existing values. A movement that appears to threaten the values of powerful and significant interest groups within the society is defined as revolutionary and may face suppression.[2]

Another type of movement is defined as neither respectable nor dangerous but as peculiar. This type, seen as odd but harmless (LGBT), faces ridicule. Social Movements may also be categorized on the basis of their strategy and methods. For instance, whether they are legitimate or underground. The popular distinction between radical and moderate Movements reflects this sort of categorization. An obvious difference between types of Movements depends upon their reliance on violent or nonviolent methods. But, a nonviolent movement may also be defined as revolutionary or radical when it engages in

1 Within the larger frame of the Freedom Movement were subsumed other Movements, such as 'Quit India'.

2 Ralph Turner, Neil Smelser and Lewis Killian, "Social Change," accessed August 8, 2018, https//www britannica.com/topic/reform movement.

civil disobedience, rather than legal or parliamentary maneuvering, as part of its strategy. The distinction between violent and non-violent Movements is a relative one because a movement may shift from one to the other as it develops.[3] Sporadic incidents of violence does not make any movement 'violent'.

Scope of Social Movements in Democracies

In Democracies, public-spirited citizens and social movements are generally ubiquitous. What have they actually achieved in terms of promoting the common good, or freedom or liberation? What has been their 'liberatory praxis'? A brief survey and analysis of some well known social movements would give us a better understanding. We begin with three of them - the *Naramada Bachao Andolan* (NBA), the *Bandhua Mukti Morcha* (BMM) and the Mazdoor Kisan Shakti Sagathan (MKSS).

1. The NBA

It is one of the most enduring and significant protest movement Independent India has ever seen. The Narmada Project Authority is building, small and big, even gigantic dams ostensibly to generate electricity and to supply drinking water and irrigation. Ancient civilizations have developed over thousands of years along its banks. Its Valley is inhabited by the Bhils and Gonds and several other tribes. At stake, therefore, are the fundamental rights of vulnerable indigenous people who are fighting for their survival; for their 'right not to be deracinated'. Theirs is a cry for the right to live with human dignity. The echoes from the Narmada have reverberated in the wider universe. What role has the NBA played? It has no doubt attracted international attention. Many prominent intellectuals of the country have increasingly enlisted their support to the movement.[4] Despite the long drawn resistance, the movement failed to stop the construction of the *Sardar Sarovar Dam*. What does that portend? Let us examine the key contribution of the NBA.

Challenging Development Models and Proposing Alternatives

The defining slogan of the NBA says it all: *'Vikas Chahiye, Vinash Nahin'* ('We want Development, not Destruction). It has re-defined the notion of 'development'. It argued, with hard data, how costs of the mega project would exceed the benefits and explained not only the environmental but also the human cost of development that would chiefly be borne by the poor.[5] The

---

3 Ralph Turner, Neil Smelser and Lewis Killian, "Social Change," accessed August 8, 2018, https//www britannica.com/topic/reform movement.

4 This writer was associated with the NBA and had in 2009 joined the long march from Harsud in Madhya Pradesh to Ferkuwa bordering Gujarat.

5 Anthony Dias, *Development and Its Human Cost-Land Acquisition, Displacement and Rehabilitation of Tribals in India* (Jaipur: Rawat Publications, 2012), 50-65.

argument that individuals and Movements that critique models of development should not also be burdened with proposing alternatives, is a good one. Nonetheless, the NBA was unique in proposing workable and eco and people-friendly alternatives. Development, it believes, must be grounded in ethics, especially Gandhian ethics.

Interrogating the State

The NBA challenged the state's power of *eminent domain*, that justifies forcible acquisition of land from their owners for public purposes. It pointed out that 'public purpose' has never been clearly defined and so is abused; that compensation has also been grossly inadequate. Constant interrogation of, and pressure on, the state has borne long-term benefits for the people and the environment. Land Acquisition, Displacement and Rehabilitation have come to be taken seriously and were put on the agenda of project authorities (PAs). Ultimately, polices and laws were changed.[6]

Re-defining Rehabilitation

The NBA expanded the notion of rehabilitation to include things needed for the oustees to recover fully their losses. 'Rehabilitation' is now firmly on the agenda of (PAs) who are now asked to make rehabilitation as a 'development opportunity' for those who were called upon to sacrifice for the nation. They are also to be the first beneficiaries of the benefits produced by the project. This contributes to the well-being and dignity of the poor.[7] For the PAs the 'poor' (the displaced, oustees, evicted persons, and so on) practically did not exist, and when they did, they were a nuisance. Thanks to NBA's initiatives, the courts developed rights jurisprudence that made PAs take displacement and rehabilitation seriously. Now, the authorities are forced to first consider non-displacing alternatives.

Espousing Gandhian Philosophy

Ahimsa, Satyagraha and the forgotten *Talisman*' of Gandhiji: The NBA has consistently pursued non-violence despite the state repression and provocation. It has developed new 'vocabularies of protests', creative, as they were unusual and bold. *Satyagraha* was part of its protest philosophy and its leaders sometimes undertook fast unto death. These languages and metaphors have caught the attention of the world. Gandhi's philosophy, embedded in

6 Rehabilitation policies were brought in and finally in the year 2013 a landmark law was notified which incorporated both the land acquisition and rehabilitation provisions.

7 For a detailed note on the contribution of the NBA, see S G Vombatkere, "Narmada Bachao Andolan, 25 Years of Resistance and Reconstruction," *Mainstream* XLIX, no. 1 (2010), 21-25.

his '*Talisman*,'[8] guides NBA's thinking and actions and it is telling the state functionaries to follow it. What the NBA is asserting is that the decisions taken by the PAs have to be based on the interest of the 'last man', the poorest and the most vulnerable.

The movement began with a few members but soon became a movement to reckon with internationally. What made this possible was the method used by its leaders, which included organizing village-level meetings to bring awareness to the people about the project that was going to uproot thousands of villagers, submerge productive land, clear-fell pristine forests, destroy delicate eco-systems, do irrevocable harm to the rivers and tributaries and result in the loss of livelihoods. This galvanized the people into forming a solid resistance front. Discussions at the village level with information and awareness being brought to them by urban activists and academics helped the cause. The leading figure of the movement, Medha Patkar, is a Gandhian. Women who were made aware became strong and woman power manifested itself in many ways.

2. *Bandhua Mukti Morcha* (BMM)

Also known as the Bonded Labour Liberation Front, is led by the indefatigable Swami Agnivesh. The BMM worked for the release and rehabilitation of bonded labourers who lead a life of slavery and debt.[9] Slavery in various forms existed in India since past many centuries. Bonded labour system is a contemporary form of slavery and it includes bonded child labour.[10] Child labour is mostly found in the unorganized sector. Millions of children are born poor, with a debt burden hanging on them because their parents had taken a debt and had not been able to repay. They are unable to go to school or play and dream like normal children because they have to work up to 16 hours a day to repay the debt of their parents. They are being sold off like commodities. This is child slavery and the BMM reached out to them.

The BMM used all methods and avenues such as elected bodies, state assemblies and legislatures, Parliament, Judiciary and the law enforcement agencies to achieve its goal. It has successfully fought legal battles in the Supreme Court of India. Indian Parliament, United Nations Human Rights Commission, ILO and UNICEF have been sensitized on the issue. Its historic Public Interest Litigation made Justice P N Bhagwati deliver his landmark

---

8 "My Life is my Message," *Gandhi Quotes*, accessed September 15, 2018, https://www.mkgandhi.org/gquots1.html.

9 Till date the organization has secured release of over 1,78,000 bonded labourers in the country of which 26,000 are children. A large number of them have been rehabilitated.

10 India is still home to an estimated 300 million bonded labourers and 65 million bonded child labourers, notwithstanding the Constitutional guarantees, prohibitive laws like Bonded Labour System (Abolition) Act 1976, Child Labour (Prohibition & Regulation) Act 1986 and other International Conventions on the subject.

judgment in 1983 declaring that all labourers who are denied common minimum wage, are to be presumed bonded labourers (3SCC 1984). The government machinery was forced to respond. As many as 7,000 houses were constructed and allotted to the labourers released from bondage. Non-formal schools and health centres have been set up.

BMM has also been campaigning for a National Minimum Wage. Most bonded labourers hail from SC and ST communities and the BMM has been making efforts to engage their members in the various creative tasks for their holistic development. Its desire to liberate people from their oppression the BMM has worked on other issues such as casteism, discrimination against women, the abominable practice of Sati, female foeticide, child marriage, drug abuse, rapes and domestic violence, religious fundamentalism and obscurantism, oppression, corruption, communalism and terrorism.[11]

3. *Mazdoor Kisan Shakti Sangathan*, (MKSS)

People Empowerment via 'non-Party Politics'

Ms Aruna Roy is the force behind this organization which engages with workers and peasants in the villages of Rajasthan. It was set up by the people in 1990 to strengthen participatory democratic processes, so that ordinary citizens could live their lives with dignity and justice. The organization was born out of a struggle for community land held illegally by a feudal landlord. Also, the struggle for minimum wages made the people understand that transparency and accountability of systems of governance are basic to access any right. It became clear that access to relevant information is a fundamental tool for ensuring transparency and accountability of the government, and of all bodies that affect public interest. There was also a demand for transparency, accountability, and redressal through social audit (physical audit by the people). The first Public Hearing the MKSS organized established the importance of information for the people, and exposed the official opposition to disclosure of records. This led to the struggle for the people's Right to Information (RTI).

RTI is an effective tool to control the arbitrary exercise of power and corruption, and to secure the government's accountability to its people. It is of utmost importance in preventing anti-people policies and is a crucial part of the larger movement to deepen democracy and ensure democratic rights, development rights and human rights. It is now recognized that this Right is necessary to enable enforcement of the citizens' fundamental rights under both the Freedom of Expression under Article 19–(l) a and the Right to Life under Article 21 of the Indian Constitution. The campaign for the Right to

11 Swami Agnivesh gave a new, in-depth and contextual meaning to terrorism by expanding its horizon. To him when state policies impoverish and kill people, it is a form of terrorism - state terrorism.

Information was born out of the MKSS's struggle to ensure that all workers receive minimum wages. A further campaign demanded a National Rural Employment Guarantee Act (NREGA) as a legal entitlement. This became law in August 2005. This law guarantees all rural households in India 100 days of employment on demand every year at minimum wages.

In a democracy, without the right to know there can be no real right to exercise power and make the Government and the State accountable to its people. The Constitution of India acknowledges that the people are the sovereign power. To exercise their sovereignty in a responsible, ethical, and effective manner, the people must have the right to know. The elected government and the bureaucracy exercise power arbitrarily. They are both riddled with corruption, without any real accountability to the people. Corruption impacts the poor and their survival. In a democratic framework, it makes a mockery of the people's right to decision making by undermining even the formulation and implementation of law and policy.

Overall Reflections and Analysis of Social Movements

Looked at from the larger perspective of what the Narmada movement has achieved, one can discern significant gains in terms of human liberation, empowerment and the understanding of 'sustainable development' that cares for persons and communities, especially the 'last man' and threatened eco-systems. It also has an intra-and inter-generational equity dimensions. The NBA has contributed a lot to the development of not only liberating ideas and concepts but has actually resulted in reasonable gains to the people in terms of obtaining for them a better deal. It has tried to put people, and not greed and profits, at the heart of development. The Narmada movement has become a modern day symbol of hope and peaceful resistance. 'Narmada' has become an inspiration for other Movements. Its liberation praxis is a guiding light for many and in many ways the philosophy and methods of the movement resonates with the central ideas of the liberation philosopher Enrique Dussel.[12]

The work of BMM was different. It resulted in 'freeing the captives from their chains'. Those who had no hope, those who were made slaves and worked in distressing conditions, and for whom life was a hell on earth, found a new meaning to their lives. In the landmark case filed in the SC, chief justice Bhagwati delivered a judgment that advanced human rights jurisprudence that was hailed by the human rights community. BMM opened the eyes of the Justices to what was happening to the poorer castes and classes in India. This helped them to understand reality from the vantage point of the poor and helped them re-interpret the law from their perspective. All this produced

12 Frederick Mills, "The Development of Human Life in Enrique Dussel's Politics of Liberation," *Inter-American Journal of Philosophy* 7, no. 1 (2016), 56-67.

some of the finest judgments that advanced the human rights jurisprudence that has become a torchbearer for lawyers, judges, writers and civil society.

The liberatory praxis of BMM is inspired by the liberating Faith-Vision or Philosophy of its leader, Swami Agnivesh, who believes that true Faith, which includes meditation, must lead to Action on behalf of the oppressed. Hence, BMM became a movement whose mission was 'to set prisoners free', 'to give sight to the blind', 'to give voice to the voiceless', to rescue women from sati (murder in the name of tradition) and free people and society from the stranglehold of caste and religious bigotry that enslave and imprison the human mind and spirit. Prophetic voices, such as that of Swami Agnivesh, denounce evil even as they announce the 'good news' of liberation to the poor. Historically, prophets have had to suffer humiliation, torture, and even death. Hence, it is not surprising that Swamiji, while he was on his way to attend a programme organized by another marginalized group - the *Pahadiyas* - in Jharkhand, he was brutally attacked by a mob belonging to the *Sangh Parivar*.[13]

The contribution, through alternative people's politics, to empowerment of ordinary citizens was done by MKSS. It is a phenomenal achievement, one which further strengthened what has come to be known as 'non-Party politics', the concept developed by India's eminent political scientist Prof Rajani Kothari. The MKSS followed non-party political process to empower people to free themselves from the yoke of corruption and governmental inefficiency and oppression. This movement got the people involved in local governance and soon ordinary people started participating in making the government machinery accountable. This empowered the people who now felt that good and corruption-free governance was their right as citizens. Democracy itself was deepened and made more robust.

MKSS's struggle to obtain minimum wages, was primarily to help people lead a dignified existence. The right to life *with human dignity* guaranteed by the Constitution would be meaningless without minimum wages. Public hearing was one of the most potent tools for further empowerment of the people, who also came to realize the power of information to make the government accountable to them. Their relentless efforts made the enactment of the Right to Information (RTI) a reality.

Right from its notification, the RTI is used by the people to demand accountability from their governments thus bringing down the magnitude of corruption. Corruption is the bane of human rights and wherever it is rampant people suffer because they do not get their rights and entitlements - such as subsidized food, oil, fuel and other basic requirements needed for survival.

---

13 For a detailed note on the attack and reflections on Swami Agnivesh's mission, see Anthony Dias, "A Condemnable Attack on Swami Agnivesh," Guest Editorial, *VJTR* 82, no. 8, (August 2018), 3-6.

MKSS is an example of how people's Movements and politics can result in favourable legislation. After the RTI law, it was the MNREGA, guaranteeing 'the right to work' was enacted. Both these pieces of legislation were revolutionary in nature helping and empowering people to check corruption, to get their right to work implemented by demanding work under the law.

The efforts made by all government to dilute the RTI speaks about its efficacy in empowering and freeing the people from oppressive governmental rules and regulations and rampant corruption. The power of the RTI is also seen in the way those who use it are being targeted by those who stand to lose. Quite a few activists have suffered on account of their relentless fight for justice using the RTI. Some of them have even been murdered. The MNREGA is also sought to be diluted by the governments of the day, which are more interested in pleasing capitalists and the business class.

Movements have been able to successfully engage with the Judiciary helping it to look at, and interpret, reality from the perspective of the poor and the vulnerable. By using PIL they have been able to bring before the Justices several things concerning the plight of the poor, or their environment. This can be termed as 'ethical hermeneutics' propounded by the philosopher of liberation, Enrique Dussel. This interpretation enabled the Judiciary to deliver comprehensive Justice and the development of a healthy jurisprudence. In the process, not only has the Judiciary's eyes been opened but they were also able to set higher standards of Justice, develop a Jurisprudence of rights that would free people from their slavery, oppression, limitation; it has given voice to the voiceless. It has expanded and deepened Art 21 of the Constitution, and has said that the right to life includes dignity. Minimum wages are needed to lead a dignified life.

Social activists and Movements have seen and experienced the misery of the people and have responded with generosity and courage. They have brought 'good news to the poor' through their understanding of the situation. Most of these 'poor' are the tribal people of India, or the dalits, vulnerable women and children, the nomadic (wandering) and de-notified ("former criminal") tribes, and others. Social Movements have been at the forefront of the project of human liberation. They wanted the people to be free from all kinds of oppression, be they human or environmental, social or political, or structural. They have won for them their freedoms through many struggles.

These Movements have been able to open the eyes of the ordinary local people and helped them see the truth. They have been able to open the eyes of the government, the public and the international community to human and environmental violations and the degradation of nature leading to a poor quality of life for the marginalized. They have been able to put international bodies such as the World Bank and IMF on notice by questioning and challenging their lending practices and by telling them to follow their own policies. Social activists and Movements have been able to 'speak truth to power' and enabled the people to do the same - the very same people who earlier were afraid to ask questions, let alone challenge state or municipal authorities.[14]

Social Movements During Democracy-deficits

In general, it can be said that because of the presence of a largely democratic space, the limitations notwithstanding, social movements have done well. However, democracy suffered it most lethal blow when former Indian PM Indira Gandhi imposed the Emergency on an unsuspecting people. Dissent was either stifled or crushed. Those who spoke up or opposed the ruling elite were either censured or tortured in prison. All the fundamental rights of citizens were suspended. People's Movements were intimidated and/or silenced. It was the triumph of democracy when Mrs Gandhi was defeated in the subsequent elections and a new government of the people was in place.

With the change of governments, and experiments with minority governments with outside support, and coalition formations, the situation in general for social movements was satisfactory. Nonetheless, Movements did suffer during this period due to various reasons. The governments of the day, no matter which political party they belonged to, were generally skeptical of people's collectivities, since these generally either challenged the state on some issue or demanded something from it. Whenever the State felt that the people were becoming too demanding, or threatening, force was used even against peaceful dissenters and protesters, among whom were women and children. Despite all this, what awaited the people after the rise of the right wing government, was something they had never imagined; only a few had seen the writings on the wall; fewer could interpret and prophesy.

Majoritarianism and Social Movements

With the stunning landslide electoral victory of the BJP in the 2014 watershed elections, the socio-economic, cultural and political landscape of the country altered dramatically. The worst fears of intellectuals and rights activists came true. The new dispensation implemented its majoritarian agenda ruthlessly. Psychological and physical attacks on dalits and the minorities were launched. The state machinery was used for propaganda. Ministers made provocative statements against minorities. The cow came to occupy a special place in the communal politics. Lynchings of Muslims on mere suspicion of either eating or storing beef or trading in it took place. Intolerance of the views of others became common and dissenting voices silenced.

14 The women of the most backward tribes known as the *Musahars*, were too afraid to talk to other men, let alone government officials. This changed after the *Lok Manch* movement started working with them. This writer is closely associated with the movement right from its inception.

Every opportunity is taken to disregard the Constitution. Sensational daylight murders of thinkers and rationalists, who were seen as threats, shocked the conscience of the nation. Most recently there was a dastardly attack on Swami Agnivesh, which sent shockwaves across the country. Most recently human rights activists across the country were arrested in a swoop that defies logic. The intent is to intimidate rights activists and social movements. Their work of empowerment threatens to disturb the *status quo* and the position of the upper castes and the business classes. After the gruesome rapes a minor in a temple in Jammu, one commentator called this kind of majoritarianism 'genocidal.'[15] One finds no remorse on the part of the perpetrators; there is only justification, and more threats. There is, therefore, a fear psychosis among the minorities and other vulnerable groups. There is also a big worry among those working among the marginalized trying to free them from oppression.

Conclusion: Towards a New Horizon of Hope

Dissent is at the core of a vibrant and robust democracy; it is not merely a 'safety valve'. It is the opposition and the dissenting voices that keeps the ruling elites on its toes. Social Movements have a bigger role to play. They have a duty to keep the entire 'political class' on its toes, because the latter have 'class interests' to safeguard. The present situation in the county has prompted several intellectuals to say that what we have in India today is an 'undeclared Emergency', far more insidious than the one openly declared by Indira Gandhi, whose ghastly ghosts have still to be exorcised. The mandate of the majority of peace loving and secular Indians has been appropriated and manipulated by a few to produce what we see now - a humungous communal monster - waiting to devour the people and the nation.

However, the Values of the freedom movement, which find expression in the democratic, socialist, secular and republican Constitution, are still alive. The intolerance towards free thought and expression and the communally charged atmosphere in the country have made many thinkers and activists rise to the occasion to save democracy, the rule of law and the Constitution. The 'award *wapsi*' by writers was one bold gesture to protest against anti-democratic and fascist forces. Swami Agnivesh, who survived the brutal assault, was soon seen protesting the arrest by the Pune police of human rights activists across the country. All over there are spontaneous outbursts of the anger of the people. Several individuals and groups have responded in many ways. Intellectuals have called the bluff of the RSS and courageously exposed

15 Ananya Vajpeyi, "What the Kathua Rape Means," *the hindu.com*, accessed Sept. 10, 2018, https://www.thehindu.com/opinion/op-ed/what-the-kathua-rape-means/article23884731.ece.

its fake nationalism.[16] The *'Caravan-e-Mohabbat'* of Harsh Mander, *'Mere Ghar me aake to dekho'* led by Shabnam Hashmi, the campaign 'Citizens against Hate', The Citizens for Justice and Peace' led by Teesta Setalvad, and so on are signs of hope. Some others are on *padayatras* to combat the grave evil of communal hatred that threatens to engulf our country. They need the support of civil society in a big way. The way forward is long and arduous but it has to be traversed.

16 Yogendra Yadav, "A Nationalism that is Anti-National," *the hindu.com*, accessed September 20, 2018, https://www.thehindu.com/opinion/lead/a-nationalism-thats-anti-national/article25041762.ece.

5

Building Capacities and Enhancing Freedoms: Movements that Foster Social Development

Ashley Miranda
Divyadaan, Salesian Institute of Philosophy, Nashik

Abstract: All true development at the end of the day must be 'human development'. Otherwise it is not development at all. 'Nothing is worth the making, and nothing is really made, if it does not make the man and the woman'. 'Human development' is about adding value to human life rather than seeking to just further economic growth under the mistaken assumption that this will automatically translate into greater well-being for all.

One cannot totally avoid conflict, if one genuinely wants change. If anything good is to be achieved, it is very unlikely that it can be achieved without conflict. But, the creation of a new world can never be achieved on the unstable foundation of prejudice and bias. Revenge, settling scores, getting even, having one's pound of flesh are not legitimate means or goals of development, by any stretch of imagination. Social Movements must always be characterized not only by a courageous standing-up to oppressive and exploitative forces but also by a honest recognition of how even in the best of people, it does not take much to convert the one oppressed into an oppressor.

What is most significant about many social movements today is that they are driven from within. Instead of allowing people to see themselves as helpless victims, who need dole and constant monetary help to survive, most social movements today encourage people to take responsibility for their own lives. The goal of every social movement must always be to create a culture where people are empowered to believe in their own potential to be agents of the change they want to see in their lives. Human life has multiple dimensions and hence it is only sensible to conclude that genuine human development is a function of the harmonious furthering of human capacities and freedoms over all these dimensions.

Social change takes time. Prophets and visionaries, revolutionaries and activists are people who make change happen because of their courage and initiative, spirit of sacrifice and commitment. However, at the end of the day, humans are always catalysts. It does not take much to make a prophet into an ideologue, and to turn an ideologue into a tyrant. No human society that is truly just and equitable can really be sustained without a firm conviction that the truth can be known, if we commit ourselves to seek it together in a spirit of dialogue with other people of good will.

Keywords: Human Development, Development, Revolution, Conflict, Violence, Dialogue, Capacity, Social Movement, Multiple Dimensions.

Introduction

India is NGO country. These NGOs, as a group, have been extraordinary agents of social change, and it would be safe to say that without their contribution, the government alone depending only on its resources, both human and material, would not have been able to achieve what it has, in the area of social transformation, over these last seventy odd years since India's independence.

Much good has happened; much good has been brought about. The contribution of the 'thousands of NGOs' to this story has been significant, but it has not always begun with them. In some situations, the NGOs came first, in the sense that an individual or a group with a plan for change or a vision for a better tomorrow, formed an NGO with specific goals that sought to tackle in a systematic manner, one or more social issues that they felt needed to be addressed, to bring about more comprehensive and systemic change. But, at some other times – most often this is the case - individuals took the initiative to address one or other social problem affecting their particular community or society at large, and these initiatives slowly grew to become Movements of social mobilization and development. The individuals who wanted to make a difference came first, then came the NGOs. Sometimes the Movements remained Movements [in the sense that they retained their informal and spontaneous character] and did not metamorphose into NGOs.[1]

1 In India we have had a rich history of social movements, big and small, that brought about revolutionary and life transforming changes, both at the micro and macro level of Indian society. In Pre-independence India, we had Movements against the social ills of sati, child marriage, caste discrimination, among others and also Movements with a positive focus seeking to promote education of girls and children of communities treated as outcastes, widow remarriage, and most importantly of all, Independence [the Freedom Movement]. Post-Independence, we have had powerful environmental Movements, workers Movements, peasant Movements, Movements for the empowerment of Dalits, etc.

On the flip side, it must be acknowledged, that not all NGOs and allied social groups formed to address pressing social problems and to work for social development have been able to retain their initial focus. Sometimes their own popularity and success has distracted them, and in some instances the lure of money, the temptation of political patronage and the inability to resist powerful and seductive forces, and the simple human foible of becoming a victim of one's own grandiosity – one's own indispensability and invincibility - has either contributed to their disintegration or dissipation. These NGOs may still be around, these social problems may still become a topic of conversation, symposia or seminars, but the fire does not remain. The survival of the NGO may become more important than the single-minded, coordinated effort to address the social issue in question and to weed out social ills from the root, so as to ensure that they do not resurface again in some other form.

The NGOs should be also on the guard against the possibility that even the best among them could become victims of their own popularity, success or greed. In order to do this, they have to address themselves some fundamental questions. What exactly is development? What is it that I/we want to achieve in terms of development through my/our work? What are my/our motives for committing myself/ourselves to the work I/we, am/are involved in? What difference do we want to bring about? What indicators do I/we have to know that I/we am/are on the right track? How do I/we know that my/our work has not been hijacked by some selfish interests, whether these are within myself/ourselves or these are within power groups within society with narrow, selfish, bigoted interests?

Progress that is oriented towards Human Development

Not everything new is progress, not all progress is development.[2] It is very easy to presume that because something [a thing or a state of affairs] is new it marks an improvement over what was in the past. Movement or change need not always be forward; there is such a thing as a 'step backward' and some changes that take place either spontaneously or through the effort of 'social agents' are most definitely retrograde. One can add to this by saying, not every step forward is a step in the right direction. Progress often comes at a price! Sometimes the price is worth paying, sometimes the price paid is not worth it. At some other times one group pays the price and another group altogether reaps the benefits.[3] When over a number of situations, the groups paying the

2 Nils Heisterhagen, "The Liberal Illusion of Automatic Progress," *International Politics and Society*, (October 11, 2018), accessed October 15, 2018, https://www.ips-journal.eu/in-focus/2018/progressive-illusions/article/show/the-liberal-illusion-of-automatic-progress-3022/.

3 Min Zhu, "Paying the Price for the Future We Want,"*IMF* (blog), (June 19, 2012), accessed October 15, 2018, https://www.ips-journal.eu/in-focus/2018/progressive-illusions/article/

price and the groups harvesting the benefits are consistently the same, then one is left with no choice but to conclude that what is happening is not progress, but loot, plunder and exploitation.

Progress and development are often used as synonyms and with good reason. The presumption is that all true progress must lead to real development. But, given the human capacity for self-deceit and rationalization, this presumption is quite often nothing more than a presumption. What we call progress, has over the years, definitely contributed to development, but this development has often been lopsided, inequitable, exploitative and even unjust. The adjectives used are antithetical to the core meaning of the term development. The issue we need to raise, therefore, is whether our use of these qualifiers has been improper or is there something not quite right with how we understand development.

Progress and development are terms that belong to the same family of words. One usually implies the other. In the sense that, progress must in some real tangible way contribute to development; while development in its turn entails that some real progress has been made somewhere, even if it is not immediately verifiable. Progress is a term that usually implies some forward movement in a definitive direction usually in the fields of economic welfare, science and technology, building of infrastructure, etc. Development too implies a movement in a definitive forward direction but it has an indispensable human dimension. All true development at the end of the day must be 'human development.'[4] otherwise it is not development at all. 'Nothing is worth the making, and nothing is really made if it does not make the man and the woman'. It is significant and appropriate that the United Nations releases every year what it calls the "Human Development Report" rather than just a "development report."[5] Explaining on its website the rationale behind its choosing to link 'human' and 'development' together it explains development is about enriching human beings rather than just adding value to the economy of which human beings are a part. 'Human development' is about adding value to human life rather than seeking to just further economic growth under the mistaken assumption that this will automatically translate into greater well-being for all. The 'human development' approach is, therefore, about promoting 'human well-being' understood as giving opportunities to people to

---

show/the-liberal-illusion-of-automatic-progress-3022/.

4 According to Amartya Sen, Mahbub ul-Haq, the noted Pakistani economist, is the one who must be credited for pioneering this concept of 'human development'. Cfr. Nermeen Shaikh, Interview, "Amartya Sen: A More Human Theory of Development,"*Asia Society*, (December 6, 2004), accessed July 5, 2018. https://asiasociety.org/amartya-sen-more-human-theory-development.

5 *Human Development Reports*, http://hdr.undp.org/en/humandev, accessed August 10, 2018.

build up their capacities and develop their full human potential, and creating conditions in which people, especially the most vulnerable, can exercise their choice about how to use their newly acquired capacities, in productive and creative ways, according to their own best judgement.[6]

Ideally, while progress and development can be considered as parallel tracks that contribute to smooth and harmonious movement of individuals and groups in a forward direction, or as concentric circles, one leading to the other, in real life situations these could very easily become divergent paths leading in opposite directions, one negating the other. Any movement, or enterprise, or NGO that seeks to bring about social change, needs to clarify for itself how its many activities contributes to genuine development. It is not enough to say that much is being done and that they are making progress; the question is, how all this is contributing to the development of the various parties involved in the activity, either as stakeholders or beneficiaries, a more fundamental question is, whether at all, this development has a human component.

Some would object to the assertion that true development must always have a 'human component' on the grounds of 'speciesism.'[7] Philosophers, like Peter Singer, think that speciesism which tends to privilege one's own species over other species is a prejudice that does not have any sound rational basis.[8] There are many social movements today in defense of the environment, in defense of 'the rights of' plants and animals, and they all have a place within the grand scheme of things. We are not in a position, in this paper, to discuss the merits of the arguments of the critics of 'speciesism', but we cannot dispute the general thrust of their argument that holds that our identity and our survival as human beings is dependent on our ability and willingness to view ourselves as intrinsically linked with the earth, with the world of trees and animals, with the world of rivers, the mountains, the coral reefs, the icebergs and the oceans. One would have to fully agree with these critics in their claim that a development that destroys and fragments the world and sees it purely in terms of its 'usefulness' to human being's relentless quest for more and more is no development at all. For a short while, we humans could perhaps get away with the destruction we take such delight in causing, but sooner rather than later, this destruction will destroy us.[9] True development must always seek the integral welfare of the human being, and to genuinely work towards the

6 *Human Development Reports*, http://hdr.undp.org/en/humandev, accessed August 10, 2018.

7 The term 'speciesism' was coined and first used by the animal activist Richard Ryder.

8 George Yancy and Peter Singer, "Peter Singer: On Racism, Animal Rights and Human Rights,"*OpinionatorThe New York Times,* (May 27, 2015), accessed August 1, 2018, https://opinionator.blogs.nytimes.com/2015/05/27/peter-singer-on-speciesism-and-racism/.

9 David Abram, *Becoming Animal: An Earthly Cosmology* (New York: Vintage Books, 2011), 3-12.

securing of the human good, we have no choice, but to seek the good of the 'earth as a whole'.

The Creation of a New Social Order

Social Movements, whether they are spearheaded by visionary individuals or by NGOs or by committed groups seek to bring about change. Whether these groups or individuals focus on local issues or problems and social ills that plague the larger society, they invariably cause a lot of heartburn. Whatever the cause, it is only reasonable to expect there will be people who feel threatened and seek therefore, to bring together like minded people to oppose the change that is sought to be brought about. One cannot totally avoid conflict if one genuinely wants change. This invariably leads to the formation of opposing parties, people who stand on opposite sides of the fence. The temptation, however, is to divide all those involved into two clearly defined groups, representing two different poles. By using terms such as victims and aggressors, oppressed and oppressors, we could very simplistically conclude that one group is good and innocent and the other group is bad and malicious. We could look for enemies to fight, for villains to vanquish. We could conclude that an individual is wrong and an adversary who needs to be shown his/her place simply because he or she belongs to a particular social group or because he or she has or does not have a certain level of education, etc. One exploiting and unscrupulous individual from a particular group does not make all members of his social group exploiters, one violent man does not make all men violent, one scheming and crooked businessman does not make all the members of his community scheming and crooked. Not every conflict between a man and a woman is an example of patriarchal dominance. Not every case of suicide – tragic though it may be – is a case of bullying companions or abusive parents. There are indeed victims and aggressors, good people and bad people but one cannot decide beforehand who is who. One would need a proper and careful investigation to reveal the truth. To prejudge would be to succumb to prejudice, which unfortunately seems to be the fashion of the day. Prejudices only entrench the many irrational biases that practically all humans are prey to, to a lesser or greater degree.

If anything good is to be achieved, it is very unlikely it can be achieved without conflict. But, the creation of a new world can never be achieved on the unstable foundation of prejudice and bias. Setting people against each other can only worsen previous misunderstandings and create suspicion. Revenge, settling scores, getting even, having one's pound of flesh are not legitimate goals by any stretch of imagination. These attitudes only worsen resentments and leave society more scarred and prone to future volatility than before. Among the greatest revolutionaries of the modern age, Gandhi and Martin Luther King (Jr.) were also fervent apostles of non-violence, forgiveness and love. The only way to break the cycle of hatred, prejudice and exploitation, they believed, was to oppose these forces with the power of dialogue and love.[10]

Becoming Aware of the Dynamics of Power

Social Movements arise to set right unjust power equations that operate between peoples, different groups or societies. Postmodernism, with its championing of concepts such as local narratives, periphery, deconstruction, has made us all acutely aware of power differentials, the tendency of majority or power groups to dominate and to exploit. The birth of social movements as a response to concrete, existential situations of oppression and the sharp focus on the injustices these Movements want to set right often gives rise to a mentality that sees things in terms of black and white. It is true that people with power tend to dominate, but it is also a fact that practically everyone has power, only different degrees and different kinds. Nietzsche understood the nature of power rightly when he said that the will to power is operative in all, the supposedly weak and the apparently strong, those who seem to be part of the herd and those who pride in taking responsibility for their lives.[11] Social Movements therefore, must always be characterized not only by a courageous standing-up to oppressive and exploitative forces but also by a honest recognition of how even in the best of people it does not take much to convert the one oppressed into an oppressor. Social Movements that only replace one set of oppressors with another set, or turn the tables on people whose ancestors once enjoyed unfair privileges are doing something that is necessary perhaps. But, this can only be considered the first stage of a longer process that seeks to bring about true justice for all and genuine harmony in society.[12]

10 Building on the words of Jesus in the Bible, Mahatma Gandhi famously said, "An eye for an eye makes the whole world go blind." Also cfr. Mark Moore, "Love and Hate according to Martin Luther King Jr.,"*Missio Alliance* (January 19, 2015), accessed August 1, 2018, https://opinionator.blogs.nytimes.com/2015/05/27/peter-singer-on-speciesism-and-racism/.

11 Emrys Westacott, "Nietzsche's Concept of the Will to Power," *Thought Co.*, accessed October 1, 2018, https://www.thoughtco.com/nietzsches-concept-of-the-will-to-power-2670658.

12 In this context it is interesting to note the differences of opinion between Frantz Fanon and Sartre on one side and Camus on the other with regard to the revolution in Algeria against the French colonial power. Fanon believed that violence is a legitimate, and even necessary cleansing force. Camus disagreed and held that the belief that peace can result from violence is a 'crime of logic'. See also: Craig DeLancey, "Albert Camus: Unfashionable Anti-Totalitarian," *Quillette* (March 26, 2019), accessed March 27, 2019, https://opinionator.blogs.nytimes.com/2015/05/27/peter-singer-on-speciesism-and-racism/.

From Condescension and Charity to Empowerment and Self Belief

When one looks at the history of social movements that have worked to bring about transformative change one notices that there has been over the years a radical shift in the awareness of those involved in these Movements about what they need to do, to bring about this change.

Initially, most Movements were characterized by the coming together of a group of highly motivated individuals, enthusiastically committing themselves to some social cause. With admitted exceptions, the approach usually was 'we' [the privileged and enlightened'] reach out and work for 'them [the oppressed, the helpless]. These selfless individuals would see themselves possessing a historic responsibility to society and to the world. At great personal cost, they worked hard to mobilize resources with which to help the community/people they had identified as needing their special care. Much good was done through their work but unfortunately it was often noticed this well-meaning work created in the beneficiaries a kind of dependence that they were not eager to let go of. They were happy to receive and oftentimes they felt very resentful when the help they got accustomed to receiving, stopped suddenly.

Social Movements, even in the present day, do need much money to sustain themselves. The difference is, now there is greater awareness that money can create unhealthy dependence, and even sometimes situations where commitment to the cause itself may be radically compromised. Now there is a greater sensitivity to the need to generate this money from within local communities as far as possible. This very rarely happens; nevertheless, the awareness that no substantial change can come about without those who presently see themselves as 'victims' or 'marginalized' taking responsibility for their own lives and destiny is itself life transforming.

What is most significant about many social movements today is that they are driven from within. Instead of allowing people to see themselves as helpless victims who need dole and constant monetary help to survive, most social movements today encourage people to take responsibility for their own lives. The focus today is on asking 'what can the community do to help itself?' There perhaps are individuals or groups of individuals so systematically exploited that they find themselves in a situation where they just cannot help themselves;[13] such groups and individuals must be helped. But the goal of every social movement must always be to create a culture where people are empowered to believe in their own potential to be agents of the change they want to see in their lives. In his vicious critique of Christianity, Nietzsche attacked what he considered to be this sense of tragic helplessness in front of evil and suffering that Christianity seemed to foster. He believed, that all humans possess the will to power, and a dignified human life is one in which

13 Victims of Human trafficking are perhaps one example of people who are radically helpless.

individuals used this 'power' within themselves in creative ways to achieve mastery over themselves and their destinies and in doing so to 'transform' the quality of their lives.'[14]

Building Capacities and Enhancing Freedoms

One of the most systematic exposes of the empowering approach which social movements that seek to foster development need to adopt is the one presented by the noted economist Amartya Sen in his writing on what he calls the 'capability approach.'[15] He holds that people are the goal of development. True development seeks to promote the integral well-being of individual human beings and their communities, by enhancing their substantive freedoms. It is not only economic poverty, but also factors such as ignorance, lack of access to health care, proper nutrition and education, social exclusion, gender discrimination, physical disabilities, environmental factors among others that restrict human freedom to live lives that are fulfilling and meaningful. Sen holds that genuine development brings together the development of capacities and the possibility of exercising freedoms. Freedom provides the space for capacities to develop. Therefore, any social movement that seeks to foster integral development must focus on 'building capacities and enhancing freedoms,'[16] without which, any other form of progress is essentially meaningless.

Numbers presented by boasting governments – whether they be GDP figures, or 'Per Capita Income' statistics, or GNP statistics usually conceal 'a multitude of sins.'[17] Viewing development purely in terms of GDP figures is like looking at the speedometer of the car to ascertain whether all is fine, without bothering to ask whether the car is headed in the right direction, whether there is enough fuel in the tank, whether the passengers are in the car and have not been left at the starting point in our eagerness to get the car moving. Human life has multiple dimensions and hence it is only sensible to conclude that genuine human development is a function of the harmonious furthering of human capacities and freedoms over all these dimensions [Physical, intellectual, emotional, spiritual, cultural, psychological, social, environmental, and of course also the economical].[18]

---

14 Emrys Westacott, "Neitzsche's Concept of the Will to Power," *Thought Co.*, accessed October 1, 2018, https://www.thoughtco.com/nietzsches-concept-of-the-will-to-power-2670658.

15 *Internet Encyclopedia of Philosophy*, Thomas Wells, "Sen's Capability Approach," accessed August 18, 2018, https://www.iep.utm.edu/sen-cap/.

16 Sen uses the term 'functionings' to refer to actual freedoms realized.

17 Ramchandra Guha, *Environmentalism: A Global History* (Gurgaon: Penguin Books, 2016), 107.

18 "Development "Beyond GDP," *Issues and Challenges in India* (April 25, 2018), accessed October 1, 2018, https://socialissuesindia.wordpress.com/2018/04/25/word-

Social Movements and The Creation of Perfect Worlds

The world needs prophets and revolutionaries. It needs visionaries and activists. As long as we live in an imperfect world, and as long as we are surrounded by injustices, there will always be need for social movements seeking to set things right. The problem arises, however, when the prophet is in tearing hurry to make his dreams of a perfect world a reality. He begins to look at problems simplistically, he comes up with quick solutions; someone has to be got rid of, someone else must be put in his place, and a third someone else must be punished. This makes of the prophet an ideologue. Jordan Peterson, speaks of the ideologue as one who begins with good intentions but who slowly gets so absorbed with his sense of self-importance and his special role in altering the story of the world that he falls prey to the temptations of oversimplification and falsification. He adopts a single axiom as a solution to the world's problems and filters out all those experiences which do not fit in with how he has chosen to look at the world.[19]

Social change takes time. Prophets and visionaries, revolutionaries and activists are people who make change happen because of their courage and initiative, spirit of sacrifice and commitment. However, at the end of the day, humans are always catalysts. It does not take much to make a prophet into an ideologue, and to turn an ideologue into a tyrant. History is full of examples of men who thought they had figured it all out; they wanted change and they wanted it immediately.[20]

A Joint Quest for the Truth and A Spirit of Dialogue

Much has changed in the world over the last hundred years or so. In fact, change has been the one constant right through the history of humankind. What is different about this century is the nature and pace of this change. Besides a leap forward in the 'quality of life' evidenced in the wonderful advances we have made in the fields of medical care, nutrition, consciousness of the rights of children and women, we have also witnessed the success of many hitherto marginalized groups in winning freedoms for themselves, which they themselves may perhaps have thought impossible not many years ago.

These advances and freedoms need to be celebrated! The more aware we are of the rights of our fellow men and women, the more committed we are to the defense of our own freedoms and the freedoms of those who belong to groups very different from the ones we belong to, the better off we are. The social movements that have made these freedoms and triumphs possible need

---

needs-development-beyond-gdp/.

19 Jordan B. Peterson, *12 Rules for Life: An Antidote for Chaos* (UK: Allen Lane, 2018), 211.

20 Jordan B. Peterson, *12 Rules for Life: An Antidote for Chaos* (UK: Allen Lane, 2018), 306-311.

to be acknowledged and commended. However, we need to pay attention to the fact that these victories have come at no small cost. Without our even realizing it, two very foundational convictions without which no just human society can be meaningfully built have been eroded from our consciousness; namely, the conviction that we can know the truth and that in order to know the truth, we must engage in a genuine and open dialogue with our fellowmen, especially those who think very differently from us. The conviction that truth can be known is replaced by an inconsistent belief that nothing is right or wrong in itself. Truth is a matter of perspective [at least that is the case with everybody else's truth except mine]. Openness to dialogue has been replaced by political maneuvering. Today some issues cannot be discussed or questioned, some things can simply not be said. Not only have marginalized groups found power [which is a good thing] but also some fringe groups have found inordinate power [way beyond their numbers]. Being politically correct today is more important than seeking the truth and trying to live by it.

There is no denying that, both in India and other parts of the world, the many social movements and the activists and prophets who have spearheaded them have rendered human society great service. By their questioning and protest they have helped us to get in touch with our humanity and to join together with our fellowmen and women to create a more free and just society. But, we need to say by way of conclusion, that no human society that is truly just and equitable can really be sustained without a humble yet firm conviction that the truth can be known, the courage to say it, even if one does not know it completely or fully, and a commitment to seek it together with other people of good will.

6

Towards a Biblical Philosophy of Liberation

Dr Martin Sebastian Kallungal
Archdiocese of Ernakulam-Angamaly, Kerala

Abstract: The main questions addressed in this paper are: First, how does the identity of philosophy shape itself up when it is done from within one or another specific tradition of liberatory praxis? Second, can the Bible be engaged philosophically? Third, what are the main aspects of a biblical philosophy of liberation? The first question followed in close conversation with the Latin American-Mexican philosopher, Enrique Dussel. Taking cues from Paul Ricoeur's ground making investigations into the relationship between philosophical hermeneutics and biblical hermeneutics, the second question about the possibility of engaging the Bible philosophically in affirmative. After clarifying the notions of 'philosophy of liberation' and 'biblical philosophy, and arguing for urgent need to seek for ways to rehabilitate philosophy in the field of biblical hermeneutics, a brief schematic presentation of a biblical philosophy of liberation is offered in the final part of the paper.

Keywords: Bible, Philosophy, Hermeneutics, Liberation, Poor.

Introduction

In this paper, we will address three questions. First, how does the identity of philosophy shape itself up when it is done from within one or another specific tradition of liberatory praxis? Second, can the Bible be engaged philosophically? Third, what are the main aspects of a biblical philosophy of liberation? In answer to the first question, which we will follow in close conversation with the Latin American-Mexican philosopher, Enrique Dussel, we propose that a philosophy, which gives thematic priority to the praxis of liberation of the oppressed and the underdeveloped, may be rightly named as a philosophy of liberation. Ironically, the first basic theme such a philosophy of liberation must take for critical-creative reflection is none other than philosophy itself. For, the condition of possibility of any philosophy of liberation as well as its first fruit is liberation of philosophy from the hands of dominant ideologists who instrumentalize it for institutional purposes. In the first part of this paper, we will explain why liberation of philosophy is of primary importance. In the second part, we will answer the question about the possibility of engaging the Bible philosophically in affirmative. Paul Ricoeur's ground-making investigations into the relationship between philosophical hermeneutics and biblical hermeneutics will be an important resource at this stage. After clarifying the notions of 'philosophy of liberation' and 'biblical philosophy', in the final part of this paper we will suggest that the primary task of a biblical philosopher of liberation is to liberate the Bible and its *others* from the practice of idolatrous reading of scriptural passages.

Enrique Dussel and Philosophy of Liberation

Dussel has made pioneering and substantial contributions to the field of philosophy of liberation. His biography is very much constitutive of his philosophical discourse because it is his life-experience which has trained him to look at the world through the eyes of *other*. Born in 1934 as the son of a country doctor, Dussel grew up in Mendoza, Argentina. From 1953 to 1957 he studied philosophy at Mendoza. In 1957, while he was travelling to Europe with the purpose of continuing his studies, he learnt for the first time in his life that he was someone from the periphery and that he did not belong to the center of the world which was Europe in his estimation. Soon after this realization, he was also deeply influenced by the French Jesuit Paul Gauthier during his stay in Israel where he learnt Hebrew and Greek. Gauthier taught him to look at history not simply from the angle of the Latin-American experience, but also from a more general perspective of the poor and the oppressed in the peripheries of the world at large. From 1969 onwards, he has been influenced by the thoughts of Emmanuel Levinas who raises the question of responsibility for the discriminated and oppressed others. In addition, he began to read Paul Ricoeur, Frantz Fanon, and Herbert Marcuse. He became convinced about the primacy of ethics and the urgency for social change. He built on their thoughts as well as the insights gleaned from his critical assessment of history, and, developed a very thought-provoking and action-inducing philosophy of liberation.[1] Dussel's ambition is to rebuild the whole edifice of philosophy. He

1 Enrique Dussel, *Philosophy of Liberation* (Maryknoll, NY: ORBIS Books, 1985).

relocates thinking practice in a spatial setting that is unfamiliar to the mainline Western philosophies, uses new categories, and develops different methods.

Periphery: The Spatial Location of Philosophy

From Edmund Husserl who stated that no one becomes a philosopher through the study of existing philosophies and that the irresistible intellectual impulse to research comes not from thoughts but from things and problems surrounding them, Dussel learnt that: "Philosophy, when it is philosophy and not sophistry or ideology, does not ponder philosophy. [...] Philosophy ponders the nonphilosophical; the reality."[2] Except in a pedagogical exercise meant for familiarizing oneself with interpretive categories, philosophers need not engage philosophies. Having, thus, decided to do philosophy differently, Dussel looks for the correct spatial setting required for the genesis and development of thought. Since philosophers need to be concerned more and more about things and less and less about thoughts, the spatial setting of philosophy must be "a territory with fixed frontiers" which, as Dussel clarifies, is "very different from the abstract idealization of empty space of Newton's physics or the existential space of phenomenology."[3] Put simply, it is socio-political peripheral space.

Exteriority, Proximity, and Praxis: Three Important Categories of Thought

All possible systems in this world have their alterities or 'the beyond'. The other is the precise notion which Dussel uses to speak about exteriority or alterity. Exteriority signifies "the ambit whence other persons, as free and not conditioned by one's own system and not as part of one's own world, reveal themselves."[4] We recognize exteriority when suddenly the face of a discriminated and oppressed other appears in our world, when the cry of the poor pierces the veil between our happy world and its periphery. Hunger, for instance, is the practical exteriority of an unjust system. To put it in Dussel's own words: "Others reveal themselves as others in all acuteness of their exteriority when they burst in upon us as something extraordinary, the enormous ('apart from the norm') – the poor, the oppressed. They are the ones who, by the side of the road, outside the system, show their suffering, challenging faces: 'We are hungry! We have the right to eat!"[5] The other not only shows its face up but also provokes justice and pronounces judgment on the system by mere self-revelation. One can either take the responsibility for the other or ignore

2 Dussel, *Philosophy of Liberation*, 3.

3 Ibid., 1.

4 Ibid., 40.

5 Ibid., 43.

the other. Since the otherness of the other is revealed in his/her exteriority, taking responsibility draws one to an existential closeness with the other. Such existential closeness is called proximity. It is much more than empathy. It is not being considerate to the other but getting contaminated by the other. When one acts responsibly for and with the other, one regains proximity. The motivation and action that bridges the gap between exteriority and proximity is called praxis. Dussel makes it clearer: "I am speaking here of approaching a person, of shortening the distance between someone who can accept or reject us, shake our hand or injure us, kiss us or kill us."[6] Indeed, praxis is about shortening the distance: "It is acting toward the other as other; it is an action that is directed toward proximity. Praxis is this, and nothing more: an approach to proximity."[7]

Re-envisioning Philosophy: Thinking out Liberatory Practices

Thanks to the inevitable reference to praxis, philosophy maintains a thick relation to the concrete historical totality from which it emerges and into which it returns. This inevitable link to contextual exigencies "places philosophy on an ideological level, where ideology is understood as "systematic whole of ideas that explain, justify and camouflage an entrenched praxis."[8] For instance, Dussel points out the pro-slavery views of Aristotle and Aquinas' the anti-feminine theological remarks.[9] Philosophical subjectivity depends on historical subjectivity. Dussel states that "the *ego Cogito* is first of all an *ego* labor*o, ego opero*, or *ego desidero* of a group, of a people."[10] This is the reason why, Dussel argues, Hegel in his *Philosophy of Right* presupposed private property to be freedom's determination.[11]

In any case, praxis determines philosophy in a very intimate manner in the choice of methods and the categories it constructs. For instance, if someone believes in and wants to reaffirm the existing system, then he/she will discard critical and dialectical methods. Praxis that reproduces the system will be

---

6 Dussel, *Philosophy of Liberation*, 17.

7 Ibid.

8 Ibid., 181.

9 In *Politics,* I,1, Aristotle says: "Nature (physics) would like to distinguish between the bodies of freemen and slaves, making the one strong for servile labour, the other upright and altogether useless for such service. [...] It is manifest, then, that some men are by nature (physei) free, and others slaves, and for that these latter slavery is both expedient and right." While talking about the transmission of original sin, Aquinas says: "Now it is manifest that in the opinion of philosophers the active principle of generation is from the father, while the mother provides the matter. Therefore, the original sin is contracted, not from the mother, but from the father" (*Summa Theologiae*, I-II, q.81, ad 5c). And, later he adds: "[...] the man's sin is the more grievous, because he was more perfect than the woman" (*Summa Theologiae*, II-II, q.163, ad 4c).

10 Dussel, *Philosophy of Liberation*, 183-4.

11 Ibid., 185.

worked out by anti-dialectical methods. A radical commitment to change will require the use of, at least, dialectical methods. But, Dussel goes a step further and proposes a still more fruitful method than the dialectical methods, which he names analectical method. "The analectical refers to the real human fact by which every person, every group or people is always situated 'beyond' (ano-) the horizon of totality."[12] He opts for an analectical method because he finds empirical-scientific methods and negative dialectical methods insufficient in approaching proximity. Scientific methods can take us to the ontic sphere, and negative dialectics can take us to the ontological sphere; but in order to reach the *meta-physical* sphere opened up by the exteriority of the other in the periphery of one's existence one needs an analectical method. Analectic or ana-dialectic is, in fact, dialectic in its positive sense. It does not deny dialectic and scientific methods; rather it goes beyond them.

All methods are to be refined and defined by an analectical moment which completes them and give them real value. Methods that lack an analectical moment are not helpful in bringing about change. Dussel writes:

> The negative dialectical methods of Marcuse, Adorno, or even Bloch is naïve with respect to the positive criticism of the utopia of the political exteriority offered by peripheral peoples, the working-class women, the oppressed youth, and the dependent societies. [...] The scientific is reduced to what is natural fact; natural fact is reduced in turn to the logical or the mathematical; and this, finally, becomes debased in scientism – extremely naïve and extremely dangerous.[13]

The analectical moment affirms exteriority and helps a system to realize what is impossible for it. It ushers in novelty, which it does by opening ourselves to "methods that not only are scientific but are not even theoretical (because analectic is a method whose point of departure is an ethical choice and a concrete historical praxis)."[14] The analectical moment in the method reconnects the thinker with praxis and converts him/her into a thinker-activist. The analectical method equips thinker-activists with "knowledge of how to operate practically on the level of public, social, governmental, [...]."[15] It is a method of transformative practice. Dussel brings out the constitutional features of this method thus:

12 Dussel, *Philosophy of Liberation*, 158.

13 Ibid., 160.

14 Ibid.

15 Ibid.

> [The] point of departure is, passively, the appeal of the other (the oppressed as exteriority); operatively, it is the denial of denial (negation of oppression), and affirmation of exteriority. The essential category of this method is, negatively (metaphysically), that of exteriority; affirmatively and operatively it is that of liberation (and not now the mere freedom of Kant). The principle of the practical method is the principle of analogy (which includes principle of distinction, passively, and principle of innovation, creatively). It concerns an operative logic that semantically refers to political, sexual, pedagogical, and other decisions.[16]

The first requirement of a practical philosophy of transformation is transformation of philosophy. Over the centuries, philosophy has often been finding fulfillment in playing a central role in the hegemonic ideological academic apparatus meticulously used by the dominant classes. One might argue that philosophy has an autonomous domain and hence it cannot be instrumentalized by the dominant classes. However, one should not forget that the autonomy of philosophical discourse is not absolute autonomy. It is relative to each philosophical subject and his/her interests; it is also relative to the praxis, especially in reference to the thematic objects, method, and categories. Liberation of philosophy starts with philosopher's (i) honest acknowledgement of the relative determinations of philosophy and (ii) the freedom and courage to shape up a thinking style that helps one to approach proximity. Dussel has warned philosophers of the danger of making philosophy "a complete abstraction, an ideological fetish that will be enshrined at the center of the hegemonic academic apparatus of the dominant classes in the developed countries."[17] A philosophy that prefers periphery to the center, a philosophy that has liberated itself from various ideological dominations, will soon evolve as a philosophy of liberation. Philosophy of liberation will give thematic priority to the praxis of the oppressed, who could be a class suffering from historical and social discrimination, a nation subjected to imposed or voluntary geopolitical isolation, a gender that is sexually oppressed by one or another ideology and practice, a text or vision that is alienated from its essence and eclipsed by idolatrous fetishism. It will be a practical, ethical discourse that takes human situation as the point of departure. For this to happen, a philosopher has to become an "organic individual" who rises above topical interests and works with the oppressed class.[18] Philosophical subjectivity has to be organically continuous with historical subjectivity. This organic continuity

16 Dussel, *Philosophy of Liberation*, 161.

17 Ibid., 187.

18 Dussel takes this idea from Antonio Gramsci.

which is a permanent way of life cannot be established with a weeklong exposure programme or just one or two socio-political experiments. One has to become part of a social movement or organization which mediates between thought and practice. Along with activist involvements, a philosopher of liberation must elabourate philosophical discourse on themes. This theoretical work is necessary for correct analysis and understanding of the situation and ideological formation of the oppressed.

Having seen briefly the constitutional aspects of a philosophy of liberation in special reference to the work of Dussel in the Latin-American context, let us now turn to the question of the possibility of biblical philosophy.

Paul Ricoeur and Biblical Philosophy

The Bible has a very complex history and unfathomable content, which necessitates diverse interpretive approaches. The mainline interpretive approaches to the Bible may be conveniently grouped as theological, historical, and literary; and, one can find amazing plurality of methods within each of these major approaches.[19] Given the heteroglossia in Biblical studies, a philosophical approach to biblical texts is formally plausible. But, apart from the formal plausibility of a philosophical reading whose rightful place is externally justified by plurality of interpretations and the conflicts among them, there is a compelling inner reason that demands a philosophical approach to the Bible. The Bible has an inner cognitive reason why it must be interpreted philosophically. None can deny that the Bible *qua* text is an interpretation. Since every interpretation calls for critical thought it is reasonable that the Bible as an interpretation also gives rise to critical thought.[20] This factual bottom-line of the actual history of the Bible-as-text-as-interpretation explains why rationality has an irreplaceable role in clarifying the content of revelation in the Bible. Having to do with interpretation, the kind of rationality that is required in a philosophical engagement with the Bible is primarily hermeneutical.

---

19 See the second part entitled, "Plurality in the Reading of the Bible" of Susan E. Gillingham, *One Bible, Many Voices: Different Approaches to Biblical Study* (Grand Rapids, Michigan and Cambridge, UK: Eerdmans, 1998).

20 This idea comes from Paul Ricoeur's principle that "symbol gives rise to thought." See his *Freud and Philosophy: An Essay on Interpretation*, trans. Denis Savage, (New Haven: Yale University Press, 1970), 38. Roger Burggraeve follows this principle in his effort to argue for a philosophical reflection of biblical texts: "As such, the text as interpretation is never a guarantee of truth, but precisely *as* interpretation it gives rise to critical thought. It is likewise for that reason that in all candidness, we reflexively explore in depth the Biblical texts and confront them with their insights from the Bible or other philosophical and religious traditions and texts. "Reading and Interpreting Holy Scripture: A Way of Thinking," in Raimond Bieringer et.al. eds, *Provoked to Speech: Biblical Hermeneutics as Conversation* (Leuven, Paris, Walpole, MA: Peeters, 2014), 101.

Nevertheless, engaging the Bible philosophically is not an easy task simply because it is not, in the first place, a philosophical treatise but a religious text with various non-philosophical literary forms which refer to concrete historical experience. The biblical texts may not seem to present a thinking style that is familiar to philosophers trained in Western academic culture largely shaped by the Greek schools of thought. What one finds in the Bible is mainly a narrative tradition. Intricate argumentative moves in various biblical genres may not be apparent to ordinary pious readers. Therefore, those who approach the Bible philosophically may have an initial discouraging feeling of alienation which Ricoeur calls 'distance of texts'. Such being the case, biblical philosophers should have a motivating conviction that "the Bible itself -from the inside out – gives rise to thought."[21] This means that the biblical texts contain within them distinct epistemological, ethical, metaphysical, and anthropological insights. It is the task of biblical philosophers to bring out the inner meaning as well as the truth-value of these insights. And, if there is one overarching theme in the Bible, it is liberation. Be it narratives or proverbs or prophecy or chronicle or epistles or hymns or parables, all the biblical genres refer to historical and existential experience of liberation from inner suffering and total oppression. The Bible is a saga of liberation-struggles of God's people.

Biblical Philosophy of Liberation: Conditions and Parameters

Most of the readers of the Bible accept the Bible as a sacred text. They call it a holy scripture. But, not everyone who venerates the Bible as a holy Scripture does it for the same reason. Many believers and scholars regard the Bible as holy for mere formal reasons. But, it is also possible to affirm the holiness of the Bible for profound material reasons. Roger Burggravae has made a helpful distinction to understand the difference in the approaches to the Bible. He says that the Bible has both "external holiness" and "internal holiness."[22] External holiness of the Bible refers to the holiness that people recognize through external signs, rituals, attitudes, etc., that accompany the Bible whenever it is read out or cited. External holiness of the Bible is sustained by different rituals, various modes of veneration, and institutional means of control which also leads the Bible to acquire unquestionable authority so much so that people consult it as the final source book and approach it as a holy thing they could swear with. The readers and hearers of the Bible receive a sense of identity from its external holiness.

On the other hand, internal holiness of the Scripture refers to the Holy One implied in the Bible when it is read and listened to. On its own the Bible cannot show its internal holiness; it needs readers to perceive its

21 Burggraeve, "Reading and Interpreting Holy Scripture: A Way of Thinking," 98.

22 Burggraeve, "Reading and Interpreting Holy Scripture: A Way of Thinking," 85-95.

internal holiness. Internal holiness is revealed to readers who make efforts to understand the biblical texts through interpretation that goes beyond historical and philological studies. Interpretation does not mean that the reader adds something to the text from outside; it is rather bringing forth *the hidden* in the text through interrogation and explanation. The act of interpretation is interrupted by the eruption of the other; and, in the course of interpretation the reader is visited by the other hidden in the text, which gives the reader a direct experience of a *beyond the same*. Every interpretation is thus marked by a radical heteronomy, which precisely introduces within the interpreter the Holy One, the ultimate author of the text.[23] In sum: in order to recognize the external holiness of the Bible, what one needs is a worship-group affiliation; but internal holiness can be recognized by only those who venture to interpret the Bible. The worshippers of the external holiness of the Bible do not and cannot approach the proximity of the biblical Other. But, the seekers of the internal holiness in their strenuous effort to understand the text through interpretation will get existentially close to the God of the Bible and his Kingdom. The first task of a biblical philosopher is to combat the reductive approach to the Bible.

It is sad to note that the reverence that the vast majority of Christians have for the Bible is motivated by its external holiness. But, it is still more sad that Christians are unaware that this wide-spread religious tendency to externally ascribe holiness as well as authority to the Bible and express the same through various ritual acts of veneration has the accompanying risk of idolatry. In fact, Scripture, as Origen and others rightly clarified, is a sacrament in which the invisible Word is available to us in visible letters. The material written letters in the Bible mediate the content of God's self-revelation. But, when the worshippers of the external holiness of the Bible do not take pains to recognize and venerate also its internal holiness, it is very likely that their worship becomes plain idolatry. In all idolatry there is an uncritical reduction of the invisible into the visible and mystery into history; or, put differently, there is an unwarranted absolutization of the known. One ends up in idolatry of the Scripture, Ricoeur observes, when one (wrongly) thinks that one has direct and full access to the divine revelation in the historical-contingent text at hand. The misconception here is that the Word of God is available in a totally transparent manner in the historically contingent words of the Bible. The primary condition of possibility of a biblical philosophy of liberation is liberation of the Bible from its idolatry reading.

Having spelled out the background condition, let us now try to identify the essential elements and basic parameters of a biblical philosophy of liberation. As mentioned earlier, the Bible has been read from liberative perspectives. Biblicists and theologians have made abundant use of scriptural insights for

---

23 Burggraeve, "Reading and Interpreting Holy Scripture: A Way of Thinking," 93-94.

developing liberation theologies in their respective contexts. George Soares Prabhu, for instance, is a biblical theologian who explored scriptural foundations for a theology of liberation and liberative actions in the Indian context.[24] However, it must be noted that liberation theologians' engagement with the scripture has been mostly thematic, not withstanding some methodological reflection soffered by way of introductions and conclusions of their works. What we are going to offer in this final section of the paper is a brief schematic presentation of a biblical philosophy of liberation; it must be fleshed out with biblical-exegetical-philosophical reflections at a later moment.

(i) *Philosophical Subjectivity*: As seen earlier, in a context of liberation, philosophical subjectivity depends on historical subjectivity. In the world opened by the Bible, history is not an indefinite movement through cycles of growth and loss, it is a definite history of liberation, redemption, salvation. The Bible is all about sufferings of the poor, their struggles for liberation, expectations for a saviour, the coming of the saviour, the victory of the saviour, the continued work of the saviour through his chosen ones, and expectation for the second coming of the saviour who will vindicate the oppressed and punish the oppressors. Considered from a Christian perspective, Jesus Christ is the Lord of history. Therefore, a Christian biblical philosopher has to shape his/her philosophical subjectivity after the person and praxis of Christ Jesus. Competence does matter in biblical philosophy.

(ii) *The Starting Point*: The starting point of a philosophy of liberation is not philosophy *per se*. Philosophers of liberation do not begin with commenting on previous philosophical works. Similarly, the starting point of a biblical philosophy of liberation is not the literal meaning of the biblical texts rather the dream of their authorial referent and the struggles of their addressees. Indeed, the Holy one is the ultimate address or of the Bible. Who are the addressees? It is important to note that all readers of the Bible are not its proper addressees. It may be contended that only those who are covered by the category of the poor are the proper and direct addressees of the Bible. The poor are the victims of injustice, exploitation, oppression, personal as well as structural sins, sickness, wars, unethical development projects, etc. Oppressors are only indirect addressees; they can become direct addressees when they realize that their identity as oppressors is due to thick structures of sin both in their inside and their outer social

24 See: Francis X. D'sa, Scaria Kuthirak kattel and Isaac Padinjarekuttu, eds, *Collected Writings of George M. Soares-Prabhu,* 4 Volumes (Pune: Jnana-Deepa Vidyapeeth, 1999-2003).

world. This immediately takes us to the question of the spatial setting of biblical philosophical reflection. It can never be an abstract space marked by the constrains of logical thinking. It is a concrete pyscho-spiritual as well as socio-political space where the sufferings and struggles of the poor are really felt.

(iii) *Exteriority and Proximity*: In sharp contrast with onto-theological and phenomenological approaches which seek for the essential core of persons and events, biblical philosophy takes exteriority seriously. A biblical philosopher joins the Word in its search for its other. Light sets out to meet with darkness and the Holy Heaven comes down to embrace the sinful earth. In biblical philosophy it is incarnation that makes proximity possible. Praxis in biblical philosophy is the passion for and the passion in meeting the other. And, in the scheme of Biblical thought, contamination is a virtue.

(iv) *Analectical Moment and Method*: The world for biblical philosophers is the daily horizon within which they live. And, this world has its ways; which is governed by empirical-scientific methods and negative dialectics. Because, the other's self-revelation happens beyond the daily horizon – it always happens in the periphery of the normal -, the scientific-dialectic methods are to be refined with an analectic moment so that the epiphany of the other is not missed. The analectic moment in the biblical thought is forgiveness. A system that lives by dialectics can forgive only on the pain of its total collapse. Think of a religious universe ruled by the law of karma. The uniqueness of the Bible lies in its capacity to bring about a new world where forgiveness is possible. Compassion (*cum* + *passio,* meaning 'to suffer with') leading to empowerment becomes, then, the analectical methodological principle.

(v) *Mediation*: Liberative thought-act in the Bible will remain unrealized if it is not mediated through a social movement. The exigency for social movement is continuous with the exigency that leads the immanent Trinity to flip over to economic Trinity, at least, as Karl Rahner thinks.[25] It is through the ongoing work of the extended hands of the Father, namely, the Son and the Spirit, the life and love in the Trinity is mediated to the human society. This mediation becomes historical in the person of Jesus. His body had been the medium in his earthly days, which continued through the Jesus movement in the apostolic times, and still continues in our time through the spiritual, social, cultural, and political Movements in/led by the Church of

25 Many Catholic theologians have rejected Rahner's views in this regard. The details of the debates, however, do not come under the purview of this paper.

Christ. The effectiveness of biblical philosophy of liberation depends on its capacity to empower the Church in her efforts to become a movement of the poor and for the poor.

Conclusion

Although, that the Bible can be interpreted philosophically and that this particular religious text has unique insights to offer to the world are apparent, one is surprised to notice that precious little has been done in the field of biblical philosophy. This is because the biblical texts are seldom subjected to rigorous rational criticism and generous interpretive imagination. Philosophy is the discriminated other that is pushed to the periphery of Biblical hermeneutics. In the forgoing pages we argued that we need to seek for ways to rehabilitate philosophy in the field of biblical hermeneutics, and, offered a brief schematic presentation of a biblical philosophy of liberation.

Part 2

Towards a Genealogy of Social Movements

7

Productive Semiotics of Social Movements

Victor Ferrao
Rachol Seminary, Goa

Abstract: Any hermeneutics or semiotics of social movements has to take the movement dimension seriously. Things are become compelling with the steady death of the *Cogito* or the isolated transcendental ego. Deleuzean film theory allows us to introduce movement into the semiosis of social movements as well as, let us work with an immanent subject. People immerse themselves in the social movements. This requires to us radicalize our becoming(s)-in-the-world. We approach the films not as a representations of the social movements but try to trace leaps of transpositions (drawing our inspiration from music) between the process of cineosis and semiosis of the social movements. This enables us to understand the cartographies of power and open pluriversal possibilities of emancipations that would enact ethical performativity emanating through the social movements.

Keywords: Semiotics, Deleuze and Gautarri, Transpositions, Cineosis , Performativity, Film Theory, Movement Image, Time Image.

Introduction

Doing hermeneutics of social movement, one may stay within classical semiotics and semantic frame work or take up more radical approach that takes movement dimension seriously and understand its impact on process of making meaning. Foucault's practices approach may assist us to enter the semiosis of dynamic social movements. All practices are theory laden. Hence, they lie within the semiotic sphere. To achieve our goal, we have to abandon the shackles of the *Cogito* that has enslaved the Western thought. *Cogito* introduces subject/object epistemology that is loaded with subjection of the object of knowledge and degenerate into what Levinas calls as egology. Lyotard has demonstrated how the saying is afflicted by the seeing/the figural. The image is never only visible but also legible. Here we shall try and radicalize our meaning making by introducing movement into it. Deleuze demonstrates it through his theory of cinema. Hence, we shall study cinema theory of Deleuze not to find representations or models of social movements but to find leaps of transpositions that will enable us to critically discern the immanent semiosis that is driving social movements.[1] He teaches that his theory of cinema attempts to depict how the world is and not just cinematic experience.[2] Following Luis Hjelmslev, he takes up semiotics that studies signs and images as independent of language and express non-language material. Time has an arrow. It is moving in a direction and gives us a sense of flow and progress. Movement image give us this sense of movement. Film images[3] are set into a movement that produces a flow of movement images and this movement image becomes the frame that produces the semiosis that draws us into the plot of the cinema. Movement also creates meaning by displacing and disrupting (deterritorialize) the images (actual and the virtual). The actual images lay down their boundaries (reterritorialize) on the amorphous image mass and enable us to draw meaning. We might take an instance of ball on a football ground in a match to understand productive semiosis/cineosis of the cinematic images. The value of the ball keeps shifting depending on its locations as well as positions of players that handle it during the match. These values/meanings irrupt from an amorphous mass/plane of possibilities. Critical books of Deleuze and those that he developed with Gauttari open us to the movement and manifests how it affects signification or meaning making. In the first part of our paper we shall study how movement produces meaning from the perspective of film theory of Deleuze. We do this because it enables us to do a semiosis of social movements that are marked also by the dynamism of movement though of a different kind. We do not see film theory as a means

1 Rosi Baraidott, *Transpositions: On Nomadic Ethics* (Cambridge: Polity Press, 2006), 5-7.

2 Gregory Flaxman, 'Introduction' in Gregory Flaxman, ed., *The Brain is the Screen: Deleuze and The Philosophy* of Cinema (Minneapolis: University of Minnesota Press, 2000), 10.

3 Deleuze teaches that cinematic sign cannot be adequately explained by the structural conditions of linguistics and post-Saussurian semiology. This is because its content is essentially tied to and motivated by pre-verbal intelligible content that it expresses. Deleuze christens this non-linguistically formed content signelectic. material which includes the sensory (visual and sonic), kinetic, intensive, affective, rhythmic, tonal and even verbal (oral and written) modulation features. Cinematic image is always constructed upon this a-signifying and a-syntatic material that is not formed linguistically but formed semiotically aesthetically and pragmatically. See also: file:///C:/Users/Victor-pc/Documents/hjelmslev%20%20semiotics.pdf accessed September 4, 2018.

of representations but one that leaps forward to transpositions in the shape of social movements.

Film Theory of Deleuze

Cinema provokes us to see, to feel, to sense and think differently. Film theory has been captive to representational thinking. Deleuze has taken cinema as one of the domains to deconstruct the power of representational categories over thinking. The rejection of representational thinking opens us to the outpouring of immanent thinking. This means images do not stand for another world at another time outside but becomes a wholesome transformative experience for audiences that become one with the sonic, visual, and narrative images on the screen.

Movement Image: The Dance of the Actual and the Virtual

Deleuze draws from Henry Bergson the idea that all images are situated in a plane of immanence where past, present and the future co-exists. These images do not stand for some other worldliness but are constantly shaping us and our world. That is, these images do not represent any transcendental world. Deleuze uses his distinction between the virtual and the actual to think images. Both actual and virtual are real and are not opposed to each other. But, only the actual find their way into the physical present. Deleuze teaches that the actual is defined by the present that passes and the virtual is defined by past that is preserved and a constant process of crystallization is taking place between the two.[4] Deleuze holds both actual and virtual images are contained in the plane of immanence. He says that it contains along with the filmic images all images relating to 'a life'. This imaging does not occur along the lines of subject and object dualism (*Cogito*) but on the lines of an assemblage (non-dual, non-unitary subject/nomadic/rhizomatic subject) that fosters connections in multiple directions. Everything is an assemblage interacting with other assemblages of images. Subject of an assemblage remains beyond binary thinking and stays fully embodied/immersed into the movement of images forming a cinematic flow of assemblages.

Movement Image: Merger of the Actor and the Spectator

The subject on the screen does not represent the subject in the audience as most film theory holds. Representation theorists usually consider films as a kind of a platonic cave. They think that the films offer the audience perceptions which are nothing but representations of world outside.[5] The representation model suggests that image reflects the world and not construct the world. Deleuze

4 Ibid., 4.

5 Ibid., 25.

rejects the denotative function of images and teaches that the subject in the audience becomes part of the flow on the screen. Deleuze presents desire not as a lack but as a wish to live and to preserve life by connecting with and relating with those things and persons that give us joy or increase our power to act. The joy is not Lacanian Jouissance/enjoyment but spinozistic power to form adequate ideas and to act. Deleuze presents a self that is becoming and is radically unstable. There is no strict distinction between who is seeing and what is being seen. The actor and the spectator are drawn into an intensive encounter with the real world that is no longer a copy.

Movement Image: Perception, Affection and Action

Movement image describes the nexus between perception, affect and action. They are the chief avtars of movement image. Perception image describes the creation of special image which is a contingent centre. It is usually brought into effect by the creation of a character (though not always) and its concomitant relation with all other images in the film. Affection image channels emotions through it. Action images describes the way in which the contingent centre defines or is derived from a determined situation or how a situation can be reconfigured by the acts of the individual. By using these three coordinates of movement images, each film organises itself. Perceptions are images acting on other images. Thus, for instance, visual perception is a consequence of light waves colliding with the retina.[6] Same is the case with tactile, olfactory, hearing and taste perceptions. All of them can be thought of as collision. The sensory input of perceptions produce actions which become complex and diverse due to intensive/extensive forces at play within/with the organism. The intensive and extensive forces are affected and are engendered by perception. Thus, our body becomes an image that distributes outside/extensive disturbance through the body (as intensive turbulence) to the components of the body to bring forth an extensive reaction.[7] Perception, affect, action are the ways we undergo cineosis.

Time Image: The Making and Unmaking of the Non-Unitary Subject

Movement images flow in the rhythm of time but time image resists the flow. There is a collapse of the coordinates into opsigns and sonsigns.[8] Opsigns and sonsigns are pure visual and auditory images that link up according to three temporal synthesis. The first is the passive synthesis that create cinematic

6 David Deamer, *Deleuze Japanese Cinema and The Atom Bomb: The Spectre of Impossibility* (New York: Bloombury, 2014), 34.

7 Ibid., 35.

8 Ibid., 224.

hyalosigns. Hyalosigns are images that appear in the now and manifests the living present and past as retention and future as expectation. But, there is a double movement of time. The double movement lets the present pass into the future while preserving all the past.[9] Hyalosign thus, create time image at the level of description. At the level of narration we have chronosigns that disrupt the temporal flow of images and order of time. This resistance of temporal continuity produces time images. While hyalosigns are indeterminate descriptions and disruptive chronosigns are narrations, noosigns involve telling a story through body and mise-en-scene (stage set). In the absence of sensory-motor (perception, affection and action) linkage between the character and the situation, through connection of the virtual linkages thought becomes us.[10] Noosigns give us dispersive narratives. To Deleuze's cinematic universe, subject is no longer the transcendental one of Descartes , whose eyes give access to representations in front of it on the screen. To him images do not represent something heroic or perverse about humanity but produce heroism or monstrosity in us. Our values and beliefs and the world we inhabit are recognized and reconfirmed by cineosis. Cinema thus, not only requires seeing of opsigns and sonsigns but also reading of lectosigns. The subject is immanent one that is an image among other images and is constructed by different perceptions and experiences.

Deleuzean Semiosis of Social Movements

There is an other reading possible of Deleuze. It is one that brackets the transcendental dimension without outright denying it. This anti-deluzeanism has to be taken in the spirit of deleuze who rejected all forms of slavishness in favour of emancipative creativity. Entering the immanent stream of social movements, we approach its rhizomatic flow of intensities. All social movements act counter to our time and act on our time and let us hope for the benevolent time to come in the future.

Mass Movements as Practice

Deleuze rejects static and sterile conception of Philosophy. We can trace this repugnance when he says "for many people, philosophy is not something that is not 'made', but is pre-existent, ready made in a pre-fabricated sky." He teaches that philosophy is a practice and not a grand theory that leads us to practice. Deleuze bridges the gap between theory and practice in his practice of philosophy.[11] Thus, he views doing philosophy in a radical immanent mode. The

9 David Deamer, *Deleuze Japanese Cinema and The Atom Bomb: The Spectre of Impossibility* (New York: Bloombury, 2014), 224.

10 Ibid., 125.

11 Gregory Flaxman, 'Introduction', 9.

hermeneutics of social movements is a practice that engages practices of social movements. Deleuze breaks down philosophy and life to what may be called the image of thought. Image for him is more than the familiar visual picture. It is a collection of sensation, a sensible aggregate that Deleuze ultimately calls sign.[12] We encounter image at the very limit of the sensible. Sensations have the capacity to derange the everyday, to short circuit the common sense and thus catalyze as different kind of thinking. This means sensations are encountered as the threshold of what may be called the thinkable. Thus, thinking is disruptive as well as irruptive. Thinking is provoked. Something in the world forces us to think.[13] We can find congruence between Deleuze and the dynamism of mass Movements. They are also provoked into being by factors external to them. It is by acting over the limits of *habitus* that social movements strives to dislodge or transform the pre-established ways of ordering the world. Thus, mass Movements are not just works of interpretations of the world but emit signs that produces the world.

The Molar, Molecular and the Mass Movements

Mass Movements can be viewed as an encounter that is embodied and is open to different kinds of connections and durations. Deleuze and Gauttari call these networks of connections assemblages. In fact they speak of inter-connected-assemblages. Inter-connected-assemblages are not melrely a link of the whole and its parts but a whole that connects with other wholes to form an inter-assemblage. These connections open us to new kind of thoughts that challenge the binary and hierarchical logic that dominates our thinking. Here we take an ethological approach that is not interested in what a body is but considers carefully the ability of a body to affect and be affected. Mass Movements can be viewed as a dynamic and rhizomatic inter-connected assemblages which are also ethological in character. These inter-connected assemblages operate on two planes, a molecular and a molar one. The molar assemblages are extensive, divisible, unifiable, totalizable and organizable while the molecular assemblages are intensive and are not unifiable, tolalizable and do not divide without changing their nature. The molecular plane has elements that are yet to be organized while the molar plane is an organizing plane that freezes movement, codifies and organizes from the molecular plane and orders them hierarchically and produces subjectivities and identities.[14] Every mass movement is an inter-assemblage that has both the molecular and molar

12 Gregory Flaxman, 'Introduction', 12.

13 Ibid., 13.

14 Teresa Rizzo, *Deleuze and Film: A Feminist Introduction* (New York: Continuum Books, 2012), 60.

dimensions. Through their molecular plane they remain open to the outside and through the molar they stay stable and acquire their identities.

Deterritorialising and Reterritorialising and The Social Movement

All social movements are disruptive and are deterritorial and reterritorial in character. Deleuze teaches that the molecular plane constantly deterritorializes the molar orderings and the molar plane constantly reterriorializes molecular movement. He teaches that oppressing orderings occur when the process of reterritorialization captures and over-codes the molecular to such an extent that renders it highly restrictive. Molecular plane deterritorializes molar orderings to varying degrees and the most extreme form of it is called lines of flight. But, even lines of flight can be reordered and coded again. Social Movements always chase the lines of flight. They interrogate and challenge the molar or unjust orderings of our society. This means they deterritorialize unjust order of things and push societies to humane becomings. The lines of flight that produces deterritorializations arise as a result of their interventions. The lines of flight are opened by the processes of deoediplizations. The social movements challenge the reining castrating law of the father and open other ways of being-in-the-world. The alternate emancipative ways of being are generated by affect. Deleuze and Gauttari name the force that either enhance or diminish the capacity of the body to act as affect. Thus, affects stands for the capacity of a body to be affected and to affect.

Image, World and Social Movement

Derrida said that there is nothing outside the text. Deleuze teaches that everything is an image. He derives his view from Bergson who teaches that image of a thing and the thing is inseparable. Deleuze teaches that image is the thing's existence and appearance. What we call thing is nothing but image. Strictly speaking there are no things but only images. This means the things are their appearances. This suggests that everything that we call material as well as our memories, thoughts and even our brain is an image. All images interact and inter-relate. A group of images can form a larger image or a larger image can become smaller images. All images are in motion. This movement is governed by what we call laws of nature. Thus, water image always flows down hill. But, there are living images that do not always obey the laws of nature. Humans (living image) for example climb the hill against gravity. Humans can use non-living images, process them and build a home. Plants can process water and minerals and build it-self. Every movement is an image. There is nothing hidden behind the image. Image does not stand for something else but to itself. All images are matter in motion. Movement image and the dynamic energy flowing matter of physic are identical. Just like matter and energy are one and they cannot be created or destroyed all images can only be traded to change. All images can be considered as matter and energy whether they are objects, humans, visual, tactile, auditory or mental. Deleuze equates image, matter and energy to light. There is light in everything and everything can be thought of as matter and light. Movement is measured in space and time. Special theory of relativity teaches that space and time are interchangeable. This means single determinate, universal line of time is not possible. We can no longer measure time along a line or as a function of space. Hence, image ultimately has time, space, motion, energy and light within it. Time intertwines as virtual past, actual present and possible future. Past, future and the present co-exist. Deleuze calls the dynamic dance of image with limitless reconfigurable possibilities as the plane of immanence. It is a field of play of images. It is a virtual universe. Now social movements have the play field of their emergence that contains everything virtual and possible for them. The way it territorializes depend on how these possibilities or waves are being driven/rode by the leaders and the followers.[15]

The Dynamism of the Social Movements

Social Movements are non-linear and complex. From the Deluzian point of view, we cannot think that social movements exist outside themselves in an ideal Platonic world. He is a philosopher of immanence and not of transcendence. To him everything is a moving image in a plane of immanence. Social Movements are embedded into planes of immanence. Everything in the world exists alongside as an inter-related flux of images. The subject is always entangled with what we may loosely call its object.

Riding the Wave and Going with the Flow

Deleuzean film theory teaches that seeing is never 'seeing as'. 'Seeing as' implies that signs are always invoked by a subject. This way of thinking denies us extra-linguistic access to the world. Deleuze opens us to the non-linguistic experience of the world. He teaches that perception may be surrounded by language but it is not reducible to language. There is always surplus that cannot be put into words. In everything that we say there is the unsaid as well as the unsayable. Following Bergson, he teaches that the world is made of images. It is these moving images that exist prior to the emergence of language. Language itself is a system of images/signs dancing into the plane of immanence whose flow we ride. Riding the wave is the way we live as humans. We ride different waves. Social movement emerge as we ride waves of confluence of images that get codified that challenge the already ossified systems or assemblages that are

15 Dryk Ashton, *Using Deleuze Cinema Books, Film Studies and Effect*, A Dissertation submitted to the Graduate College of Blowing Green, State University, in partial fulfilment of the requirements for the degree of Doctor of Philosophy, 2006, 83-95.

unjust and oppressive. Riding the wave is molecularising. All molecularising contests the stagnant and decadent molar systems in our society.

Anti-Oedipality of Social Movements

All social movements are anti-Oedipal.[16] They are following an anti-cannibal philosophy that does not digest or reduce otherness to some kind of substantive essence or sameness. They are riding intense waves of immanence. Movements are always on a dynamic move and are based on an already–not-yet philosophical vision that energizes them. Movements have anti-narcissus seeds though often they are also hijacked by some people to meet their narcissistic ends. All Movements are embedded in ideological debates that animate social formations. These ideological debates contest the reigning politics of *status quo* that legitimate oppression and exploitation. All Movements thus have an anti-Oedipal character that courageously takes on the forces that threaten to castrate dissent, freedom of thought and action. Anti-oedipal energy that animates social movements seeks emancipation for all and is profoundly political. It is a practice that enforces a continuous war against enslaving modes of being human. There is strong epistemo-political reflexive circle that animates social movements that continuously strives to wash them clean of all oppressive stains.

Epistemo-Political Circle in the Social Movements

Epistemo-Political Circle operates like a hermeneutical circle and becomes the rudder that guides and directs the social movements. It is a reciprocal nexus of theory and practice. It opens us to the intellectual space and the creative and forceful space of action or engagement of a social movement. All understanding and actions form inter-assemblages. This is why epistemo-political circle forms part the inter-assemblages that anchors or territorialises on the plane of immanence of specific movement. Different Movements have different epistemo-political circles in which they move and have their being. The dynamism of the epistemo-political circle can open it to rhizomatic or non-linear dynamism of social movements though often they seem to be linear and predictable. This opening of the anti-Oedipal force takes it, is beyond the either/or (contrastic) binary logic that often enslaves the social movements. This means the social movement often Oedipalise as the other of the same. It means the social movements attempt to become the other in merely contrastive sense and become a diametrical opposite image of the oppressive regime or assemblage that they are fighting. Deleuzian semiotics makes it possible

16 Gilles Deleuze and Felix Guattari, *Anti-Oedipus: Capitalism and Schizophrenia* (Minneapolis: University of Minnesota Press, 1983). Pg No.

of going beyond the either/or structure of our thought and embrace other emancipative options and ways of being humans.

Multiple Emancipative Options

The actualized/terriorialized regimes on the plane of immanence are a manifold. The actual and the virtual both exist on the plane of immanence. Deleuze thinks that everything is political. All territorlizations and deterritorializations are political and are a result of the struggles of divergent forces. How do we work with theses divergent forces and change the world? This means we have to ask: can we change the mode of our existence? Mass Movements can be viewed as struggles to institute new emancipative planes of immanence. We have to understand this without putting immanence into a transcendent frame. Deleuze thinks immanence as immanent to it alone. This does not just change the linguistic registers of thought and adds active dynamism to thought itself that does not have to be a representation/copy of something else. Hence, thinking becomes inventive not in accordance to what the world is but what the world is capable of becoming. This makes thinking productive. Deleuze is most radical when he teaches that thought it-self becomes the world.[17] Hence, we can change the world not by standing outside it or standing against its flows but driving the waves on the plane of immanence that would institute new emancipative planes of immanence.

Riding the Productive Wave

Deleuze attempts to reverse Platonism, undo classical theories of representation and avoid relativism by grounding his theory of subjectivity into radical immanence. The post binary thinking of Deleuze refuses to set a transcendental subject against the world but place the subject in radical relationship of immanence into an emanating world. Overcoming the dichotomy of the body and mind, Deleuze sees self not in monadic essentialist sense as a singularity but invites us to view it as always in a networks waves/ aggregates of relationships. This means identities are assemblages and can be deassembled and reassembled. Social Movements are striving to bring such productive and emancipative changes.

Breaking the Prison of Desire

Delusion thinking of desire opens multiple options. Desire is not a lack to be fulfilled as Lacan would have us think. Desire is productive in Deleuze and Gauttari.[18] It is akin to Nietzsche's will to power. It leads actual to the

---

17 file:///C:/Users/Victor-pc/Documents/Thiele_DeleuzeStudies.pdf, accessed September 14, 2018.

18 Gilles Deleuze and Felix Guattari, *Anti-Oedipus*.

possible. It is endless, immanent and rhizomatic. Desire is underlying force similar to Freud's libido. Desire precedes the subject and its various relations. Deleuze teaches that modern capitalist society produces Schizoid humans. Capitalist relations produces Schizos just as it produces shampoos or cars. Only difference for now is that these human Schizos are not saleable.[19] Subject is no longer unified and based on fixed essence but is cracked, split into pieces and assembled of various entities. Subject is indeed a subjected subject. This means desire is not outside relations. It produces our being-in-the-world. This does not mean we are condemned to the wimps and fancies of desire that produces us. Desire being productive offers us possibilities of riding alternated waves and lead our actuality to possibilities that are emancipative. We are not prisoners of desire but are able to ride the lines of flight and produce new planes of immanence that world organize new assemblages of the self and our society. This is what social movements do. We can think of Movements as composed of little assemblages/sub-assemblages (machines) that compose slightly bigger assemblages. These in their turn, produce bigger assemblages. These components can be joined to other assemblages like philosophies, theories, assemblages of people which then might open emancipative as well as oppressive possibilities. Aligning of the productive semiosis of assemblages opens multiple emancipative potentials in our social movements.

Playing on the Plane of Immanence

Different images both virtual and real occupy the same plane of immanence. Deleuzean thought has no transcendental gap between body and mind, and no ontotological difference between thought and action. The nodes of activity, the chain linking humans and non-humans are described as a machine assemblage. All images and the assemblages exist on the plane of immanence. The plane of immanence is the machine assemblage of movement images. It is changes that we ride on the machine assemblage that bring about what Deleuze calls becomings. He prefers to three kinds of becoming: Becoming a woman,[20] becoming an animal[21] and becoming a minor. All social movements are machine assemblages on the plane of immanence. The immanence within such planes open non-linear and centre-less dimensions of play and generate transposed modes of being/becomings. These different machine assemblages are products of libidinous play of non-unitary subjects who are actively producing new assemblages. Social Movements are also aesthetical, ethical as well as libidinous. They are never isolated or even self contained. They do

19 http://citeseerx.ist.psu.edu/viewdoc/download?doi=10.1.1.520.9170&rep=rep1&type=pdf, accessed September 14, 2018.

20 Rosi Baraidott, *Transpositions*, 43-91.

21 Ibid., 96-138.

not exist in mutual exclusive ways. This view opens to us trans-atomistic and non-dual conception of self and society which influence our thinking of all Movements. They are not only entangled with their opponents but are also with other Movements that are riding other emancipative or even oppressive goals. This way of thinking allows us to move away from all forms of essentialisms and even universalisms and leads us into the flow of pluriversalisms which can only enrich the social movements themselves. They can derive inspiration as well as new direction from this entanglements. It can open us to new domains of resistance and new Movements for emancipation.

Cartographies of Power and The making of the Self and it's Other

Power can be restrictive (*potestas*) and power can be productive (*potentia*) force. It brings about relations of exclusions and inclusions. We need to adopt non-linearity to develop cartographies of power that account for the complexities of our time. The power formations set the norm, the norm-al and the norm-ative and let loose flows of pejorations, exclusions and exploitations. This logic of the same is oppressive and has to be countered. Old ethical theories seem to be inadequate to address these flows of oppressions, discriminations and dehumanisations. We need new ethics to face our complexities. Such a new ethics will provide road maps to social movements which are also often framed in the traditional philosophical visions contaminated by anthropocentrism, patriarchy, racism/casteism or ethnocentrism. The new ethics envisions a non-unitary subject in place of self-contained subject of Descartes. In its place, it thinks of the subject in non-unitary terms who is nomadic and transient in character. This approach inserts dynamism as well as being-in-the-world (spatial/contextual) dimensions to the new non-unitary subject. Thus, this new vision brings us to a new enlarged sense of self and its other alongside its dynamic relations. The other of the subject has been always conceived in non-unitary terms. Thus, for instance woman is thought in terms of a sexualized bodies, back/white are racialized bodies, non-human other/earth is also a naturalised body/thing. But, the self-contained authoritarian self marks its distance and subdues this other who is thought in non-Unitarian terms. The new ethics that we envisage here will enable us to address all shades of the ills of self-centred individualisms that afflict us today. But, this does not take us into conservative communitarianisms as it opens possibilities of multiple belongings. Thus, we arrive at ethical transpositions of inter-webbed 'subject and it's others' that would provide positive sources of resistance to social movements.

Dissensus and Ethical Perfomativity

Lyotard teaches that consensus is unethical. He teaches that ethics is produced by dissensus. All social movements embody dissent. Lyotard opines that consensus is only one particular state of dialogue, debate and discussion and not its ultimate goal or end. Its end, he says is paralogy.[22] Dissensus interrupts and redistributes claims, counter-claims as well as roles and subject-positions. There is an ethical performativity in the dissent, dissident and dissensus. Being embodiment of dissensus, all social movements are profoundly performative. But we need to avoid performative positivism that ascribe performative emancipative dimension to all social movements and stay open to the fact that they could be becoming vehicles of vested interest. The semiosis of social movement as dynamic inter-assembled assemblages that continually link and delink with other assemblages might provide us an insight. Semiosis is a multi-modal sign process. If we consider the sub-assemblages within the assemblages of the social movements, we can understand how dissensus embodied by the social movements can allow us to understand and choose to forge emancipative assemblages and disassociate/delink from the oppressive assemblages that might constitute social movements. Social Movements can also have a contingent centre like the cinema that is generated by the sub-assemblages that assemble, deassemble and reassemble. Besides, this dynamism can generate emotions as well as motivate people to action. Thus, in several ways the multiple assembling, deassembling and reassembling of the inter-assemblages shape all people that assemble to form social movements. These sub-assemblages that constantly assemble and disassemble are semiotic resources that enact ethical performativity that may be emancipative.

Conclusion

Our study attempts to seek a relation of transpositions between the film theory of Deleuze and the social movements and thus open the doors for a productive semiotics. With the death of the *Cogito* of the West, our study opens us to the perfomativity of the non-unitary Subject in relation to the anti-Oedipal or dissenting nature of the social movements. Being attentive to the cartographies of power, we are enabled to seek pluriversal possibilities of emancipations that would enact ethical performativity emanating through the social movements.

22 Sara Ahmed, *Differences That Matter: Feminist Theory and Postmodernism* (Cambridge: Cambridge University Press, 1998), 48.

8

Religious Beliefs and Practice: The Philosophical Treatment after Wittgenstein

Jose Nandhikkara
Dharmaram Vidya Kshetram (DVK), Bangalore

Abstract: Philosophical investigations took a decisive 'linguistic turn' in twentieth century, examining the nature of human languages and its relation to human existence and nature. Learning from Wittgenstein's investigations on 'Rule Following' I suggest that linguistic turn was in fact a 'praxis turn', showing the fundamental importance of practice in our complex forms of life. Language-use is an objective and normative practice, with regularity across time, place and persons, and relates to fundamental ways of life. This fundamental aspect of language use is applied to throw light on the relation between religious belief and practice in the life of the believers, showing the importance of the characteristic features of the framework – objectivity, regularity and normativity – and the internal empirical and logical relation between belief and practice. Only in the context of a religious forms of life in which a religion is objectively, regularly and normatively practised, the relation between religious belief and practice is seen and understood.

Keywords: Belief, Form of Life, Language, Linguistic Turn, Normativity, Objectivity, Practice, Regularity, Stream of Life, Wittgenstein.

1. Introduction

Philosophical investigations took a decisive 'linguistic turn'[1] in twentieth century, examining the nature of human languages and its relation to human

1 Richard Rorty, *The Linguistic Turn* (Chicago: University of Chicago Press, 1967), 13. Rorty refers to G. Bergmann, *Logic and Reality* (Madison, Wisconsin: University of Wisconsin

existence and nature. Language is examined as both the means of thinking and medium of thought. This has in turn also illuminated the nature and role of philosophy itself with the conclusion that philosophical problems are problems which may be solved (or dissolved) either by an ideal conceptual language or by understanding more about the actual use of language. For the philosophers who have taken the linguistic turn philosophical investigations are predominantly "critique of language,"[2] rather than, as traditionally held, "the truth of things."[3] The linguistic turn, however, should not be seen as trivialising philosophical investigations as mere play of words, reducing reality to words, and semantics exhausting ontology and epistemology. *Homo loquens* do not replace *homo sapiens*. Both thinking and language-use are fundamental facts of a living human being.

The linguistic turn initiated new ways of investigating philosophical problems. According to Wittgenstein, who has influenced the most the linguistic turn, wrote:

> The object of philosophy is the logical clarification of thoughts.
> Philosophy is not a theory but an activity.
> A philosophical work consists essentially of elucidations.
> The result of philosophy is not a number of 'philosophical propositions', but to make propositions clear.[4]

The 'logical clarification of thoughts' and 'making propositions clear' contributed significantly in the fields of epistemology, aesthetics, ethics, metaphysics, philosophy of religion, philosophy of science, and philosophy of mind, etc., Linguistic philosophy works with the motto 'Look Closer' and follows the method of analysis for the set goal of clarity. Because language is a human construct and philosophical problems are linguistic problems, by using a logically perfect language for systematic analysis linguistic philosophers were confident that the problems could be solved/dissolved.

This 'linguistic turn' was in practice a 'semantic' turn seeking consistently and insistently for meaning. According to Dummett,

> Because philosophy has, as its first if not its only task, the analysis of meanings, and because, the deeper such analysis goes, the more it is dependent upon a correct general account of meaning, a model for what the understanding of an expression consists in, the theory

Press, 1964), 177 for the title of his book.

2 Ludwig Wittgenstein, *Tractatus Logico-philosophicus* (London: Routledge, 1922), 4.0031.

3 Thomas Aquinas, *In Aristotelis libros De caelo et mundo*, trans., Fabian R. Larcher and Pierre H. Conway, I.22.228, accessed January 22, 2018, http://dhspriory.org/thomas/english/De Coelo.htm#1-22.

4 Wittgenstein, *Tractatus*, 4.112.

> of meaning, which is the search for such a model, is the foundation of all philosophy, and not epistemology as Descartes misled us into believing.[5]

Accordingly, the pursuit of truth was given to positive sciences and philosophy was left with the task of clarifying meaning.

Learning from Wittgenstein's investigations on 'Rule Following' I suggest that linguistic turn was in fact a 'praxis turn', showing the fundamental importance of practice and clarifying who we are and throwing light on why do we do what we do in our complex forms of life. As Wittgenstein said, "In order to describe the phenomenon of language one has to describe a practice, not a one-time occurrence, whatever it might be."[6] This fundamental aspect of language use is further applied to throw light on the relation between religious belief and practice in the life of the believers. They are related to each other not just empirically but logically. "The motto here is always: Take a wider look round."[7]

2. Wittgenstein and Linguistic Turn

Wittgenstein assumed in the *Tractatus* that problems of philosophy rested on "the misunderstanding of the logic of our language"[8] and used an *a priori* logical method to analyse the depth grammar of any possible language. In contrast, the *Philosophical Investigations* used a descriptive method: "One cannot guess how a word functions. One has to look at its use and learn from that."[9] He moved from the realm of logic and formal conceptual language to that of ordinary language and actual use, and from analysis to description of 'language-games', 'family resemblance', and 'stream of life'. He observed: "Philosophy may in no way interfere with the actual use of language; it can in the end only describe it. For it cannot give it any foundation either. It leaves everything as it is."[10]

Language, as we use it, is a fundamental human practice that is rooted in nature and developed in collabouration and conversation with fellow human beings. It is the development of the natural propensities of living human beings, a joint venture of nature and nurture. Language-use is also neither a finished product nor is it unfinished; it is an open-ended process, like human beings who use language in various ways in the stream of life in conversation

5 Dummett, *Frege: Philosophy of Language* (London: Duckworth, 1973), 669.

6 Wittgenstein, *Remarks on the Foundations of Mathematics*, eds, G. H. von Wright, R. Rhees, G. E. M. Anscombe (Oxford: Basil Blackwell, 1978), 335.

7 Wittgenstein, *Remarks on the Foundations of Mathematics*, 127.

8 Wittgenstein, *Tractatus*, Preface.

9 Wittgenstein, *Philosophical Investigations* (Oxford: Blackwell, 1953), 340.

10 Wittgenstein, *Philosophical Investigations*, 124.

and collabouration with others. Our language-use is both dynamic and stable and rests on agreement in our form of life,[11] which includes both agreements in actions and judgements. In learning a language, thus, we do not merely learn the pronunciation, spelling and syntax of words, but the forms of life which make those sounds and ink marks the words they are, play their roles in the respective language-games – asking, thanking, cursing, greeting, praying, etc.[12] It is agreement in judgement and practice that makes the noises and scribbling meaningful words in the complex forms of human life. "Only in the practice of a language can a word have meaning."[13]

According to Wittgenstein, "Language relates to a way of living,"[14] how human beings live, move, and have their being in the world. It is a practice with characteristic elements of objectivity, regularity, and normativity. Language-use is objective; it is not just something that we think but something that takes place in the sphere of actual behaviour of living human beings and its foundations are in the stream of our lives. Wittgenstein has successfully shown that there is no *private* language that "to refer to what can only be known to the person speaking," as there is no possibility of distinguishing between what seems to be the case and what is the case in such a *private* language.[15] Neither the world of objects, nor the Platonic Ideas, nor the Cartesian *res cogitans* provide the foundations for our language use.[16]

The bedrock of our practices, including language use, is the regularity of practice and agreement in acting and judgement. Unless there is regularity in the use of a word, it cannot function as a word in any language. "The phenomenon of language rests on regularity, on agreement in acting."[17] It is a regularity of our lives that is based on the regularity of nature. Though regularity of nature is necessary for language, it is not sufficient; we need regularity of human nature - agreement in acting and judgement. For example, the sound of thunder is not the name of lightning. It is a regularity across time and persons – not something that only one person does only once. Though "Language did not emerge from some kind of ratiocination,"[18] they are not without reasons; once language-games are established there are reasons. Moreover, children learn

11 Wittgenstein, *Philosophical Investigations*, 241.

12 Ibid., 23.

13 Ibid., 344.

14 Ibid., 335.

15 Wittgenstein, *Philosophical Investigations*, 243.

16 Jose Nandhikkara, *Being Human after Wittgenstein: A Philosophical Anthropology* (Bangalore: Dharmaram College, 2011), 158-167.

17 Wittgenstein, *Remarks on the Foundations of Mathematics*, 342.

18 Wittgenstein, *On Certainty*, eds, G. E M. Anscombe and G. H. von Wright (Oxford: Basil Blackwell, 1969), 475.

language from the grown-ups by being trained to its use. Language is, thus, a product of nature and nurture and could be seen as part of our second nature.

Wittgenstein's point is that the bedrock of our linguistic use is our regularity and agreement in actions rather than ratiocination. "It is our acting, which lies at the bottom of the language-game."[19] The crucial point is the normativity – the distinction between what is the case and what ought to be the case - that is shown by the agreement in acting and in judgements. "Here it is of the greatest importance that all of us, or the overwhelming number, agree on certain things. For example, I can be sure that the colour of this object will be called 'green' by most people who see it."[20] "If there was no agreement in what we call 'red', etc., etc., language would come to an end."[21] Without agreement the words would be meaningless; they would not be words but just sounds and ink marks. "The sounds and marks would not have a meaning independent of his production of them – which comes to saying that would not have meaning in the sense that words have meaning."[22] If there were no overwhelming agreement in applying a word, it would have no role in a language. "If language is to be a means of communication there must be agreement not only in definitions but also (queer as this may sound) in judgments."[23]

Both regularity and overwhelming agreement in judgements are to be seen as part of the framework on which the working of our language is based. They provide a system of co-ordinates for the practice of a language. This is not merely an epistemological point but a metaphysical aspect of there being any language use. Wittgenstein wrote: "Our language-game only works, of course, when a certain agreement prevails, but the concept of agreement does not enter into the language-game."[24] It is part of the framework of having any language. This is true also about regularity of practice. Regularity and agreement are not inserted between a word and meaning to bridge them. Meaning is not a Platonic, Cartesian, or social entity. It is our actual use of the word that is highlighted by drawing attention to the role of regularity and agreement of the members of a community. A community is not external to the word use; it is part of the characteristic surrounding and framework of language use.[25] They are interdependent.

---

19 Wittgenstein, *On Certainty*, 475, 204.

20 Wittgenstein, *Remarks on the Foundations of Mathematics*, 342.

21 Ibid., 196.

22 Norman Malcolm, *Wittgenstinian Themes: Essays,* 198-89, ed., G. H. von Wright (New York: Cornell University Press, 1995), 165.

23 Wittgenstein, *Philosophical Investigations*, 242.

24 Wittgenstein, *Zettel*, eds, G. E M. Anscombe and G. H. von Wright (Oxford: Basil Blackwell, 1967), 430.

25 Wittgenstein, *Remarks on the Foundations of Mathematics*, 323.

First of all, if there are no similarities in the world, human beings could not see similarities and classify them; there would not be any language. Secondly, if there are no human beings with capacities to see and judge similarities, there could not be any seeing of similarities and classification without which there could not be any language. "The seeing of similarities underpins patterns of language use" and these "patterns of word use... emerge from our ongoing practice."[26] This is something fundamental to human living. Thirdly, if there are no human beings who quietly agree on a vast variety of judgements concerning regularity in nature and in human actions, there would not be any language because language is a human practice and practices are by nature objective, regular, and normative. Languages are not human inventions or discoveries but practices that evolved as a joint venture of nature and nurture. Things are similar and they are seen and judged as similar, not by just one individual but all who share in a form of life. Our concepts, in general, depend on the fact that human beings would respond in similar ways under similar circumstances, pressing for which (similarities, seeing similarities or judging similarities) is basic or reducing one to the other is a philosophical obsession rather than philosophical investigation. It is futile to separate between elements of nature and nurture in human practices. They are interwoven to give shape to our complicated forms of life.

"Wittgenstein's position is simply this: what I mean is determined by my natural use of words, so that we cannot sensibly ask whether my use really conforms to what my words mean."[27] My natural use of words is interwoven with the rest of my life. It is formed by nurture and becomes my second nature. Calibration is made possible by my regularity in patterns of use. Given the same training, human beings respond in certain regular ways; we agree in acting and in our judgements. Other beings may respond in different ways. It is also possible that a particular human being or a group of people may respond differently. "Such a case would present similarities with one in which a person naturally reacted to the gesture of pointing with the hand by looking in the direction of the line from finger-tip to wrist, not from wrist to finger-tip."[28] In such situations, there cannot be normative practices including language use.

To the question, "How could human behaviour be described?" Wittgenstein answered: "Surely only by showing the actions of a variety of humans, as they are all mixed up together. Not what one man is doing now, but the whole hurly-burly, is the background against which we see an action, and

---

26 Michael Luntley, "Patterns, Particularism and Seeing the Similarity," *Philosophical Papers* (November 2002), 274, 271.

27 C. McGinn, *Wittgenstein on Meaning* (Oxford: Basil Blackwell, 1984), 87-88.

28 Wittgenstein, *Philosophical Investigations*, 185.

it determines our judgment, our concepts, and our reactions."[29] Applying it to linguistic use, Malcolm wrote:

> To speak a language is to participate in a way of living in which many people are engaged. The language I speak gets its meaning from the common ways of acting and responding of many people. I take part in a game ... To follow the rules for the use of an expression is nothing other than to use by those many people who take part in the activities in which the expression is embedded. Thus, the meaning of the expression is independent of me, or of any particular person; and this is why I can use the expression correctly or incorrectly. It has a meaning independent of my use of it.[30]

Wittgenstein himself admitted: "One can of course imagine someone who lives alone and sketches pictures of the objects around him (say on the walls of his cave), and his picture language could be easily understood."[31] For our language use we need not only multiplicity of instances, "the whole hurly-burly of human actions" but also "the actions of a variety of humans, as they are all mixed up together."[32] Language, thus, relates to practices - ways of living.

3. Following a Religion

Wittgenstein's investigations into meaning and use, and rules and rule-following help us to clarify the nature of following a religion. Though there are differences between belief and practice - like meaning and use, rule and rule following - they are not two entities, one conceptual and the other empirical, that are brought together externally. They are not two things that can be grasped independently of one another. Like the relation between a true proposition and the fact that verifies it or a desire and something that satisfies it,[33] the relation between a belief and practice is internal. To understand a belief is to recognize what acts are in agreement or in conflict with it, just as to understand a description is to understand what would be the case if it were true or false. There is no gap between them. There are obviously important differences between practices with belief and those without belief. Believers could rightly

29 Wittgenstein, *Zettel*, 567.

30 Malcolm, *Wittgenstinian Themes: Essays,* 198-89, 164.

31 Wittgenstein, *Nachlass: The Bergen Electronic Edition* (Oxford: Oxford University Press, 2000), MS, 165, 105.

32 Wittgenstein, *Zettel*, 567.

33 Ludwig Wittgenstein, *Wittgenstein and The Vienna Circle*, ed., B. F. McGuinnes (Oxford: Blackwell, 1979), 157.

ask: "What greater difference could there be?"[34] There is also an important difference between what we do and what we ought to do in religious matters. From Wittgenstein's investigations on rules and following rules, I argue that "Following a religion is a practice."[35] My aim is to show that the important elements of objectivity, regularity and normativity that are interwoven in the concept of practice are operative in what we call 'following a religion' as well. Religions make sense only in the context of objective, regular and normative practices.

First of all, following a religion is objective; there is a distinction between thinking that one is following a religion and actually following it. Objectivity safeguards the distinction between seems/thinks so and is so. Whatever seems religious to me is religious is not an acceptable position. Following a religion is something that a believer actually does, not merely something that seems so to the agent. It is only in the actual practice of a religion that a religion is understood and followed. Following a religion is not a matter between the believer and God only in such a way that only the believer knows that she/he follows her/his religion and only she/he can follow that religion. The idea that following a religion is a practice secures the distinction between thinking that one is following a religion and one is actually following it. Without that distinction thinking that one is following a religion would be the same as following it, which does not make sense. Practices provide the objective criteria for following a religion. A believer's sincere belief that she/he is following a religion, though necessary, is not sufficient to judge that she/he is actually following a religion.

It is often wrongly thought that what is essential to religion is carried out in the inner realms and any overt actions are mere symptoms of something deeper and mysterious. The external behaviour, according to this view, gets its religious value only because of the inner – intention, attention, devotion, etc. Without this inner factor, rituals are merely gestures and vocal prayers are just noises. The inner is what makes those gestures and word-use part of religious practice; it gives life. Religion is something inner, according to this pervasive picture. Religion, however, is not restricted exclusively to the inner realms; it is something the believers do and what we do is connected with the rest of our lives. Though Wittgenstein's remark that "It is our acting, which lies at the bottom of the language-game"[36] is true about religion, it cannot be restricted to outward behaviour either. It is neither exclusively a spiritual nor a bodily activity. It is something that living human beings ought to do involving the

34 Wittgenstein, *Philosophical Investigations*, 304.

35 Ibid., 202.

36 Wittgenstein, *On Certainty*, eds, G. E M. Anscombe and G. H. von Wright (Oxford: Basil Blackwell, 1969), 204.

whole of their lives. The first commandment, according to the Bible, is "You must love the Lord your God with all your heart and with all your soul and with all your mind and with all your strength."[37] This love is shown in various ways in the stream of a religious life.

A belief in God is expressed in the behaviour and a belief ought to make a difference in the life of the person. The religious faith informs and transforms the life of the believer. If it does not affect one's way of life, it is impossible to judge one's belief as religious. A belief is judged by the role it plays in the life of the believer. The notion of belief without corresponding practices, like the love without expressions, is incoherent. Both would lack objectivity.

Secondly, there is regularity, meaning. Following a religion is a repeatable procedure. In order to describe the phenomenon of religion one has to describe a practice, not a one-time occurrence, whatever it might be.[38] Like other practices, it is repeatable over time (and place) and across persons. It can be taught and learned. A human action that cannot be logically repeated across time (and place) is incoherent. What is possible for one person to repeat over time cannot be logically impossible for others to do. As one human being cannot follow just one rule just once in a lifetime, one human being cannot follow a religion just once in his life.

One action does not make a practice, religious or not. As I am not justified to judge on the rule-following character of a creature on Mars who looked at something like a signpost, and then walked parallel to it,[39] I have no justification to judge on its religiosity by observing one action, even if I knew all its feelings at that moment. It must behave in a certain regular way. I need to see the action being repeated a number of times and more importantly its connection with the rest of the Martian's life.

Whether I would be able to judge the action of the Martian depends on how much I know about its various forms of life. An action, like a word, can be judged only in the stream of life. Following a religion involves the mastery of many interrelated practices and a whole web of human behaviour. One cannot do an action just once and claim that it is a religious act. One may participate in a religious ritual just once; but the person will not be following a religion by that act alone. The whole circumstance would make the point clear, especially what preceded and followed that act. What in a complicated surrounding, we call 'following a religion', we would not call it so if it stood in isolation; it relates to a way of living. Indeed, religious acts will have their significance only in the context of a regular human life. The bedrock of our practices, including following a religion, is the regularity of practice and agreement in

---

37 Gospel of Mark 12:30.

38 Wittgenstein, *Remarks on the Foundations of Mathematics*, 335.

39 Wittgenstein, *Nachlass*, MS 124, 187.

judgements. This is something fundamental. Following a religion takes place in the sphere of actual behaviour of living human beings and its foundations are in the stream of our lives. This cannot be restricted to be a matter between God and soul alone. Religion relates to a regular way of living involving God, community and the world. As in the other cases of practices, we need normative regularity, not just natural regularity. That is our third point, normativity.

Normativity, here, means that regularity is subject to standards of correctness. Following a religion is concerned with how we ought to live rather than stating how we live. The distinction between is and ought to be kept here; there is a correct way of following a religion. Religious practices are not just regularities of behaviour but regularities that have a normative force, ways believers ought to act. It is manifested in a regularity that is normative which presupposes understanding and judgement from the part of the religious believer. The judgement itself is possible only where an established pattern of behaviour is discernible. It is essential to have such standards of correctness to specify the scope and content of any religious practice. This does not rule out creativity, growth and development in religious belief and practices. As in other practices, we not only inhabit these patterns but also shape them as we go on responsibly and creatively. Believers are active agents living in the world in contact with God in conversation and collabouration with other fellow human beings.

Although, practices and beliefs are internally related and like other aspects of life, and religion is also "characterised by what we can and cannot do,"[40] the ultimate source of normativity in religion is God. Religion, though lived within the contingencies of nature, transcends them. In religion, one has to make a leap of faith, involving a personal judgement and passionate commitment. Though a religious believer belongs to a community, one has to make it for oneself; one has to make a commitment, a fundamental option in life that affects the whole life. A believer's ultimate support in this judgement is God. Wittgenstein wrote,

> So, this can only come about if you no longer support yourself on this earth but suspend yourself from heaven. Then everything is different and it is 'no wonder' if you can then do what now you cannot do.[41]

For a believer the sanction and confirmation from God is fundamental. God is the bedrock where all explanations come to rest in religion. At the bedrock level, however, the religious beliefs do not stand alone; they are interwoven with other empirical claims and value judgements and held together

40 Wittgenstein, *Zettel*, 345

41 Wittgenstein, *Culture and Value*, 39.

by what lies around them. They are shown in their lives in their attitudes to the world, fellow human beings and God.

4. Conclusion

Wittgenstein wrote:

> One can freely compare a firmly rooted picture in us with a superstition; but one can also say that one must always come to a firm ground, be it now a picture or not so that a picture at the source of all thoughts must be respected and not be treated as superstition.[42]

Religious pictures that are at the source of all thoughts and explanations are to be accepted at their face value; they do not stand for something else. Whether individuals take the picture at the basis as superstition or as truth is a personal judgement, supported by nature and nurture and most importantly by God. Because of the nature of religious beliefs there is no such thing as bringing evidence to demonstrate their correctness or to prove their validity. Evidence may play a role in establishing the nature of the case at issue, but how one should judge the case cannot itself be deduced from any particular evidence. One has to make a judgement and a faith commitment. If there is an argument, "Its purpose is not to convince positively, or convert, but to remove erroneous notions and prejudices."[43] While there may be 'proofs' within a particular religious framework, that framework will itself not be founded; from a logical point of view, it is simply one possibility among others; one may take it as superstitious or true faith.

Wittgenstein wrote: "If someone asks: How could the surroundings force the ethical in someone? – the answer is that he may indeed say, 'There's no such thing as must,' but at the same time under such circumstances such and such will be done."[44] This is true about religious faith; one cannot force someone to follow a religion. One has to rush up and seize the rescue-anchor on one's own accord and not be led by the hand of the instructor.[45] This free response believers take as something that they ought to do. The point remains, however, though many reasons could be offered, at some stage one has to make a fundamental, personal and religious judgement. This could be the result of nurture in a religious environment, years of personal study and search or may be due to a momentous religious experience.

---

42 Wittgenstein, Nachlass, MS 138, 32b-33a. 20.5.1949.

43 A. Ambrose, ed., *Wittgenstein's Lectures, Cambridge 1932-35: From the Notes of Alice Ambrose and Margaret Macdonald* (Oxford: Basil Blackwell, 1979), 63.

44 Wittgenstein, *Nachlass*, MS 173, 17r. 30.3.1950.

45 Wittgenstein, *Culture and Value*, 73.

Furthermore, I may be unable to specify the basis of my belief, and yet my belief is not without a basis; indeed, from a religious point of view it has the strongest basis possible. The believer "will treat this belief as extremely well-established, and in another way as not established at all."[46] On the one hand, he may cling to it in the face of evidence which would shake any empirical belief, but on the other, he may recognize that his grounds for so doing are nothing like what we ordinarily call 'evidence'. Here we don't talk of probabilities and hypotheses – the nature of a being a believer is entirely different. The belief forms the basis of our lives, the way in which we see the world.

Though these three elements, objectivity, regularity and normativity, are constitutive of religious practice, they do not make the sufficient and necessary conditions for following a religion. From a Wittgensteinian point of view, they are not elements in the practice but belong to its framework.[47] Our attitudes to the world, fellow human beings and God are fundamental. They are not mere opinions that can be proved right or wrong in further investigations. There is a certain 'indefiniteness' and 'variability' with regard to human behaviour,[48] including religious practices. As Wittgenstein observed with regard to judging the genuineness of expressions of feelings, it is most difficult here to put this indefiniteness, correctly and unfalsified, into words.[49] This is not, however, ignorance, but a fact of life. Like other practices, the background against which we describe a religious practice, "is the bustle of life. And our concept points to something within this bustle."[50] It makes sense to talk of understanding and following a religion, only in the context of a stream of life in which a religion is objectively, regularly and normatively practised; it "cannot be replaced by the appearance of a practice."[51]

46 Wittgenstein, *Lectures and Conversations on Aesthetics, Psychology and Religious Belief*, ed., C. Barrett (Oxford: Basil Blackwell, 1966), 54.

47 Wittgenstein, *Remarks on the Foundations of Mathematics*, 323; See also: Wittgenstein, *Philosophical Investigations*, 240.

48 Wittgenstein, *Remarks on the Philosophy of Psychology*, Vol. II, eds, G. H. von Wright and H. Nyman (Oxford: Blackwell, 1980), 626-627.

49 Wittgenstein, *Philosophical Investigations*, 227.

50 Wittgenstein, *Remarks on the Philosophy of Psychology*, Vol. II, 625.

51 Wittgenstein, *Nachlass*, MS 180a, 36.

9

Critical Theory and the Youth Movements of the Sixties: A Privileged and Complex Relationship

Nishant A. Irudayadason
Jnana-Deepa Vidyapeeth, Pune

Abstract: This paper examines the relationship between the critical theory of the Frankfurt School developed by Horkheimer, Adorno and Marcuse, and the student protest movement of the sixties in Europe. This paper explores how the student movement of 1968 the sixties embodied the critique of the authoritarian personality, the critique of the consumer society and of the culture industry, the fight against sexual repression and for a new kind of liberation, one which is both collective and individual.

Keywords: Revolution, Marxism, Cultural Industry, Rationalization, Authoritarianism, Consumer Society, Liberation, Enlightenment.

Introduction

The question of the relationship between theory and practice, between intellectual development and social movements is one of the most fascinating, yet complicated. In this paper, I shall deal with the relationship between the critical theory of the Frankfurt School and the youth Movements of 1960s. The question has many aspects and deserves a detailed treatment.[1] We shall touch

1 On this subject, the most complete work is in German. It is that of W. Kraushaar eds, *Frankfurter Schule und Studentbewegung. Von der Flaschenpost zum Molotowcocktail*

only on a few key points, aimed at supporting a very precise hypothesis: the critical theory of the Frankfurt School was the theoretical perspective which, more than any other theory, could provide a horizon of self-understanding to youth Movements of the sixties. This is because the critical theory, developed by the long-term work of the Frankfurt School from the 1930s to the 1960s, was the most structured attempt to develop a critique of the capitalist society that could offer something new and different from what the classical Marxist critique of bourgeois society offered. The Frankfurt School was grafted onto an intellectual horizon strongly structured by the Marxist tradition, but from this basis it was able to produce a series of relevant theoretical innovations, which went far beyond what other traditions had managed to do.

But (and this is the second aspect of my hypothesis) the relation between the critical theory and the youth Movements of the sixties was equally difficult and complex. The meeting between the critical theory and the youth Movements was essential especially in the light of the events of May 1968, which if proceeded otherwise, would not have been a mass movement, but a pure academic discussion. To become a mass movement, had to rely on historically consolidated elements of contradiction including the fighting ability of the working class in European societies and the anti-imperialist conflict in Vietnam, and adapted itself to a critique of the more traditionally Marxist tradition. Thus, the Movements ended up being part of the search for a renewed Marxism, which was nevertheless able to go beyond Marxism through the elabourations of the Frankfurt School. On one hand, we must emphasize the great proximity of the Movements to the themes of the Frankfurt School and, on the other, the contradiction that emerged between the two poles. Therefore, we need to talk about a privileged but complex relationship.

The Diffusion of the Theses of the Frankfurt School in the Sixties

There is a first confirmation of the strong link between the theories of the Frankfurt School and the movement of 68 in the dissemination of the texts of Adorno, Horkheimer and Marcuse in the circles of the youth protest. The story is interesting and has paradoxical aspects. The most important theoretical works of the Frankfurt School namely the articles of Horkheimer and Marcuse published between 1932 and 1941 in the Journal of the Institute for Social Research, the *Zeitschrift für Sozialforschung*, and *Dialectic of Enlightenment*, the collabourated intellectual work of Horkheimer and Adorno, published in 1947 were, in the early sixties, completely forgotten and untraceable,

---

1995; Vol.I, Chronik, Vol. II, *Dokumente*, Vol. III, *Aufsätze, und Kommentare, Register* (Hambourg: Rogner & Bernhard, 1998).

including in Federal Germany.[2] Habermas (1992 [1988]) recollects, "when I became Adorno's assistant in 1956, the intellectual past of the Institute for Social Research was not accessible to the new students. [...] Horkheimer had a great fear that we would get to the crate in the Institute's cellar that contained a complete set of the *Zeitschrift*."[3] The true "rediscovery" of the critical theory was, as Habermas explains, due to the radical students: "It was only the intelligent young people of the late sixties who took up the first Critical Theory [...]" And it is not at all a painless rediscovery: *The Dialectic of Reason*, that Horkheimer did not want to reprint, was published in 1968 by a publishing house De Munter in Amsterdam linked to the movement and was republished by Fischer. The same publishing house reprinted under the title *Kritische Theorie* the most radical writings Horkheimer dated between 1939 and 1941,[4] which he had earlier excluded from the two volumes. In Italy too, the rediscovery of *The Dialectic of Reason* was made by a representative of the heterodox left, Renato Solmi, who had it published by Einaudi publishing house. However, as Horkheimer had imposed certain cuts and modifications, Solmi withdrew his name and the translation appeared signed with a pseudonym. From 1968, Horkheimer's and Adorno's main texts were again available in Germany, and massively translated in Italy. The English and French translations were later, although they also appeared within a few years.

As for Marcuse, the diffusion of his works was even faster: *One-dimensional Man*,[5] published in the United States in 1964, was translated into Italian in 1967 and French in 1968, and suddenly became the best-seller of movement, reaching impressive sales. *Eros and Civilization*,[6] published in the US in 1955, appeared in Italy in 1964 and France in 1968. Soon, all of Marcuse's other works were translated and published.

Themes of the Critical Theory Influencing the Movement

It is important to devote some thought to the most interesting aspect of the rapport between the critical theory and the movement of the sixties and that is the presence of many themes that the Frankfurt School had tackled during

2 Theodor W. Adorno and Max Horkheimer, *Dialectic of Enlightenment*, trans. John Cumming (New York: Herder & Herder, 1972).

3 Jürgen Habermas, "The Dialectics of Rationalization," in Habermas ed., *Autonomy and Solidarity: Interviews with Jürgen Habermas* (London and New York: Verso, 1992) 96-97.

4 Max Horkheimer, "The German Jews," in *Critique of Instrumental Reason: Lectures and Essays Since the End of WWII*, trans. Matthew J. O'Connell and Others (London: Verso, 2012), 101–118.

5 Herbert Marcuse, *One-Dimensional Man: Studies in the Ideology of Advanced Industrial Society* (New York: Routledge & Kegan Paul, 1964).

6 Herbert Marcuse, *Eros and Civilization: A Philosophical Inquiry into Freud* (New York: Routledge & Kegan Paul, 1955).

thirty years of research (research which, as we have seen, had been relegated by the very will of the first and most recognized director of the Institute for Social Research, Max Horkheimer) in the documents of the youth Movements in the sixties. The students picked up these themes and applied them effectively, especially in the first phase of the movement in 1968. We shall briefly go through some of the most important themes.

Anti-authoritarianism

The slogan of anti-authoritarianism is the most obvious starting point. Anti-authoritarianism was the most original and characteristic theme of the 68 movement: it characterizes the early phases of the student movement and differentiates it from so many other Movements that preceded or followed it. Anti-authoritarianism was the first true banner of the youth movement, which launched this arrow from the University campuses to all areas of society. The rebellious youth questioned all the constituted authorities, inaugurating what was in many ways a general revolution which took an extremely strong hold on all aspects of a closed society.

But who, in the 20th century, had more than anyone undertaken the analysis and criticism of authority? Without doubt the Frankfurt School. The reasons are obvious: this orientation of social research had developed in Germany in the early thirties (the Nazis took power in 1933). As a result, the great question of social theory, for the proponents of the Frankfurt School, was to understand how authoritarian power could win the support of broad masses, including those of the lower middle classes. Researchers at the Frankfurt School, confronted with the phenomenon of mass adherence to authoritarian dictatorships (notably those of Hitler and Mussolini), felt the need to find explanations that classical Marxist theory did not provide for this 20th century phenomenon and to find how, from this, had been born a broad consensus to deal with authoritarian leaders and dictators.

The theme of authority and the exploration of the psychological mechanisms that are the basis of the obedience of the individual, including against his or her own interests, were thus central to the Frankfurt school, which devoted its most important social or psycho-social researches to it published as *Studien* über *Autorität und Familie* (can be translated into English as *Studies on Authority and the Family*, but no English translation available for this work) in 1936[7] and *The Authoritarian Personality* in 1950.[8] While, for the Frankfurt School, the critical inquiry into the patriarchal family and its

7 Max Horkheimer, *Studienüber Autorität und Familie: Forschungsberichte aus dem Institutfür Sozialforschung* (Paris: Librairie Félix Alcan, 1936).

8 Theodor. W. Adorno and Others, *The Authoritarian Personality* (New York: Harper & Brothers, 1950).

crisis explained the processes of formation of authoritarian or sadomasochistic individuals who gave their consent to the dictatorship, in the movement of the sixties, this theme was applied to all establishments and was integrated into the daily life of a whole generation.

In federal Germany, between 1966 and 1968, the youth movement was precisely defined as an anti-authoritarian movement: it was struggling against the repression of the Nazi past, against the consensual society that was emerging as part of the grand coalition of 1966 between Christian Democracy and Social Democracy, and in a battle that lasted for years against the *Notstandsgesetze*, a state of emergency law was passed in June 1968 which provided for the possibility of limiting constitutional freedom. The student movement, after its failure to stop the emergency legislation, began quickly unravelling in 1969. The students strongly perceived the risk of an authoritarian trend in German society, which was denounced by young radical intellectuals like Oskar Negt and Johannes Agnoli: "Today's fascism", wrote Rudi Dutschke, the leader of the movement, "no longer manifests itself in a party or in a person, but it takes root in the fact that everyone is trained daily to become an authoritarian personality, takes root in education."[9] The structures of the authoritarian personality, according to Dutschke, had survived the defeat of fascism and continued to fuel anti-communist ideologyin the sixties.

The question of anti-authoritarianism is also central to the birth of the youth movement in Italy: in what constitutes the true "manifesto" of the movement, Guido Viale in his article "*Control'Università*" (Against the University) wrote:

> The roots of academic authoritarianism, as of all forms of authoritarian rule, lie not only in a series of institutional and economic structures, but above all, first and foremost, in the consent of those who suffer the power. The university is organized to create and maintain consent [...] Authoritarianism is the political form of the system: it constitutes the political node around which to concretize the struggles, and also the unitary ground for the massification of the struggles themselves.[10]

9 Rudi Dutschke and Others, *Die Rebellion der Studentenoder die neue Opposition* (Hambourg: Rowohlt, 1968).

10 Guido Viale, "Control' Università," *Quaderni Piacentini* 33 (1968). On this subject, see also C. Donolo, "La politicaridefinita." Note "sul movimento studentesco,"*Quaderni Piacentini* 35 (1968). We can now find these texts in G. Fofi and V. Giacopini, *Prima e dopoil'68. Antologiadei"Quaderni Piacentini"* (Rome: Minimum Fax, 2008). For a good historical reconstruction of the movement in Italy, see G. Crainz, *Ilpaesemancato. Dal miracolo economi coaglianni Ottanta* (Rome: Donzelli, 2003).

It must be said, however, that the Movements quickly passed the "anti-authoritarian" phase (characterized also by the choice of participative democracy in preference to representative democracy), to move towards a more "orthodox" anti-capitalism. Nonetheless, the anti-authoritarianism of 1968 started a powerful process of transforming the gaze of authority into all major social institutions: from the family to the University, from church to army, from school to psychiatric hospitals: all these "disciplinary" structures were subjected to a radical attack and criticism that profoundly changed the ways of life and relationship within them, leaving very deep traces in the fabric of our society.

Consumer Society

Although, now banal, this is another significant theme. This novel theme was developed in the 1930s and 1940s by the critical theory of the Frankfurt School. Forced into emigration to the United States, Horkheimer and Adorno encountered a type of society completely different from what they had known in Europe; mass consumption was already a reality, whereas it would only become so in Europe after the World War II. The two leaders of the Frankfurt group then set themselves the goal of thinking of the global social changes brought about by the new expansion of consumption. To understand how important this question was in their reflection, it is sufficient to re-read the passages from *Dialectic of Enlightenment*, in which Horkheimer and Adorno explain that the problem is not that consumer goods simply liquidate the old metaphysics, but that they themselves become a new metaphysics, an ideological curtain which, assimilating the individuals to one another in as many consumers, masks the real relations of class and power within the society.[11] As Marcuse wrote in *One-dimensional Man*, "The people recognize themselves in their commodities; they find their soul in their automobile, hi-fi set, split-level home, kitchen equipment. The very mechanism which ties the individual to his society has changed, and social control is anchored in the new needs which it has produced."[12] With this awareness, social criticism has changed its direction. Unlike the tradition of social and labour Movements, it is no longer the social bases of wealth that are attacked in a demand for more equal redistribution of goods and resources. It is no longer a question, on the part of the lower classes, to say: "We demand the goods that the ruling classes want to reserve for themselves," but, on the contrary, to affirm: "We do not wantwhat you have, we do not want to enter into your spiral of consumption, we do not want to be caught up in the mechanism of induced needs, which is really a way to get us into relationships of domination; we want to experiment

11 See Adorno and Horkheimer, *Dialectic of Enlightenment.*

12 Marcuse, *One-Dimensional Man*, 11.

with different ways of living and consuming, which waste less human and natural resources." In Paris in 1968, a document of the Action Committee, "We are on the move", proclaimed that in contemporary capitalism, individuals were stolen twice, the first time as workers, the second as consumers: "In paying for advertising, the worker-consumer pays with the fruit of his productive work a pure void: the creation of his own needs."[13]

In short, social criticism no longer presents itself as a demand for the redistribution of material affluence, but as the refusal of a certain form of consumption, which is also reflected in the search for alternative lifestyles. This aspect is very present in the student movement of the sixties and cannot be thought of without referring to the social criticism of the Frankfurt School. The paradox, however, is that the ideology of consumption and self-identification through the choice of consumer goods were so strong, so integrated into the social fabric of the sixties, that the young people of the 68 identified themselves through several objects of consumption and thus marked their difference from previous generations. They formed a community by opting for a certain way of dressing and hairstyle; the use of Renault 4 and padded jackets became symbols that were born out of a critique of the consumer society but ended up contributing to the birth of a new model of consumer.

Cultural Industry

This theme is related to the preceding one and was prophetically addressed in the research works of the Frankfurt School, especially in *Dialectic of Enlightenment*, which devotes an entire chapter to it, becomes central to the movement of 68. Here again, the criticism is born of a reflection of Horkheimer and Adorno from their American experience: arriving in the United States, the two friends from Frankfurt settle near Hollywood in 1941 and discovered the world of American cinema, as well as the models of life and consumption that it conveys. The significant presence of radio and television: all impelled them to undertake a new and much deeper reflection on the media. The discovery of the centrality of these issues, which became evident today, was then a real novelty because it moved the terrain of conflict on the cultural level.

By giving a central place to the theme of the media, the reflection brings out a new reading of society: the bases of the adhesion to the dominant powers in the society of late capitalism are new and stronger than in the past, because they rest, on one side, on the fetishist cult of the commodity and, on the other, on the enormous and dazzling apparatus of ideological and media manipulation. Coming from Marcuse (and Guy Debord), this theme was structuring the Movements of the sixties. The widely held idea was that, in the society of late capitalism, social antagonisms were largely masked or diverted

13 Action Committee Report, *Quelleuniversité? Quellesociété?* (Paris: Seuil, 1968).

by a new power of manipulation of consciousness. In a way, it emerged from a reading of society as based on manipulation - the only way to explain why the lower classes no longer perceived their interests as antagonistic to those of the dominant. On this point, there is a strong convergence between the critical theory and the movement of 68, which puts the question of the means of mass communication at the centre of its fight and takes the media as one of its privileged targets (the titles of the Springer group in Germany, the *Corrieredella*in Italy).

Individual Liberation and Critique of Repression

This is also an important theme transported from the critical theory of the Frankfurt School to the youth movement of the sixties. It is the only current of "Marxist" thought (Wilhelm Reich, the theorist of the sexual revolution) that succeeded in fully integrating not only Freudian critique but also Nietzschean critique of the repressive nature of the institutions of bourgeois society, starting with the family. The Frankfurt School, though born within Marxism, manages to appropriate the content of the critique of the repressive society from another theoretical horizon. The youth movement of 1968 tried to transform these themes into life practices and, here again, positioned itself in a very different way from other struggles or revolutions. Two theses distinguish it from other social movements before. First, the idea that there is no collective liberation without liberation of individuals from the repressive relations in which they are retained. Second, the idea that, to free oneself from these repressive relations, individuals must also fight against themselves, that is to perform a work of self-transformation. The impulses and demands of collective liberation and equality cannot be separated from those of individual liberation: refusal of repression at school and in the family, and the claim on sexual freedom. In March 1967, with the constitution of the *Kommune 1*, the movement of "communes", began in Berlin, whose basic principle was that "every group that wants to reorganize society on an anti-authoritarian basis, must organize itself on anti-authoritarian, egalitarian and community bases". In the universities and in the occupied schools, young people give birth to new relationships in which they feel free, organize alternative courses of sexual education and reading the texts of Reich, Fromm or Marcuse. We begin to understand that a dynamic of social liberation can fail only if it does not bring about a change in each individual, and that politics cannot be separated from a profound upheaval of individual behaviour. This is the new idea that will bear fruit particularly in feminist Movements, which will break with all the rituals of the old politics and rethink it based on the idea of "starting from oneself".

This theme is also an opportunity to reflect on a particular characteristic of a part of critical thought that circulated in the sixties: its proximity to Friedrich Nietzsche, that the previous Marxist traditions had generally condemned and refused. For the Frankfurt School, Nietzsche constantly remained an important reference, from *Studies of Authority and Family* to *Dialectic of Enlightenment* and even beyond. Nietzscheism has also left a certain mark in the working-class tradition, for example in the writings of Mario Tronti. Nietzsche is also fundamental for an author like Foucault and, later, for all post-structuralism. Naturally, the uses of Nietzsche in these different perspectives of critical thought are extremely heterogeneous. But, they have in common to use the author of *Thus Spoke Zarathustra* as a powerful antidote against humanism and social democratic progressivism, against the conciliatory ideologies that deny the radicality of domination and conflict or dilute them. The crudeness of his gaze on bourgeois society is perceived as more accurate than the "soft" visions that fuel the gradualism and reformism of the workers' movement.

Moreover, for critical theory, the reference to Nietzsche becomes constitutive of a rebellious or insubstantial subjectivity that appears to be destructive of the dominant social order, but which carries strong elements of ambivalence. If we look at the long-term effects of the youth Movements of the sixties, we see that the Nietzschean demand for a radical and irreducible subjectivity that does not try to surpass itself to go towards an ideological horizon of progress, but claims to affirm its hedonism in an immediacy, to release its own needs, on the one hand, feeds critical themes like those of sexual liberation and the refusal of the principle of performance, but on the other hand, flows perfectly into the developments of contemporary society. In a sense, it can be said that hedonism and narcissism, this self-centred subjectivity, in search of small pleasures, which emerged in the years 1980-1990, is also born from this type of protest, from the reaffirmation of subjective needs against the prevailing order and authority. So, the legacy of 1968, on the one hand, is in sharp contrast to recent developments in society (just think of the critique of the performance principle that is dominant in the contemporary neo-liberal society) but, on the other hand, it is congruent to it, once cut off from its solidarity and communitarian aspect.

Different Rapport of the Scholars of the Frankfurt School with the Movement

Though the major themes of the Frankfurt School are found in the Movements of the sixties and play a fundamental role, the various personalities of the School of Frankfurt have maintained different kind of rapport with the movement of 1968. From this point of view, the figure of Herbert Marcuse is emblematic: unlike Horkheimer and Adorno, he remained in the United States after the end of the Second World War and became a kind of figurehead of youth in revolt, not only with the strange slogan "Marx, Mao, Marcuse", but above all with books like *One-dimensional Man, Eros and Civilization* and A *Critique of Pure Tolerance*.[14]

Marcuse's rapport to the movement was totally different from Adorno's. The author of *Minima moralia* was read and studied, he became an important theoretical reference, but remained resolutely on his "pessimistic" positions, which eventually led him to confront the most radical of his pupils, especially with the student leader Hans Jürgen Krahl. Thus, Adorno was fiercely disputed. He suffered the occupation of his own research institute and lived the classic conflict, which was observed almost everywhere at the time, that of the professor and his students.[15] This conflict between Adorno and the movement çan obviously seem paradoxical if one thinks of what he himself had written so far and of the decisive theoretical reference he had become for the youth of the sixties, at least in Germany. However, we must also understand the position of Adorno: beyond his fundamental refusal of political commitment, his lack of confidence in a supposed "revolutionary" potential of the Movements and his certainty that, given the situation, any social transformation was absolutely impossible, he considered that certain forms of provocation and struggle implemented by the movement were in fact counterproductive, because they could help to awaken in German society an authoritarian potential and a demand for repression without being able to bring about concrete positive changes. After initial sympathy, Adorno received from his students an attitude of criticism and refusal, which is also noticeable in his last writings such as "Marginalia to Theory and Praxis,"[16] and "Resignation"[17] directed against a blind "activism" that Adorno called "pseudo-activity".

Marcuse's position was totally different. After formulating, in 1964, the diagnosis of a "one-dimensional" closure of the society of late capitalism, Marcuse had seen it denied with pleasure not only by the strength of the Vietnamese liberation struggle, but also and especially by the youth movement that was developing in the United States. From this movement, Marcuse had sought to redefine various aspects of his thought, engaging in a close dialogue with one of the leaders of the protest, Rudi Dutschke.

The clash with Adorno was therefore inevitable, and the letters they exchanged between February and August 1969, are a testimony of a certain

14 Robert Paul Wolff, Barrington Moore and Herbert Marcuse, *A Critique of Pure Tolerance* (Boston: Beacon Press, 1969).

15 For criticisms made on Adorno and his responses to them, see Chapter 14 of Stefan Müller-Doohm's well-documented and useful book, *Adorno: A Biography*, trans. Rodney Livingstone (Cambridge: Polity Press, 2005), 242-272.

16 Theodor W. Adorno, "Marginalia to Theory and Praxis", in *Critical Models* (New York: Colombia University Press), 259-278.

17 Theodor W. Adorno, "Resignation", in *Critical Models* (New York: Colombia University Press), 289-294.

dramatic intensity. Adorno died in Switzerland on August 6, 1969 and his final text is probably the letter he addressed to Marcuse that day, to "prevent a catastrophe", the radicalization and publicization of the disagreement between Marcuse and the Adorno-Horkheimer duo. To his old friend Adorno, Marcuse had instead written: "We cannot abolish from the world the fact that these students are influenced by us (and certainly not least by you)—I am proud of that and am willing to come to terms with patricide, even though it hurts sometimes."[18]

Marcuse did not share the pessimism of Adorno; on the contrary, he sought to interpret with the instruments of critical theory the new processes to which the Movements had given life. The aspects he emphasized were, on the one hand, revolution in values, sensibilities, forms of life, and the rejection resulting from the competitive and dehumanizing aspects of modern capitalist society, its "false needs" and its defence of "performative principle", on the other hand, the idea of a change of the subjects of the social conflict, in which the student, the intellectual, the marginal figures who would change framework of conflict significantly.

Conclusion

If what we have developed so far is convincing, we can conclude that, in a certain sense, the critical theory is the theory of motion of 68. Empirical evidence confirms this. Thus, in Germany, the most important leaders of the movement are directly students of the Frankfurt School. In the Western world, the only large-scale critical theorist who was taken as a reference for the movement (although he was obviously also strongly criticized) is the Herbert from Frankfurt. In Marcuse, the Frankfurt School and the movement of 68 were fused, with a force that existed for no other theoretical current. This remains true, even if other supporters of the Frankfurt School, like Adorno, have violently clashed with the movement.

It is also necessary to understand, as we know in the introduction, why the movement of 68 could not be "Frankfurt." The fact is that such a movement, especially in Italy, but also in France, although opened the way for a profoundly innovative social criticism, could only support the more "heavy" and more traditional forces of conflict, the working class inside (hence the quest for student-worker unity) and anti-imperialism at the international level (needless to point out how much the Vietnam War was fundamental to the development of the movement in the United States). But, at this point, we need to leave the framework of the Frankfurt School, which insisted too much on integration, or *latency*, of the working class and its ability to struggle, while it

18 Adorno and Marcuse, "Correspondence on the German Student Movement" (123-126), *New Left Review* 233 (1999), 125.

showed too little confidence in the correctness of the anti-imperialist struggles and powers (Soviet Union and China) that supported them. It must be said that, from this point of view, history has given reason to the oldest of the Frankfurt School, whose pessimism has proved more realistic than the optimism with which the Movements of 68 read the struggles against imperialists.

By thinking of itself as revolutionary in the classical sense of the term, the movement would have come closer to the renewed or recycled Marxism rather than critical theory. Yet, this meant the loss of the most innovative themes of the movement, which in many ways, continued to influence European and American societies in the following decades. Such a movement has undoubtedly been decisive in the profound changes it has brought to society. It ended up thinking of itself as the vanguard of a revolutionary process of fundamentally Marxist inspiration, but in reality, it represented something very different, a social upheaval of which we do not yet have an adequate interpretation. From this point of view, we can say that the destiny of the movement of 68 was paradoxical: conquered like political movement, it triumphed through many transformations that it initiated in the culture, in the ideas and in the forms of the social life. Revolution failed or perhaps, one could say, revolution remained a dream. Nevertheless, the movement carried within itself the seeds of two victorious revolutions, the feminist revolution against the patriarchal society and the revolution that brought an end to the authoritarian archaism of the Soviet bloc in 1989. To conclude, I think we can say that the movement of 1968, as it often happens in the great historical processes, was both a success and a failure: success because its vein of anti-authoritarianism and freedom could meet, often in a confrontational mode, the tendencies towards individualisation and the development of a "negative freedom" which are peculiar to the developed Western societies; failure because it has undoubtedly lost on the other fronts, that is to say in the battle against hyper-consumerist global capitalism and against the society of the spectacle (whose forces have only increased), and for a more participative democracy and less representative, for a society based on different values like ecological solidarity. The question therefore arises: did the Movements of the 1968s fail for lack of being a credible alternative or because the opponent was too strong to handle or for both reasons at the same time? This is not, in my opinion, the least important question that the movement of 1968 has bequeathed to us. Based on the reflections of Immanuel Wallerstein, one could say that the movement of 1968 was an end and a beginning. The end of 19th century politics. But the beginning of what? It is far from clear yet.

It can be observed that in India too we had student unrest Movements in 1960s which shaped the political consciousness of the masses. This was particularly evident in the student protest in the present day Tamil Nadu against the imposition of Hindi. The movement has to be seen not only as a linguistic concern but beyond, namely a reaction to a culture of imposition. Such Movements have been sporadic in many parts of India but was strategically contained geographically not to make impact in other parts of India. Political parties have appropriated such momentum for their electoral gains only later to dampen the spirit of such Movements. Recent history also shows the great potentiality that the student Movements can have in shaping the socio-political ethos. To name a few, student protest demanding justice for Nirbhaya in Delhi, the JNU student uprising against suppressing alternative voices, student protests in different parts of Andhra Pradesh and Telangana against subtle discrimination against Dalits in institutions of higher learning following the suicide of Rohit Vemula, the student unity to let the state and central governments to act swiftly to revoke the ban on Jallikattu—an important moment in history to reclaim local self-reliant economic practices. The major difficulty in sustaining all these Movements is a lack of a consistent theory that would co-ordinate praxis. The intellectuals of India are saddled with an immense responsibility to work out theories that can be paradigmatic of social revolution even though in the present political climate realizing this task seems a distant possibility. But, it is time that we began.

10

'Not without Difference': Re-visiting Emmanuel Levinas on Racism

Jojo Varakukalayil CST, PhD
Little Flower Institute of Philosophy and Religion, Aluva

Abstract: In deconstructing the ordinary concept of race beyond different disciplines, social circumstances, biological theories, and exclusivist political viewpoints we argue that philosophical analysis of the ordinary concept of race doesn't accord to the essentialist logic of interpretation. This article argues that the ordinary concept of race and the development of its meaning through racialist's appropriation is malevolent; and the sullying of its meaning is not the logical conclusion of it. As a result, the logical core does not afford to a rationale for racism. Racism, for Emmanuel Levinas, is the denial of the otherness of the other. The diabolical criminality of the monstrosity of evil of Hitlerism was one of the most vivid avatars of racism. Nazism considered the phenomenology of difference as a point of reducing the other as different to the ego/self or Nation/State. Jews, exclusively, are the other race defiling the purity of the Germanic Aryan blood. The other person, in various forms of racism, is the threatening other. This difference of the other remains a point of attack and an antagonism is nurtured against the other in racism. It's not difference that makes alterity, holds Levinas, rather alterity makes the difference. The other persons' difference cannot be reduced to the mere 'whatness', namely, the 'face' to a 'form'; yet, more truly, one doesn't want to be recognised detached from one's difference. Anyone wants to be respected as 'who' irrespective of 'what' i.e., one is 'not without difference'. The face of the other - difference - stands as moment of the ethical signification of the other as the absolute other; and this radical alterity of the other remains beyond any intentional *Cogito*. True humanity of the humans begins in this recognition, before any cognition of being, before ontology and it happens in this event of difference!

Keywords: Race, Racism, Face, Alterity, Otherness, and Difference.

Introduction

1. Deconstructing the Ordinary/Essentialist Concept of Race

Philosophical analysis of the ordinary concept of race argues that the ordinary concept[1] of race is not essentialist. Why? A philosopher will think beyond the conceptual frame work of the different disciplines such as social constructions, biological descriptions, essentialist's view points and an analysis of the ordinary concept of race will point to the internal theoretical dilemmas inherent in different disciplines. Given this we attempt to deconstruct the ordinary concept of race. What does it mean to deconstruct the ordinary concept of race? Hardimon rightly opines that: "Why not leave race to the experts-biologists, anthropologists, or social theorists-researchers whose discipline and training provides them with special expertise? To begin with none of these disciplines are concerned with the ordinary concept of race *as such*."[2] Internally critiquing or in "critical intimacy"[3] the concept of race and racial theories one could learn that there are discrepancies and disputes among the concept of race and its well approved theories.[4]

Critical mind could state that the logical core of the differing and different racial theories does not imply that there is an intrinsic connection between physical features and humanly important traits of intelligence and moral character. It does not imply racial hierarchies or moral and intellectual superiority of one race over the other. The racialists deem the visible physical features of race as reliable markers of humanly important differences. Ashely

1 Naomi Zack writes that "the ordinary concept of race purports to refer to an individual's body." Reading Zack's argument implies that race and human bodily appearance are interlinked. Phenomenology of difference gives way to reductionist ontology and there is an immediate identification and designation of someone as s/he appears in and through his/her body. Racism manifests in attacking the other in his/her body as physical violence. Naomi Zack, *Race and Mixed Race* (Philadelphia: Temple University Press, 1993), 9.

2 Michael O. Hardimon, "The Ordinary Concept of Race," *The Journal of Philosophy* 100, no. 9 (2003), 438.

3 Gayatri Chakravorty Spivak, "Critical Intimacy – Interview," *lareviewofbooks.org*, accessed April 30, 2019, https://lareviewofbooks.org/article/critical-intimacy-interview-gayatri-chakravortyspivak/?fbclid=IwAR1ytviRmlyIYOILzBrX5lxUq0rYT6EfEVbR0j8Qjw5FKaCbj7AbwQaCdQ#.
Spivak, in her interview with Steve Paulson, explains deconstruction as follows: "It's not just destruction. It's also construction. It's critical intimacy, not critical distance. So you actually speak from inside. That's deconstruction."

4 Hardimon, "The Ordinary Concept of Race," 451-452.

Montagu argues that there is any indissoluble relation between mental and physical traits and racial superiority of one race and inferiority of the other.[5] But, in the case of the racialist approaches the body is seen through the naked eyes and it remains as a reason for the logic of difference. Hence, the phenomenology of difference becomes the immediate access point to make out or find the person next to him/her as different from you and accordingly to arrive at his/her racial identity. One's phenomenality remains under permanent threat and attack. The visibility/body, for a racist, seems to work as the reason to find the racial difference implying that "[r]ace is *essentially* manifest."[6]

Such an essentialist view cannot be adopted since there exist no reason for a superiority of one race over the other or any hierarchical gradation of races or any grounds for racial discrimination.[7] However the core of the racialist interpretation is essentialist claiming a racial hierarchy and the consequent subordination of "lesser" groups (minority groups in India at present times). It works in effect as a basis for all kind of hatred and racial discrimination[8] and attack on minority as is the case in India in the preset times. This sullying of meaning is not the logical conclusion of the ordinary concept of race, for it is because the logical core does not afford a rationale for racist agendas or terrorists attacks or any kind of totalitarian move. The racialist misinterpretation of the meaning of the concept race and their professed claim of the hierarchical superiority of one race (majority vs. minority; natives vs. immigrants) over the others is a fallacious position giving rise to racial discrimination, apartheid, slavery, colonialism, fundamentalism, castes, genocide as ethnic cleansing and to the misconception of racial purity. In deconstructing the ordinary concept of race and its logic we learn that any such reductive logic is a misappropriation and distortion of the concept of race to serve the racist agenda and ideology. Such an imperialistic ideology is at work today in Indian socio-political fabric of the society as religion is politically corrupted and politicians take religion as the tool for political gain. Political Hindutva Movements of BJP, RSS and VHP in India are the avatar of evil of violence and communal carnage. The logic of racism reincarnates under the disguise of any kind of atrocities of humans against humanity of the other humans.

---

5 Ashley Montagu, "The Concept of Race," *The Concept of Race*, ed., Ahley Montagu (New York: The Free Press of Glencoe, 1964), 24.

6 Hardimon, "The Ordinary Concept of Race," 442.

7 S. L. Washburn, "The Study of Race," *The Concept of Race*, ed., Ashley Montagu (New York: The Free Press of Glencoe, 1964), 242.

8 Michael Banton, *Racial Consciousness* (London, New York: Longman, 1988), 145.

2. The Logic and the Issue of Racism

Racism refers to hatred, hostility, contempt and harmful intentions in a persons' heart and mind expressed through conscious attack of the other by killing, or discriminating. The classic form of racism is one of deliberate harming of the other person who are different in terms of their particularities or certain characteristics. Michael Banton notes that "the deterministic ascription of real or supposed negative characteristics to a particular group is generally seen as a central characteristic of racism as ideology."[9] This was the logic of the racist rhetoric of imperialism. Hannah Arendt writes, "Racism has been the powerful ideology of imperialistic policies since the turn of our century."[10] The Nazi ideology has been one of such violent form of racism launching genocide and extermination of other who are different.[11] This monstrosity of the evil of racism was incarnated in the diabolic criminality of the Nazi theory of Aryan superiority and of Jewish inferiority popularized by Adolf Hitler.[12] This imperialist ideology is still camouflaged and manifested in violence as inhumanity of humans against one another in the Political Hindutva Movements of RSS or the ISIS attacks upon the innocent people (The most recent attacks and self bombing in Colombo, Sri Lanka remains a very concrete proof for the hatred of humans against the other). Contemporary racism goes far beyond any fixed biogenetic theories, physiological differences and blood relations. It is at this juncture that the other person's difference as visibility is taken as a condition for his/her identity. The logic and the rhetoric of racism manifest today in excluding the other as the foreigner, the refugee, the outsider, the migrant, the other state worker, the Dalit, the Advasi, the lower caste and the like. The difference is what is not of the same, i.e., s/he is not of my race, class, caste, creed, culture, nation, state, parish, rite, context, etc., and the other as the outsider is gowned as the image of the enemy. Here one moves from a phenomenology of difference to a reductionist ontology of imperialist domination.

3. Racism and the Logic of 'Difference'

The difference of the other person is interpreted as a reason for exclusion of the other and not taking difference as the other persons' being as such. The racialists fix unalterable biogenetic factors as a reason for exclusion and thus

9 Michael Banton & Robert Miles, "Racism," *Dictionary of Race and Ethnic Relations*, ed., Ellis Cashmore, 3rd edition (London & New York: Rutledge & Kegan Paul, 1996), 310.

10 Hannah Arendt, *The Origins of Totalitarianism* (Orlando, Austin, New York, San Diego, London: Harvest Book, 1996), 158.

11 Naomi Zack, *Thinking about Racism*, 2nd edtion (Australia: Thomson Wordsworth, 2006), 46-47.

12 Adolf Hitler, *Mein Kampf* (Mumbai: Jaico Publishing House, 2010), 257-299.

fail to accommodate differences; rather they dominate and destroy difference by perpetrating violence. Roger Burggraeve writes "one accepts differences only in so far as they are a matter of accidental particularities or specificities within a same genre or basic design, in which individuals differ from one another within a same 'sort' only very relatively (for example, character, taste, intellectual level), and in which their deeper affinity is not at all tested."[13] This rejection of the other is there in every level and it has become one of the key factors of present day political strategies.

The other embarrasses and threatens the safety and security of the solipsistic ego. "The figure of the 'Other'", writes Sturat Hall, "was constructed as the absolute opposite."[14] For Malik, "[e]quality has come to be redefined from the 'right to be the same' to mean 'the right to be different.'"[15] And "Differences can exist or not exist. Differences are not in themselves good or bad. One is not racist or anti-racist in pointing out or in denying differences, but one is racist in using them against someone to one's own advantage."[16] Hence, racists hold a logic of exclusion by virtue of the difference that makes the other as the other. However, one must overcome any such logic of domination and exclusion that does violence to the other on account of the difference. Emmanuel Levinas, in his philosophical affirmations, provocatively, questions the logic of the Western ontological thought leading to the imperialism of thinking and being.

4. The Diabolical Criminality of Hitlerism and the Evil of Racism

In Levinas' "Reflections on the Philosophy of Hitlerism,"[17] he writes that "National Socialism revealed the diabolical criminality, the absolute evil, of what cannot be called 'thought.'"[18] Hitler's move propagated the idea of Aryan race as the superior [*Uber Mensch*], the "overman"[19] and only people of a

13 Roger Burggraeve, *The Wisdom of Love in the Service of Love – Emmanuel Levinas on Justice, Peace, and Human Rights*, trans. Jeffrey Bloechl, (Milwaukee WI: Marquette University Press, 2007), 59.

14 Sturat Hall, "The West and the Rest: Discourse and Power," *Formations of Modernity: Understanding Modern Societies*, eds, Sturat Hall and Bram Gieben (Cambridge: Polity Press, 1992), 289.

15 Kenan Malik, "Universalism and Difference in Discourses of Race," *Review International Studies* 26, (2000), 175.

16 Albert Memmi, "Racism and Difference," *Theories in Racism and Racism: A Reader*, 2nd edition. eds, Les Back and John Slomos (London, New York: Rutledge, 2009), 131.

17 Emmanuel Levinas, "Reflections on the Philosophy of Hitlerism," trans. Sean Hand, *Critical Enquiry* 17, (1999), 63-71.

18 Emmanuel Levinas, "As If Consenting to Horror," trans. Paula Wissing, *Critical Inquiry* 15, (1989), 487.

19 Friederich Nietzsche, *The Will to Power*, trans. Walter Kaufmann and R. J. Hollingdale, (New York: Vintage Books, 1968), 463.

higher race can create lasting civilizations that lasts forever. Taking Levinas's view into account we argue that in every form of racism, the other is the enemy as such, and from this perspective all forms of violence remain as modalities of the denial of the other as the other. The Jew, in the case of the anti-Semitic thinking, is an enemy just as for racism the other is an enemy due to the very fact of his/her difference. This cannot be considered simply as a rare event that happens at times but rather, in the effort of being, the *connatus essendi* of the being, of which Spinoza[20] speaks about, the dynamic existing of the being, where one is inclined to oneself and safeguarding oneself, the 'nature', one is potentially racist. It separates and categorizes the other as different from the self/ego and this categorization is further embedded with hierarchical order, and consequently it manifests in discrimination, segregation, subordination, elimination, extermination and the like. Hitlerism was the quantitative extension of this evil manifested as the pure form of racism. It represents the concretization of the effort of existing, the reduction of the other to the same. Levinas finds this permanent possibility of racism woven into our being in the effort of being as "non-reciprocal determination of the other."[21] Everyone is potentially racist, a permanent possibility woven into the 'axiology of one's being' and to one's 'ontological nature' when one moves inexorably toward oneself as self-affirmation of oneself denying the other.

5. Racism as Denial of the Otherness of the Other

The fundamental problem of racism, for Levinas, consists in the failure to appreciate the difference of the other in his/her unique unrepeatability. Here racism consists in embracing what is of the 'same, and excluding what is different, namely, the 'foreign'. The only type of otherness found acceptable is the otherness within one's own 'genere' i.e., the otherness within one's own blood, soil, one's family, origin, nation, society, church, club, parish, rite, caste and the like. Difference, for the racists, is that makes the other 'the other'. On the other hand, for Levinas, "the recognition of the other happens beyond being, beyond essence…"[22] One cannot however reduce the other's otherness to his or her phenomenology of difference as whatness; rather it is his/her alterity that accords value and worth to the identity of the other as the Other. "It's not difference that makes alterity," Levinas argues, "alterity makes difference."[23] In racist relation to the other, there is no guaranteeing or appreciation of the

20 Baruch Spinoza, *Ethics* (Oxford: Oxford University Press, 2000), 48.

21 Emmanuel Levinas, *Totality and Infinity: An Essay on Exteriority*, trans. Alphonso Lingis, (Pittsburgh: Duquesne University Press, 2007), 99.

22 Ibid,.

23 Emmanuel Levinas, "The Vocation of the Other," Is *it Righteous to be?* Interview with Emmanuel Levinas, Jill Robbins, ed. (Stanford: Stanford University Press, 2001), 106.

otherness of the other as his/her difference as his or her radical alterity rather it remains a relationship in terms of reducing the otherness/whoness to whatness. This event happens in the face-to-face relation with the self and the other in proximity.

The epiphany of the face manifests his/her absoluteness beyond comprehension. The self cannot hold the other within the limits of reason as Kant wanted. It opens towards the limitlessness of the other from the beyond. For Levinas "[y]ou turn yourself toward the Other as toward an object when you see a nose, eyes, a forehead, a chin, and you can describe them."[24] Such an approach to the other in terms of knowledge and perception is not ethical and rather it is reductive. What is the difference then: person *qua* persons are who's. In racism one misrecognises this 'whoness' to 'whatness' i.e., what the other is. It is constantly operative in international political relations and strategies of different governmental policies where all the others are outsiders, the foreigners. We maneuver under the pretext of such a logic that legitimizes our human relations inherent with racist tendencies. Against this relation Levinas argues that "the best way of encountering the Other is not even to notice the colour of his eyes! When one observes the color of the eyes one is not in social relationship with the Other."[25] Although, in inter-human relations one immediately does not tend to reduce the other; nevertheless, the act of facing is different from the act of seeing that leads to calculative thinking. "The eye", Levinas writes there, "does not shine; it speaks."[26] The eye speaks a voiceless voice that arrests the self-absorptive tonality of the imperialist self. Hence, the other is not to be approached as an object of perception or rather as another ego like me. In calculative thinking (as in Heiddeger) the being of the other is appropriated by the same. Such relation to the other is totalizing and is diametrically opposed to the ethical moment. It entails the fact that whenever one considers the other in terms of her difference as a point of exclusion and elimination one does violence to the other by bigotry. A relation dominated by the visibility of the other fall short as a true relation a 'relation-less-relation' owing to the fact that the other is reduced to his differential identity. In short, the other is an object rather than an alter ego who signifies in proximity.

Racism is the "reduction of the otherness of the other to the non-human-otherness of a totality, of a species in which Otherness loses its singularity and is simply treated as one more of a kind."[27] In understanding the other from

---

24 Emmanuel Levinas, *Ethics and Infinity: Conversations with Philippe Nemo*, trans. Richard A. Cohen, (Pittsburgh: Duquesne University Press, 1999), 85.

25 Ibid., 85-86.

26 Levinas, *Totality and Infinity*, 66.

27 Rudi Visker, *The Inhuman Condition: Looking for Difference after Levinas and Heidegger* (Dordrecht: Kluwer Academic Publishers, 2004), 180.

his/her characteristics is to render the other, the other than you, or other than something else. Its otherness is relative as it is defined in terms of 'for me'. The difference is approached as not-of the same. It implies that the other is approached from a non-personal realm where the other person is not approached *qua* face but reduced to his/her visibility its 'form', as having such and such characteristics, and makes them belong to a particular race different from the same, and thus inferior. The face, however, is a speaking; it is not visible or doesn't appear as a phenomenon, but it is invisible in its rectitude and dignity. The other signifies before me in his/her own light which is a revelation of the face.[28] The transcendence of the other is announced in immanence, but neither reducible nor containable to it.

The other has alterity as such, as a characteristic which implies that the alterity of the other is something that the other already has i.e., the other is already someone before I meet. The other solicits me to treat him/her as someone and as a 'who', in her unique identity as the other. When such an ethical demand from the other is not met, s/he is denied of his/her unicity. I am unique but you discriminate me for what I am/my visibility: 'form', 'context', 'visage', 'nationality', 'religion', 'context', 'culture', caste, rite and the like. The other has an absolute alterity and when one fails to respond to the signification of the face s/he does violence to the other by treating the other as a relative other hence Nazism, racism, casteism etc. Rudi Visker argues, "[r]acist language de-humanizes the Other; it de-faces people by denying them dignity to which Levinas gives expression by distinguishing the face from the outward visage, from the 'form'. Racism denies persons this capacity to 'break through' or 'rent' the form that announces them. It de-figures them by reducing them to fissures that are not so fissured."[29]

The face, for Levinas, cannot be reduced to the form and it bursts opens the form. The first command unspoken from the face is "do not kill me"[30] that is, do not reduce me to a 'form'. The egoist self is forbidden by the unspoken command that *thou shalt not* reduce other's alterity to mere visibility and difference. The twofoldness of this ethical command and demand speaks: 'do not reduce me to a form' and 'respect me for who I am'. This appealing of the face is ethical prayer of the face which the self cannot escape. There is an asymmetry between self and the other; a relation with the other, i.e., a relation-less relation, I am invested with untransferable responsibility to regard and respect the other as a unique for "he is not under category."[31] Being irresponsible would mean not to do what you ought to have done.

28 Levinas, *Totality and Infinity*, 199.

29 Visker, *The Inhuman Condition*, 180.

30 Levinas, *Totality and Infinity*, 197.

31 Ibid, 69.

6. 'Not-without Difference' Revisiting Levinas

In short, racism, for Levinas, is the denial of the otherness of the other or the failure to appreciate and regard the other's difference; and avoiding racism would, then, entail respecting the other as a face without colour, caste, context, creed, culture, etc. Given this argument on racism, I learn that there is something that Levinas' overlooks in this regard; namely the independence of 'whoness' and 'whatness'. There seems to be something misplaced within it. When I am a racist I reduce the 'whoness' to 'whatness'. What I need to do for Levinas here: Avoiding racism would be respecting you as a face and not even to notice the color of your eyes. I would respect you as a human being without gender (sexism), without noticing your characteristics (racism), without taking note of your context (nationalism), without taking into account of your creed (fundamentalism) etc. Levinas would stand even beyond the claims of those who reject difference and those who praise difference[32] by arguing that 'it is not difference which makes alterity, for Levinas, alterity makes difference'.

Hence, racism as absolute negation of difference is defined as heterophobia; anti-racism, on the other hand, is the absolute affirmation of difference is heterophilia, i.e., the naturalization or essentialization of difference.[33] Difference is the humanity's most precious capital, but for Levinas he does not stand with the anti-racist logic rather he stands for the claim of the transcendence of the other that 'separates' the self and the other. Levinas writes, "the other is not other because he would have other attributes, or would have been born elsewhere or at another moment, or because he would of a different race. The other is other because of me; unique and in some manner different than the individual belonging to a genus."[34] In re-considering this account of Levinas Visker remarks that "a person does not want to be reduced to his/her ('different') skin-color, etc., *but also refuses to be detached from it* – insists on something that, in not being a thing, escapes full understanding, is not possessed, cannot be determined (the way one determines whether a thing, has such or such a quality)."[35] That is to say, no one wants to be regarded as 'who' irrespective of 'what' and to recognize the Other as a face 'without any cultural adornment' i.e., 'what' is to refuse their unique difference. In re-reading Levinas' philosophy of racism, one should ask, can one pay due respect to the other without taking into account of one's characteristics or his/her difference?

---

32 Pierre-Anderé Taguieff, *The Force of Prejudice: On Racism and Its Doubles*, *Contradictions*, Vol. 13, trans., and ed., Hassan Melehy (Minneapolis, London: University of Minnesota Press, 2001), 20-29.

33 Taguieff, *The Force of Prejudice*, 20-29.

34 Levinas, "The Vocation of the Other," 106.

35 Visker, *The Inhuman Condition*, 181. The emphasis is in original.

In reconsidering this Visker argues that the "inscriptions which, in their own way, thus make them irreplaceable" and for him, "to be different" – "is to be inscribed."[36] These inscriptions to which one is 'tied to' or 'inscribed into', one may not know about it and this not knowing does not imply that they are detached from it either. Hence not reducing to his/her characteristics or detaching from them remains the irreducible dignity of the other. Hence one is 'not without' difference. It speaks about who (*quis*?) and whatness (*quid*?). Someone's unique human dignity is something which escapes one's access and yet something which one does not want to refuse too, for the reason that refusing them would mean to deny something of which we are part of. The irreducible alterity as difference of the other does not give in to any transcendental consciousness. You bump what it means to be you, who? and if you go against this limit, you betray yourself. It stands for one's unicity which is one's relationship to one's difference. One cannot give this up, or no transcendental *Cogito* can hold it either. One is tied to such transcendence beyond reduction.

Levinas argues that other is without form and cannot be approached from the context. But, can one respond to the ethical appeal of the other in a very abstract way; the ethical response to the other has to be concrete and, thus, responding to the individual who stands face to face. The social relation to the other is not noticing and observing, rather it is the ethical openness in terms of letting good to the other i.e., in being fissured from within at the entrance of the other and the egoist self is radically altered by the transcendence of the other in proximity. Here morality, at first, for Levinas, is a matter of not of the Right but of the Good. This is the moment of the infinite responsibility as substitution, expiation despite oneself happens.[37] For Levinas "the recognition of the other happens beyond being, beyond essence [...] The possibility of respect and of goodness are extraordinary possibilities with regard to nature, with regard to the perseverance in being: the possibility of holiness which is beyond perseverance of a being in its being, would recognize the priority of an irreducible alterity. The true humanity of man begins in this recognition, before any cognition of being, before ontology."[38] Being awakened by the radical alterity and heteronomy of the other in proximity the self is taken beyond its essence to an otherwise than being.[39] Philosophizing as a radical critique to the imperialistic autonomy by the heteronomy of the other serve as a tool for transformative praxis be it in India or across the globe.

36 Visker, *The Inhuman Condition*, 181. The emphasis is in original, 181-182.

37 Emmanuel Levinas, *Otherwise than Being or Beyond Essence*, trans., Alphonso Lingis, (Pittsburgh: Duquesne University Press, 1998), 48.

38 Levinas, "The Vocation of the Other," 106.

39 Levinas, *Otherwise than Being or beyond Essence*, 109.

7. Conclusion

The discourse on race and racism cannot be limited to inhuman situations based on the fixedness and unalterable biogenetic factors and even on ethnic, class, caste, rite basis alone. The global situation of migration of people to different countries in search of work and living make the earth one of living with difference; a country like ours where there is a dancing of differences makes the nation as an idea of being together provokes us to think beyond the borders but not without differences. The present day Indian political situation muddled with the religious question raises burning issues of new forms of racism under the disguise of political Hindutva and Hindu Nationalism. Such fascist regimes are pouncing upon the minorities in the name of religion, caste, nationalism, region and the like. Philosophizing in India at the present moment becomes the task of every thinker. In thinking difference beyond differences would invite us to stand up for the birth of a new way of being and becoming. On becoming authentically human in India in present times is the commitment to the wisdom from within. As a result, living with difference in India in the present times would invite ACPI to think without/beyond borders without letting one's difference to be lost in the iron clutches of imperialistic servitude and such a philosophy remains true to transformative praxis in the inter-human realms.

11

"Royce's Beloved Community: An Antidote to Globalizing India"

Dr Francis Abraham Aykaraparampil CMI
Darsana Institute of Philosophy, Wardha

Abstract: Royce's conception of "Beloved Community" provides a global vision in which every individual has unique meaning and significance through the process of interpretation within the context of community governed by the principle of love, in contrast with a vision of the globalized and globalizing India where materialist individualism, homogenization, and devaluation of communion governed by an attitude of profit-making prevails. At the outset, the above statement has two parts: i) The conception of the Beloved Community is a global vision and an ideal where everyone is united in love and communion through interpretation. ii) The Beloved Community is understood as a Roycean response to the globalized and globalizing India and the world at large.

Keywords: Absolute Idealism, Being, Beloved Community, Christianity, Critical Rationalism, Community, Community of Interpretation, Globalization, Great Community, Idea, Idealism, Individual, Interpretation, Interpreter-Spirit, Invisible Church, Love, Loyalty, Mysticism, Pragmatism, Realism, Royce, Self, Self-Representative System, Universal Community, Will to Interpret.

1. Introduction

Josiah Royce (1855-1916),[1] in his *Lectures on Modern Idealism*, wrote: "A philosophy is inevitably an expression of a mental attitude which one assumes towards life and towards the universe."[2] He lived at a time in American history when individualism was promoted in all walks of life. During his time, people especially the new migrants from England were withdrawing from their social life and were turning towards themselves and building their lives by working mainly in the gold mines. Royce wanted to have a change in this tendency of individualism by asking himself some of the fundamental questions of life. For instance, in a letter to Elizabeth Randolph, his daughter-in-law, Royce wrote: "If I then ask: 'Why must I live?' the answer is always ready: 'Because my cause needs my help'. If I still ask: Why choose a cause?, the answer is, 'Only thus can my life get sense, only thus can I help my fellows to give sense to their own lives.'"[3] He wanted to move from the extreme individualism, exploitation and devaluation of communion of his social milieu to a community of communion and harmony where each one's meaning is found by respecting and living for others. Even from the beginning of his academic life, Royce proposed his philosophy of community. He also invited us to fulfil our role as members of the Universal Community or the Beloved Community as Royce prefers to call it, known and willed by the Absolute.

There are two paradigm shifts in the academic life of Royce, first from the postulate of absolute unity to ethical self by the influence of G. H. Howison,[4] and from ethical self to the universal community by the influence of Charles Peirce.[5] For him, each one is invited to focus on how to live a moral life in this Universal Community founded on the principle of love and thus actualizing the ideal of the Beloved Community. He challenged the American society and the world at large to have a positive outlook towards life, whereby we discern the presence of the Spirit, an absolute point of reference that opens up new

1 This article is indebted to my own book on Royce: Francis Aykaraparampil, *Beloved Community: A Roycean Response to* Globalization (Bangalore: Dharmaram Publications, 2017), 1-10, 199-225, 259-285.

2 Josiah Royce, *Lectures on Modern Idealism*, ed. Jacob Loewenberg (New Haven, Conn.: Yale University Press, 1919), 241.

3 John Clendenning, ed., *The Letters of Josiah Royce* (Chicago: The University of Chicago Press, 1970), 550.

4 G. H. Howison, "Introduction" and "Comments" to *The Conception of God: A Philosophical Discussion Concerning the Nature of the Divine Idea as a Demonstrable Reality*, by Josiah Royce, ed. Randall E. Auxier (Bristol and Virginia: Thoemmes Press, 2000), ix-xxxviii, 79-132.

5 Charles S. Peirce, Review of *The World and the Individual*, by Josiah Royce. *Critical Responses to Josiah Royce, 1885-1916*, vol. 2, *Reviews and Articles*, ed. Randall E. Auxier (Bristol and Virginia: Thoemmes Press, 2000), 70-80.

horizons of meaning to this life and all the human affairs. Royce's conception of Beloved Community provides a global vision in which every individual has unique meaning and significance through the process of interpretation within the context of community governed by the principle of love, in contrast with a vision of the globalized and globalizing world where materialist individualism, homogenization, and devaluation of communion governed by an attitude of profit-making prevails. At the outset, the above statement has two parts: i) The conception of the Beloved Community is a global vision and an ideal where everyone is united in love and communion through interpretation. ii) The Beloved Community is understood as a Roycean response to the globalized and globalizing India, and globalizing world at large.

Royce lived in a time of American history where it had been too individualistic. He was very sad about the hyper-individualism and selfish living of the miners. His point of departure is the desire to have a change in this tendency of individualism. Royce, holding an ethical and sociological ideology from the beginning of his academic life, was convinced that without an eternally complete knowledge of reality, in which we ultimately participate, there could never be a full extension of positive meaning for human beings. If there is no eternal dimension to existence, we may feel that there is more freedom, but it could never be totally fulfilled. Royce was not interested in hyper-specialization of a discipline. He dealt with almost every discipline such as metaphysics, epistemology, ethics, pragmatism, and sociology, and tried to make bridges between different worlds of thought and develop his own synthesis. In fact, Royce was true to his own words that "the philosopher, in the world of thought, is by destiny forever a frontiersman."[6] Being a Calvinist with a Puritan background, Royce was a bold and colourful thinker who sought a theoretical and practical bond between the individual and community. Hence, we can make the following assertions: i) The human beings long for meaning and harmony in their lives both within and without. ii) The meaning is found and the harmony is possible only when unique loyal persons come together in love, and engage in the building of a genuine community. iii) All have an authentic human existence harmonized in the spirit of the Beloved Community through the process of interpretation.

2. Being, Self and Community: Three Central Notions of Royce's Philosophical Pursuit

In his first book, *The Religious Aspect of Philosophy*, Royce wrote: "The sense of community, the power to work together, with clear insight into our

---

6 Josiah Royce, *The World and the Individual*, vol. 2 (New York: The Macmillan Company, 1900), 3.

reasons for so working, is the *first* need of humanity."[7] Moreover, the sense of community occupied the centre of Royce's mental stage out of the living experiences with his family at Avon Farm near Grass Valley, California, the hard teenage life at the San Francisco Grammar School, and the fruitful long teaching career at Harvard University. The wholeness of Royce's conception of the Beloved Community spread throughout his philosophical writings.[8] In this process, we employ a descriptive-critical approach to his works as a single whole belonging to the three stages and develops three central notions of his philosophy, namely "Being" from the Early Period (1885-1897), "Self" from the Middle Period (1898-1907), and "Community" from the Later Period (1908-'1916).[9] Though sometimes we experience them as disconnected or contradictory, Royce was always a man of synthesis. In the early period, Royce began his philosophical life from "being," and then continued with "self" in the middle period and "community" in the later period. He tried to understand being by means of "idea," the self by means of "interpretation," and community by means of "loyalty." The result of his philosophizing is the conceptions such as "the Absolute unity" from the early period, "the ethical self" from the middle period, and "the universal community" from the later period,[10] and we come to the conclusion that Royce's understanding of being

7 Josiah Royce, *The Religious Aspect of Philosophy: A Critique of the Bases of Conduct and Faith* (Boston: Houghton, Mifflin, 1885), 175.

8 A bibliography of Royce's works, composed shortly before his death, contains twenty-three books and ninety-four articles. Ignas K. Skrupskelis, "Annotated Bibliography of the Publications of Josiah Royce," *The Basic Writings of Josiah Royce*, vol. 2, ed. John J. McDermott (New York: Fordham University Press, 2005), 1167-1226.

9 Royce's philosophical pursuit is divided into three periods. The early period (1885-1897) is comprised of books such as *The Religious Aspect of Philosophy: A Critique of the Bases of Conduct and Faith* (1885), *The Spirit of Modern Philosophy: An Essay in the Form of Lectures* (1892), and *The Conception of God: A Philosophical Discussion Concerning the Nature of the Divine Idea as a Demonstrable Reality* (1897). The theme of this period is the metaphysical and epistemological insights of Royce and the intervention of Howison. In the middle period (1898-1907), Royce wrote books such as *Studies of Good and Evil: A Series of Essays upon Problems of Philosophy and of Life* (1899), *The World and the Individual*- 2 vols. (1899, 1900), *The Conception of the Immortality* (1900), and *Outlines of Psychology: An Elementary Treatise with Some Practical Applications* (1903). Here, the self is understood as an ethical concept, and its meaning is found in "interpretation." The intervention of Peirce also happens during this time. The later period (1908-1916) consists of works such as *The Philosophy of Loyalty* (1908). *The Sources of Religious Insight* (1912), *The Problem of Christianity* (1913), and *The Hope of the Great Community* (1916) in which Royce proposes his sociological understanding; where the principles of "loyalty and love" play a major role in the understanding of his philosophy of community and eventually the Beloved Community.

10 Frank M. Oppenheim, *Reverence for the Relations of Life: Re-imagining Pragmatism via Josiah Royce's Interactions with Peirce, James and Dewey* (Notre Dame, Indiana: University of Notre Dame Press, 2005), xii-xiii.

is the foundation, the self is the principle of meaning, and community is the centre of Beloved Community. Through the development of these paradigm concepts, he provides us with a philosophy of community towards the Beloved Community, a community united in "love." With the help of Royce's concept of the Beloved Community, we try to find the meaning of life, the meaning of each unique individual, and how each might live move and have their being in a Beloved Community. In the final analysis, we affirm that the Beloved Community is an axiom to make this world 'beloved' and an ideal for human realization in the globalized and globalizing world.

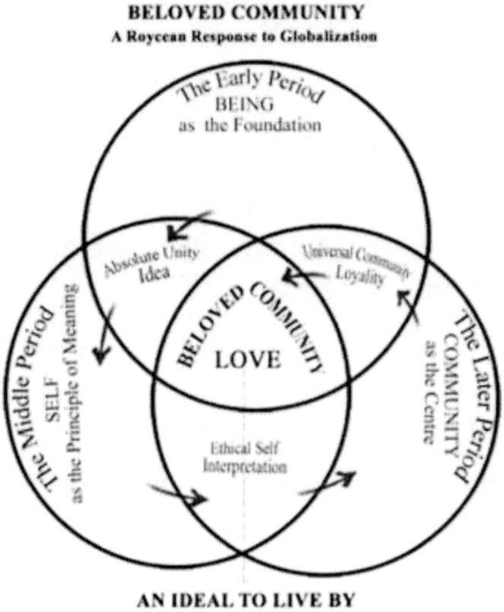

3. The Eight Tenets of the Beloved Community

The following eight points are indeed conceived as a recapitulation of Royce's whole philosophy and the eight tenets of Beloved Community.

i) Royce argued for an eternal dimension throughout his philosophical pursuit. The moral and religious meanings are found in this eternal dimension.

ii) He held the proof for the existence of this eternal dimension through the reality of human error which points to an Infinite Thought who possesses all truth. Hence, the eternal dimension is the ultimate expression of the internal meaning of an idea and the complete fulfilment of the human purposes.

iii) After the intervention of Howison, he started to think about the finite beings and proceeded with the argument for the existence of the selves, and held that it is neither an actual experience nor a substance, but a meaning or purpose embodied in a conscious finite life.

iv) Under the influence of Peirce, he tried to widen his philosophical vision from the ethical understanding of the self to a loving community of interpreting selves.

v) Royce believed that all our experiences are not personal but social; and a community is not merely a group of selves, but a union of loyal selves conscious of their own role in the community. He stressed the role of loyalty and love in constituting a Beloved Community by which each self is invited to widen their horizons and actualize the beloved communion.

vi) Royce was convinced that the eternal dimension or the Interpreter-Spirit is the beginning of philosophical as well as community life.

vii) He finally came to the conclusion that the Beloved Community is the ideal paradigm community and defined it as "the genuine love of the unity of the great community to which all civilized men, when enlightened, consciously belong."[11]

Royce invites us to recall our dearest friendships and build up genuine communities holding on to the principle of love in the following words: "Your Christian love is much more than mere pity... Your love will then become the Charity that never faileth. For its object is the Beloved Community, and the individual as ideally a member of that community."[12] This can be presented graphically as follows:

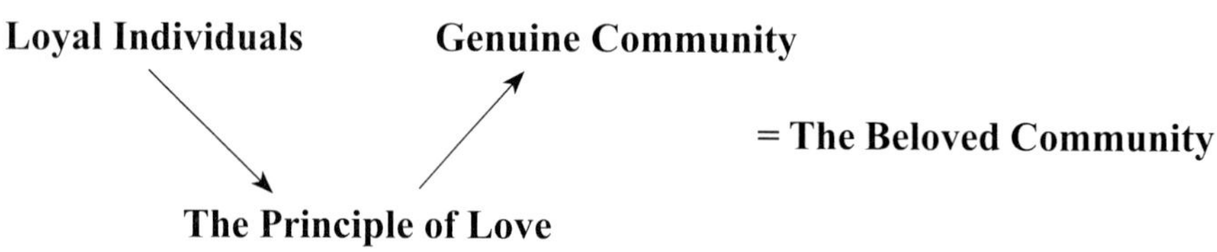

At this juncture, I also join with Smith in articulating Royce's philosophy as a story of the co-operation and tension between individual and community.[13] He called upon philosophy to take up the responsibility of a moral educator by cultivating a "deeper sense of companionship with the world."[14] His philosophical outlook was clear in the following words: "Arise then, freeman,

11 Josiah Royce, *The Hope of the Great Community* (New York: The Macmillan Company, 1916), 38.

12 Josiah Royce, *The Problem of Christianity* (New York: The Macmillan Company, 1913; reprint edition, Washington D.C.: The Catholic University of America Press, 2001), 197.

13 John E. Smith, *The Spirit of American Philosophy* (New York: Oxford, 1963), 91.

14 Josiah Royce. *The World and the Individual*, vol. 1 (New York: The Macmillan Company, 1899), 418.

stand forth in thy world. It is God's world. It is also thine."[15] In spite of its ambiguities, we must acknowledge Royce's genuine effort to give individual meaning, worth, and dignity to every finite being and his continuous task of seeing individuals as needing the Beloved Community.

4. Philosophical Investigations after "Beloved Community" for Globalizing India

It is a fact that there is an underlying thought of a philosophy of community in all of Royce's writings. It also proves that there is an ideal of the Beloved Community in the back of Royce's mind from the beginning of his academic life, though he explicitly enumerates it only in the later period. The immediate reasons for articulating it were: the plight of the migrants in the gold mines, the miseries of the World War I from 1915-16 and the torpedoed *Lusitania* that has killed four Harvard graduates.[16] Today, Royce's philosophy of community can have an extensive discussion on the inspirations from the Beloved Community especially for today's globalized and globalizing world, and the ideal of the Beloved Community can be a Roycean response to its negative social effects. Globalization is marked by the expansion of the national and global markets, erosion of social, religious and political barriers, and a bundle of unlimited possibilities.[17] On the one hand, we are optimistic on account of its enormous employment opportunities, bigger markets, varied and quality products, cheaper prices, better education, communication and transportation. On the other, we are doubtful about its claims especially in the context of uneven wealth distribution, cut-throat competition, exploitation, homogenization, financial insecurity and environmental problems. According to Royce, the Beloved Community is a postulate to look up to and an ideal to live by especially in this context of most individualized and individualizing situations which he himself experienced in the gold mines. His ethico-social philosophy or the ideal of the Beloved Community is attractive as to seek communion, and to build up communities in this extremely individualized and individualizing world. Hence, we propose the ideal of the Beloved Community to gather inspiration as much as we can and go forward with new resolutions to make this globalizing India a better one. In this context, we try to discuss globalization and its economic, political and cultural impacts in India.

---

15 Royce, *The World and the Individual*, 470.

16 *Lusitania* was a British ship launched in 1906, and the world's biggest of its kind. It was sunk by Germans in 1915 causing thousands of deaths. This incident became an iconic symbol of the World War I. Josiah Royce, *Metaphysics*, eds. William Ernest Hocking, Richard Hocking and Frank M. Oppenheim (Albany: State University of New York Press, 1998), 14-25.

17 Sumit Roy, *Globalization, ICT and Developing Nations: Challenges in the Information Age* (New Delhi: Sage Publications, 2005), 14.

Economic globalization, according to Steger, is "the intensification and stretching of economic interrelations across the globe."[18] Our country, being a nation with its socialist roots, was sceptical about the merits of globalization. However, the organizations such as International Monetary Fund (IMF) and World Bank (WB) pressed India to enter into the New Economic Policy (NEP) of 1991; and it was the first stepping stone to globalization in India. The new policy brought far-reaching changes in every sphere of the society. For example, Foreign Direct Investment (FDI) has played a vital role in the fast growth of Indian economy; and as a result, so many international companies have invested in India, benefited from an increased flow of communication and a greater speed and ease of transportation, started their own firms, and created crores of job-opportunities. Hence, the young people are now motivated to have higher education to get better jobs and salaries. This is only one side of the coin; on the other, economic globalization has brought about uneven distribution of wealth, cut-throat competition, income inequality, exploitation and environmental degradation. In today's globalized world, "laws are legislated for the advantage of the stronger."[19] Though they seemingly offer financial assistance to the weak and needy, actually they set the ample context in which the powerful few dictate the terms for the powerless majority.[20] Moreover, half of the wealth is managed and enjoyed by the superpowers. They want to make it more; so they approach the developing and poor nations with their promises and assurances. In brief, the growing inequality across the country and the environmental issues are on the rise. In praxis, the globalization never attains the goal of a global community; rather it creates a global market in which there are no citizens, only consumers. In this scenario, the economic globalization is not a sufficient solution to establish a just society rather it creates an unjust society. If we take the case of India, we had a paradigm shift in the early 90s; twenty eight years later, a genuine introspection would reaffirm that though we have gained a lot, the rich became richer and the poor became poorer.

Political globalization is "the intensification and expansion of political interrelations across the globe."[21] It promotes social and political contracts between different countries, breaking the barriers of continents, culture, race

18 Manfred B. Steger, *Globalization: A Very Short Introduction* (New York: Oxford University Press, 2003), 37.

19 Joy Ainiyadan, "From Globalization to Global Democratic Community," *Rehumanizing the Human: Interdisciplinary Essays on Human Person in Context*, ed., Augustine Pamplany (Bangalore: Asian Trading Corporation, 2006), 82.

20 Johnson Puthenpurackal, "The Question of the Human: In the Postmodern Context of Growth of Technology and Birth of Globalization," *Rehumanizing the Human: Interdisciplinary Essays on Human Person in Context*, ed., Augustine Pamplany (Bangalore: Asian Trading Corporation, 2006), 37.

21 Steger, *Globalization*, 56.

and colour, to promote the cause of an international community based on mutual respect and trust. When each country's governmental actions takes place on a global level to make sure the welfare of the citizens and economic growth, it certainly indicates that global political activity has transformed the barriers of national divisions and is entrusted upon international political organizations like G8, G20, EU, and BRICS. Many nations help each other in the building up of the cities and villages and also for military operations and environmental protection. In fact, the breaking of national boundaries positively affected the democratic countries like India. For instance, in India, we have very many projects that are sponsored or undertaken by countries like Japan, US and Germany. In a way, we are more connected to the global space and take advantage of the favourable climate in the international political scenario.[22] In view of political globalization, there are several issues to solve for the countries such as undermining the governing power of the nations by global markets and international trade policies, the problem of immigration and the security, etc.[23] The question that we have to ask here is, if capital can flow among nations in political globalization, why not people and labour? It shows that political globalization is for the benefit of the developed countries. Rao rightly puts it: "Globalization is successfully breaking national boundaries when it is actually building up nothing more than a vast international colony exclusively for the benefit of the developed countries."[24] Hence, we must consider seriously the issue of the loss of sovereignty of India, as a state and the survival of a democratic and autonomous India whenever we deal with political globalization.[25]

Cultural globalization is "the intensification and expansion of cultural flows across the globe."[26] In a way, it promotes wider interactions and better adaptations between cultures and works on the principle that we all grow together through interpersonal relationships and mutual give and take. For example, Indians are tempted to taste Italian and French cuisines and wear Jeans and T-shirts, whereas Americans and Europeans practise yoga and try Ayurvedic treatment. The Indians learn Chinese and the people of China learn Hindi. It also helps in the development of a plural society and better interconnectedness among different cultures through which people across the globe try to overcome the barriers of continents, race and colour and enjoy

---

22 Steger, *Globalization*, 67.

23 Ibid., 62-63.

24 Srinivasa Rao, "Philosophical Perspectives: Challenges of Globalization," *Vijnanadipti* 4, (2001), 252, as cited in Puthenpurackal, "The Question of the Human," 36.

25 Antony Kalliath, "Globalization: Colonization Perpetuation: A Critique of the Marginalized," *Religion and Politics: From Subaltern Perspective*, ed., Thomas Kadankavil (Bangalore: Dharmaram Publications, 1999), 120.

26 Steger, *Globalization*, 69.

a life of mutual respect and greater confidence. Steger writes, thus, "we are not moving towards a cultural rainbow that reflects the diversity of the world's existing cultures. Rather we are witnessing the rise of an increasingly homogenized popular culture underwritten by a Western 'culture industry' based in New York, Hollywood, London, and Milan."[27] In other words, the homogenization process stands for "the reduction of cultural diversity, not cultural integration."[28] The so called "Americanization of the world" or "McDonaldization" a term coined by American sociologist George Ritzer, or cultural imperialism seems to be conquering the whole world.[29] There is no cultural integration taking place; rather only systematization and uniformity towards the Western style of life, neglecting the beautiful pluralistic fabric of the democratic nations like India.[30] Hence, cultural globalization invites the danger of identity-crisis, cultural and ethical demoralization, religious terrorism and a reaction to the supremacy of the developed nations. It never believes in a give-and-take policy, rather it tends to impose their baggage of claims, beliefs and practices. Consequently, there is resistance from some countries, cultures and religions individually and collectively to reject the imposition from the West.[31] For example, the insurgence of the jihadist groups like Al-Qaeda, ISIS, etc., with their intention of creating an Islamic State, free of any Western influence, is in a way the result of such cultural intrusion.

As we have discussed above, globalization, with its economic, political and cultural dimensions, created golden opportunities in India, and at the same time a chaotic situation which is not conducive for genuine human communities. However, globalization is not a movement to be rejected completely. Human beings are endowed with amazing ingenuity and an inner urge to be productive. They are always in search of new avenues to gratify their enormous ambitions and noble aspirations. They try to use the unused and exploit the unexploited to make profits and create a consumerist world. We cannot just ignore the opportunities or reject the positive potentialities that globalization contains, and think of a stagnant world. On the one hand, globalization is a moment of creative innovation, and on the other it could be a danger or threat to humanity as it generates individualism, corruption, and mono-culture. Together with the positive potentiality and profitable productivity of globalization, India has to deal with all its inherent negative effects. Globalization also creates a moment of crisis where each person is called

---

27 Steger, *Globalization*, 70.

28 Antony Kalliath, "Cultural Globalization and Identity Constructions," *Journal of Indian Theology* 1, no. 2 (May-August 2008), 61.

29 Steger, *Globalization*, 71.

30 Puthenpurackal, "The Question of the Human," 38.

31 Roy Lazar A., "Wrestling against Shadows," *Jeevadhara* 34, no. 199 (January 2004), 90.

to make right decisions at the right time. Here, we understand globalization not in contrast with the Beloved Community rather we try to consider the Beloved Community as an ideal in a globalizing India, in a globalizing world, which boosts our aspirations, potentialities and productivity, purifies our world from its malignant tendencies, and makes it a better world.

Having lived through two world wars, social turmoil, and racism, and now going through terrorism and religious fundamentalism, many now feel in need of a universal spiritual community in which all people love unconditionally and live happily. However, looking closely at Indian scenario, we understand that human society seems utterly fragmented by ethnic, racial, regional, and religious conflicts, each small group demanding its own territory, identity, rights and even supremacy.[32] At present we see the world engaged in a fight to define who wins. Some groups desire to destroy others, though human beings basically have the desire "to bring harmony, coherence, rationality, and unity of insight into their lives and into their world."[33] If the people of India are ready to assimilate the true meaning and purpose of life and act accordingly, the Beloved Community will begin to take its roots immediately. Here, each person must do it individually; and each administrative set-up must do it collectively.

From a critical point of view, the Beloved Community is a postulate, giving tentative conclusion to Royce's line of thought. In other words, in Beloved Community, he is having a point of unity as an answer to the meaninglessness of life. Royce did not stop with this postulate; rather he desired to make it personal. Thus, for him, the Beloved Community became an ideal that speaks of loving each other, being interested in others, and having communion and mutual respect. It has no religious flavour. It is not the institutionalized Church. It is simply an ideal to live by. Royce's conception of Beloved Community is synonymous with a philosophical vision to realize. It is a hope, an ideal for humankind, and it has a message to the globalized and globalizing India and the world at large, whereby the whole humanity would be unified in loyalty and love, strengthened in spirit, brought together in harmony.[34]

5. Conclusion

Royce presented the Beloved Community as an ideal to inspire his own people to turn away from the individualistic tendencies and lead them to a life of beloved communion. When we have the same situation in our

32 Jacquelyn Ann K. Kegley, *Genuine Individuals and Genuine Communities: A Roycean Public Philosophy* (Nashville and London: Vanderbilt University Press, 1997), 3.

33 Peter Fuss, *The Moral Philosophy of Josiah Royce* (Cambridge, Massachusetts: Harvard University Press, 1965), 248.

34 Clendenning, ed.,*The Letters of Josiah Royce*, 649.

present globalizing India, our investigation could be whether the concept of Beloved Community is a fitting Roycean response to the individualizing tendencies of globalization. Hence, the ideal of the Beloved Community is arguably a "philosophy of transformative practice." Royce was convinced that the philosophers are given the serious responsibility of transforming the present selfish world into a beloved one where there is communion, loyalty and diversity of cultures. Those philosophers who hold on to the Christian and human values can articulate it easily. The secular-minded philosophers also can utilize the Beloved Community as an ideal to look up to which can inspire and make positive changes for a better tomorrow. Summarily, we, as philosophers, can inspire the people and the nations like India in their search for meaning of life and of all the human affairs by presenting the Beloved Community as a philosophy of transformative practice. We may not succeed in uplifting the whole India to the status of "beloved", but we can certainly make a difference at least in our outreach. In brief, Royce's Beloved Community, urges us to focus more on our moral and community life, challenges to discern the presence of the Interpreter-Spirit, who each day accords new horizons of meaning, offers rays of hope, renders strings of harmony in the universal community and invites us to be members of the Beloved Community in this globalized and globalizing world. If we are united in love and loyal to this ideal, the Beloved Community, the world is going to be better, peaceful, just, secure, and a beloved communion to the fullest sense.

Part 3

Praxis: Programmatic and Pragmatic

12

Śaraṇa Movement: A Revolution for the New Society

Ivan D'Souza
Diocese of Mangaluru, Karnataka

Abstract: The *Śaraṇa* Movement was organised by Basavaṇṇa in the 12th century AD in Karnataka. It was a revolutionary religious renaissance which raised its voice against the oppressive structures of the society such as caste hierarchy, gender and class inequality, temple cult and brahminic orthodoxy. The followers of Basavaṇṇa vehemently opposed the practice of untouchability and rules of pollution. The present paper sheds light on the *Śaraṇa* Movement spearheaded by Basava and taken forward by galore of saints. It explains about the background, context, development, policies, philosophy and politics involved. It tries to evaluate the strength and weakness of the movement and calls for our involvement and propagation to build up an egalitarian society.

Keywords: Śaraṇa, Basavaṇṇa, Vīraśaivism, Liṅgāyatism, Vacana, Karma, Kāyaka, Liṅga

Introduction

From the background of the recent developments in Indian scenario we can see revolutionary ideas being implemented for a free and liberated society. The Supreme Court has opened the doors of Sabarimala temple in Kerala for women, through its historic judgement, amidst a wave of opposition. It has reiterated the need for safety of women and protection of their basic rights. The rights of

LGBTQA[1] are upheld and gay sexuality is legalized. These are the pointers for a new society. On the other hand, the problems like fundamentalism, lynching, killing and intolerance are on the rise. People are being held prisoners by the religious centres and persons, in nexus with anti-social elements. Such was the crisis and conflict in Karnataka, during the time of Basavaṇṇa[2] (1105-1197 A.D.) in the 12th century. In this context we pose the question: Can *Śaraṇa* Movement be a liberating force to humans who are imprisoned by social evils and human rights' violations? Can it be a paradigm for a new society?

The *Śaraṇa* Movement was a revolutionary religious renaissance which raised its voice against the oppressive structures of the society such as caste hierarchy, gender and class inequality, temple cult and Brahminic orthodoxy. The followers of Basavaṇṇa vehemently opposed the practice of untouchability and rules of pollution with a vision of new society. The present paper sheds light on the *Śaraṇa* Movement spearheaded by Basava and taken forward by a band of inspired seekers. It explains about the background, context, development, policies, philosophy and politics involved. It tries to evaluate the strengths and weaknesses of the movement and calls for our involvement and engagement, to build up an egalitarian society.

1. Origin and Context of the *Śaraṇa* Movement

There was rivalry between Jains and Śaivites in the middle of 11th century in Karnataka. The *Sallekhana*[3] vow of Jains and the lack of respect for women led to the decline of popularity of Jainism among masses.[4] At this juncture, Basava rose to the occasion and propounded a new faith which was accommodative and inclusive in nature.

The new system of philosophy and praxis advocated by Basava is called as *Vīraśaivism* or *Liṅgāyatism*. The followers of *Vīraśaivism* are expected to be the heroic followers of Śiva as it is suggested by the very name itself. *Liṅgāyatism* is the religion of those who wear *liṅga*, which is originally thought as the phallic symbol for Śiva. For *Liṅgāyats* it represents inner conscience of a person. *Liṅgāyatism* is influenced by the then existing sects of *Śaivism*

1 The terms Lesbian, Gay, Bisexual, Transgender, Queer, Intersex and Asexual are used to refer to the sexual and gender identities of people.

2 Basavaṇṇa is also called by names such as Basava, Basaveśvara (the Lord of Basava). Basava is derived from *Vṛṣabha* which means bull. Basaveśvara is a title of reverence whereas Basavaṇṇa is a title of affection.

3 It is the Jain religious practice of voluntarily fasting to death by gradually reducing the intake of food and liquids.

4 M. B. Hugar, *Sharanara Andolana Hagoo Hosa Samajada Parikalpane* (Belgaum: Vimochana Prakshan, 1995), 25-26.

namely, *Kālāmukha* and *Pāśupata*.[5] Basava has also has drawn inspiration from the sixty-three saints (*Nayanmārs*) of Tamil *Śaivism*.[6] He is considered as the incarnation of Śiva. *Liṅgayata* means one who is beloved of *liṅga*. *Liṇga* is the personal emblem of Lord Śiva (*iṣṭaliṅga*). The *iṣṭaliṅga* is the symbolic representation of *Liṅga*.

The terms *Vīraśaivism* or *Liṅgāyatism* were used interchangeably to denote to the new movement pioneered by Basavaṇṇa. Till the end of 19th century there was no confusion between *Lingāyata* and *Vīraśaiva*. Of late there has been longstanding controversy in the use of these terms. Hence, the term *Liṅgāyatism* is used in this paper as denoting the actual sense of the *Śaraṇa* Movement. The followers of new faith initiated by Basava are known as *Śaraṇas*. *Śaraṇa* in general signifies a devotee who has surrendered to the Lord for a cause. It also means the one who has reached the fifth stage of *Śatsthala* system and has accomplished maturity in *Bhakti*. There are different opinions among scholars about the origins of the *Śaraṇa* Movement. The scholars who favour brahminism and follow caste hierarchy opine that Basava is not the founder of *Śaraṇa* Movement. According to them, Basavaṇṇa continued the tradition of five scriptural scholars. But, another opinion says that Basavaṇṇa is the founder of the new movement to establish a society of equality and justice.

2. *Vīraśaivism vs Liṅgāyatism*

There has been a debate whether *Vīraśaivism* (*Liṅgāyatism*) is an independent religion or whether it is a branch of Hinduism. Therefore, there are traditional and non-traditional views with regard to the origin of *Vīraśaivism*. According to the first, it is asserted that *Vīraśaivism* existed even before the times of Basavaṇṇa. It owes its origin to the five great sages (*pañcācāryas*): Revaṇārādhya (Reṇukācārya), Maruḷārādhya (Maruḷasiddha), Ekorāmārādhya, Paṇḍitārādhya and Viśvārādhya who were considered to be emerging from the head of Śiva.[7] *Vīraśaivism* accepts *Vedas*, class hierarchy and *karma* theory. Dr M. Chidananda Murty's work *Vīraśaiva Dharma: Bhāratīya Saṁskṛti* shows that *Liṅgāyatism* is part of *Hindu-Vīraśaivism*.[8] The traditionalists propose that Hindu is *Vīraśaiva*, *Vīraśaiva* is *Liṅgāyata* and therefore *Liṅgāyata* is Hindu.

5 *Kālāmukha* is one of the dominant schools of *Śaivism* in Medieval Karnataka whereas *Pāśupata* sect was founded by Lakulisa.

6 Basava calls them as *Purātanaru* in his mystical aphorisms.

7 The word '*ārādhya*' is a reverential title added to the names of the persons, as in the case of Viśvārādhya. See: Kanti Chandra Pandey, *An Outline of History of Śaiva Philosophy*, R. C. Dwivedi ed., (Delhi: Motilal Banarsidass, 1986), 43.

8 M. Chidananda Murty, *Vīraśaiva Dharma: Bhāratīya Saṁskṛti* (*Hindu Liṅgāyata*) (Bangalore: Minchu Prakashana, 2000).

According to the second view, Basavaṇṇa is the founder of socio-religious movement called *Liṅgāyatism* which aimed at freeing the people from the clutches of Brahmanical domination and exploitation.[9] He is regarded as a social and religious reformer. Dr M. M. Kalburgi who was assassinated by fundamentalist groups was a strong adherent of *Liṅgāyatism*. The view that Basavaṇṇa as the founder of new *Śaiva* sect was not supported by the Sanskrit works of post-Basava period like *Siddhāntaśikāmaṇi*, *Śrīkarabhāṣyam* of Śrīpati etc.[10] Once such Sanskrit texts were written the original *Liṅgāyatism* had to distinguish itself from *Vīraśaivism*. The *Lingāyatism* established by *Śaraṇas* in the line of Basavaṇṇa is entirely different from the *Vīraśaivism* proposed by Sanskrit texts. The *Śaraṇa* Movement advocated monotheism, rejection of caste system, denial of rites and rituals, opposition of animal sacrifices, rejection of the Vedas, equality of gender, work, charity etc. *Vīraśaivism* influenced by Brahminism stressed on polytheism, rites and rituals, necessity of caste system (*varṇśrama*), life lived by acceptance of offering etc.[11]

It has to be borne in mind that *Vīraśaivism* and *Liṅgāyatism* have different focus and perspectives. There have been constant and continuous efforts to equate *Vīraśaivism* with *Liṅgāyatism* to perpetuate the vested interests of Brahminism. Hence, we see a lot of misinterpretation and misrepresentation of the whole philosophy of *Śaraṇas*. *Liṅgāyats* are not *Vīraśaivas* because *Liṅgāyatism* is based on *vacanas* (sayings of *Śaraṇas*) whereas *Vīraśaivism* is based on *Āgamas*. It has to be noted that till 14th century, the term '*Vīraśaiva*' was not used by any writers. It is not at all found in the writings of Basavaṇṇa, Cennabasavaṇṇa and Allama Prabhu. In 1368, Bhikmakavi wrote *Basavapurāṇa* on the basis of Telugu work *Basava Purāṇamu* of Palkurike Somanatha. He used the word 'Vīramāheśvara' instead of 'Vīraśaiva' for the first time.[12]

3. *Vacanas*: Literature of *Śaraṇa* Movement

Vacanas are the spontaneous utterances of different mystics of *Liṅgāyatism*. *Vacana* (what is said) of *Liṅgāyatism* is opposed to *śruti* (what is heard) and *smṛti* (what is remembered) of Vedic Hinduism. The sayings of Basava and his colleagues are called as *vacanas* and their collection is *vacanaśāstra*. *Vacanas* are filled with parallelism, repetitions and recurring formulae. They are written

9 V. Rathinasabapathy, *Perspectives in Virasaivism: From Tamil Sources*, Mruthyunjaya Swamigal Memorial Lecture Series (Dharwad: Institute of Kannada Studies, Karnataka University, 1982), 1.

10 Rathinasabapathy, *Perspectives in Virasaivism: From Tamil Sources*, 3.

11 N.G. Mahadevappa, *Lingayataru Hindoogalalla* (Gadag: Ladai Prakashana, 2017), 6.

12 Ramjan Darga, *Lingavanta Dharmadalli Enuntu Enilla?* (Dharwad: Ladai Prakashana, 2017), 29. Also see: Ramjan Darga, *Basavanna mattu Ambedkar haago itara Lekhanagalu* (Gadag: Ladai Prakashana, 2015), 153.

in simple colloquial Kannada for the benefit of the common people as against Brahminic tradition of Sanskrit literature. Each *vacana* ends with a signature (*ankita*) which gives a clue of the author. The *vacanas* are direct, spontaneous and challenging utterances.[13]

Around twenty-one thousand *vacanas* are available today. Out of which fifteen thousand were written in 12th century itself.[14] Most of the *vacanas* were composed by people of working class. It is interesting to note that many women who have trodden the path of Basavaṇṇa have also composed *vacanas*. *Śaraṇas* like Siddharamesvara, Akkamahadevi, Jedara Dasimayya, Ambigara Chaudayya, Madivala Macayya, Allama Prabhu, Mahadevamma, Aidakki Lakkamma etc. have composed many *vacanas*. The *vacanas* of Basavaṇṇa end with '*Kuḍala Sangama Deva*' (Lord of the confluence of the two rivers, Krishna and Malaprabha in Bijapur, Karnataka), Akkamahādevi's *vacanas* end with '*Cennamallikārjuana*' (Lord white as beautiful Jasmine) and Allama Prabhu's *vacanas* end with 'Guheśvara' (Lord of caves). Basavaṇṇa has written around 1400 *vacanas*.

It has to be noted that *Śaraṇas* have also upheld the learning of Sanskrit to break its Brahminic monopoly. But, the scholars like M. Chidananda Murty have considered this move as to assert view that *Vīraśaivism* is the extension of Vedic Hinduism.[15] What Brahmins had deprived to the Śudras and Dalits of, was provided by the *Śaraṇa* Movement. The centres of learning Sanskrit were encouraged as a sign of protest and a voice of dissent against Brahminical hierarchy.

Śaraṇas have condemned the *karmakāṇḍa*[16] of the Vedas. They have opposed all types of animal sacrifices and violence. They have proved wrong the idea that God is pleased with those who have learnt the Vedas and the Scriptures. One of the *vacanas* of Basavaṇṇa expresses, "Veda was shivering. Why? Because our *Kūḍalasaṅgamadeva* ate at the house of Mādāra Cennayya."[17]

4. Focus and Praxis of *Śaraṇa* Movement

Philosophy and practice go hand-in-hand. *Śaraṇa* Movement is essentially a socio-religious movement. It has its own rich and unique creed and doctrine. Its special feature is the supreme importance to *Śivaliṅga* or *liṅga*. The important

13 Henry D'Almeida, "Basava: Service to Humanity is Service to God," *Jeevadhara* 32, no.188 (May 2002), 174-190.

14 Mahadevappa, *Lingayataru Hindoogalalla*, 67.

15 M. Chidananda Murty, *Vīraśaiva Dharma* (Bangalore: Bharatiya Samskruti Prakahsana, 2000).

16 The section which deals with the rites, rituals and sacrifices of the Vedas.

17 Basavaṇṇa who was a Brahmin ate at the house of the lower caste Mādāra Cennayya.

doctrines of this movement are: fivefold ethical codes (*pañcācāra*), eight aids to faith (*aṣṭāvaraṇa*) and six stages of spiritual journey (*ṣaṭsthala*). *Pañcācāras* highlight the responsibilities and duties of the persons. *Aṣṭāvaraṇas* safeguard one from the worldly attachments and *Ṣatsthalas* aim at growth and well-being of the person.

The *Śaraṇa* Movement propagated by Basavaṇṇa questioned and challenged the existing inequality, dehumanizing caste, class and sex discrimination. The galore of seekers who followed Basavaṇṇa advocated an egalitarian ideology based on the path of devotion and equal access to spiritual goods. We shall see the revolutionary ways adopted by the *Śaraṇa* Movement in the following:

4.1 New Vision of Religion

Śaraṇas have conscientised people about the irrelevance of superstitions and occult practices, and the meaninglessness of mere rites and rituals of Brahminic religion, by proposing an alternative in the understanding of religion. Basavaṇṇa utters:

> Seeing a snake of stone,
> they say: 'Pour milk, do!'
> Seeing a real snake,
> they say: 'Kill it!'
> If a Jaṅgama who can eat arrives,
> they say: 'Away!'
> and serve their dainties to a Liṅga that cannot set! (194)[18]

Śaraṇas believe in one God Śiva and reject all kinds of idol worship. For them, understanding is the teacher, the teacher is God, God is swami (spiritual preceptor) and swami is permanent. There are no offerings of things such as lemon, coconut, ash gourd for worship.[19] Hāvināḷa Kallayya says, "Understanding is teacher, good conduct is disciple, knowledge is *liṅga*, result is *tapas*, equanimity is *yoga*."[20] According to Basavaṇṇa, good conduct or virtuous life is heaven and evil conduct or life of vices is hell (239). There is no place for those aspects of merits and demerits which create desire for *svarga* and fear of *naraka* as in Hinduism. Those who are initiated into ordination through *iṣṭaliṅga* are reborn and they are liberated in this life itself.[21]

---

18 The number in the parenthesis indicates the *vacanas* of Basavaṇṇa as found in H. Deveerappa, ed., *Vacanas of Basavaṇṇa*. trans., L.M.A. Menezes and S.M. Angadi (Sirigere: Annana Balaga, 1967).

19 Darga, *Lingavanta Dharmadalli Enuntu Enilla?* 21.

20 Ibid,, 18.

21 Ibid., 23.

Iṣṭaliṅga constitutes everything that is in the *Brahmāṇḍa* (creation). Worship of *iṣṭaliṅga* refers to containing the whole cosmos in one's being. Hence, nothing is outside and none is outsider to the one who adheres to *liṅga*. All creatures are *aṅga* (part) of *liṅga*. *Liṅga* welcomes and accommodates all in itself. The unity we attain with the one in our inner core is *liṅgāṅgasāmarasya* (unity between *liṅga* and *aṅga*). In other words, it is the mutual relationship between matter and spirit.[22] *Liṅgāyatism* speaks about two types of *Śivayoga* or union with the divine: first, for *ātmakalyāṇa* (the well-being of self) and second, for *lokakalyāṇa* (well-being of the world). Basavaṇṇa distinguishes between two words, *bhavi* and *bhakta*. *Bhavi* says, "this is mine," whereas, *bhakta* says, "this is ours."[23] *Bhavi* asks, "*ivanārava*" i.e., who is he? whose? But *bhakta* asks, "*iva nammava*" i.e., he is our own person (62).

Liṅgāyatism interpreted and critiqued the teachings of Hinduism. *Manusmṛiti* says, "*dharmo rakṣati rakṣitaḥ*" (MS 8.15) i.e., "religion protects those who protect it." It has indirectly caused the perpetuation of caste system. It has led to the protection of *varṇaśrama dharma* which ascertains the superiority of Brahminic classes than the protection of people of lower castes and the underprivileged.[24]

4.2 Body as the Temple

Śaraṇa Movement rejected the privileged temple cult of Brahmins which exploited and misused the poor men and women belonging to the lower strata of the society. It propounded a new way of worshipping God through the worship of personal *liṅga* worn in one's body. Basavaṇṇa meaningfully states,

> The rich
> Will make temples for Śiva.
> What Shall I, O Lord,
> a poor man, do?
> My legs are pillars,
> the body the shrine,
> the head cupola of gold.
> O Lord of the Meeting Rivers,
> listen, O Lord:
> Standing things shall fall,
> that which moves shall stay.[25]

---

22 Ramjan Darga, *Basavanna Eke Beku?* (Gadag: Ladai Prakashana, 2017), 56.

23 Darga, *Basavanna Eke Beku?* 47.

24 Darga, *Basavanna Eke Beku?* 74.

25 K. V. Zvelebil, trans., *The Lord of the Meeting Rivers: Devotional Poems of Basavaṇṇa* (Delhi: Motilal Banarsidass, 1984), 820.

This poem upholds the dignity of every human being by affirming body as the temple of God. It instils new hope and gives solace to those people who face the prohibition of entering into the temple. God is not present in the structures. The construction of temples perpetuates the priestly class. They get their share for daily living from the offerings of working class.[26] Basavaṇṇa identified himself with the poor and the exploited, with the new concept of the body as the temple. This put an end to all kinds of evil and corrupt practices in the temple such as *Devadāsi* system, the free and obligatory offerings of farmers to the priests etc.

4.3 Equality of Caste, Gender and Profession

Śaraṇa movement propounded equality of all by promoting casteless and egalitarian society. It vehemently opposed the clericalism, dogmatism, priestcraft, ritualistic barriers and all kinds of exclusions in terms of class, color and gender. One of the *vacanas* of Basavaṇṇa which expresses solidarity and equality with the people of lower caste and outcast goes thus:

I am Mādāra's son
Him, who derives his pedigree
Down from the ancient saints and claims
Has as the founder of his stock
My father it was who washed my dirt
This taint of caste!
I am good Sir, Mādāra's son
O Kuḍala Saṅgama, thou serpent collared Lord
Thy grandsire's grandsire's sire
is Cennayya[27] (347)

Basavaṇṇa announces the futility of the caste system in the following aphorism:

Clinging to caste, you seek impurities;
You look for darkness, while you cling to light
Why you, you silly man!
You claim to be superior by caste:
Is there any benefit
By a hundred billion priests? (594)

The *varṇā* system was challenged by Basava by promoting *varṇasaṅkara* or *jātisaṅkara* (inter-caste marriage). Vedic religion considers *varṇasaṅkara* as an obstruction to *dharma*. But, *śaraṇas* treat it as a sign of

26 Hugar, *Sharanara Andolana Hagoo Hosa Samajada Parikalpane*, 100-101.

27 In the *vacana*, Madara stands for Cennayya, a low caste. Hara is Śiva. Basavaṇṇa considers Śiva as his real father.

socio-religious revival and reform. Caste or origin should not be the criteria for any kind of relationship or interaction.

In *Lingāyatism*, instead of *maṭha* (monastery) there is *mahāmane* (great house) which proclaimed universal brotherhood. *Mahāmane* welcomed and accepted the people of different castes, occupations and professions such as traders, weavers, craftsmen, peasants, oilmen, ferrymen, farmers, hunters, shepherds, fishermen, carpenters, woodcutters, shoe makers, barbers, toddy sellers, folk artists, scavengers, prostitute and some brahmins. Basavaṇṇa declares:

> Of one who eats food blessed by you, wherever he be,
> What is the caste?
> Of one who is fit for your service, O Master,
> What is the caste?
> Of one who is drawn to your bosom, O God,
> What is the caste?
> O Lord of the Meeting Rivers.[28]

4.4 Work Liberates

Śaraṇa Movement upheld the dignity of labour. It believes in the motto "*kāyakavekailāsa*" i.e., "work is the means of liberation" as pronounced by Āidakki Mārayya.[29] 'Hard work is final accomplishment and spiritual pursuit' is its manifesto. "If you are engaged in work, forget the vision of teacher, forget the worship of *liṅga*" says Aidakki Marayya. People should not hesitate to undertake any kind of bodily work. There is no division of classes or castes for work. Even *guru* attains liberation through work. The work done by struggle and striving not only sustains one's daily needs but also contributes towards the welfare of the society.[30] *Lingayatism* suggests that what is obtained through work is *liṅgaprasāda*. It has to be distributed in the society and economic inequality has to be destroyed. In the context of *Śaraṇa* Movement, the significance of work, exertion and service has to be seen as a means of becoming self-reliant without being dependent on the King. The monarch may employ force, power, authority, violence etc. but the people through their work should establish peace, harmony, prosperity and tranquillity in the society. One of the poems says,

> Work on the soil, toil hard with your limits-
> Consecrate to the Lord

---

28 Deveerappa, ed., *Vacanas of Basavaṇṇa*, 241.

29 Darga, *Lingavanta Dharmadalli Enuntu Enilla?* 15.

30 Deveerappa, ed., *Vacanas of Basavaṇṇa*,139-140.

The food that you thus earn
And share it with others[31]

All the works are dignified and honourable. No profession can be considered as inferior one. Basavaṇṇa writes,

The father of Vyāsa was a fisherman;
Mārkendaeya's mother, an outcaste;
And Mandodari was the daughter of a frog.
O look not to caste! For who could say, anyway
What he had been born in births past.
Indeed, Agastya was a fowler;
Durvāsa, a mason; Kaśyapa, a blacksmith;
Kaundinya there, as everyone knows,
Spent his lives cutting hair.
'So what if one had been a dog-eating outcaste?
'The devotee of Śiva is born into a good family.'
So says our Lord of the Meeting Rivers.[32]

Through the principle of *kayaka*, *Śaraṇa* Movement strongly condemns the theory of *karma*. *Karma* theory says that every action has an effect either good or evil, depending on its morality. *Karma* decides the future whereas *kayaka* concerns the present. In other words, nothing depends on *prārabda* (past *karmas* which decide the present birth) except *prayatna* (effort). *Karma* can be understood in three ways: Firstly, it indicates to the rites, rituals and sacrifices of Vedic times (*karmakāṇḍa*). Secondly, it denotes the results of the action. Good actions result in merits and evil action cause demerits. This decides one's rebirth. Finally, it stands for desireless action (*karmayoga*). *Liṅgāyatism* says that actions without desire demotivates the doer.[33] *Śaraṇas* say that work has to be paid just wages, neither more nor less. Thus, they have proposed a movement for the workers' security and protection of their rights.

Śaraṇas reject the theory of the world as *māyā* (illusion or unreal) and assert that world is real. Basava remarks:

This world is the Lord's Mint
The coin that is good here,
will be good in heaven.

31 *Śrī Basaveśvara: A Commemoration Volume* (Bangalore: Government of Mysore, 1967), 73.

32 Deveerappa, ed., *Vacanas of Basavaṇṇa*, 192-193.

33 T. R. Chandrashekara, *Lingayata Thatva Pranalike* (Gadag: Ladai Prakashana, 2017), 16.

One who is accepted as good in this world
is acceptable in heaven as well.[34]

4.5 Charity or *Dāsoha*

Dāsoha is the practice of charity exercised through *kāyaka*. Literally it means, imbibing the spirit of *dāsa* (servant). It is giving to others the remaining portion of earnings after one's needs are fulfilled. In other words, the work done just to fill the belly is employment and the work done for the service of oneself and the society is *dasoha*. It contributes to the equal distribution of wealth and facilities in the society. *Dāsoha* challenges the culture of '*dāna*' which was prevalent in the Hindu society. In such almsgiving the giver shows pride and receiver feels inferior. But in *dāsoha* all have the role to give or receive. It places a check on the unnecessary accumulation of wealth by the rich and deprivation of wealth and necessities to the poor. Once Aidakki Marayya brought home some extra rice to which his wife Aidakki Lakkamma said, "Which devotee of Śiva has the greed other than the King?"[35]

4.6 *Anubhāva Maṇṭapa*-Hall of Spiritual Experience

Anubhāva stands for mystical and metaphysical experience as against *anubhāva* which consists of worldly experience. *Anubhāva Maṇṭapa* was a colloquium to discuss theological, mystical and philosophical aspects of *Liṅgāyatism*. It was a place where all were welcomed without the barriers and boundaries of caste, creed, sex and occupation for spiritual discourses and to experience Śiva as present in all. The initiative had gained its momentum under the leadership of Basavaṇṇa, Allama Prabhu, Cennabasava, Siddharama and others. The deliberations and discussions were conducted under the spiritual guidance of Allama Prabhu and was carried out in Kannada. There were many women mystics and philosophers who made remarkable contributions through their writings and learned discourses such as Akkamahadevi, Muktayakka, Akkanagamma, Lakkamma, Nilamma etc.

Anubhāva Maṇṭapa tried to replace the concept of *mandira* (temple). It promotedcollective leadership, collabourative action and motivated all those who were in the margins to be in the mainstream of the society. Basavaṇṇa and his followers moved from kingly set up to the collegial and cordial company. It is said that there were 770 leaders in the spiritual parliament which had *Vacana* literature as its constitution. It believed in the maxim, "*ariveguru*" i.e., "realisation is the teacher".

---

34 Sadashiva Wodeyar, "History and Theology of Veerasaivism," *Religion and Society* XXXIX, nos. 2 & 3 (June-Sept 1992),10.

35 Darga, *Basavanna Eke Beku?* 59.

Anubhava maṇṭapa also paved the way for the education of adults, women, dalits, backward classes and working folks. This enabled them for union, protest and revolution. They began to compose poems. Both men and women had equal right for learning and discussions. The practice of *Liṅgadīkṣa* (ordination or initiation) to all discarded gender discrimination.[36]

5. *Śaraṇa* Movement: A Way Forward

American sociologist, Herbert George Blumer identifies four phases in the life-cycle of social movements. They are: Emergence, Coalescence, Bureaucratization, and Decline. The reasons like success, organizational failure, co-optation, repression, establishment within mainstream society etc. may result in the decline of the social movements.[37]

The *Śaraṇa* Movement has undergone these stages. The working of any Movements has ups and downs. It is confronted with the zig-zag routes of success and failure, strengths and weaknesses. It emerged as a reaction to the then social conditions of inequality, domination and discrimination. It tried to address the issue of the masses in their own language, culture and ethos. Then it became more organized due to the following of people in large numbers. The popularity of *Śaraṇa* Movement began to spread so rapidly that it reacted strongly against its oppressors and exploiters. Then there was the formalization of the Movement with many of counter-strategies, ideologies and well-planned programmes of conscientization. It mobilized the people and made them realize their own dignity, worth and respect. Though there is much more to be achieved by *Śaraṇa* Movement, due to the hidden agendas and hindrances, false allegations and brainwashing its voice becomes shrill. Hence, it has experienced a stage of stagnation, struggle and suffering. But, since its aim is not a short-term goal it rises more powerfully every time when it suffers setback. Today there is a need for *Śaraṇa* Movement to show its liberative and transformative potential in the mainstream of our country.

The work *The Land of the Liṅgam* by a soldier in British India, Arthur Miles explains about Basava, his *Śaraṇa* Movement and its growth in the following way:

> … he was the first Indian free-thinker. He might be called the Luther of India. The acknowledged leadership of the priests was in full swing when Basava came upon the scene, and there was a movement on foot to replace caste and priestly authority with intelligence and free-thinking. Basava, a Śivaite Brahman, was in

---

36 *Śrī Basaveśvara: A Commemoration Volume*, 153-154.

37 Jonathan Christiansen, "*Four Stages of Social Movements,*" *EBSCO Research Starters* (2009), 2-4, accessed October 12, 2018, https://www.ebscohost.com/uploads/imported/thisTopic-dbTopic-1248.pdf.

> the camp of the liberals, lie mounted the rostrum for the abolition of caste and ceremonies, and preached that all men were by birth equal, that one sex was as important as another, that child marriage was wrong, and that widows should be permitted to remarry. He promised the Liṅgyāts, the freedom of individual action. All wearers of the divine liṅgam were to occupy a common level; they were to eat together and to intermarry. For a while the simplicity of his teaching appealed to the people, but soon, as they increased in wealth and numbers, they wanted their old distinctions back, as these increased their importance. Ceremonies and elabourate ritual crept into their worship, and thus, as new converts entered they were placed on a lower strata, while the priests got back their old power and again became the privileged caste.[38]

The initial rigour and enthusiasm of the *Śaraṇa* movement in the 12th century gradually calmed down at the latter stage from second half of 14th century onwards because of Brahminisation and Sanskritsation of its philosophy, practice and literature. It became a parallel structure to that of the Brahmins. Eventually it was under the clutches of *maṭhas*. The so-called political and religious leaders have proclaimed themselves as the custodians and ambassadors of *Liṅgāyatism* and justified that it is not different from *Vīraśaivism*.[39]

The very reason for which *Śaraṇa* Movement emerged, has become the obstacle for its growth, leading to its stagnation and irrelevance. There is a strong and well-organized political undercurrent working behind this, to silence the power of the movement. Today *Liṅgāyatism* itself has become a caste of Hinduism with groups like weavers, Gauḍas, Reddys, etc. Though it does not support any sort of caste system, it is not free from any caste and sub-caste system. Most people think that they are Hindu *Liṅgāyats*.[40] If commoners do not acknowledge themselves as part of Hinduism, then they are persecuted and neglected in every area. In reality, *Liṅgāyata* indicates separate religion and *Vīraśaiva* is construed part of Hinduism.

There is a demand by the lower class and many other categories of people to declare it as a religion of minority so that many facilities can be availed of, by them. In the recent past there has been an attempt by the Karnataka state government to declare it as a separate religion. But, the political parties try to fish in troubled waters. Since it involves approval and verification by Central government and other administrative bodies, it remains a distant dream.

---

38 Arthur Miles, *The Land of the Lingam* (London: Hurst & Brackett Ltd., 1933), 111.

39 Darga, *Basavanna Eke Beku?* 16.

40 Chandrashekara, *Lingayata Thatva Pranalike*, 46.

Conclusion

Liṅgāyatism is the only religion of Karnataka, though officially it is not declared as a religion by the government of India. Progressive thinker, Dr M. M. Kalburgi who was killed in the recent past, who belonged to the *Liṅgāyata* tradition, was a staunch proponent of *Liṅgāyatism*, as a separate religion. No doubt that *Liṅgāyatism* became an alternative to the people who were subjugated for their caste and status, as dictated by *Manusmṛti*. It has been successful to address the religious, social, economic and cultural needs of the common folk. The *vacana* is still relevant and has answers to the problems including terrorism, fundamentalism, ritualism, casteism and extremism, which are affecting the several parts of our country. There is an urgent need to take forward the spirit of *Śaraṇa* Movement in the society today. *Liṅgāyatism* has shown paradigm shifts from temple to *anubhava maṇṭapa*, from monastery to *mahāmane*, from caste to justice, from *karma* to *kāyaka*, from *dāna* to *dāsoha*, from superstition to rationality, from inequality to equality, from patriarchal dominance to genderless society and from violence to non-violence.[41] But. it is sad to see that *Śaraṇa* Movement is once again crushed under the strong clutches of vested political interests. Though it struggles hard, to shake itself free of the evil forces that deter it, the movement itself finds hard, to regain its primordial élan. Is it not true, that it is being marginalized by majority Hindus? The major difficulty is that, it got fixated to the regional boundary and thus, has not spread itself to the national level.

41 Darga, *Lingavanta Dharmadalli Enuntu Enilla?* 25-26.

13

Bhakti Movements in Contemporary Religions

Fr Dr Biju Pallippadan V.C.
Morning Star Regional Seminary, Baarackpore, Kolkata

Abstract: Etymologically the term *Bhakti* comes from the root *bhaj* which means to serve. *Bhakti* as a religious concept means devotional surrender to a personality conceived supreme God for attaining salvation. *Bhakti* is defined as a devotion or passionate love for the Divine. There are number of reasons for the emergence of *Bhakti* movement. Hinduism lost its simplicity and has become complex. The existence of caste system, untouchability, inequality in the society etc. has contributed for the coming of *Bhakti* Movements. Besides, the coming of Islam and their monotheistic concept of God also set the background for the development of *Bhakti* Movements. In this paper we shall deal with origin, development and the present world. How the contemporary gurus carried forward the same flame of devotion (*Bhakti*).

All the *Bhakti* Movements in one way or other highlighted five major beliefs as its pivotal principles. They taught that God is One (*Ekam Sat)* and therefore shall not be any barrier for worship. It insisted that worshipping God with devotion is better than performing religious ceremonies. The nature of *Bhakti* is absolute love for God; *Bhakti* is supreme attachment to the Lord. To worship God, man must serve humanity without considering the religion and caste he or she belongs to. We are going to make a study of *Bhakti* Movements origin, causes and present leaders or Movements of *Bhakti* in contemporary India.

Keywords: *Bhakti* Movement, Upanishads, Bhagavad Gita, Monotheism, *Advaita*, Sufi Movement.

1. Introduction

Etymologically the term *Bhakti* comes from the root *bhaj* which means to serve. *Bhakti* as a religious concept means devotional surrender to a personality conceived as supreme God, for attaining salvation. *Bhakti* is defined as a devotion or passionate love for the Divine. The word is first mentioned in Rigveda which indicates worshipping Indra and Surya.It gives expression to a feeling of intimacy with the highest God. Later in Upanishads, *Para Bhakti* is stressed, which is directed to Vishnu and Siva.[1]

1.1 Origin of *Bhakti* Movement

The word '*Bhakti*' means devotion to God. *Svetasatara Upnishad* speaks of the highest devotion to God. We have references to *Vishnu Bhakti*, *Krishna Bhakti* etc. in ancient texts. In the epic Ramayana, we have the reference to *Guru Bhakti*. In the Bhagavad Gita, there is emphasis on love and devotion to God. *Bhakti* Movements originated in south India between 7th and 12th century. They had a countercultural undercurrent.[2] The Bhaktas of God did not believe in any sort of caste distinctions. They advocated love and devotion to God and discarded all sorts of rituals and ceremonies. They preached oneness of God and "that all religions were but roads leading to the same goal."[3]

1.2 Causes of *Bhakti* Movements

Hinduism had lost its simplicity and had become more complex. Many philosophical schools like *Vaisnava, Saiva* and the *Sakti* cult had appeared on the scene. The existence of caste system, untouchability and inequality in society, etc. had contributed to the emergence of *Bhakti* Movements. Besides, the coming of Islam and their monotheistic concept of God also set the background for the development of *Bhakti* Movements. The persecution of Hindus by Muslim rulers, who tried to convert them to Islam, led to the preservation of their religion through *Bhakti* movement. In the context of saints, they preached equality of castes as far as devotion to God is concerned. Elabourate rules and rigour in religion were not liked by common man. The

---

1 Anto Cheramthuruthy, *Contemporary Indian Thought* (Kottayam: OIRSI Publications 2017); Also see: Anand, "Sufi and Bhakti Movement in India," *historydiscussion.net*, accessed October 2, 2018, http://www.historydiscussion.net/history-of-india/sufi-and-bhakti-movement-in-india/3052.

2 Kunal Chakrabarti, "The Lily and the Mud: D. D. Kosambi on Religion," *Economic and Political Weekly* 43, no. 30, (July 26, 2008), 60-70, where the author, in his discussion on the approach of Kosambi, to history, brings in the discussion on the genealogy of the Bhakti Movement, in dialogue with eminent historians like Romila Thapar, M. Hiriyanna, M. A. Mehendale, Thapar, Suvira Jaiswal, Arvind Sharma and G. C. Pande and N. N. Bhattacharyya.

3 G.M Bailey, ed., *Bhakti Studies*, Vol. 1 (Bombay: Sterling Publishers, 1992).

enthusiasm and inspiration of the *Bhakti* saints enabled them to remove the evils of society. In the sphere of religion and normal thinking in law, in literature and even in political ideals, a new life came into being in India by the middle of the 16th Centuary.

1.3 Major Principles and proponents of *Bhakti* Movement

However, the development of *Bhakti* started in South India between the seventh and the twelfth century. During this period the Shaiva Nayanars and the Vaishnavite disregarded the austerities preached by the Jains and the Buddhists and preached personal devotion to God as a means of Salvation. They also disregarded the rigidities of the caste system and unnecessary rites and rituals of the Hindu religion.

They carried their message of love and personal devotion to God to various parts of South India by using the local languages. Although, there were many points of contact between south and north India, the transmission of the ideas of *Bhakti* Saints from South to north India was a slow and long drawn-out process. It was mainly due to the fact that Saiva Nayanars and the Vaishnavite Alvars preached in the local languages. And use of Sanskrit language was still less. However the ideas of *Bhakti* were carried to the north by scholars as well as by saints. Among these mention may be made of Namadeva, Ramananda, Ramanuja, Nimbarka, Vallabhacharya etc.

1.3.1 Namadeva

Namadeva was a Maharashtrian Saint who flourished in the first part of the fourteenth century. He was a tailor who had taken to banditry before he became a saint. His poetry which was written in Marathi breathes a spirit of intense love and devotion to God. Namadeva is said to have travelled far and wide and engaged in discussions with the Sufi Saints in Delhi.[4]

1.3.2 Ramananda

Ramananda was also a Maharashtrian Saint who belonged to the period between the second half of the fourteenth and the first quarter of the fifteenth century. He was a follower of Ramanuja. He was born at Prayag (Allahabad) and lived at Benares. He was a great devotee of Lord Ram and therefore he substituted the worship of Ram in place of Vishnu. He was dead against caste system in India. He picked up disciples from different castes of Indian Society. He taught his doctrine of *Bhakti* to all the four Varnas, and disregarded the ban on people of different castes cooking or eating their meals together. Among his

4 Cheramthuruthy, *Contemporary Indian Thought*, 143.

disciples there were a cobbler, a weaver, a barber and a butcher. His favorite disciple was Kabir who was a weaver.[5]

1.3.3 Ramanuja

Ramanuja was a great preacher of *Bhakti* cult. He flourished in the early part of the twelfth century. He belonged to South India. He was a follower of Vaishnavism. His great disciple was Ramananda. He preached that devotion to God was the only way to attain Salvation. He disregarded caste system and longed to be entertained by the low caste people.[6]

1.3.4 Nimbarka

Nimbarka was another great preacher of *Bhakti* Cult. He belonged to the South, but spent most of his life in Mathura. He was a great devotee of Lord Krishna and Radha. He preached the doctrine of Self-Surrender. Vallabhacharya was another distinguished preacher of the *Bhakti* Cult. He was born in a Telugu Brahman family in Benares in 1479. He was a great devotee of Lord Krishna. He spent most of his time at Vrindavana, Mathura and Benares and preached Krishna *Bhakti* or devotion to Lord Krishna. He was the founder of the *Pushti Marga*, the path of divine grace.[7] He preached that the follower of *Pushti Marga* or the path of divine grace will definitely get the highest bliss. Besides these great preachers of *Bhakti* Cult, there were other three prominent exponents of the cult, who, by their sincere efforts not only popularised the *Bhakti* Cult but also immortalised themselves in the history of India. They were Kabir, Guru Nanak and Sri Chaitanya.

1.3.5 Kabir

Among those who was most critical of the existing social order and made a strong plea for Hindu-Muslim Unity, the name of Kabir stands out. Kabir was a Champion of the *Bhakti* Cult. The teachings of Kabir were very simple. He first of all emphasized on the unity of God. He said, we may call the God by any name such as Rama, Hari, Govinda, Allah, Sahib etc. it makes no difference. They are one and the same. Kabir said God is formless. He strongly denounced idol-worship. He also did not believe in incarnations (Avatara) of God. He disregarded formal worships and practices like idol-worship, Pilgrimages, bathing in holy rivers.[8]

---

5 Cheramthuruthy, *Contemporary Indian Thought*, 143.

6 Ibid.

7 N. N. Bhattacharyya, *Medieval Bhakti Movements in India* (New Delhi: Munshiram Manoharlal Publishers Pvt. Ltd., 1989).

8 Krishna Sharma, *Bhakti and the Bhakti Movement* (New Delhi: Munshiram Manoharlal Publications Pvt. Ltd., 1987), 45-55.

He advised people not to give up the life of a normal house holder for the sake of a saintly life. He said that neither asceticism nor book knowledge could give us true knowledge. Dr Tara Chand says that the mission of Kabir was to preach a religion of love which would unite all castes and creeds.[9] He disregarded the outer form and formalities of both Hindu and Islamic religion. Kabir strongly denounced the caste system. He gave emphasis on the unity of men and opposed all kinds of discrimination between human beings. His sympathies were with the poor man, with whom he identified himself. The teachings of Kabir were appealing to both Hindus and Muslims. His followers were called as *Kabir panthis* or the followers of Kabir. His poems were called as *dohas*. After his death, his followers collected his poems and named it Bijak.[10]

1.3.6 Sri Chaitanya

The *Bhakti* Movement of Sri Chaitanya is based on the concept of love between Lord Srikrishna and the milk-maids of Gokul, especially Radha. He used the love between Radha and Krishna in an allegoric manner to depict the relationship of Love, in its various aspects of the individual soul with the Supreme Soul. In addition to love and devotion as a method of worship, he added the musical gathering or Kirtan which can give a special form of mystic experience while praying Him (God).Through this method of worship one gets himself detached from the outside world. According to Chaitanya, worship consisted of love and devotion and song and dance which produced a state of ecstasy in which the presence of God, whom we called Hari, could be realised. He said that such worship could be carried out by all, irrespective of caste, colour and creed. The teachings of Sri Chaitanya had profound impact in Bengal and Orissa. His love and form of worship crossed all the manmade boundaries of the Indian Society and he welcomed the people into his fold irrespective of caste, creed and sex.[11]

He was also called Goura, as he was white in complexion. Chaitanya's birth place Nadia was the centre of vedantic rationalism. So, from an early life he had developed an interest in reading scriptures. He had acquired proficiency in Sanskrit literature, logic and grammar. He was a great lover and admirer of Krishna. His biographer Krishna Das Kabiraj says "Sri Chaitanya used to say, O Krishna! I don't want education, power or followers." Give me a little faith

9 Anand, "Sufi and Bhakti Movemets in India," http://www. historydiscussion.net/history-of-india/sufi-and-bhakti-movement-in-india/3052.

10 Friendhelm Hardy, *Viraha-Bhakti* (Pondicheryy: Oxford University Press, 1983), 86.

11 Cheramthuruthy, *Contemporary Indian Thought*, 144-145.

which will enhance my devotion to you. He was very unfortunate from family point of view, as he had lost his parents and his wife at an early age.[12]

However at the age of 22 he visited Gaya where he was initiated into the Krishna cult by a recluse. He became a god-intoxicated devotee who incessantly uttered the name of Krishna. Chaitanya is said to have travelled all over India in spreading the Krishna Cult. He spent most of his time in Puri, Orissa on the feet of Lord Jagannath. His influence on the people of Orissa was tremendous. He is said to have initiated Prataprudra Dev, the Gujapati king of Orissa into his cult. He is still worshipped as Gauraong Mahaprabhu as the very incarnation of Krishna and Vishnu. He is said to have disappeared in the temple of Lord Jagannath in 1533 A.D.

1.4 Guru Nanak

Guru Nanak, the founder of Sikhism was one of the great exponents of *Bhakti* Cult. He was born in 1469 in the village of Talwandi (now called Nankana) on the bank of the River Ravi in the state of Punjab. Nanak from his very childhood showed a religious bent of mind and later preferred the company of Saints and Sadhus. Although, he married early and inherited his father's profession of accountancy, he did not take interest in either. He had a mystic vision and forsook the worldly life. He composed hymns and sang them with stringed instrument which was played by his faithful follower named Mardana. He is said to have made wide tours all over India, even beyond it, to Sri Lanka in the South and Mecca and Medina in the west. He attracted a large number of crowds wherever he went. His name and fame spread far and wide and before his death in 1538 he was already known to the world as a great saint.[13]

1.4.1 Philosophy of Nanak

First of all like Kabir, Nanak laid emphasis on the oneness of Godheads. He preached that through love and devotion one can get the grace of God and the ultimate Salvation. He said, "Caste, creed or sect have nothing to do with the Love and Worship of God."[14] Like Kabir, he said, "God does not live in any temple or mosque. One cannot realize Him by taking bath in holy rivers or going on pilgrimages or performing rites and rituals. One can attain him by complete surrender. Therefore, like Kabir, he strongly denounced idol-worship, Pilgrimages and other formal observances of the various faiths. However Nanak laid great emphasis on the purity of character and conduct as the first condition of approaching God. He also laid emphasis on the need of a Guru for

12 Sharma, *Bhakti and the Bhakti Movement*, 122.

13 Bailey, ed., *Bhakti Sudies*, 168.

14 A. J. Appaswamy, *The Theology of Hindu Bhakti* (Madras: CLS, 1970), 49.

guidance. He spoke about the universal brotherhood of man.[15]

Muslims. It has been argued that the old forms of religion continued almost unchanged. It also did not affect any major change in the caste system. Of course his ideas in course of time gave birth to a new creed called Sikhism. However in a broader sense it can be viewed that both Kabir and Nanak could create a climate of opinion which continued to work through the succeeding centuries.

1.4.2 The Sufi Movement

They were called Sufis as they wore garments of Wool (suf) as their badge of poverty. Thus the name 'Sufi' is derived from the word Suf. They consider love to be the only means of reaching God. Historian Tara Chand says, "Sufism indeed was a religion of intense devotion, love was its passion; poetry, song and dance, its worship and passing away in God its ideal". The Sufis did not attach importance to namaz, hajj and celibacy. That is why they were misunderstood by orthodox muslims. They regarded singing and dancing as methods of inducing a state of ecstasy which brought one nearer to realisation of God. There were some leading Sufi Saints like Khwaja Muinuddin Chisti, Fariuddin Ganj-i-Shakar, Nizam-ud-din Auliya etc.[16]

2 Contemporary Leaders

There are many gurus or leaders still who follow the path of *Bhakti* Marga suchas Mata Amritanandamayi, Sri Sri Ravi Shankar, Sathya Saibaba etc., Let us see their ways in brief.

2.1 Mata Amritanandamayi

Sudhamani Idamannel, born on September 27, 1953, popularly known as Mata Amritanandamayi or *The Hugging Saint*, is not only revered as a spiritual leader by her followers, but also respected for her philanthropic and social services by the general public. She smiled when she was born, unlike most who cry. At five, when other children preferred to play, she would sing devotional songs. At nine, her schooling was terminated, and she had to take care of her younger siblings at home, which she accepted with a smile.

2.2 Philosophy of *Amma*

For Amma, Advaita (non-dualism) is not a mere philosophy, but something to be lived. As such, Amma's every thought, word and deed resound with that greatest of truths: Everything within and without is divine. Accordingly, Amma oversees a massive matrix of humanitarian activities. Hospitals for

15 Bailey, ed., *Bhakti and the Bhakti Movement*, 169.

16 Anand, "Sufi and Bhakti Movemets in India," http://www. historydiscussion.net/history-of-india/sufi-and-bhakti-movement-in-india/3052.

the sick, homes for the homeless, disaster relief, orphanages, hospices, free pensions, suicide-prevention, employment programmes. The list is endless. Influenced by Amma's example and experiencing her pure love, thousands upon thousands of people from around the world have been inspired to take up a life of service giving whatever time or money they can spare in order to help others.

This has been Amma's vision from the beginning. Amma says, "In today's world, people experience two types of poverty: the poverty caused by lack of food, clothing and shelter, and the poverty caused by lack of love and compassion. Of these two, the second type needs to be considered first—because, if we have love and compassion in our hearts, then we will wholeheartedly serve those who suffer from lack of food, clothing and shelter." This is the secret behind the success of Amma's charitable mission and how its expansion seems to be constant and without end. And the brilliance of Amma's grand scheme is that not only are the downtrodden uplifted but also the volunteers, as the selflessness of their actions purifies their minds, helping them to gradually progress along the spiritual path. Amma's charitable social services cross all barriers of nationality, race, caste and religion, and have drawn the attention of the world community.

2.3 Sri Sri Ravishankar

According to Sri Sri Ravishankar`s philosophy, God lies within every heart. He says that, each one of us has God lying inside. He is of the opinion that God is an integral part of our lives and we cannot go away from him. He teaches that spirituality is that which enhances human values such as love, compassion and enthusiasm. It is not limited to any one religion or culture. Hence, it is open to all people. He feels the spiritual bond we share as part of the human family is more prominent than nationality, gender, religion, profession, or other identities that separate us. According to him, science and spirituality are linked and compatible, both springing from the urge to know. The question, "Who am I?" leads to spirituality; the question, "What is this?" leads to science. Emphasizing that joy is only available in the present moment, his stated vision is to create a world free of stress and violence. His programs are said to offer practical tools to help accomplish this. He sees breath as the link between body and mind, and a tool to relax the mind, emphasising the importance of both meditation/spiritual practice and service to others. In his view, "Truth is spherical rather than linear; so it has to be contradictory."[17]

17 Pravin Agrawal, "Sri Sri Ravi Shankar,"*speakingtree.in*, accessed September 21, 2018, https://www.speakingtree.in/allslides/an-introduction-to-sri-sri-ravi-shankar-713469.

2.4 Sri Sathya Sai Baba

Bhakti is love towards God without any expectations. Give and take is involved in *Bhukti,* not in *Bhakti.* In the Bhagavad Gita in *Bhakti* Yoga, true *Bhakti* is explained by Shri Krishna as loving everyone and having compassion towards all, without having hatred or envy towards anyone, and knowing that God resides in everyone. This is true *Bhakti* or devotion. To whomever we prostrate or offer obeisance, it reaches God. In the same way, whomever we blame or disdain also reaches God. It is important to love all. The divine quality is to truly love even those who hate us. We must love even those who blame us, bring us loss and suffering. That is true *Bhakti*

Our life should be like a river. There could be humans, animals, sinners or saints who want to drink water from the same river. But for the river, there is no difference. It does not feel that it flows in order to quench the thirst only of the saint. The five elements (Earth, Water, Fire, Air and Space) bestow equally upon all without any discrimination. Nature, which is born out of divinity, represents the divine quality and divine nature. Nature exemplifies divine selfless love. But *Vyakhti or* human who is born out of *Srushti,* Nature, is unable to understand this principle. As a result of narrow-mindedness and inability to love everyone equally, man is living a very selfish life.[18]

2.4 Christianity

Recent decades have witnessed a remarkable movement throughout the Christian church. Springing up spontaneously across the full field-from Protestant to Roman Catholic to Greek Orthodox - the charismatic renewal now involves millions of people on every continent. The charismatic renewal is not strictly a movement like many others described. It cannot be traced to one outstanding leader, or even a small group, with a well-defined set of doctrinal and organizational convictions. This renewal has sprung up from the grassroots in a wide variety of forms.

The charismatic renewal takes its name from the Greek word charisma, a gift. In the New Testament this gift involves all that God gives us in his grace through Jesus. But, most often this word is used for a specific way the Holy Spirit shows himself within the Christian community. The apostle Paul uses the picture of the body when he writes about spiritual gifts. Christians are members of the body; Jesus is the head. Just as parts of the human body have different functions, so Christians experience a variety of spiritual gifts. These are given by the Holy Spirit to strengthen the body of Christ in its worship, witness and service (1 Corinthians 12:12-31). At the heart of the charismatic

18 Jayaram V., "What Is Bhakti?" *saivrinda.org*, accessed September 21, 2018, https://saivrinda.org/discourse-summaries/what-is-bhakti-summary-of-divine-discourse-on-2-July-2016.

renewal stands the conviction that the full range of spiritual gifts in the New Testament is meant for the church today.

2.4.1 Khrist Bhaktas

On every Sunday and second Saturday, thousands of people, who are not baptised as Christians, come to worship Jesus in *Matridham, a Catholic āśram in Varanasi, Uttar Pradesh, North* India. These people, who are now called Khrist Bhaktas (devotees of Christ), are mainly Hindus belonging to several caste groups. They gather in the āśram to listen to the Word of God preached to them. They come from the neighbouring villages, cities, and districts and even from neighbouring states (provinces). The number of devotees has grown enormously and has taken the form of a movement, now called the Khrist Bhakta Movement. This is happening in Varanasi, a holy city for the Hindus and a city known as the religious and cultural capital of India. Though it was started as āśram movement it has adapted number of ways of *Bhakti* Movements, preaching word of God, singing Bhajans and Holy Eucharistic adorations etc. The charismatic elements are seen at large in this movement.[19]

2.4.2 *Bhakti* Movementin Catholic Church

As of 2018, the Catholic Charismatic Renewal exists in over 230 countries in the world. The Charismatic element of the Church is seen as being evident today as it was in the early days of Christianity. Some Catholic Charismatic communities (Vincentian Congregation, IMS, Capuchins, diocesan priests) conduct healing services, gospel power services, outreaches and evangelizations where the presence of the Holy Spirit is believed to be felt, and healings and miracles are said to take place. The mission of the Catholic Charismatic Renewal is to educate believers into the totality of the declaration of the gospels. This is done by a personal relationship with Jesus Christ; a one-to-one relationship with Jesus is seen as a possibility by the Charismatic. He is encouraged to talk to Jesus directly and search for what The Lord is saying so that his life will be one with Him; to walk in the Fruit of the Spirit in (Gal 5:22-23). This is what the Charismatic understands by giving their life to Jesus. Conscience is seen as an alternative voice of Jesus Christ.[20]

2.4.3 The Results of *Bhakti* (Charismatic) Movement

The results of the *Bhakti* movement are far-reaching. First and the foremost result was that it minimized the differences and distinctions between the Hindus and the Muslims. The people of one religion tried to understand the

19 C.J. Kuttiyanikkal, *Khrist Bhakta Movement: A Model for an Indian Church? Inculturation in the Area of Community Building* (Berlin: LIT Verlag, 2014), 253.

20 Bhattacharyya, *Medieval Bhakti Movements in India*, 87.

people of other religion. Secondly, the caste system gradually lost its previous importance as the *Bhakti* preachers disregarded it. Thirdly, the spiritual life of the people became very simple and more developed than before. Lastly, the movement had tremendous impact on the literature and language of the country. It helped the regional languages to get enriched in spreading the cult of Radha and Krishna. *Bhakti* Literature was produced in plenty in different regional languages. And this *Bhakti* movement has lasting influence on the people of India and outside. Even Akbar the great, was greatly influenced by the *Bhakti* and Sufi Philosophers, which made him follow a secular strand in the field of religion.[21]

2.5 Critical Appraisal, Praxis and Conclusion

Loving devotion gives the devotee a greater and more valuable knowledge of the Lord than any intellectual process of meditation or reflection.[22] All the *Bhakti* Movements in one way or other highlighted five major beliefs as its pivotal principles. They taught that God is One (*Ekam Sat)* and therefore shall not be any barrier for worship. It insisted that worshipping God with devotion is better than performing religious ceremonies. The nature of *Bhakti* is absolute love for God; *Bhakti* is supreme attachment to the Lord.[23] To worship God, man must serve without considering humility. The idea of Equality

Presently we are passing through an era of growing intolerance in society, for various reasons, resulting in 'Honor killings', disrespect towards women, abandonment of the girl child, growing caste discrimination, polarisation of society, based on religion, affecting the national peace. And ultimately, the intolerance in the 'Art of living' is causing increase of greed, leading to massive corruption in section of the society. We have become very selfish towards each other, instead of thinking for others; we only bother for self only.

The *Bhakti* movement encouraged the devotees, to keep aside the age old traditions of rituals and castes and only to express their love for god. The *Bhakti* Movements had great countercultural and positive impact on the Society, with the flowering fort of new religious and cultural vision, with a broad spiritual and mystical outlook. Due to the *Bhakti* Movement, India was enriched with a rich collection of literature of spirituality, faith and devotional hymns. *Bhakti* also promoted the growth of the popular religiosity, and through it, vernacular prose and poetry.

---

21 Cheramthuruthy, *Contemporary Indian Thought*, 153.

22 De Smet and J Neunner, ed., *Religious Hinduism* (Bombay: St Paul's Publications, 1997), 305.

23 See: Narada Bhakti, *Sutra 2: Sadilya Sutra*, 1.1.2.

14

Gandhian Movement for Women's Liberation in India

Bishop Lawrence Pius D.D.
Bishop of Dharmapuri Diocese in Tamil Nadu

Abstract: Unlike many who wrote and worked with the principle of sexual equality in mind, Gandhi sought to bring about a revolutionary change in the status of women in the first half of 20th century. He was pained at the oppressed status of women. His inspiring women personalities were taken from Hinduism namely Sita, Draupadi, etc. Liberation of women has to start with the family, with woman claiming "complete right over her body". Marriage should not be just for sensual enjoyment. He condemns strongly child marriage, purdah, dowry, prostitution and the devadasi system. Widow remarriage and sanctity of womanhood should be upheld. Liberation of women does not lie merely at the family level. Women education should be given top priority for social and national service. This should include also rural women. Men and women should accept responsibilities at the national level although women should play a complementary role. Equality means upholding the rights of women although it may not imply equality of occupation.

Keywords: Dharma, Gandhi, Movement, Praxis, Women, Politics, Beauty, Dowry, Education of, Equality of, Exploitation of, Legislature, Liberation of, Marriage, Poverty, Problems of, Purdah, Sanctity of, Urban/Rural, Widows, Remarriage of

Introduction

A close reading of Gandhi's life would explicate how Gandhi integrated moral principles and philosophical ideologies meticulously. It is a philosophy in praxis as he firmly believed that theory cannot be divorced from practice.[1]

Undoubtedly Gandhi transcended all his contemporaries and to a great extent he became successful in conscientizing the big masses of India especially the women folk, who were enslaved by superstition and immorality, which eclipsed their social and personal conscience. Before the advent of Gandhi, the attitude towards women, though sometimes sympathetic, was patronizing. But for Gandhi woman was the source of insurmountable power and if they came together they could display such a heroic non-violence as to kick away the atom bomb like a mere ball.[2]

Social Movements in India have been classified into nine categories based on the participants and issues involved: peasants, tribals, dalits, backward castes, women, students, middle class, working class, and human rights and environmental groups.[3]

Here an attempt is made to study Gandhi's initiatives as well as his views on women's movement which helped to free them from the numerous injustices wrought against them by tradition. More than that our concern here is to explicate the principles that underlie his movement for changing the condition of women in India.

My paper will consist of three parts: (1) Women's status in the past Indian society (2) The various instances of Gandhi's movement towards freedom of women (3) Gandhian Approach to Women's liberation

PART I

1. Women's Status in Indian Society in the Past

Women and Harijans were rightly seen by Gandhi as the two most depressed sections of society. The significance of Gandhian movement for women lies in its attempt to uplift them from the then socio-political, cultural and economic malaise. Gandhi's effort will be grasped better when projected against the societal background of his times. The social framework, social structures, cultural norms and value systems influenced the social status of men and

---

1 Shoba Raguram, "A Critical Appraisal of Gandhi's Views on Women," in *Gandhi and Social Action Today*, ed., Mercy Kappen (Bangalore: Sterling, 1990), 57.

2 Joseph Raj A," Ceaseless Crusader," in *Prose*, ed., Swaminatha Pillai (Chennai: Tamil Nadu Text Book, 2018), 50.

3 Ghanshyam Shah, *Social Movements in India: A Review of Literature*, 2nd and enlarged edition, (New Delhi: Sage Publications, 2004).

women. Exploitation of women, vulnerability, economic disability, Poverty, Violence, Educational Deprivation and Enforced Widowhood[4] are some of the areas where the consequences of the oppression of women were greatly felt.

A. Exploitation of Women

Women were victims of humiliation, torture and exploitation. Rape, murder, dowry, burning, wife beating and discrimination in the socio-economic and educational fields were the abominable crimes the society inflicted on them. Indian male chauvinistim exploited women in every sphere of their being.

Women were considered to be the primary under-dogs of an exploitative society. Women did more hazardous manual labour than men. Yet men were considered to be the "bread winners". These genes of slavery were passed on to succeeding generations.[5]

The most widespread and dehumanizing discriminating assault was done against women at the psychological level, at her childhood. She had been taught to be docile and subservient. Usually baby girls were given bangles, anklets etc. thus communicating to them a sense of fragility. Moreover a woman's value was judged, not in terms of her worth as a person with rights and dignity as in terms of her utility to man.[6]

B. The Vulnerability of Rural Women

When compared with women in cities and towns the condition of women was more miserable in rural India with respect to various socio-economic aspects.

Poverty was the identity of India and the worst afflicted were women. Better health care and higher educational opportunities were farfetched dreams. A woman was treated as a "silent lamb" born to suffer all evils.[7] The misogynistic society had a preference for the male child. Sons were regarded as social security while daughters were considered a liability. Women were paid half or three-quarters of the money which their male counterparts earned for the same job. In India, a predominantly agricultural country, women had been doing more than half of the total agricultural work and worked for 15 to 16 hours a day, unpaid at home and underpaid outside.

4 Shah, 1. This does not mean that the situation has changed substantially today.

5 Ibid.

6 Shodhganga: A Reservoir of Indian Theses, Jawaharlal Nehru University http://shodhganga.inflibitnet.ac.in/bitstream/10603/8562/707/chapter%202.pdf.2.

7 Ibid., 8.

PART II

Gandhian Movement for Women's Liberation

A. Characteristics of a Women's Movement

Though there are many women Movements, there are certain characteristics which define the viability of a movement.

1. The members should aspire to bring new legislations or to bring changes in the legislations to give justice to women and control violence.
2. They should demand implementation of the legislations meant for women and avoid the misuse of the power conferred by implementation
3. The movement should nurture the level of consciousness of women of different strata of the society. It should lead the women to take up self analysis of every individual member in such a way that she enjoys the fruit of the movement and is motivated to move ahead.[8]

B. Preliminary Notions on Gandhian Movement for Women's Liberation

Gandhi had a far and wide experience in leading several Movements in South Africa where he fought against the evil forces of discrimination based on colour and origin of the citizens. His protest against the government on aborting the validity of marriages other than the Christian marriages evoked a positive response from every quarter of the land i.e., from the natives, the whites and the Indians.

His weapon of *Satyagraha* (non-violence) made the government to finally yield. As he persuaded women to join the *Satyagraha* struggle along with their husbands, to his great surprise, they were all glad to enter the struggle, despite the fact that one of them was pregnant and six of them had young babies in arms. Women's imprisonment worked like a charm upon the mine-labourers near Newcastle and other places. When they all joined the strike, it finally contributed to the success of the *Dharma-yuddh*a in South Africa.[9]

It is very important to note that Gandhi had been striving to bulldoze all the social evils done against women one by one. He wanted women to get liberated from every form of slavery, so he employed all his potential skills to banish the evils as well. We shall discuss the problems pertaining to women one by one.

---

8 Shah, 2-3.

9 Pushparajan A, "Gandhi's Approach to Women's Liberation," *Journal of Dharma* Vol. XIII, no.1 (1988), 41.

1. Women's Problems

According to Gandhi, male domination was the primary element which must be addressed. He understood that legislations were done mostly by men and so they should be revisited at their origin.

Moreover it was the women themselves who contributed to their own degenerated status. They were believing that they were inferior and accepted to be subservient in many ways. Yet the seers among men recognized the equal status of women with men.[10] Man regarded woman as his plaything and she found it to be easy and pleasurable to be such, because when one drags another in his fall the descent is easy.[11] Gandhi argues, "Woman is not helpless, she must never regard herself as weaker than men. She should not therefore, beg for any man's mercy nor depend upon him."[12]

2. Gandhi's Solutions to the Specific Problems of Women in India

The root cause of women's slavery is the male domination and her refusal to accept her own nobility. These could be rooted out only when she learns that she has equal status with man. The specific problems pertaining to women are enlisted in the following passages.

a) Poverty

While speaking to the woman who did not have alternative dress to wear, Gandhi decided to bring economic autonomy to women and to do so, *khadi* would serve as the powerful instrument that would promise livelihood and a dignified dress. He claimed that it would serve as a livelihood for the poorest and a loving companion for the educated and well-to-do women. *Khadi* served as a call for a paradigm shift in the understanding and dignity of women in society.[13]

b) Deliverance from the Child Marriage

Regarding child marriage, Gandhi observed: "It is a pernicious system of marriage. They are *ab initio* null and void and as such no marriage."[14] To Gandhi, child marriage is an abuse of womanhood. "It is irreligion and it is not religion to give religious sanction to a brutal custom and by doing so we recede from God as well as swaraj." When woman's marriage age was fixed to be 14 by '*Sarada* Act' he personally wanted it to be raised to 16 or even 18.

10 Pushparajan, "Gandhi's Approach to Women's Liberation," 52.

11 Ibid.

12 *Anand* T Hingorani and Ganga A. HIngorani, "Woman," *The Encyclopedia of Gandhian Thoughts*, (New Delhi: Sh. Jitendira Prasadam, 1983), 377.

13 Pushparajan,"Gandhi's Approach to Women's Liberation," 41.

14 T.D. Kirupalani, *Gandhi – His Life and Thought* (Faridabad: R K Jain, 1970), 393.

The authenticity of the texts that promote child marriage, the *Smriti,* must be questioned.[15] It is undiluted animalism. Further, he believed that child marriage should be totally wiped out of our society and it could be done not by mere legislation but by enlightened public opinion of the parents.

When they become adults, child widows should be allowed to remarry with all their freedom, without any odium. Gandhi queried: "Marriage is a sacrament. If it is a symbol of pure love, then marrying children and ill matched partners cannot be considered a sin?"[16] He reiterated that by not countenancing such customs, we would recede from God as well as "*Swaraj.*"[17]

c) Remarriage of Widows

Perpetual widowhood cannot be enforced on widows.[18] The widows lived in seclusion and in big danger of being exploited. They were disrespected and despised at home and in society and it was the unwritten law that they should carry a mark that would be easy for anyone to find their identity. To such a superstitious anomaly Gandhi would say that widows need not have any external marks. Thus his opinion was grounded only in natural justice and not in the immortality of the soul.[19] He conscientized the false protectors of religion and insisted: "We cry out for cow protection in the name of religion but refuse protection to human cow in the shape of girl widow."[20]

He recommended that every widow had much right to remarry as every widower. Voluntary widowhood was a priceless boon in Hinduism and enforced widowhood was a curse.[21] For those who could not have control their passions he advised them that it would be better to marry rather than to sin in secret.[22]

d) *Devadasi* System

Gandhi was against the age old system of *Devadasi*. It was the other form of legalized prostitution, he believed. He appealed to the people: "Let the Indian men ponder over the fate of the thousands of sisters who are destined to a life of shame for this unlawful and immoral indulgence."[23] He denounced the men who contracted a relationship with them and urged that it was unlawful

15 S.R. Bakshi, *Gandhi and His Social Struggle* (New Delhi: Print India, 1986), 177.

16 Pushpa Joshi, *Gandhi on Women* (Ahamedabad: Navajeevan, 1988), 39.

17 K.S. Bharathi, *Socio Religious Thought of Gandhi* (Nagpur: Dattsons, 1989), 153.

18 Manmohan Choudhdri, *Exploring Gandhi* (New Delhi: Gandhi Peace,1989), 224.

19 Choudhdri, *Exploring Gandhi*, 223.

20 Mercy Kappen, "The Gandhian Contribution to Woman's Liberation," in *Gandhi and Social Action Today*, ed., Mercy Kappen (Bangalore: Sterling, 1990), 43.

21 Ibid., 154.

22 Madhu Kishwar, "Gandhi on Women," in *Debating Gandhi: A Reader*, ed., A. Raghuramaraju, (New Delhi: Manushi, 1985), 312.

23 Pushparajan, "Gandhi's Approach to Women's Liberation," 46.

and a sin against their own wives. He requested them to "refrain from making them objects of their lust. Secondly let everyone join in the crusade against the existence of this system."[24] However, he maintained that these devadasis could not marry.[25]

e) Loss of Authority

Gandhi, in the male chauvinistic society of India, maintained: "Ultimately woman will have to determine with authority what she needs. She must muster enough courage to denounce being dominated and to do what she thinks right."[26] He set a role model in that he never abused the service attitude of *Kasturba* his beloved wife. In the question about untouchability, he never imposed his power that his wife should give them the same treatment as he gave. He respected her freedom to its greatest measure. Gandhi the patriarch was confident that he would never abuse authority and trust vested in him.

f) *Purdha*

Gandhi detested the practice of *purdha* system in India. A religious script that forces women to wear *purdha* would not be a genuine text but an interpolated one, he believed. For the Hindu religion, the time when the women were compelled to wear *purdha* was the time of decline of its glory.[27] Chastity could not be contained by *purdha,* he staunchly believed. For him "Chastity is not a hot house growth, it can't be imposed, it cannot be protected by the surrounding wall of the *purdhas*, and it must be capable of withstanding every unsought temptation."[28] He basically asks a question why fear had taken hold of most of us that we could not look at woman without evil thoughts.[29]

g) Dowry

Dowry would be an inhuman way of treating women and it is a heartless custom. The scapegoats were the women. So he observed that this "insidious discrimination done against the female sex is an anachronism."[30] He strongly advocated that those who practiced dowry should be excommunicated from society. However it cannot be wiped away from the society at once but only by employing pedagogical ways could we help out the situation.

24 Kishwar, "Gandhi on Women,"133.

25 Pushaprajan, "Gandhi's Approach to Women's Liberation," 47.

26 Kappen, "The Gandhian Contribution to Woman's Liberation," 48.

27 Bharathi, *Socio Religious Thought of Gandhi*, 153.

28 Kirupalani, *Gandhi – His Life and Thought*, 394.

29 Kappen, "The Gandhian Contribution to Woman's Liberation," 222.

30 Kirupalani, *Gandhi – His Life and Thought*, 394.

PART III

Gandhi's Approach towards Women's Movement

Gandhi's uniqueness lies not only in tackling the different issues regarding women, but in attacking the basic problem underlying those issues and suggesting a fundamental solution to the same. He distinguished himself from all his pioneers concerning women's liberation. Whereas the former ones wanted "liberation from", Gandhi wanted "liberation for". Gandhi had a prophetic[31] thrust by which he denounced some elements and advocated some.[32]

1. The Problem

Gandhi, after his very long experiments with his life situations discovered that the most important problem to be addressed was the problem of inequality between the genders. He understood that it would be not possible for any single person to win but collectively it was a possibility. Therefore he urged all the members of his women movement to understand the problem and grasp their own worth.

2. Towards a Solution

a. Equality

Although, through *Varnanshrama* he believed in the stratification of society,[33] he maintained the equality of women to men. Being created by God as Christianity believes, Hinduism puts it in a different way: "All beings arise from Him, live in him and are absorbed in Him."[34] If this was true, then all that is created i.e., men and women also must be equal. Most of the problems arise due to lack of this sense of equality, he believed. He said, "To call woman a weaker sex is a libel. It is injustice done to woman."[35] In his words: "Just as is fundamentally man and woman are one, their problems must be one in essence. The soul in both is the same. The two live for the same life, have the same feelings. Each is complement of the other. The one cannot live without the other's active help."[36] He called upon men to understand the essence of

31 Samul Rayan, "Gandhi: Selected Writings of Samuel Rayan," in *Spirit and Truth, India Christian Reflections on Sprituality and Worship,* ed., Kurien Kunnumpuram (Mumbai: St Paul's, 2012), 210.

32 Pushparajan, "Gandhi's Approach to Women's Liberation," 51.

33 Richards, *Philosophy of Gandhi* (London: Curzon, 1982), 84.

34 Dr. Chandaradhar Sharma, *Critical Survey of Indian Philosophy* (Delhi: Motilal Banarsidass, 1987), 57.

35 Hingorani, "Woman," 377.

36 Hingorani, "Woman," 208.

woman and treat them equally instead of looking lowly at the women as an object of play or lust.

Men and women are a peerless pair being complement to one another. Equality should never be understood in physical terms but in a spiritual sense. Woman will not make her contribution to the world by mimicking or running a race with men.[37] He believed that woman would occupy her proud position by the side of man as his mother, sister and silent leader.[38]

b. Real Beauty

Gandhi wanted to do away with the awe for external beauty and beauty that was offered by ornaments. He instructed women that men had taught them the ways of dressing, behaving which might please them. Woman had not seen in all that her slavery and her degradation. "Real beauty is of the heart."[39] He added: "Grace of woman lies in her character and modesty."[40] He further observed: "Woman is nothing if she is not self-sacrifice and purity personified."[41] Thus, Gandhi was able to connect her most beautiful element of purity with self-sacrifice so that she might consider both as the two sides of the same coin.

c. Marriage

Gandhi subscribed for a simple ritual-free marriage which he christened as "Gandhi *Lagan*". On coercion, he was bold enough to say, "No society or relatives of the parties concerned have any right to impose their will upon them who may contract the marriage."[42] He adds: "If society fails to recognize the marriage of the people who rightly agree among themselves, then it should be the height of tyranny to drive them to suicide.[43] We know that till this date this sort of tyranny continues in different parts of the nation.

In ancient India, *Manushutra* declared that a woman must do whatever the husband asks her to do whether that be in accordance with "*dharma*" or opposed to it. But, Gandhi rewrote the understanding between the parties in a different way. The husband is not a "guru" or "god" and the marriage bond should be built on mutual fidelity.[44] He lamented that "men have condemned themselves to be the lords and masters of women instead of considering them

37 Bharathi, *Socio Religious Thought of Gandhi*, 157.

38 Kirupalani, *Gandhi – His Life and Thought*, 396.

39 Kishwar, "Gandhi on Women," 211.

40 Priya Ranjan, "Mahatma Gandhi's Concept of Women," *in Nari: Facets of Indian Womanhood,* ed., CM Aarwal (Delhi: SK Garg, 2000), 13.

41 Hingorani, "Woman," 376.

42 Nirmal Kumar Rose, *Selections from Gandhi* (Ahmedabad: Navjeevan, 1972), 276.

43 Ibid.

44 Choudhdri, *Exploring Gandhi*, 231.

as their friends and co-workers. Woman is not a competitor of man or an inferior.... but only complementary to her male partner."[45]

The ideal marriage aims at "spiritual union" through the physical union. For Gandhi: "You are being united as friends and equals."[46] He concluded that man and woman should not come together unless there is openness for creating new life. However the parties should transcend their vocation for the cause of the nation.

d. Education

Gandhi insisted that illiteracy could not be a ground to underestimate women and their rights. He argued: "What is all the education worth if in marriage they are to become mere dolls for their husbands and permanently engaged in the task of rearing which could be meaningless."

Education is always liberative in nature. He wanted, by and large, that all women must be educated. He asserted that education is one of the sure ways to independence. As M Chidambaram says: *"It is the most effective tool for women's empowerment by enhancing their self-esteem and self-confidence."*[47]

The quality of education imparted to the girl children must be future oriented, Gandhi believed. Parents should make their sons and daughters self-reliant, well able to earn an honest livelihood by the sweat of the brow."[48]

e. Imitating the Inspiring Models

Gandhi was motivated by the fundamental metaphysical and religious purpose of life beliefs which he derived from the Hindu way of life.[49] He very often recalled the names and the characteristics of inspiring women viz., Sita, Damayanthi and Draupadi. These were shown as the models in order that a woman must be able to imitate them. One should give up the idea that one is helpless.[50]

Women should follow Draupadi because she showed how a woman could become self- reliant. Sita, Draupadi and Damayanthi must be imitated because they are prototypes of yore.[51]

---

45 Kirupalani, *Gandhi – His Life and Thought*, 146.

46 Ibid., 152.

47 Farzana Alim and Sameena Sultana, "Woman's Education and Empowerment,"*Woman's Link* 17, no. 2 (2003), 2-4.

48 Kishwar, "Gandhi on Women," 215.

49 Richards, *Philosophy of Gandhi*, 30.

50 Choudhri, *Exploring Gandhi*, 220.

51 Kishwar, "Gandhi on Women," 271-272.

f. The Sanctity of Womanhood

Women are custodians of all that is pure and religious in life.[52] The best means to attain the liberation of women is *Ahimsa*. They could be apostles of nonviolence in the world, better than men. In his own words: "Woman is the incarnation of Ahimsa. Ahimsa means infinite love, which again means infinite capacity for suffering. Who but woman, the mother of man, shows this capacity in the largest measure? Let her forget that she ever was or and can be the object of man's lust and she will occupy her proud position by the side of man as his mother, maker and silent leader."[53]

Gandhi wanted women to become the "sisters" of humanity by serving the poor and unfortunate. He created a new "horizon" where women could link their aspirations with the "national interest" He further legitimized the contribution of women in the development of the whole world. He believed that every Indian girl was not born to marry, but to serve and dedicate herself to service in the world. He added that women could stay unmarried and channelize their energy to involve in an altruistic way of living.[54]

3. The Remarkable Features of Gandhi's Approach to Women Movement

Being a charismatic leader, Gandhi was competent enough to put forth his real and exalted understanding of women. He was considered to be the messiah and champion of the oppressed women because he was able to discover the most precious element of their being, the soul force.

By the force of *satyagraha* he awoke the dormant conscience of women and so too men. He emphasized that women could render service to humanity by a higher level of living, not by coercion or just by mimicking men but by self-realization striving forward to self-actualization.

Because of Gandhi's movement, many legislations were enacted in the glorious history of nations and specifically India. His conscientizing program led to a chain reaction among women. After being enlightened, women were lighting the other women's candles of hope and courage and encouraged one another to create a new world which was ruled by the laws of *satyagraha* and *swadesi*.

52 Bharathi, *Socio Religious Thought of Gandhi*, 148.

53 Hingorani, "Woman," 376.

54 Kishwar, "Gandhi on Women," 278.

4. The Role of Gandhi's Women Movement in Different Areas

a. In *Swaraj*

On the significance of spinning *Khadi,* he would say, "The restoration of spinning to its central place in India's peaceful struggle for deliverance from the imperial yoke gives her women a special status." He told women: "The economic and the moral salvation of India rests mainly with you."[55]

b. Untouchability

It is another realm where women could contribute substantially, Gandhi thought. "If the Hindu heart is to be cured of the taint of untouchability, women must do the lion's share of the work." It involved not only the women as a group but individually also. He questioned: "Untouchable because they perform sanitary service? What mother has not performed such service for her children?"

However we know that his wife *Kastruriba* had not accepted the *Harijans* at her home. She took to *Satyagraha* against his views in silence. At the nearer end of her life of course she accepted to admit them in the *Ahsram*. That his convictions could not change the heart of his own wife can be said to be an irony.

c. The Salt Strategy

Gandhi's choice of salt as a symbol of protest made many wonder-struck. He made use of every chance that attracted women towards his movement. Salt serves as one of the best companions of women because she is the provider of food at home and every food item demands salt. So, as the protest started from Gandhi the women joined. It was headed by many women. The learned were in front but the whole *Dandi* march was marked by the participation of innumerable women across the country. "Woman volunteers carried *lottas* of water from the Chowpatty beach to make salt at home and many others went out onto the streets selling this contraband salt at fancy prices."[56]

We would not be able to avoid an important question, i.e., whether the women who participated were all enlightened. In point of fact only a few had understood the real meaning behind the *swaraj* and the objective of *Dandi* march whereas the majority of the women folk would not have understood the full implications. Further it was not that all the women were accepted to play a vital role in the struggle and at times we come to know that the struggle of ordinary and poor ladies who headed the long march against the imperialistic

55 Kishwar, "Gandhi on Women," 282.

56 Ibi., 292.

British were simply forgotten as it happened with *Kanthapura,* a village where the political struggle led by two widows was ignored.[57]

d. Picketing

Women and children were the immediate victims of alcoholism. Gandhi therefore appealed to the hearts of women to rise against the liquor shop owners and the manufactures. He made women to lead and said that "men should be in strict subordination to them."[58] Women played a prominent role in picketing toddy shops and booths and demonstrating against their owners. They boldly faced the *lathis*, molestation and many other hardships. However, women's involvement in the movement would lead to the neglect of household duties. To respond to Gandhi's call could well mean a break with one's family and very few did make the break.

e. Representation in the Legislatures

Systematic denial of the representation of women in the legislatures by the British was withdrawn as Gandhi jumped into politics. Nevertheless the sudden, massive entry into politics by women earned them representation in the political arena. With Gandhi's intervention free India had two women ministers in the new India Cabinet. He further reiterated that women must have votes and an equal legal status. But the problem does not end there. It only commences at the point where women begin to participate in the political deliberations of the nation.[59]

In 1931, the Congress party passed a resolution at its annual session in Karachi committing itself to the political equality of women, regardless of their status and qualifications. It is significant that at that time, women in most European countries had not yet won the right to vote, despite a much longer history of struggle on this issue.

However one cannot deny that women were in fact preferred by Gandhi himself for more peripheral roles only.

5. Critical Approach on Gandhian Women Movements

Apart from his influence and his call to participate in different demonstrations, Gandhi seemed to have some black spots too. Womens activity and discussion focused on spinning, wearing *khadi*, fund raising, enrolling new members, picketing and fitfully working for the removal of untouchability and for promotion of Hindu-Muslim unity. The role of women remained in the national movement as auxiliary and supportive. He described their contribution as

57 Kishwar,"Gandhi on Women," 23.

58 Ibid., 286.

59 Ibid., 288.

"the women were heroines whose "mute" work the nation will never know." They continued to play a supportive and nurturing role for the men in the movement.[60]

Gandhi's movement can be critically evaluated in two ways. Firstly and more accurately, one can ascertain that it was Gandhi who helped to loosen the traditional biases to such an extent that the rare exceptions among these women groups could stand up against any odds and assumed the power and responsibility equal to men. Concerning Congress, the women viz., Dr Annie Besant and Sarojini Devi already assumed the highest honorus in the party presidentship.

Secondly, though Gandhi did not come up with a manifesto for the downtrodden women, he succeeded in raising the question of their depressed condition as a moral question for society to reckon with. He made women to become aware of their saddened situation in the society and it served as an implicit call for a "self actualization" of all her potentials and capacities.[61]

6. Critical Aspects of Gandhi's Approach towards Women and Women Movements

Gandhi advocated that the women folk should do child rearing whereas men should earn the daily bread. Wile he could see clearly that women should be freed from slavery, he forgot to acknowledge the inherent interconnection between most forms of authority and injustice or between the enslavement of women and the denial of economic independence to them by keeping them confined to the household as their main sphere of activity. He failed to revise his concept of the natural division of labour between the sexes. He could not see this division as a part of the same self-interested teaching of man which had resulted in the confinement and subordination of woman.

His dual attitude of obedience and rebellion against authority is evident in every single movement of campaign he led and in the very philosophy of non-violent *Satyagraha*.

As he invited women to participate in public life to serve as "Sisters", simultaneously he wanted them to renounce married life but a little later he would call them to be *Sitas* and *Damayanthis*. More clearly he wanted them to come to public life but the status of being "married" should serve as the prerogative to be like Sita and Damayanthi. He seemed to contradict himself with his views.[62] While idealizing women as the people of capacity of silent suffering, should the women opt to subordinate themselves and suffer so that they may possess the quality of "silent suffering" forever? When Gandhi calls

60 Kishwar,"Gandhi on Women," 293.

61 Pushparjan, "Gandhi's Approach to Women's Liberation," 51-57.

62 Kishwar, "Gandhi on Women," 300.

them "sisters of mercy and mothers", doubts arise whether he wanted them to continue to act as moral guardians of society as social workers and do-gooders without competing with men in the sphere of power and politics because that would be a reversion to barbarity.

It is important to note that the women liberative movement remained successful to throw away the British Empire and some social evils in society by legislation. However, it was unfortunate that after obtaining freedom from the British, Gandhi himself could not act against many of the social evils either by legislation or by public opinion. It is a sad fact to note that even today the untouchables, including women, beg for concessions to get their participation in the decision making process validated and to realize their rights as well.

Conclusion

As regards women's liberation was Gandhi a reformist or revolutionary? There are reasons to say that he was both in some aspects.

Positively, Gandhi is one of the few leaders whose practice was far more radical than the words he used for describing it. Where Gandhi remains unsurpassed in terms of impact and influence even today is in the fact that in the national mainstream women acquired a new confidence, a new self-view, and a consciousness that they could themselves act against oppression. From passive objects, women could become active subjects or agents of reform not only of their own predicament but of the whole society.

Negatively, the participation of women in the freedom movement was limited both quantitatively and qualitatively. Particularly rural women could not enter the main stream of social and political action.

Further, because of Gandhi's influence, the All India Women's Conference in the 1930's decided not to belong to any political organization nor take active part in party politics.

Added to this Madhu Kishwar observes that Gandhi can be said to have seen the male and female in terms of the "active-passive" complementary which has been an important ideological device for denying women any chance to acquire power and decision-making ability in the family and in society.[63]

While harping on women's equality, Gandhi often gave them only a subordinate role. Again, as Madhu Kishwar points out, he encouraged "tokenism" at the very top without bringing about any real changes at the bottom.

In the ultimate analysis, it can be said that Gandhi was deeply concerned about women and their dignity and gave them an exalted status but finally ended up as a benevolent patriarch in his attitude towards women as he was often unable to look beyond their subordinate role vis-à-vis man.

63 Kishwar, "Gandhi on Women," 296.

15

The Chipko Movement and Its Aftermath: A Few Reflections Based on Environmental Philosophy

Gregory Mathew Malayil CMI
Dharmaram Vidya Kshetram, Bengaluru

Abstract: The Chipko movement, informally originated in Uttar Pradesh's Chamoli district (now in Uttarakhand) in 1973, aimed at conservation of forests in the Himalayan areas, spread over to other regions within no time and conscientized the society on the relevance of sustainable development. As a social and environmental movement, it influenced the governments in making special legislations to protect the environment. However, the Chipko movement was not a mere agitation with certain goals of achieving a few demands or abolishing certain practices. Though the very purpose of the movement might be economic in the beginning, later it became instrumental in forming the moral conscience of the individuals and groups, to provide due care for the environment. Gradually, its after-effects caused radical transformations in the attitude of the society; and environmental ethics became a major concern before any new endeavour in agriculture, forestry, constructions etc., being taken up. Apart from its role in educating the society about the intrinsic value of the environment and the rights and duties of human beings as citizens of the environment, the Chipko movement is unique and outstanding in its social concerns such as non-violence and women empowerment. Also, the Chipko prompts us to reflect on our moral obligations and to be aware of the environmental citizenship which we all are endowed with.

Keywords: The Chipko Movement, Environmental Philosophy, Women Empowerment, Ecological Citizenship, Ecological Conversion.

Introduction

The Chipko movement which is very unique among the environmental Movements in India has far reaching consequences in policy making and legislations related to environment. Apart from its impacts in the governmental as well as political levels, the Chipko influenced the society to form its collective moral conscience. The beginning of many other Movements in different regions of the nation attests this fact. This paper is a modest attempt to explore the contributions of the Chipko in transforming the environmental conscience of India. The Chipko being a social environmental movement, it would be helpful to have a conceptual clarity of the dynamics as well as the factors driving such Movements

Environmental movement is a type of "social movement that involves an array of individuals, groups and coalitions that perceive a common interest in environmental protection and act to bring about changes in environmental policies and practices."[1] The emergence and development of social movements depend on the dynamic interaction of three factors. i) The broader political constraints and opportunities unique to the national context in which they emerge. ii) The organizational resources, informal as well as formal which mobilize people into collective action and sustain a social movement. Resources may include pre-existing organizations, such as informal networks, voluntary associations, and religious groups. iii) The collective process of interpretation, attribution, and social construction which give meaning and value to collective action. By bringing shared meanings and definitions to their situation, people who feel aggrieved about some aspect of their lives can become more optimistic that, by acting collectively, they can redress their problem.[2]

Environmental Movement: Definitions

The environmental Movements are conceived as broad networks of people and organizations engaged in collective action in the pursuit of environmental benefits.[3] They are understood to be very diverse and complex, such as their organizational forms ranging from the highly organized and formally institutionalized to the radically informal, the spatial scope of their activities ranging from the local to the almost global, the nature of their concerns ranging from single issue to the full panoply of global environmental concerns. Such an inclusive conception is consistent with the usage of the term amongst

1 Yanki Tong, "Environmental Movements in Transitional Societies: A Comparative Study of Taiwan and China," *Comparative Politics* 37, (2005), 167-168.

2 Ibid., 169-170

3 Christopher Rootes, "Environmental Movements: From the Local to the Global," *Environmental Politics* 8, (1999), 1-12.

environmental activists themselves and enables us to consider the linkages between the several levels and forms of what activists call the environmental movement.[4]

The collective action can be at three levels: i) the local grassroots movement level; ii) the social movement level; and iii) a cycle of protest.[5] A Local Grassroots Environmental Movement (LGEM) as a movement, is to fight against a particular instance of pollution in a geographically specified region. LGEMs have a limited range of goals that are tied to specific pollution problems. The identification of each level of movement activity is critical to understanding the political environment in which an LGEM operates.[6]

Old and New Movements

The social movements may be classified as old and new according to Luke Martell.[7] Old social movements are associated to political parties and political hierarchies. Any new social movement including the environmental movement has a dual aspect: a general aspect and a particular aspect.[8] Padam Nepal argues that the new social movements in India emerged because of the failure of the established oppositional forces in India's national politics, in giving direction and care to the subaltern and marginal groups.[9]

The environmental Movements that are characterized by the features of both old and new social movements have been critically described by Luke Martell.[10] The features of environmental Movements that fit them in the category of 'New' Social Movement include: i) non-hierarchical forms of organization in their movement, playing down the role of hierarchy of leaders. ii) Grass roots based decentralized form of participation. Major features of 'Old' Movements include: i) The concern to get politicians as the associates. Politicians also would be interested in such collabouration as it may facilitate their march to power. ii) The view that formal leadership structures and hierarchies are the most effective way to pursue political change. Some scholars categorizes environmental Movements under various labels such as

4 Christopher Rootes, "Environmental Movements: From the Local to the Global," *Environmental Politics* 8, (1999), 2.

5 Paul Almeida and Linda Brewster Stearns, "Political Opportunities and Local Grassroots Environmental Movements: The Case of Minamata," *Social Problems* 45, (1998), 37-60.

6 Ibid., 38.

7 Luke Martell, *Ecology and Society: An Introduction* (Cambridge: Polity Press, 1995), 112-114.

8 Ibid.

9 Padam Nepal, *Environmental Movements in India: Politics of Dynamism and Transformations* (Delhi: Authors Press, 2009), 98.

10 Martell, *Ecology and Society: An Introduction,* 114.

'tribal or peasants movement' or 'new social movements', some even title them as 'middle class' or 'elitist Movements.'[11]

Significance of Local Environmental Movements

According to Christopher Rootes,[12] local environmental campaigns are ubiquitous and recurrent, even in times when environmental issues were not significant on national agenda. Yet their relationship to trans-local environmental Movements and issues has been relatively neglected. Local environmental campaigns are related to national and local organizations in different ways, and at least one factor that would vary be certain special issues of the concerned locality. The relationship between local campaigns and global environmental issues is problematic, but the ways in which local mobilizations often combine issues of environment, economic justice and democracy, mirror the emerging agenda of trans-national environmentalism.[13] Environmental Movements in India, mostly were initiated centering on dams, displacement and rehabilitation. These Movements in general, effectively registered their protest against the forces and agencies whose actions had affected the environmental balance adversely. Further, the issues raised by the actors of the ecology and environment movement suggest that the ecology movement is not a mere exercise in romanticism nor a movement relating to food, fodder and fuel alone. In India it is also seen that the ethnic practice of worshipping planets, trees, forest, and rivers reflects the natural and social domains and the wisdom of seeing unity in the living and the non-living world in the Indian tradition.

Environmental Movements can contribute to development and in India we have a good number of models. Along with the *Chipko*, Save the Bhagirathi and Stop Tehri project,[14] Save the Narmada Movement, the Appiko movement in the Western Ghats; the campaign against the Silent Valley Project; and the opposition to the Gumti Dam in Tripura, to mention a few.

The Chipko Movement: Background and Objectives

Chipko Movement, started in April, 1973 at Mandal of Chamoli district of Gharwal division of Uttar Pradesh, was raised out of ecological destabilization

---

11 Ratna Reddy V, "Environmental Movements in India: Some Reflections," *Journal of Indian School of Political Economy* 10, (1998), 685-695.

12 Christopher Rootes, "Acting Locally: The Character, Contexts and Significance of Local Environmental Mobilisations," *Environmental Politics* 16, (2007), 722-741.

13 *Ibid.*

14 B. Manu, "Between Two Sacred Rivers, Tehri Dam Project," *India Magazine* 4, (1984), 44-51.

in the hills.[15] The fall in the productivity in forest produces forced the hill dwellers to depend on the market which became a central concern for the inhabitants. The continuous natural distress like flood, and land slide due to Alakananda river and many other devastations adversely affected the ecological balance of the region. Reasonably it could be assumed that such natural calamities were consequences of over mining of forest resources in different time periods.

In 1973, the State Forest Department gave a lease of forest trees to Simon Company, a manufacturer of sporting goods from far off Allahabad.[16] The relationship between the erosion and floods and mass scale felling of trees - was already recognized. Decision was taken to *Chipko* that is 'to hug' the trees that were threatened by axe, and that was the beginning of the *Chipko* Movement. This movement has multifaceted conflicts over forest resources, at the scientific, technical, economic, and, especially, the ecological levels.[17] Major demands of the *Chipko* were not merely to protect timber, fuel, fodder and small slumber but the preservation of soil and water. The primary objectives of the *Chipko* Movement were to ensure an ecological balance and the survival of the tribal people, whose life was totally revolving around these forests. Public meetings were held in the region and the felling of trees by the company was stopped. In initial days villagers were lured by the company but failed to attract them. In 1974 Sunderlal Bahuguna the '*Chipko* Messenger' visited the entire region taking the *Chipko* message from village to village. In subsequent period the local people did not allow anyone for cutting trees even for home industries. Thus, one finds a change in the Chipko, from economic to ecological. It has been successful in forcing a fifteen year ban on commercial green felling in the hills of Uttar Pradesh and generated pressure for a national forest policy that is ecologically more sensitive. Women were very active and came out of their homes to take lead in the movement.

Although, the *Chipko* Movement is now practically non-existent in its region of origin, it remains as one of the most frequently deployed examples of an environmental and an eco-feminine movement. A great number of books, articles and research papers have appeared on the *Chipko*, in the years since the movement began.[18] This large quantum of literature on the *Chipko*, indicates

15 Jeffrey Haynes, *Politics in the Developing World: A Concise Introduction* (New Jersey: Wiley Blackwell, 2002), 229.

16 Mishra, A and S. Tripathy, *Chipko Movement: Uttarakhand Women's Bid to Save Forest Wealth* (New Delhi: Gandhi Peace Foundation, 1978).

17 Vandana Shiva and J. Bandopadhyay, "The Evolution, Structure and Impact of the Chipko Movement," *Mountain Research and Development* 6, (1986), 133-142.

18 Sya Kedzior, "A Political Ecology of the Chipko Movement," A Master's Thesis submitted to University of Kentucky, April 2004, accessed September 10, 2018, https://uknowledge.uky.edu/cgi/viewcontent.cgi.

that most of the aspects of the movement have already been explored. One can learn several lasting lessons from the *Chipko*. This paper tries to analyse the *Chipko*, not just as an event that happened at some point of time at certain geographical locations, but as the enkindling of thoughts and reflections on environmental philosophy, though not sparked consciously, that which would transform the society beyond the immediate goals of the movement.

Certain Unique Features and Important Insights

The movement made people conscious of the value of the forest, its preservation and the need for maintaining ecological balance. The movement has established the importance of the need-oriented programmes, indigenous strategies, self-reliance and structural changes that resulted in high degree of people's participation with the help of appropriate small scale technologies. To a certain extent the *Chipko* put an end to the exploitation of resources of forests and the development process biased in favour of the urban industrial complex and against local needs. The philosophies of the movement has spread beyond Uttarakhand hills and linked to many social activists. The Chipko could go beyond the social and cultural boundaries. It caused to unite people irrespective of their caste, ethnic and financial status, political ideologies, gender and age groups. Among the various features, the eco-feminism or women empowerment and non-violence are remarkably outstanding.

Women Empowerment

Chipko movement offered women a platform to realise command over public power and authority. Women who were treated as a weaker section of the society took the lead, both as leaders and the participants in the Chipko. The experiment could make people believe that participation of women in the development process can be achieved by an ideological commitment and with certain organizational methodology.[19] Like independence movement of India, people of all stages, viz., children, youth, adults, old and students, all sacrificed ambitions of their life and took part in taking ahead the concepts and the processes of the Chipko movement. It was experienced that the Western model of development reflected in the form of large scale infrastructure, have marginalized the women to the level of labour delivering products. But, the *Chipko* Movement proved that women who produce all subsistence goods can maintain the *status quo* by retaining the traditional eco-system. The women were aware that conservation of forest was their only source of living and survival. New ecological concepts were brought through this movement that made women to grasp these issues which were earlier controlled by their male

19 S. Jain, "Women and People's Ecological Movement: A Case Study of Women's Role in the Chipko Movement in Uttar Pradesh," *Economic and Political Weekly* 19, (1984), 1788-1794.

counterparts. This has resulted in various changes in the gender relations in rural Gharwal region in performing the household and social responsibility. The new concept of ecological challenges became more concerned for the women.[20]

Non-Violence

In all the Movements, it has been observed that the people adopted the Gandhian ideology of non-violence. These Movements have established the fact that common property regimes of the people play crucial roles in the daily subsistence activities of poor peasants in India. All these issue are being debated at local, national and international levels, where social scientists are playing central role in debates at various levels, including national and international levels. Concrete convictions in non-violence, cooperation and self-help, helped the *Chipko* Movement to move forward. Further, it was a fact that women who were away from the intricacies of public power and political activities genuinely believed in the ideas of cooperation and self-help. The principle of non-violence as a natural and more effective weapon imposed on people as a moral pressure helped them considerably to make the *Chipko* Movement a grand success.

Advanced Technology in Data Collection

Though, not a direct impact or consequence of the Chipko, this aspect cannot be ignored. A few methods, for example, satellite imagery, both synchronically and diachronically, were used to identify ecological hot spots, by multi-disciplinary teams.[21] The Geographical Information System (GIS) studied the micro situations relating to human and environmental features. The anthropological perspective would be different and adaptable to the local specificity with respect to the ecological and cultural diversities.[22]

Beyond the Chipko

Environmental Movements are not an end in themselves and so too, with the Chipko. Of course any environmental movement begins with practical, localized and concrete issues, which may usually tamper the sustainable development. Solving the local issue alone is not the soul of the Movements.

---

20 S. Jain, "Women and People's Ecological Movement: A Case Study of Women's Role in the Chipko Movement in Uttar Pradesh," *Economic and Political Weekly* 19, (1984), 1788-1794.

21 Conrad Kottak P and E Colson. "Multilevel Linkages: Longitudinal and Comparative Studies," in Assessing Cultural Anthropology, ed. Robert Borofsky (New York: McGraw Hill, 1994), 396-412.

22 Glen Green M and Robert W Sussman, "Deforestation History of the Eastern Rain Forests of Madagaskar from Satellite Images," *Science* 248, (1990), 212-215.

Any movement passes on certain messages to the society, and any movement will bring certain values and awareness to the community at large. The problem may be a temporal or physical or economic with a mix of culture. But, the aftermath of the issue has many more points to make. How far that awareness is subsequently conveyed is very important. The uniqueness of forests in ecological balance, our moral obligation to protect the environment, the concept of ecological or environmental citizenship, and the ecological conversion that we need to undergo as Pope Francis presents in *Laudato Si* are certain relevant themes in the aftermath of the Chipko. Reflections on the said themes would provide the ongoing and dynamic message perpetuated by the Chipko, and the reflections would be considered as part of environmental philosophy as well as environmental ethics.

Forests as Means of Environmentally Sustainable Development

In the context of the Chipko movement, it would be very meaningful to have an understating of the resourcefulness and uniqueness of forests as a component of our ecosystem. Forests constitute a very precious, renewable natural resource and an important component of the ecosystem. Unsustainable developmental process have been reflected through, deforestation, reduction in forest cover and ultimate desertification in many areas.[23] Multi-pronged pressures have been exerted on the forest ecosystem through growing population, cattle grazing, fuel and fodder collection, industry and forest fires. These amply demonstrate the impact of unsustainable development on forests. As regards India, forest cover is estimated to be only 11% and the desirable forest area should be 33% of the total land area (as specified by the national Forest Policy). It may be stated that till the late 1970s forests were targeted for resettlements, agriculture and industrialization. Such a trend was considerably checked by the forest conservation act of 1980. Of late, however there has been the emergence of wide scale consensus on the ill effects of deforestation and hence policies are being adopted at all levels for restoration of this precious resource. The importance of forests in sustaining various species of life, both plants and animals, and thereby maintaining bio-diversity is unquestionable. Steps are also being taken in the direction of promoting afforestation and increasing the area under forests. Forest cover may be increased by: i) improving canopy cover in the forest land ii) undertaking large scale afforestation, particularly in the non-forest and degraded lands. Although, steps taken in this direction have yielded positive results, we are yet to achieve the desired extent of forest cover or afforestation. An enhanced awareness of the issues would do much in this respect.

---

23 Raj Kumar Sen, Amit Mukherjee and Pran Krisna Pal, *Environment and Sustainable Development in India* (New Delhi: Deep and Deep Publications Pvt. Ltd., 2010), 195.

Moral Obligation

In a broader sense, environment may be defined as everything that envelopes me. It is the natural world in which people, animals and plants live. The study of environment is confined to the system of interacting living and non-living components. The philosophical question involves the moral question: why is it morally wrong to pollute and to destroy the environment? If that is wrong, is it simply because a sustainable environment is essential to human well-being? Or is such behaviour also wrong because the natural environment and its denizens have certain values in their own right which ought to be respected and protected?[24] The distinction between instrumental value and intrinsic value is of central importance in answering these questions. Instrumental value is the value that the things have in virtue of being a means or instrument to service some other ends. Intrinsic value in the sense of non-instrumental value is the value that things have as ends in themselves, that is in their own right and regardless of whether they are useful as means to other ends.[25] The forest and products related to it had an instrumental value in the life of the people of the Uttarakhand hills and no doubt that concern prompted them to hug the trees from felling down. People who initiated the *Chipko Andolan* might not be aware of the intrinsic value of the forest in itself. They might not have thought about the intrinsic value of life the forest contains, independent of its prospects for furthering some ends such as wood, resources for food or the pleasure from aesthetic experience. The intrinsically valuable is good as an end in itself. So, it is commonly agreed that something's possession of intrinsic value generates a moral duty on the part of moral agents to protect it, or at least to refrain from damaging it. It is not because of the fact that environment is essential for the existence of the human being. Rather than a necessity, we must see that we are integrated to the environment; specifically, the forest in the case of the people who were the proponents of the Chipko movement. The central message we must learn from this movement is: the environment is an essential and constitutive component of being holistically human and morally responsible as its stewards.

We are not complete in ourselves. The environment also has a role in moulding our personality. At the same time speaking about the environment is meaningless if there are no humans. So, without humans the environment also is not complete in itself. There is mutuality between the environment and the human beings. From a Christian religious point of view human beings are created in the image and likeness of God. Anthropocentricism views human

24 Brennan Andrew and Lo, *Understanding Environmental Philosophy* (Durham: Acumen Publishing Ltd., 2010).

25 Gregory Malayil, "A Thermodynamic Approach to the Kinetics of Environmental Pollution" *Journal of Dharma* 39, (2014), 285-299.

beings as the centre of ethical concern and the environment is seen as a useful resource. Non-anthropocentrism does not place human beings above or below other beings and it attaches intrinsic value to the human beings as well as non-humans. Ignoring the contrivance between the two views, it is obvious that humans have intrinsic value. If human beings have an intrinsic value, there is no doubt the environment or ecosystem where they are an integral part, also must have an intrinsic value. So, we have moral obligation to protect our environment. The intrinsic value of the non-humans is relative to that of humans as values are human centred. Finally, the message of the intrinsic value and moral duty should be communicated to the society and the collective conscience is expected to form accordingly. Otherwise the Chipko Movement will not have any impact beyond the constraints of time and space. The Chipko could create a new awareness and lead us to valid conclusions.

Ecological/Environmental Citizenship

The one important difference between the environmental Movements and other emancipation Movements is the notion of responsible environmental citizenship. It is not only rights and entitlements but also duties, obligations and responsibilities.[26] Citizenship necessitates a conditional set of rights and obligations as part of the community concerned. We live in times of revolution, an ongoing revolution in which the perils of the future dictate the change of everything now. Whether we cycle, recycle, buy local, or write academic papers on the meaning of the environmental crisis, we are already repositioned through these acts and newly acquired habits in a joint effort and in trends of communal change. This makes for change in the meaning of citizenship and the roles of the citizen, now understood as an ecological citizen in the times of environmental crisis and a silent spring of political revolution.[27] Once we grow to the stake holders of the citizenship, the agitations or political controversies related to the environment will disappear. But, several reports we hear about deforestation and land encroachments from various places of our nation, whatever be the reason, raises doubt about our genuineness as practicing citizens of environment. It seems that we still need the Chipko or its latest versions to deal with the environmental issues.

The ecological or environmental citizenship has been proposed by British political theorist Andrew Dobson to construct a new concept of citizenship.[28] According to Dobson, who prefers the term ecological to environmental

26 Dahrendrof R., "The Changing Quality of Citizenship," in *Condition of Citizenship*, ed. B. Van Steenbergen (London: Sage, 1994), 146.

27 Andrew Dobson and Ángel Valencia Sáiz. "Citizenship, Environment, Economy-Introduction," *Environmental Politics* 14, no. 2 (2005), 157-162.

28 Andrew Dobson, "Ecological citizenship: A Defence," *Environmental Politics* 15, no. 3 (2006), 447-451.

citizenship, this kind of citizenship is centred around an obligation to reduce one's ecological footprint, an obligation that carries the status of citizenship from the public sphere to the private one. After all, much of our energy consumption and waste production take place at home. It is a non-territorial citizenship, departing from the nation-state as the source of citizenship.[29] Yet, Dobson emphasizes, those who reside in the regions of greater negative impact on the ecosystem have a greater obligation to reduce their own ecological impact.[30]

The obligations of ecological citizenship follow very obviously from the discussion of ecological non-territoriality. The space of ecological citizenship is the ecological foot print and the ecological footprints of some members of some countries have a damaging impact on the life chances of some members of other countries as well as members of their own country. The principal ecological citizenship is then to ensure that ecological footprints make a sustainable, rather than unsustainable impact. This formulation also gives an answer to the question: to whom or to what are the obligations of ecological citizenship owed. Once again the answer flows from the ecological non territoriality. Ecological footprints are an expression of the impact of the production and reproduction of the individuals' and collectives' daily lives on strangers near and far. It is these strangers to whom the obligations of ecological citizenship are owed.

Obligations of ecological citizenship are due to anyone who is owed ecological space. A critical implication of these types of obligation and to whom they are owed is that they contain no explicit expectations of reciprocity. If my ecological footprint is an unsustainable size, then my obligation is to reduce it. They are owed because of an unjust distribution of ecological space and they end when that imbalance has been addressed.

Ecological Conversion

The 'Ecological Conversion'[31] presented by Holy Father Pope Francis in his Encyclical *Laudato Si* is very relevant in this context. The question whether we have undergone any conversion by imbibing the spirit of the Chipko and other similar Movements or not, challenges our integrity as responsible citizens of the environment.

Holy Father rightly observes that external deserts in the world are growing, because the internal deserts have become so vast. "So what they

---

29 Andrew Dobson and Derek Bell," Introduction," in *Environmental Citizenship,* ed., Andrew Dobson and Derek Bell (Cambridge: The MIT Press, 2006), 1-17.

30 Andrew Dobson, "Citizenship," in *Political Theory and the Ecological Challenge*, ed., Andrew Dobson and Robyn Eckersley (Cambridge: Cambridge University Press, 2006).

31 Pope Francis, *Laudato Si* (Encyclical Letter, 2015), 217.

all need is an 'ecological conversion', whereby the effects of their encounter with Jesus Christ become evident in their relationship with the world around them. Living our vocation to be protectors of God's handiwork is essential to a life of virtue; it is not an optional or a secondary aspect of our Christian experience."[32]

This conversion calls for a number of attitudes which together foster a spirit of generous care, full of tenderness.[33] It also entails a loving awareness that we are not disconnected from the rest of creatures, but joined in a splendid universal communion. As believers, we do not look at the world from without but from within, conscious of the bonds with which the Father has linked us to all beings.

Conclusion

As in the case of many of the environmental Movements, the Chipko also had its origin in the context of certain local issues. Though the initial motivation was economic concern or livelihood of the local people, the movement went beyond local and particular apprehensions and transformed into a moral force which conscientized the society about its obligations to the environment. Though the Chipko is not alive as a movement now, still its vibrancy persists like never-ending ripples. How far we internalized the message of the Chipko and similar environmental Movements is a pertinent question. Similar to the felling of forests and its far reaching consequences which triggered the Chipko movement, still there are regional as well as global issues related to the environment. The challenge before us is to transform ourselves with the right attitude to protect the environment. Recurring environmental Movements is not the genuine solution to protect the environment.

We need to have an introspection as individuals and collectives whether we sincerely love the environment and really convinced of the fact that we are really integrated to the ecosystem where we live. As citizens of the ecosystem or environment we have rights and duties and are obliged to exercise our duties to the environment and privileged to enjoy our legitimate rights. If a reflection on the nuances of the Chipko movement prompts us to follow the environmental ethics with all our steps in the ecological space we occupy, no doubt we are faithful citizens of the environment in every respect. Environment indeed is real and safe home where we all live in harmony as fully human and mutually accountable. The Chipko and similar Movements will certainly help us all to be closer to our mother nature, to protect her in all possible ways, and to love her with the right passion and the just pride.

---

32 Pope Francis, *Laudato Si* (Encyclical Letter, 2015), 217.

33 Ibid., 220.

16

Alternative Media Movement

Francis Arackal Thummy
Mount St Dominic's, Mangalore

Abstract: It can be safely said that some form of alternative media did exist from the time the so-called 'mainstream media' came into being. From the inception of mainstream media at least a section of it has been observed as failing to perform its designated role in society – inform, educate, and entertain. More so in the 20th century and the initial decade of 21st century when media came to be controlled, almost completely, by the wealthy and the powerful – culturally, financially, politically, and socially. Social Movements felt abandoned by this dominant mainstream media. Hence, social movements have been left with no other go than turning to alternative vehicles of communication giving rise to alternative media movement. Present contribution aims to look into the various aspects of this media movement.

Keywords: Activist media, Alternative Media, Alternative Media Movement, Alternative Press, Democracy, Film, Freedom Movement, Free Speech, Independent Film Makers Association, Indymedia, Information Communication Technology, Interactive Media, Mainstream Media, New Social Movement, Participatory media, Radio, Social Media, Social Movement, Television.

Introduction

Alternative media are varied, spring from a wide variety of motivations and causes and are full of contradictions, and given the limited scope of this paper, almost impossible to present a comprehensive account. I would like to affirm the claim of Roger Silverstone[1] that alternative media "have created new spaces for alternative voices that provide the focus both for specific community interests as well as for the contrary and the subversive."[2] Alternative media movement encompasses all these – the community, the contrary and the subversive. Mass media is employed "to pursue a critical or alternative agenda, from the margins, as it were, or from the underbelly of social life."[3] Some of the finest examples of alternative media are the underground press of the 1960s such as *Village Voice* and *The Rat* in the Unites States, *Oz* and *It* in the United Kingdom. They arose from the communitarian and subversive needs of the society of the time and in turn gave rise to social movements and served as further impetus for an increase in alternative media movement in many parts of the world. This paper would like to first of all examine as to what is alternative media, consider its origin taking apart each medium – Press, Radio, Films, Video and Television, and the Internet. The paper will also show that alternative media movement is very much related to social movements. Hence, a consideration of the philosophy of social movements, its impact, and a brief study of the new social movements are due. Finally, the paper highlights the wide use of social media as alternative media.

1. What is Alternative Media?

'Alternative Media' is the term used to describe non-mainstream media forms that are independently run and community focussed, such as zines, pirate radio, online discussion boards, community run and owned broadcasting companies, and activist publications such as *Communalism Combat*, *Health Action*, *Secular Indian* etc., (Coyer et al., 2007). "Alternative media are media produced by the socially, culturally, and politically excluded: they are always independently run and often community-focused, ranging from pirate radio to activist publications, from digital video experiments to radical work on the web" (Coyer et al., 2007: Back cover). Alternative media used to be understood as underground, radical or oppositional media. Today it also accounts for newer cultural forms such as blogs, fanzines, and personal websites (Atton, 2001). There is another view according to which Alternative Media are those providing a timely corrective to media theorizing which focuses almost exclusively on the output of the media conglomerates.

It is important to ask how and why people produce and use alternative media. Some answers could be: to make meaning, to interpret, and to change the world in which they live. Scholars of journalism and media studies have illustrated the production of alternative media as a means for activists to

1 Author of *Why Study the Media?* (London: Sage, 1999).

2 Chris Atton, Alternative Media (London: Sage, 2002), 1.

3 Ibid., 1.

generate dissent, while communication scholars have examined activists' performances and view events as challenges to dominant power structures (Atkinson, 2009). Atkinson in his work *Alternative Media and Politics of Resistance: A Communication Perspective* (2009) demonstrates the role of alternative media in the performance of resistance against power structures by contemporary activists. Specifically, he explores the role of alternative media in the establishment of activist networks in local communities; the role of alternative media in the construction of strategies of resistance by networked activists; and the role of interactivity between local and global networks in production of alternative media content.

2. Origin of Alternative Media

Tracing the origin of the alternative media is a task not easily achieved. Due to the limited scope of this paper we shall trace its history by focusing only on two English speaking countries – India and Britain – easily the two leading democracies of the world.

2.1 The Alternative Press

Press, more than other media, has provided a voice to those on the social and political margins. Nancy Fraser, in her essay 'Rethinking the public sphere' argues that alternative press form part of a 'subaltern' public sphere which continually interacts with the mainstream to create what she terms 'emancipatory potential.'[4] The history of the press in India began with the publication of Hicky's *Bengal Gazette* in 1780. Since then both the Britishers and the Indians published pamphlets, magazines, and newspapers. Some of the notable ones are: *Calcutta Gazette*, *Bengal Journal*, *India Gazette*, *Bombay Herald*, *Bombay Courier*, and *Madras Courier*. In the context of the Freedom Movement those brought out by the Indians served as alternative press. It served as an alternative to the propaganda unleashed by the Britishers against the Freedom Movement and its leaders. At the same time, it is noteworthy that almost all the pioneer journalists in India were Englishmen, but they did not refrain from pointing out the bitter truth about the rulers of the time.[5] For instance, James Silk Buckingham of *Calcutta Journal*, William Carey of *Friend of India*. Raja Ram Mohan Roy of *Sambad Kaumudi* & *Mirat-ul-Akhbar* (Mirror of News) and Gangadhar Bhattacharya of *The Bengal Gazette* followed their great journalistic example and gave great impetus to the freedom movement.[6]

---

4 Kate Coyer et al., *Alternative Media Handbook* (London: Routledge, 2007), 47. As cited in Angela Phillips, *The Alternative Press*.

5 Francis Arackal, *The Indian Media: How Credible?* (Bombay: Better Yourself Books, 2010), 33-47.

6 Ibid., 35-37.

In Britain *The Village Voice* was born in 1955 as an anti-establishment post-war publication. Six years later the satirical magazine *Private Eye* was launched. Within a year it had a circulation of 35, 000. For it published stories that no one else would touch. Both these publications represented a new voice which would go on to define post-war attitude towards authority.[7] When Oz–an Australian Magazine–came to London through its editor Richard Neville, it was an instant hit, especially with the young for it provided one of the first, and perhaps the best, "one of the fiercest and most compelling cries of rejection of the choice offered to the young within welfare capitalism."[8] *It*, a child of London's emerging cultural 'underground' movement, was launched in 1966. In 1968 a group of left-wing activists started *Black Dwarf*. Later on there were publications such as *Ink*, and *7 Days*. By the early 1970s alternative publications were springing up in every university town in Britain. Since then the alternative publishing movement has gone on.

2.2 Radio

As far as the medium of Radio is concerned it was the 'Radio pirates'[9] who opened the path to alternative broadcast airwaves. Hind and Mosco (1985) argue the first radio pirates were actually the early inventors of the 1900s like Guglielmo Marconi and Reginald Fessindon, themselves unlicensed because, of course, there was no license to be given out since the medium was only just being invented![10] In the 1920s, it has been estimated, upwards of 250,000 people in Britain alone were involved in amateur radio in some fashion. They most vociferously opposed the state monopoly on radio, lobbied against a commercial system and came up with home-made crystal radio sets. Virtually anyone with a transmitter and an interest in broadcasting had access to the airwaves. Pirate radio stations of various hues in many continents came up, including Women's Scéal[11] Radio in Galway, Ireland, at various times. In the second decade of the 21 Century amateur broadcasters are still very active.[12] Today licensed community radio works as an alternative media especially in the rural hinterlands of many countries, including India. In the age of online, internet radio is serving as an alternative medium and independent producers are finding more outlets through online distributed networks. Out of alternative radio activity a network of organisers, producers, and collabourations has

7 Coyer et al., *Alternative Media Handbook*, 49.

8 Ibid.

9 'Radio pirates' are those who broadcast without a license.

10 John Hind and Stephen Mosco, *Rebel Radio: The Full Story of British Pirate Radio* (London: Pluto Press).

11 Scéal in Irish means gossip/stories.

12 Coyer et al., *Alternative Media Handbook*, 15.

emerged.[13] "Taken together, community/micro-radio and pirate radio best demonstrate the notions of alternative media."[14]

2.3 Film, Video, and Television

"There is inevitably a relationship between media and the ever-shifting social and political context which in large part determines its form, content, modes of production, exhibition, and distribution. Alternative film, video, and television are by definition a response to the politics and media landscape contemporary with them."[15] The context that we are considering is between 1965 and 2005, during which a great variety of alternative film, video, and television was produced. Due to colonial influences our knowledge of the existence of such alternative platforms naturally takes us to the home of the colonizer – UK – where from the 1970s and 1980s there was the community video movement and Left, Feminist, and Black film, and video workshops. In recent years globalization issues and radical politics found their voice in the Internet-based organizations such as Indymedia, FreeSpeech, Democracy *Now*! and One World. All these have had a considerable, invariably inspiring, effect on practices in India too. In the realm of Indian Indymedia, it is the independent film makers and their work that have been prominent.

According to Alan Fountain, "The birth of video in the late 1970s, the development of low-cost digital equipment in the 1980s and 1990s and the results of digitalization over the last decade have all made decisive contributions to an extraordinary growth in the number of alternative producers worldwide and the breadth, creativity and potential political effect of their activities."[16] Scholars term the period between 1965-1980 as one of 'utopian dreams'. Films, videos, and television of this period drew upon the heady mix of issues and attitudes that were prevalent in the Western world particularly in the US and the UK. 'Workshops' were the forums in which ideas for independent film, videos, and television germinated and exchanged. The independent creators of the time were very strong on theory: New Marxist ideas, along with semiotics, structuralism, and psychoanalysis. By 1974 an Independent Film Makers' Association (IFA) was formed in Britain. This Association embraced all shades of alternative/independent filmmaking practice. "IFA aimed to strengthen the oppositional space for its work of

13 Coyer et al., *Alternative Media Handbook*, 25.

14 Chris Atton, *An Alternative Internet: Radical Media, Politics and Creativity* (Edinburgh: Edinburgh University Press, 2004), 115.

15 Alan Fountain, "Alternative Film, Video and Television 1965-2005" in Kate Coyer et al., *Alternative Media Handbook* (London: Routledge, 2007), 30.

16 Fountain, "Alternative film, video and television 1965-2005," 29.

production, exhibition, distribution, and education while at the same time mounting a critique of mainstream media ...."[17]

The new video portapack technology enabled non-professionals to produce videos to voice their own views and campaigns directly. In this connection Fountain is of the view that it was the video rather than film workshops which prioritized the development of 'participatory media' which led to the 'democratisation' of media both in terms of production and distribution.[18] "This commitment to enabling more people to become involved in expressing her, his or their own voice became the consistent and main motivation of what might be called 'video access groups' through the 1970s, 1980s and 1990s."[19]

From the 1970s a weekly programme, *Open Door*, on BBC gave access to a variety of community groups in television distribution. This represented the first use of the BBC as a means of enabling non-professionals to be fully involved in representing their concerns on British national television.[20] The arrival of Channel Four in 1981 was a significant moment in the realm of alternative television in Britain for it enabled many radical voices to find space. At this time, there were also many varied alternative and radical film and video Movements across the world. Advances in technology, particularly the rapid expansion of video as a means of low-cost production and distribution, enabled thousands more people to become active participants in the production process.[21] By the mid-1990s radical activist media projects devoted to global political activism and the spread of counter-information have had considerable impact. Two outstanding examples of this is: *Outfoxed: Rupert Murdoch's War on Journalism* and *Walmart: The High Price of Low Cost.*

2.4 The Web and Interactive Media

The story of the origin of alternative media on the internet is brief as the general availability of the technology itself is barely 30 years old. Even so, within this short time there have been thousands of alternative media projects on the web. The invention of the World Wide Web (WWW) in 1989 not only widened the access to information on the Internet, it also improved the presentation and downloading of information. Alternative media on the internet are helping humanity rethink media and journalism in 21st century.[22]

---

17 Fountain, "Alternative film, video and television 1965-2005," 33-34.

18 Ibid., 34.

19 Ibid., 35.

20 Ibid., 35.

21 Ibid., 37.

22 Chris Atton, "A Brief History: The Web and Interactive Media" in Kate Coyer et al., *Alternative Media Handbook* (London: Routledge, 2007), 59.

The use of the Internet by the Zapatista movement in Mexico to send communiques out to the rest of the world has been cited as a potent demonstration of autonomous electronic communication to share information about the situation in Chiapas.[23] Manuel Castells has called the Zapatistas the "first informational guerrilla movement."[24] Since Chiapas a range of groups, Movements and causes have used the web "to present mobilizing information, alternative news reports, video and webcam feeds, Internet radio, archives, discussion lists, chat rooms, bulletin boards and sound files."[25]

"Alternatives arise from Movements. They do not create Movements."[26] Hence Alternative Media Movement can be considered as a part of/result of Social Movements as its aim is also to achieve some form of social change. "Dissenting voices do not die away when the moment of social change dissipates because the need to speak, to be heard, and to belong are powerful impulses through which we create our sense of ourselves individually and collectively."[27] This brings us to the question as to what Social Movements are.

3. What is a Social Movement?

"Social Movement is a grouping of people who have become involved in seeking to accomplish, or to block, a process of social change. Social Movements normally exist in relations of conflict with organizations whose objectives and outlook they frequently oppose."[28] Giddens writes: "Social Movements come in all shapes and sizes. Some are very small, numbering no more than a few dozen members; others may include thousands or even millions of people. While some social movements carry on their activities within the laws of the society in which they exist, others operate as illegal or underground groups."[29] Social Movements often arise with the aim of bringing about change on a public issue, such as expanding civil rights for a segment of the population. Social Movements such as the environmental movement, is an example of an effort to bring about practical reforms, with considerable success.

3.1 Philosophy of Social Movements

Social Movements are numerous. But what are they? Do they fit in with the democratic ethos of a society/nation? There has been a general agreement that

23 Atton, *Alternative Media*, 133.

24 Manuel Castells, *The Information Age: Economy, Society and Culture - The Power of Identity*, Vol. 2 (Oxford: Blackwell, 1997), 79.

25 Atton, *Alternative Media*, 133.

26 Angela Phillips, "The Alternative Press" in Kate Coyer et al., *Alternative Media Handbook* (London: Routledge, 2007), 48-48.

27 Angela Phillips, "The Alternative Press," 48-49.

28 Anthony Giddens, *Sociology*, 4th Edition., (London: Polity Press, 2001), 699.

29 Giddens, *Sociology*, 439.

relatively little philosophical attention has been dedicated to social movements as such. Other than emphasizing the roles and activities of social movements, philosophers have not dwelt on the nature of social movements per se. An account of social movements must draw on political philosophy and the theory of democracy; social ontology and action theory; as well as bodies of work in sociology and other social sciences.

Kolers (2016) is of the view that "philosophers have had much to say on issues impinging on social movements but much less to say on social movements as such."[30] To do a philosophical overview of social movements one may have to consider the nature of shared agency and collective action, social epistemology, democratic theory, and the theory of individual responsibility for structural injustice. More recently of course, philosophers have paid more attention to the role of social movements in the achievement of justice and in the political life of democracies. According to Kolers (2016), "contemporary analytic philosophy has considerable work to do if it is to account for the nature, epistemology, ethics, and politics of social movements."[31]

3.2 Impact of Social Movements

According to Giddens, "Often, laws or policies are altered as a result of the action of social movements. These changes in legislation can have far reaching effects. For example, it used to be illegal for groups of workers to call their members out on strike, and striking was punished with varying degrees of severity in different countries."[32] Eventually, however, the laws were amended, making the strike a permissible tactic of industrial conflict. Social Movements are among the most powerful forms of collective action. Well-organized persistent campaigns can bring about dramatic results. The American civil rights movement, for example, succeeded in pushing through important pieces of legislation outlawing racial segregation in schools and public places. The feminist movement scored important gains for women in terms of economic and political equality. Environmental activists have won important concessions from governments and corporations. For instance, in the case of genetically modified (GM) foods.[33]

4. New Social Movements

For nearly four decades there has been an explosion of social movements in various parts of the world. They ranged from Movements for Civil rights,

30 Avery Kolers, "Social Movements," accessed August 18, 2018, https://onlinelibrary.wiley.com/doi/full/10.1111/phc3.12351.

31 *Ibid.*

32 Giddens, *Sociology*, 439.

33 *Ibid.*

Dalit rights, Gay rights, Women's rights, Ecological awareness, freedom of expression and so forth. Some social commentators refer to them as 'new social movements (NSMs)'. Such designation seeks to differentiate them from those that preceded them in earlier decades, about which we shall discuss still later.

New social movements (NSMs) have been loosely defined as Movements emerging in post industrialist or advanced industrialist society. Examples of such would be Movements regarding the environment, women's rights, animal rights, alternative religions, alternative sexualities, and so on and so forth.

The growth of NSMs is evidence that citizens in contemporary society are not apathetic or uninterested in politics (not the traditional one), rather there is a belief that direct action and participation is more effective than reliance on politicians and political systems. This way NSMs are helping to revitalize democracy in many countries.[34]

As Johnston et al. (1994) write, in NSMs "the grievances and mobilizing factors tend to focus on cultural and symbolic issues that are linked with issues of identity rather than on economic grievances that characterized the working-class Movements."[35]

Haenfler et al. expound upon the differences between NSMs and traditional social movements indicating that traditional Movements target state apparatuses, typically in protest cycles, whereas NSMs "target cultural codes and individual practices" regardless of moments in which political action is most favorable (elections, national/international meetings, legislation barring or passing equal rights, etc.).[36] Rather, NSM theory presents Movements in terms of struggling over:

> postmaterialist values, identities, and cultural practices rather than class-based economic concerns and material resources. And that NSM theories have expanded the focus from movement organizations and conventional politics, pointing to broader definitions of Movements based on loosely organized networks, collective identities, and cultural challenges.[37]

---

34 Giddens, *Sociology*, 440-441.

35 Hank Johnston, Larana, E., & Gusfield, J.R., eds, "Identities, Grievances and New Social Movements," *New Social Movements: From Ideology to Identity* (Philadelphia, PA: Temple University Press, 1994), Also see: 1-35. <https://scholar.colorado.edu/cgi/viewcontent.cgi?article=1034&context=jour_gradetds> accessed September 19, 2018.

36 Ross Haenfler et al., "Lifestyle Movements: Exploring the Intersection of Lifestyle and Social Movements," *Social Movement Studies* 11, no. 1 (2012), 7.

37 Ross Haenfler et al., "Lifestyle Movements: Exploring the Intersection of Lifestyle and Social Movements," *Social Movement Studies* 11, no. 1 (2012), 4.

Thus, NSMs are observed to be a unique product of contemporary society differing in their methods, motivations, and orientations. In a way they highlight the new challenges being faced by contemporary world. This is partly because traditional political institutions and their leaders seem unable to cope up with the challenges before them. They find it impossible to respond creatively to the threats to ecology, the potential dangers of nuclear energy, genetically modified organisms, the powerful effects of the cyber age and the Internet, and the looming dangers of artificial intelligence. The cumulative effects of all these impart a kind of sense to individuals and societies that they are losing control over their lives; they begin to feel less secure and more isolated. This in turn leads to powerlessness and helplessness. By contrast, corporations, governments, and the media appear to be dominating more and more aspects of people's lives heightening the sense of risks and uncertainty.[38]

4.1 Communication Technology and New Social Movements

Technological innovation can have a large impact on the ways in which communities communicate and mobilize. As with the Arab Spring uprising, social media, particularly Twitter, a medium accessible on cell phones when Internet access was restricted by the government, played a tremendous role in organizing protestors. Information Communication Technology (ICT) has enabled new social movements around the world "to join together in huge regional and international networks comprising non-governmental organizations, religious and humanitarian groups, human rights associations, consumer protection advocates, environmental activists and others who campaign in the public interest."[39] The speed and reach of this technology have helped to access and share sources of information (through messaging and live-streaming), and then on to put pressure on corporations, governments, and international bodies. One of the most striking instances of this has been the huge protests against the World Trade Organization (WTO) in Seattle in 1999. More specifically, it is the invention of the Internet that has facilitated the internationalization of protest Movements. Grass roots activists from Alaska to Australia can meet online to share information, exchange experiences and coordinate joint action. This ability to coordinate international political campaigns is what that has rattled corporations and governments and the most encouraging and inspiring to participants in new social movements. Some of the noteworthy campaigns have been: one against landmines, another in favour of cancelling Third World debt. Some observers argue that the Internet

38 Giddens, *Sociology*, 439-440.

39 Giddens, *Sociology*, 441.

has enabled a 'migration' of power away from nation-states into new non-governmental alliances and coalitions.[40]

4.2 New Social Movements and Alternative Media

Different forms of media can disseminate information on behalf of all of the types of networks and organizations described above. In more formal networks, access to the resources of traditional media, such as television and radio, can be achieved more readily by organizations that have more clout and public visibility. However, with the advent of new media making alternative media available to a larger audience, new social movement actors in the informal and loosely organized networks are able to leverage their voices in myriad ways to contribute to the new social movement at large. While traditional media have certainly served its purpose in the spreading of radical and alternative messages, particularly social movement theorists studying the use of pamphlets and newsletters in social movements of the 1960s and 1970s, alternative media in the post industrialist era tends to centralize less around the one-to-many model, and emphasizes the liberatory effect of new media technologies that allow a many-to-many model to reach dispersed networked communities. In earlier social movement theories, media were seen as tools to help organize the movement, however, in later conceptions of NSM theories, media are observed as spaces in which the organization takes place, rather than as additional resource opportunities for communication.[41]

As Lievrouw aptly notes, new media technologies serve a multitude of purposes based on the needs of particular groups, specifically as it pertains to users adopting existing media tools for their own needs, but more importantly, by expanding upon the pre-existing structures to 'remix' the media for re-presentations and adaptations of new media messages, referred to as reconfiguration and remediation. She writes, "reconfiguration and remediation allow people to work around the fixity of traditional media technologies and institutional systems, and to negotiate, manipulate, and blur the boundaries between interpersonal interaction and mass communication."[42] Thus new media technologies can be situated in the postmodern free-flowing paradigm in which the 'fixed' institutions are deconstructed to reveal the lack, particularly as it pertains to alternative representations that do not fit into the normative.

Manuel Castells, discussing the features available in multimodal communication models writes, "the characteristics of communication processes between individuals engaged in the social movement determine the organizational characteristics of the social movement itself: the more

40 Giddens, *Sociology*, 441.

41 Leah A. Lievrouw, *Alternative and Activist New Media* (Polity Press: Cambridge, 2011).

42 *Ibid.*, 5.

interactive and self-configurable communication is, the less hierarchical is the organization and the more participatory is the movement."[43] For Castells, the autonomous feature of the Internet allows leaderless Movements to occur in spaces that are away from the dominant institutions that seek to change; however, he notes that while organizing online allows these types of cultural Movements (as opposed to protest Movements) to flourish and expand, it is not the only route that Movements need to move, particularly highlighting the need for face-to-face gathering to work out the most important issues and occupy physical spaces.

Reworking new media definitions, Lievrouw adopts a definition that is useful for the analysis of media projects in alternative and activist communities, specifically the ways in which the medium functions in terms of its assets and tools, the ways in which people use these media, and the ways that people are structured or organized around these media systems: 1) The material artifacts or devices that enable and extend people's abilities to communicate and share meaning 2) The communication activities or practices that people engage in as they develop and use those devices; and 3) The larger social arrangements and organizational forms that people create and build around the artifacts and practices.[44]

New social movement theory tends to situate the oppositional actors in these Movements as "knowledge workers," coming from highly educated backgrounds seeking out cultural and symbolic justices rather than material goods. Lievrouw writes, "participants in NSMs have been precisely those members of society who are most involved in the production and circulation of culture, including media culture and information technology."[45] The scope of alternative media in NSMs also varies, from individual run campaigns to a small network that parse out information amongst volunteers. These small-scale Do It Yourself networks then provide a sense of intimacy and trust amongst these networks; it is much easier to get comfortable with issues of cultural diversity and sexuality when you feel the person on the other end of the medium is not just an anonymous Internet user, but a real person identifying in the same way you are.

The macro and micro effect of media communication and usage in NSMs points to the intersection of broadcasting and dissemination of information, as well as the interpersonal and collective identity building that takes place on these media networks thus making "engagement via new media both symbolic

---

43 Manuel Castells, *Networks of Outrage and Hope: Social Movements in the Internet Age* (Cambridge, UK: Polity Press), 15.

44 Lievrouw, *Alternative and Activist New Media*, 7.

45 Ibid., 42.

and material."[46] The mobilization that takes place due to this online/offline, micro/macro relationship is what helps move the movement, a term that Lievrouw calls 'mediated mobilization'.

5. Social Media as Alternative Media

The beginning of the 21st century saw the coming into being of multiple social media sites: Face Book, WhatsApp, QQ, WeChat, QZone, Tumblr, Instagram, Twitter, Reddit and so forth. In 2018 one can count sixty plus social networking sites. Many of these social networking sites have been used as or turned into activist media, autonomous media, citizens' media, radical media, tactical media – in one word alternative media. They are being used so by activists, citizen journalists, Movements of various types for innumerable causes and goals. One very recent example of this is the use of social media in the unprecedented floods that wrought indescribable havoc in 12 out of 14 districts of the Indian State of Kerala. When mainstream media could not reach or had to be shut down due to the flood fury, it is the social media that played a great role in transmitting the necessary information and coordinating the relief operations. Social media was used to mobilize relief materials of all kinds from throughout India and abroad. The State could bounce back to a semblance of normalcy with the wide-spread use of social media.

Conclusion

In the foregoing pages, we have tried to present the relevance of alternative media and how it fits in with the other social movements. Alternative media movement got an impetus with the arrival of the Internet. As a result every individual is able to be a media person (citizen journalist) enabling multifarious alternative voices. But, lately the Internet itself has come under the control of giant corporations (E.g., Google, Microsoft, Amazon …) which seek to do the gate-keeping so as to set the agenda regarding the data that will pass through it. Besides, these data grabbing and data storing corporations (in the age of Big data business, economics, and politics) are creating hurdles for net neutrality. So, even the Internet which was expected to serve as a vehicle for the voice of the voiceless and an instrument of democratic participation, and above all, a public sphere, is turning out to be another medium of domination by corporations, governments, and other vested interests putting spokes in the wheel of the alternative media movement.

46 Lievrouw, *Alternative and Activist New Media*, 158.

17

From Sudra to Servanthood: Reimagining Education in India

Jose D. Maliekal SDB
St John's Regional Seminary, Kondadaba

Abstract: This Paper builds itself on the assumption that the Social Movements, being collective and individual learning processes, leave their critical impact on the society at large. So an interrogation of the process of educative imagination of our nation, under the throes of Neo-Liberalization, as to its "social movement" orientation, is in order. Against this backdrop, as indicated by the programmatic title, "From Sudra to Servantood: Reimagining Education in India", question is posed, as to whether the hermeneutical optic, to understand the Christian interventions in society, should be that of the *Sudra*, the traditional service-providing caste, or whether it should not be that of *Servanthood,* capable of evoking a consciousness and praxis of service for the downtrodden, as the response-ability of all citizens. Responding to this challenge, a socio-economic and political audit of the Christian engagement in the ministry of education is being attempted, so as to reimagine the terrain, under the shift of keys from "Sudra to Servanthood". After capturing the present educational scenario, the discussion turns towards an alternative counter-narrative, from the point of view of Christian engagement in the mission of education. The paper concludes, summing up the process, and highlighting its emancipatory thrust.

Keywords: Sudra, Servanthood, Education, Neo-Liberalization, Performance, Function, Pedagogy of the Oppressed/Encounter, Dalits, Subalterns, Indigenous Knowledge, Deprevational Perspective, Common Good, Paulo Freire, Felix Wilfred, Culture/Human Rights, Partnership, Christian, Capitalism, Trickle Down Theory, Fraternity, Ambedkar, Private/Public.

"Nihil humani a me alienum Christianis."
("Nothing human is alien to a Christian.")
–Tertullian

Introduction

This Paper builds on the assumption that the Social Movements, especially New Social Movements, being collective and individual educative/learning processes, leave their critical impact on the society at large.[1] So, a reflection on their educative component is in order. And consequently, an interrogation of the process of educative imagination of our nation, under the throes of Neo-Liberalization, as to its "social", as well as "movement" orientation, is called for.

Now, to a note of explanation on the title, "From Sudra to Servanthood: Reimagining Education in India". It is inspired by the challenge thrown by the contextual and public theologian, Felix Wilfred, to Christianity and society at large, towards overcoming a Post-Liberalization amnesia of the poor. In this regard, he calls for a transformation of consciousness, on the part of Christians, by making the journey from being a "Collective Sudra" to becoming a facilitator of the spirit of servanthood.[2] His assertion is that Christians, in India, have been always looked upon, as playing the role of the *Sudras*,[3] who have been providing services to the other castes,in the traditional caste hierarchy of South Asia. But, the services provided by the Christians, in the areas like education and health, do not evoke a change of consciousness in the people, in such a way that they would feel impelled to engage themselves in the same kind of service, for the benefit of the poor and the marginalized.

In other words, it will not be by increasing our services, but rather, by creating a general spirit and culture of servanthood that the Christians will radically promote the cause of the poor and the marginalized. Christian

---

1 Randolph Haluza-DeLay, *Education, Social Movements and Environmental Learning (from Developing a Compassionate Sense of Place: Environmental and social Conscientization in Environmental Organizations*), accessed September 27, 2018, http://csopconsulting.tripod.com/sitebuildercontent/sitebuilderfiles/2RHDeducation.pdf; see also Dip Kapoor, "Subaltern Social Movement Learning and the Decolonization of Space in India," *International Education* 37, no. 1 (2007), 10-41, accessed July 24, 2018, http://trace.tennessee.edu/internationaleducation/ vol37/iss1/2 .

2 Felix Wilfred, "The Poor in the Age of Globalization: Challenges to Christianity," in *Asian Dreams and Christian Hope: At the Dawn of the Millennium*, ed., Felix Wilfred (Delhi: ISPCK, 2000), 44-76.

3 Sharad Patil, *Dasa-Sudra Slavery, Studies in the Origins of Indian Slavery and Feudalism and Their* Philosophies (New Delhi: Allied Publishers, 1982); See also: B.R. Ambedkar, *Who Were the Shudras? How They Came to the Fourth Varnas in the Indo-Aryan Society?* (Bombay: Thackers, 1970).

interventions on behalf of the marginalized will carry impact, only when the poor will cease being viewed as an occupational speciality of the Church and voluntary agencies alone, but rather, the issues of the poor will start being seen as the responsibility of every citizen.

If the involvement of the Church goes along the direction of promoting servanthhood, its contribution will be truly a spiritual one. Spirituality is something deeper than ethics. Especially given the contemporary mood of globalization, marketized liberalization, ethical appeals fall on deaf years. The logic of financial capitalism and the market does not fall within the purview of ethics. Ethical language could make little difference, in terms of transformation. What is called for is a deeper spiritual transformation, at the individual and collective level, wherein both individuals and groups would follow policies and praxis, that are sensitive to the poor, the last and the least. This will lead to a culture of non-exploitative and service-oriented praxis,[4] which will have as its hardware, as strong sense of advocacy, on behalf of the marginalized, the Dalits, Tribals, women and the other marginalized. The Church has to be participatory agent and a catalyst in this process, moving beyond welfarism, which the Church is accustomed to.

To translate this challenge into the horizon of the social movements would be to raise the question, whether the Church is a catalyst in/for the Social Movement(s) for the poor, in the mood and mode of the ethics of participation and responsibility.[5] In the vision of Paulo Freire, progressive social movements are important vehicles of social change, Movements that can contribute to counter-hegemonic globalization, a 'globalization from below'. In Gramscian terms, 'a war of position', challenging the hegemonic order, finding spaces for "swimming against the tide."[6]

What is being attempted in this work is only a modest endeavour towards a socio-economic and political audit of the Christian engagement in the ministry of education, so as to reimagine the terrain, under the shift of keys from "Sudra to Servanthood", under the broader thematic of the transformative potential of social movements. Of course, the implicit assumption is that this internal audit will have a parabolic effect, in placing the proper interventions in the civil society, in interrogating the wider educational scenario.

I intend proceeding with this paper, in three stages. After presenting in broad strokes, the present educational scenario, under the impact of globalization, the discussion will turn towards an alternative counter-narrative,

---

4 Felix Wifred, "The Poor in the Age of Globalization," 57.

5 Avery Kolers, "Social Movements," *Philosophy Compass*, 11, no. 10 (2016), 586-588.

6 Peter Mayo, "Paulo Freire, Globalization and Emancipatory Education," accessed April 7, 2018, https://www.google.co.in/search?ei=2gm6W6qwIcXsvgSzyJgg&q=Paulo+Freire%2C+Globalization+and+Emanicipatory+Education.

from the point of view of Christian identity and engagement in the mission of education. This will be undertaken, with an eye towards, reimagining the Christian educational enterprise, into something of parabolic and transformative impact in the India of today. In the process, it is hoped that a few signposts for the Indian Christianity, for be-coming a Social Movement, will emerge, a movement that will network with other Movements, which are part of the critical civil society.[7] This will be followed by a conclusion, summing up the process, and highlighting its emancipatory thrust.

Education under the Neoliberal Rubric: Amnesia of the Poor

India is perhaps home to the most numerous institutions of higher education in the world, with around 30,000 according to some estimates. The exponential growth of higher education in India is the result of new hopes, in the context of a market oriented globalized economy. Even with all the expansion in education, the Gross Enrollment Ratio (GER) in the country is about 13%, much lower than the developed countries.[8] As the state is not able to respond to the growing demands of higher education, private providers have entered the fray, in a massive way, with self-financing colleges and deemed universities.[9] The scenario is not much different in the fields of primary and secondary education, where also the private sector has made inroads, in a big way. While the rationale for Private-Public Partnership is inefficiency of the government, the means offered to overcome it actually promise no relief or improvement. Private-Public Partnership (PPP) is not an idea, but rather an ideology which promotes privatization as a means of reducing the government's responsibility to increase the number of schools.[10]

"The ideas of the ruling class are in every epoch the ruling ideas."[11] As in every sector, those who possess power also define what education is and determine its content and methods. Naturally, those in power opt for the kind of education that will replicate the present society and set their eyes on the benefits that they can derive from the maintenance of *status quo*. There is the phenomenon of cultural invasion of the oppressed, by the dominant, by which the oppressed are made to adhere to the values of the privileged. Paulo Freire's

7 Felix Wilfred, "Christianity and Ambiguities of Civil Society," in *Margins: Site of Asian Theologies*, ed., Felix Wilfred (Delhi: ISPCK, 2008), 245-264.

8 For comparison with a few other countries, see Semmalar Selvi, "Higher Education Budget: The Impact on Dalits," *Jeevadhara* 42, no. 247 (January, 2012), 46 – 57.

9 On the various aspects of present-day educational scenario in the country, see the special issue of *seminar* 624 (August 2011).

10 Krishna Kumar, "Partners in Education,"*Economic and Political Weekly* 43, no. 3 (January 19, 2008), 11.

11 Karl Marx, *The German Ideology*, ed. David Mclellan (Oxford: Oxford University Press, 1984), 176.

insightful comment, "Whether they are in the nurseries or universities", the oppressors are prepared "to become the invaders of the future,"[12] is relevant here. There is at work, a "nutritious approach to education", by which those who have power are fed and over-fed to become "intellectually fat". On the other hand, those at the margins of the society are made to starve.[13]

Though Christian missionaries have been instrumental in imparting literacy, and through it, empowerment, to the illiterate Dalit Subalterns in different parts of India, from colonial times,[14] as regards higher education, the stance of the Christian missionaries has been ambiguous. Education was seen part of the civilizing mission of Christianity. Moreover, the missionaries believed in the "Trickle Down" theory, according to which, the education imparted to the elites and high castes would slowly percolate to the lower castes and classes, and would bring about a great change. It is this elitism that has, by and large, characterized the history of Christian education, which prevented it from being sufficiently radical.[15] "Education was offered to the higher castes who were then invited to take what *they* wanted from it without having to forego their essential elitism."[16]

If Christianity is to shed its elitism and its colonial vestiges, and decolonize its imagination, especially in the field of education, Christian institutions of education, have to challenge the mode of education, which serves the *status quo*, kept in place by the forces of globalization and the market. The prophetic challenge for the Christian institutions is to swim against the current and project a policy re-orientation of education that will effect socio-political, cultural and economic transformation.[17]

Weaving a Christian Counter-Narrative of Education

While dealing with the theme of reimagining education, especially in our Christian institutions of learning, discussion could be had on issues like, access,

---

12 As quoted in "Engaging Freire's Pedagogy for a Critique of Indian Education," accessed April 7, 2018, http://shodhganga.inflibnet.ac.in/bitstream/10603/135427/9/09_chapter%204.pdf .

13 Paulo Freire, *Education for Liberation and Community* (Melbourne: Australian Council of Churches, 1974), as quoted in Felix Wilfred, "Higher Education and Christian Identity," in *The Sling of Utopia: Struggles for a Different Society*, ed., Felix Wilfred (Delhi: ISPCK, 2005), 261.

14 See P. Sanal Mohan, *Modernity of Slavery: Struggles Against Caste Inequality in Colonial Kerala* (New Delhi: Oxford University Press, 2015).

15 Felix Wilfred, "What is "Christian" about Christian Colleges?" in *Christians for a Better India*, ed., Felix Wilfred (Delhi: ISPCK, 2014), p. 189.

16 J.C. Ingleby, *Missionaries, Education and India* (Delhi: ISPCK, 2000), 274-275.

17 Felix Wilfred, "Higher Education and Christian Identity," in *The Sling of Utopia*, 261-262.

equity, governance, quality, evaluation, research, partnership and financing,[18] I would like to turn our attention, to some systemic issues.

Education as a Common Good

Common good should be the overarching framework and commanding vision for any educational institution, especially in a Christian college. This needs to be stressed in these times when, in the context of the capitalist economy and liberalization, education is viewed more and more as a tradable private good. The relationship of the educational institution and the students becomes one of suppliers and consumers of intellectual goods. In fact, this is what it has become at the international level with WTO entering into the field of education as a tradable service across borders.[19] Closely connected to this is the consideration of knowledge and education for its economic value, and the benefit it could bring in terms of material advancement. Education, which, in the context of globalization, is being treated as merchandise, must be treated as a means of humanization and emancipation.

Drawing on Radhakrishnan Report (1949) and Kothari Commission Report (1964-1966), the National Policy on education (1968 & 1986) set the goal of community and national development as the major objective. This community-orientation remains the foundational principle for all educational institutions, and the Christian ones will make their contribution, the more they adhere to this foundational policy of national education. Beyond a perspective of "neutrality of knowledge", Christian institutions, must display a "Positional Objectivity" by fostering all sciences, especially research in basic sciences, not neglecting the human and social sciences, going beyond the servitude to the market.[20] Christian institutions should engage themselves in community-oriented researches. This holds good also for policies of admission, where we will have to shed our colonial, now globalization-oriented elitism, to project a proactive and preferential option for the poor, promoting a culture of inclusiveness. Restricting higher education only to the well-to do is neither good for the growth of the country nor is it Christian in spirit. It would contradict the letter and spirit of the national policy of education which speaks

18 For a critical inquiry into access and inclusiveness, in Indian education, especially the disparity in the GER (Gross Educational Ratio), see Sukhadeo Thorat, "Higher Education in India. Emerging Issues Related to Access, Inclusiveness," Nehru Memorial Lecture (Mumbai: University of Mumbai, 2006).

19 V.T. Patil, *Higher Education in India: The International Engagement* (Delhi: Authors Press, 2010).

20 See in this context, path-breaking approaches to higher education, in the optic of "Multiple Intelligences", "Disruptive", beyond the run of the mill, "Integrative" approach to knowledge in Saikat Majumdar, *College Pathways of Possibility* (New Delhi: Bloomsbury, 2018).

of "education for equality."[21] The National Policy on Education of 1986 states unmistakably this goal, by placing special emphasis on the removal of disparities and equalization of opportunities, by attending to the specific needs of those who have been denied equality so far.[22]

Socially and Politically Conscious Higher Education

Economic liberalism anaesthetizes social consciousness. Therefore, in a market-driven model of education one may not expect any serious concern for common good or effort to reach out to the marginalized. In line with its spirit of pragmatism, this model of education keeps at bay social and political issues.[23] The responsibility towards community and practice of solidarity could become effective only when deep social consciousness is nurtured among students and staff. The bourgeois higher education of today is politically and socially "illiterate", in spite of all its impressive market-oriented specialization. The lack of social and political awareness results in teachers and students becoming simple transmitters and recipients of knowledge and information, with no regard to the social significance of the knowledge produced and transmitted. This neglect facilitates the promotion and maintenance of class and caste structures of educational institutions.

It is then a serious obligation on the part of Christian institutions to instill a critical sense about society, and free the students from the social and political naiveté and anesthetized state of consciousness. More than ever before, a critical social consciousness is required precisely because, through its philosophy of individualism and its consumerist allurement, liberalization functions as a deterrent of social consciousness.[24]

Ecology, Ecosophy and a Culture of Partnership

Growth in ecological consciousness is another task, which has to be woven into the Christian counter-narrative to tide over the profit-orientation and the exploitation of the neo-liberal capitalism, plaguing the educational scenario. There is need of countering the culture of individualistic neo-liberalism, with an interrogation of the culture of consumerism, with its 'manipulative reasons' and its attempts to explain away poverty, in terms of laziness and inefficiency of

---

21 Felix Wilfred, "What is "Christian" about Christian Colleges", 190-92.

22 *National Policy on Education 1986* (as modified in 1992), (Delhi: Government of India, Department of Education, Ministry of Human Resources Development, no. 41).

23 Sudhanshu Bhushan, "Higher Education in 12th Plan: Paradigm Shift in favour of 'For Profit,'" *Economic and Political Weekly* 48, no. 4 (January 26, 2013), 19-23; See also: Binay Kumar Pathak, "Critical Look at Narayana Moorthy Recommendations on Higher Education," *Economic and Political Weekly 49*, no. 3 (January 18, 2014), 72-74.

24 Felix Wilfred, "What is "Christian" about Christian Colleges?" 197.

the poor,[25] and not as a result of structural injustice. This also calls for knitting into our educational narrative, a culture of partnership between, women, men and nature, and helping the staff and students, grow in feminist consciousness and gender sensitivity, challenging the structures of patriarchi(es).

Culture of Human Rights, Constitutional Morality and Dissent

Of late, it was heartening to hear that the Catholic Church has decided to teach the Indian Constitution, in all the schools, run by the Church. It will go a long way in making the staff and the students, politically conscious and in enabling them to stand for their rights and the rights of others, as mentioned earlier. When efficiency and profit are the dominant *mantra*, the violation of human rights are perpetrated with impunity. The process of globalization heavily impinges on the practice of human rights. At a time, when the dignity of the minorities, labourers and workers are threatened in many gross and subtle ways, often in connivance with the state power, Christian institutions are called upon to bear witness to their Christian character, by respecting the rights of the faculty, workers and even students, which include freedom of expression, association and dissent.[26]

There is growing awareness of constitutional morality in the country today, especially brought about by the grounded interpretation of the Constitution by the judiciary, though what has been applied in the context of repealing section 377 of Indian Penal Code has not been shown in the case of manual scavengers, who die by the hundreds, in the sewages of India. "The issue of the rights of sweepers and scavengers has never entered the mainstream legal consciousness in the country," wrote Upendra Baxi in *Law and Poverty: Critical Essays*. Outgoing Chief Justice of India Dipak Misra set out four cardinal corners of the Constitution: Individual autonomy and liberty; equality sans discrimination; recognition of identity with dignity; right to privacy. He also underscored the centrality of fraternity to the constitutional value system. These signposts require us to contemplate and act on the meanings and expressions of "intrinsic dignity" for conservancy workers and *safai karamcharis*.[27]

This new trend in stressing the constitutional morality, can be traced to Ambedkar and his resistance to caste and untouchability, rooted in his stress on Fraternity[28] and social endosmosis, as much needed virtues for the grounded

25 Pierre Bourdieu, *Acts of Resistance: Against the Tyranny of the Market* (New York: The New Press, 1998), 42ff.

26 Felix Wilfred, "Higher Education and Christian Identity," 269-270.

27 Kalpana Kannabiran, "The Scope of Constitutional Morality," The *Hindu*, October 4, 2018, 8.

28 Smaran Shetty and Tanaya Sanyal, "Fraternity and the Constitution: A Promising Beginning in Nandini Sundar V. State of Chhattisgarh," accessed September 25, 2018, http://docs.

practice of democracy, as much as, equality and liberty. Along with these bulwarks of democracy, the right to dissent,[29] the safety valve of democracy, as opined by Justice Chandrachud, is embedded in the lived reality of democracy.

Why I have delved into the aspect of constitutional morality, inscribed by fraternity, in relation to the forgotten plight of the manual scavengers is for emphasizing, especially in the Christian institutions, on the need to help our students, as citizens, to acquire a *deprivational* perspective, in the study and practice of the Constitution, and making the state accountable for the same. In this context, the culture of dissent also acquires importance.

Art of Negotiation: Education towards Inter-religious Dialogue, Tolerance, Conflict- Resolution and Secularism

Negotiation is the ability for border-crossing. This is indispensable for education in multi-cultural and multi-ethnic societies of Asia. India is not a monolithic civilization, but a celebration of different civilization(s), not a metanarrative, but a pluralistic cascade of mini-narratives. India has been breathing the air of mystical pluralism, in a spirit of living and lived dialogue. Constant re-living and reinterpretation of this reality, through symbolic celebrations and dialogue of the hands in actions for justice, on behalf of the marginalized, have to be knit into the texture of our educational processes, as an antidote to the tendencies towards, monolithic, authoritarian religio-cultural and majoritarian nationalism. Here again, we have to inculcate in the students, a sense of fraternity, cutting across the adherence to various creeds and cultures and languages. This calls for "Pedagogy of Encounter", and education for peace and conflict resolution, for which UNESCO has taken several initiatives in the past few decades. There is an Asian and specifically Indian approach to secularism, which is quite different from the majoritarian nationalism, which tends to subsume and obliterate all difference of identities, on the one hand, and the soft-Hindutva practised by certain political parties, on the other. True secularism is a defence against all types of fundamentalist and communalist trends.[30]

Valorization of Indigenous Knowledge(s) from Subaltern Locations

At the outset, it may be made clear that by indigenous knowledge here, is not meant, knowledge, which is exotic, as opposed to the native, not even, knowledge of native origin, as opposed to the Western knowledge, like what

manupatra.in/newsline/articles/Upload/1A226E6F-4443-472F-9E7E-CB70EA7C3744.pdf

29 See: Anuradha Raman in Interview with Soli Sorabjee, "'If dissent is not allowed, it'll take different forms,'" *The Hindu*, September 27, 2017, 9; see also: Zoya Hassan, "Restricting Protest, Stifling Dissent," *The Hindu*, June 26, 2017, 9.

30 *Secularism and Its Critics*, ed. Rajeev Bhargava, (Delhi: Oxford University Press, 1999).

was connoted by "national education", during the Independence struggle or what is being exalted as Vedic knowledge, as the fount of all sciences, as claimed by the 'Pundits' of the *Sanghparivar*. What is meant by indigenous knowledge here has different epistemological presuppositions, as regards its sources and ends. Knowledge is not reducible, to something that is derived from a few elites and specialists. People and community are resources of knowledge, and today one has come to realize this more sharply in connection with environmental issues and sustainable use of the gifts of nature.[31] A less known but important fact is that indigenous knowledge has today a lot of economic potential which needs to be tapped. This knowledge embedded in the life and practices of the people is widely made use of:

> World Bank found that after several decades of massive developmental efforts, two-thirds of the world's population still could not survive without indigenous knowledge of plants, animals, insects, microbes and farming systems (UNDP 1994). The World Health Organization noted that up to 80 per cent of the world's population depends on traditional medicine for is primary health needs (WHO 1998).[32]

To tide over underutilization of traditional knowledge, education and research in Christian colleges need to be community-based. Promoting indigenous knowledge, in a transdisciplinary way, will chart a new course, in the field of higher education, by furthering the goal of sustainable development. Pursuit of indigenous knowledge helps, among other things, conservation of biological diversity, equitable sharing and sustainable use of natural resources, thus paving way to the holistic development of the entire community. This evidently challenges the notion of development, which, under neo-liberalism, is tilted towards the rich, at the cost of the neglect of the poor and the community orientation of resources.[33]

Christian colleges can forge linkages with the social movements and civil societies, like feminist and environmental Movements, which are producing first rate knowledge, in interaction with the locations at the peripheries, with their own fresh theoretical perspectives and analytical instruments. Valorization of this local fund of knowledge, gathered from the rough

31 *Indigenous Traditions and Ecology*, ed., John A. Grim (Cambridge M.A.: University Press, 2001).

32 Nirmal P. Sengupta, *Economic Studies of Indigenous and Traditional Knowledge* (Delhi: Academic Foundation, 2007), 22.

33 Felix Wilfred, "What is "Christian" about Christian Colleges?" 201-202.

ground of Indian realities, will go towards the empowerment of the subaltern communities and assist them in their struggle for identity assertion.[34]

Conclusion

As I conclude this paper, an incident related to a Catholic community and its leadership, including the parish priest, which happened in Bardez, in Goa, as narrated by Peter Ronald deSouza, comes to my mind. The Catholics, among whom was also a Zilla Parishad member, made up 25% of the village population. When approached by concerned parties, following a dispute about the use of the newly installed crematorium, by the Dalit Mahars of the village, their stance was, "It is internal matter of the Hindus. We have nothing to do with it." Desouza's observation on the event is that, by brushing aside the dispute as 'internal' to the other religion, a "Private" and not a "Public/Secular" matter, they were eclipsing the element of discrimination of the Dalits, which should have been a common concern.[35]

This Paper has been an attempt at showing how the Christian community, with its leadership, has to realize its identity, as an interlocutor in the civil society.[36] There is nothing private about religion, which would warrant our insular mindset, preventing us from "Speaking to" and "Speaking out" on the issues, affecting the victims. *Private/Personal* is *Public*.

The counter-narrative to the selling of knowledge-ware mode of Marketized Education, we have attempted weaving, has called for the reimagination of education as a common good, socially and politically conscious, promoting ecology, ecosophy and a culture of partnership, the culture of human rights, culture of constitutional morality and dissent, the art of negotiation and border crossing and the valorization of indigenous knowledge(s) from subaltern locations. The arena of education, which is a site of contestation, which we chose to interrogate, is one among many available strategic and subversive entry points, to tame the Economic Leviathan of the globalized market. It is also a trigger for Christianity to be ever a disciple, in the teacher-student-student-teacher mode,[37] contesting hegemonies, as advocated by Paulo Freire, in his pedagogic optic of the Pedagogy *of* the Oppressed, and not *for* the Oppressed. Christianity is a social movement-ever-in learning, networking with other Movements, in *performance* in

34 See Kancha Ilaiah, "Productive Labour, Consciousness and History; The Dalitbahujan Alternative," in *Subaltern Studies: Writings on South Asian History and Society – IX*, eds, Shahid Amin and Dipesh Chakrabarty (Delhi: Oxford University Press, 1997), 165-200.

35 Peter Ronald deSouza, "Humiliation in a Crematorium," in *Humiliation: Claims and Context*, ed. Gopal Guru (Delhi: Oxford University Press, 2013), 126.

36 Felix Wilfred, "Christianity – Interlocutor in Civil Society," in *Asian Dreams and Christian Hope*, 181-207.

37 As quoted in "Engaging Freire's Pedagogy for a Critique of Indian Education."

the public sphere, beyond the *function*, around the ritual,[38] living up to the ethics of refusal of domination and exploitation, characteristic of the social movements. The constraints, by way of counter-strategies by the state-market nexus would be many, but the task is to *invent* spaces, within the constraints. That is precisely, the journey from being a Sudra, in the market of commodified services, to becoming Symbols of Servanthood, believing with Jon Sobrino, the liberation theologian, that, "*Extra pauperes nulla salus.*"("**There is no salvation, outside the poor**.")

38 Peter Beyer, *Religion and Globalization* (New Delhi: Sage, 1997), 86-96, for the distinction he makes between the dimensions of *function* and *performance*, while dealing with the relevance and continuity of religion in the context of globalization. Functional relates to the rituals, moral injunctions and the rituals of a religion, as part of the maintenance of the system, that is religion, whereas the performative relates to what a religion is, and what it becomes in relation to the society, its questions and concerns, especially in relation to the service of those who are left behind by the systems of the society.

18

The Emerging Phenomena of Contemporary Inter-Faith Harmony Movements in Urban India

James Ponniah
University of Madras

Abstract: To the situation of increasing religious fanaticism across the globe, contemporary religious subjects do not remain as mute spectators. Rather, they see themselves as agents of change who need to intervene to save the situation. Based on the fieldwork done in the city of Chennai, this paper shows how contemporary inter-faith harmony Movements today are gaining momentum in the city of Chennai through study of activities of three different religious organizations, namely, the Hindu organization of 'Sri Vishnu Mohan Foundation,' the Muslim organization of 'Islamic Foundation Trust' and the Christian organization of 'Institute of Dialogue with Cultures and Religions'. It describes how inter-religious initiatives in the city of Chennai has been advancing in new direction. Moving beyond the idea of cultivating religious tolerance through formal inter-religious dialogue, the current efforts of these organizations focus on celebrating religious differences that are already present in Indian societies, just as they seek to debunk fanatics' campaigns of religious bigotry. This essay employs the framework of social and spiritual capitals to understand and analyse the phenomena of contemporary inter-faith harmony Movements in urban India today.

Keywords: Religious organisations, peace, interfaith harmony, social capital and spiritual capital.

Introduction

In recent years, religious peace-building initiatives have become more visible, more urgent, more numerous, and more recognized. Diplomats, governmental and non-governmental bodies, international and global organizations, journalists, and funding organizations pay increasing attention to the possibilities of religious peace-building and of positive co-operation with religious leaders to address specific problems, including war, conflict, and violence. Also, religious actors themselves—ranging from laypersons and individual religious leaders of denominational structures to inter-denominational and multiple religious bodies—seem more open and encouraged to take up a role as peace-builders, exploring their own faith traditions and developing their resources and practices for peace. They increasingly develop an intentional, systematic, and proactive approach to peace-building, often in cooperation with other religious or confessional organizations.[1]

The quotation above from Katrien Hertog's book *In The Complex Reality of Religious Peacebuilding* highlights a surge of interests among people of various backgrounds including religious groups that advocate peace in the world. This book discusses the phenomena of inter-faith harmony Movements that are working on the ground across the globe under different circumstances and in differing intensities. Since 1990 there have emerged across the world many organisations and initiatives that focus exclusively on the relationship between religion and peace-building. Some studies have been undertaken to explore their methods, strategies and contributions of these organisations. Organizations and centres that focus exclusively and solely on peace are only a few in India. Writings on peace-making in India have largely focused on major events of conflict between Hindus and Muslims during partition of India in 1947 and after the demolition of Babri Majsid in 1999. Such works on peace-making in India had mainly dwelt upon the Gandhi's idea of ahimsa and the views, methods and strategies of Gandhi and of his followers like frontier Gandhi. It was personality-centred. As a result, 'organisational or movement approach to peace' is missing in India. In Post—Ayodhya India, religious peace initiatives have become an visible movement that not only characterizes the centres that are solely dedicated to peace, but also that peace has become an important component of various secular or religious institutes that address the question of religious harmony in some way or the, through their programmes and activities. This paper is a small attempt to explore and analyse the inter-religious peace movement advanced by the centres and organisations in Chennai to overcome differences and conflict in India,

1 Quoted in, Katrien Hertog, *In The Complex Reality of Religious Peace-building: Conceptual Contributions and Analysis* (Lanham, MD: Lexington Books, 2010), XV.

and to bring about unity and harmony in their own small ways. Taking into account the potentiality of religion to combat conflict and engender peace, this paper, in Part I, seeks to explore how interreligious harmony in the city of Chennai is promoted by three different religious organizations. They are the Hindu organization of SVMF (Sri Vishnu Mohan Foundation), the Muslim organization of IFT (Islamic Foundation Trust Chennai) and the Christian organization of IDCR (Institute of Dialogue with Cultures and Religions). Part II of the paper employs the framework of social and spiritual capitals to understand and analyse the phenomena of contemporary inter-faith harmony Movements in urban India today.

PART I

A. The Muslim Organization of IFT

The Islamic Foundation Trust (IFT) was established way back in 1979. One of the objectives of the foundation is to make Islam a living reality in modern times and to build bridges of understanding between different faiths and peoples. Its mission, originally, was to reach out to Muslims and non-Muslims primarily through the publication of vernacular Islamic literatures in Tamil. Since late 1990s, its publications began to address the issue of religious and social harmony in more than one way. It produces many relevant books entitled, *Ontray Kulam Oruvane Thevan* (One Race and One God) *Emmathamum Sammathamay* (All Religions are Acceptable), *Islam Manitha Urimaihalin Kavalan* (Islam: The Custodian of Human Rights), *Saathi Oliya Samathuvam Malara* (Let caste go so that equality can blossom) etc., to further the cause of religious harmony and social emancipation. They publish materials to eradicate misconceptions about Islam and Muslims, and thus create communal amity. They also publish *samarasam* (peace), a bimonthly periodical which is circulated in 3000 government libraries all over Tamilnadu. The editor claims that 40% of the periodical's content is addressed to Muslim readers, 30% to non-Muslim readers, and the rest 30% is on current issues. A quick survey of the contents of *samarasam* speaks volumes for IFT's breadth of vision on a range of issues that affect the nation and its common people as we find in the essays such as 'Islam against Terrorism,' 'GST-A War waged in the Midnight,' 'Kollaiyanae Veliaru' (Let the robbers quit)—an essay that analyses the issue of Gas plant in Kathirmangalm (Tamilnadu), "India Afflicted by Religious Fanaticism" 'Islam's Influence over Women,' 'Kiladi-An Excavation for Dravidian Civilization,' and so on.

Realizing that in contemporary society, people are strongly influenced by mass media, IFT embarked upon the domain of mass media in 2000 by establishing CCC (The Creative Communication Chennai). It first took cognisance of the all pervasive nature of mass media and its "intrinsic and inherent power to make or mar news, to broadcast or narrowcast information, to develop or destroy sanity among people, to build or blast relationships, to communicate truthful, constructive, useful and beneficial information, or to spread false, utterly harmful, downright destructive information or concepts."[2] Against this background, while it portrays Prophet Muhammad as their role model who "not only adopted effective and efficient means of communication but he had also been the most powerful influencer and creative communicator – even in this age of 21st century. He is the Living Communicator in the sense that his message is still influencing and inspiring, touching and transforming billions of people the world over,"[3] it also calls upon Muslim Ummah "to communicate the teachings of Islam to all mankind."[4] Its rationale in this regard is: "Non-communication of Islam and non-commitment in this important field would be tantamount to signing our own death warrant! The global scenario today is that, Islam is the most misunderstood and the most misinformed civilization....Given this global 'phenomenon,' it becomes all the more necessary to present Islam as it is to the people of the world."[5] To achieve this goal, it made its services available in electronic media through *Manuda Vasantham* (Human Spring), an Islamic Television Programme, aired since 2000 through the satellite channels. One of its main goals is to dispel misunderstandings regarding Islam and Muslims and to present Islam as common to all human beings. The Q and A programme entitled '*Kelvi Pirandadu Inru*' by Dr K. V. S. Habeeb Muhammad, an eminent Islamic scholar, has become so popular in that it not only addresses the biases against the Muslims but also serves as a platform for Islamic advocacy and lobbying in support of causes and issues that concern the common people of the state.

Further, the organization periodically invites renowned non-Muslim writers both to release and review their books, especially, on Islam. In an effort to promote religious harmony, the foundation holds every year an Eid get-together for non-Muslim writers and journalists, some of whom address the gathering on Islam and communal harmony. Additionally, they hold conferences in different parts of the state which unequivocally condemn fundamentalism and radicalism in Islam. Thus it plays the role of what Kraybill would call as "truth-teller,"[6] while "raising a voice of moral outrage against

---

2 http://ift-chennai.org/creative-communication-chennai-ccc, accessed October10, 2018.

3 Ibid.

4 Ibid.

5 Ibid.

6 As quoted in: Cynthia Sampson, "Religion and Peace-building" in *Peacemaking in International Conflict: Method and Techniques*, ed., William Zartman (Washington, DC: United States Institute of Peace, 2007), 281.

what are seen as ...wrongful acts committed by a party to the conflict."[7] In the context of peace-building process, truth-telling is seen "distinctly an act of moral advocacy on the part of the religious actor."[8] Such conventions also take up common people's issues such the menace of TASMAC (liquor shops run by Tamilnadu state government), atrocities against women and price-hike etc.

IFT's contribution is not restricted to the production and dissemination of knowledge alone. They also extend their works to social service and charity that is aimed at the benefit of the poor and the needy and the disadvantaged, irrespective of religion, thus fostering inter-religious harmony. It started a unit called Health Care Services India, popularly known as HECSI in 1992 at Madrasand runs a Mobile Medical Service to provide free medical service to a cross section of the slum and village folk, irrespective of caste, creed and community, towards health care and human development. They network with Hindus and Christians to visit hospitals and old age homes. During natural calamities such as Tsunami and Chennai floods they undertook relief works. With the help of Muslim AID, a UK based charity organization, Islamic Foundation Trust (IFT) had built 100 homes to the Tsunami victims. It also runs three women empowerment centres in the city where they train poor women, irrespective of religion, in computers, handicrafts and tailoring. In their charity works, they are motivated by Prophet Muhammad. Explaining this, one of my interlocutors said that Prophet Muhammad has clearly stated the "the best among you is the one who is kind to every human being."[9]

B. Christian Organization of IDCR

Earlier known as *Aikiya Alayam* (Temple of Unity) since its inception in 1967, the rechristened IDCR is now located at Loyola College since 2005. The renewed institute's objective is "to promote a genuine spirit of unity among and respect for all religions and their followers, to engage in breaking differences and building bridges, to resolve conflicts ensuing peace and forgiveness among and between the believers and others going beyond the boundaries of caste, creed and culture."[10] To actualize this goal, the institute runs several workshops, conferences and retreats on inter-cultural and inter-religious relations and conflicts, training programmes and religious education programmes. As Cynthia notes, one of the important roles religion plays in the process of peace-building is education:

---

7 As quoted in: Cynthia Sampson, "Religion and Peace-building" in *Peacemaking in International Conflict: Method and Techniques*, ed., William Zartman (Washington, DC: United States Institute of Peace, 2007), 281.

8 Ibid.

9 In an interview with the sub-editor of *Samarasm,* March 2018.

10 Director, *Institute of Dialogue, Culture and Religions* (Leaflet) (Chennai: IDCR, 2010).

> Education and training play a role during each stage of conflict transformation, whether to sensitize a society to inequities in the system; to foster an understanding of and build the skills of advocacy, conflict resolution, democracy, or living with diversity; or to promote healing and reconciliation. The key to this activity is the dimension of preparation—of teaching or in some way providing a learning experience for others from a position one step removed from direct involvement in conflict intervention.[11]

In this regard, one of its most successful flagship initiatives of the IDCR is the creation of 'Peace Rangers,' an inter-collegiate student movement in 2007. To orient the college students as peace rangers, IDCR began to conduct many training programmes such as 'Breaking Differences and Building Bridges' (BDBB) and Interreligious Awareness and Practice (IRAP) in 2012. IRAP is a 6 day workshop and it provides open space for college students not only to reflect on their own religious beliefs and practices but also to understand those of others. It is specially designed to building inter-religious awareness while it strives to enlighten students on the faith traditions of others. In the workshops of IRAP, "students are exposed to different styles of prayer and a broad range of beliefs and styles of devotion, thus creating a safe environment for religion through interactive sessions."[12] Through seminars by learned scholars, various aspects of different religions are learnt, discussed and rationalized, while field trips to various religious sites help the participants to get exposed to the religious world of other traditions. Having been trained through workshops, peace rangers are equipped to conduct similar types of programmes for the youth and children in schools and colleges. They also seek to promote peace and harmony in Chennai city by conducting events and open campaigns in public places including road-shows on different themes related to conflict and peace in the country. To list only a few of their programmes: 'Trekking for Peace at Velliangiri Hills' (which involved meeting with a Hindu Sadhguru at Isha Foundation to discuss ways of building peaceful society), joint-celebration of 'Harmony Day' with Brahma Kumaris marked by bi-cycle peace rally, 'Breaking Differences: Harmony Within' (a training programme for young lawyers to work towards the reduction of stigma and discrimination of HIV positive children), Inter-religious meditation and prayer (IMAP) etc. Out of such positive experiences by the youth in IDCR was born Blink in 2014. Blink Foundation is a college student's forum which brings together college students, school students and the educators "to nurture a society that celebrates the dignity of difference. To achieve this, Blink enables action through both

11 Cynthia Sampson, "Religion and Peace-building," 292.

12 http://blinkfoundation.org/all-project-list/inter-religious-awareness-practices-irap/, accessed October 10, 2018.

contact and content by offering value Education programme in schools, and web portal that acts as Knowledge Depository."[13] It works with a vision : "To nurture a society that celebrates the dignity of difference."[14] and a mission: "To facilitate a virtual and real platform to connect, converse, contribute, and co-act and celebrate a well informed and incisive society."[15] To materialize its vision and mission, it trains 'change agents.' Change agents are college student volunteers—motivated and passionate young men and women—who are trained by Blink to evolve a new vision for social transformation. Upon the completion of training they become agents of CHANGE and impart this knowledge and experience to the younger generation. Blink employs various strategies and organizes various programs to promote values of tolerance, understanding, acceptance and celebration of difference. To name a few: it conducts 'sports for equality,' 'Campaign Castaway' (event to eradicate social evils by painting social messages on garbage bins), 'Every Smile Counts', 'Flash Mob performance' (to emphasise gender equality) and 'Learning with Disabilities'(Teacher's workshop for 'Understanding Students with Learning Disabilities')

C. Hindu Phenomenon of Sri Vishnu Mohan Foundation

The third phenomenon, Sri Vishnu Mohan Foundation, started in 2009, is a research foundation that carries forward the message of a woman guru, Sri Sathguru Sarasvathi. It aims at bringing to fore the transformational knowledge traditions of India that come from its teachers, gurus, seers and books. Drawing from cross cultural and religious contexts, SVMF strives to harness interdisciplinary approaches to rediscover, formulate and create pathways to transforming lives. One of the goals of the foundation is to forge well-meaning and relevant partnerships with organizations and individuals who promote 'humankind's ideals of equality, coexistence and selflessness.'[16] To achieve its goals, the organization under the leadership of Swamiji Sri Hariprasad is networking with people of other faiths and good will. The collabourative efforts of the swamiji are also quite conspicuous by his presence and support in various fora across India and the world (Malaysia, USA and Europe) where he shares dais with Muslims, Buddhists and Christians and join in their efforts of harmony and peace in society.

To pursue one of its objectives of 'promotion of knowledge to the benefit of human well-being,'[17] it conducts every year a seminar on Peace since 2016.

---

13 http://blinkfoundation.org/, accessed October 10, 2018.

14 Ibid.

15 Ibid.

16 http://svmf.in/objectives.html, accessed October 2, 2018.

17 Ibid.

The first seminar was titled 'Peace, Philosophy and Religion' The second year conference in 2017 was 'Peace and Reconciliation: Perspectives from Religion and Philosophy.' In the third year 2018, the conference's main focus was on the theme 'A Just and Lasting Peace Springs: From A Just And Peaceful Society.' The annual international conference on peace and reconciliation has its roots in a simple gem (idea) from Sri Sathguru Swami Gnanananda Sarasvathi: When a devotee came to meet her with friends from other faiths, she said: "God realisation is like a mountain peak. From the top, you can see all the paths leading to it. All are arduous but all lead to the summit. Only the people on the summit or who approach the summit know that all paths lead to it. It is the people at the foot of the mountain who fight over which path is superior."[18] It was this seed that has grown into the annual conference, where peace is addressed from all perspectives. These annual conferences bring together eminent people, scholars, activists and the common people from civil society. For instance the first annual conference in 2016 was inaugurated by Dr K. S. Radhakrishnan, Chairman of the Kerala State Public Service Commission. The keynote address was delivered by Dr S. R. Bhatt the Chairman of the Indian Council of Philosophical Research and special address was given by H.E. Fabig, the Consul General for Germany. The 2017 conference became a global phenomenon as it presented speakers and thinkers from across the globe and religious traditions which included: Respected Esin Celebi Byru of Turkey (22nd descendant of the Sufi mystic Jalaludin Rumi), Respected Haji Syed Salman Chisty of the Chisty Foundation, Ajmer

Ven. Somphong, H.E. Hasan Nooriyan, Consul General of Iran from Hyderabad, Most Rev. Archbishop Thomas Menamparampil, former archbishop of Guwahati, Mr. Wajahat Habibullah (I.A.S), Former Chairman, National Commission for Minorities and Dr Yajneshwar Shastri, Vice Chancellor of the Sanchi University of Buddhist-Indic Studies. Such conferences address wide range of issues connected with peace such as 'Ethics of peaceful coexistence,' 'Exploration of peace in the Mahabharata', 'Enforcement of peace—administrative aspects,' 'Peace and the Jews of Kerala,' 'Solution of modern life problems through Ayurveda and Spirituality' and 'Public religion Vs private religion.'

18 In an interview with Sami Hariprasad in Chennai on September 10, 2017.

PART II

Inter-religious Peace Movements Viewed through Social and Religious Capitals

In this section, I would explore how the religious organisations and Movements mentioned above function as arms of peace-making by employing two theoretical tools, namely social capital and religious capital. By social capital I mean social trust and reciprocity produced out of a set of norms, values and attitudes that get operated at the level of social relationships.[19] The locus of social capital can be either individuals or institutions or both. Thus, it is the outcome not of the individuals but also of organisations, and thus becomes both personal and structural. Two important functions of the social capital is bonding and bridging. While social capital produces closeness, intimacy and care resulting in bonding between in-group members, it can also function as a channel of positive relationship between the in-group and the out-group members by bridging the social distance between the two and strengthening social cohesiveness.[20]

Against this understanding of social capital, let us take stock of the functions of the three peace organisations we have mentioned above. Various topics covered in the talks, seminars, events, the programmes and the written literatures of IDCR, IFT and VMF include key values such as repentance, forgiveness and reconciliation that are capable of bridging the social gap between the in-group and the out-group and the engendering collabouration between the two thereby facilitating social cohesiveness in society. Thus, what is common to all three organisations is that that all exhibit greater capacity for peace by forming alliances and collabourations in local community. Through their initiatives they strengthen social cohesiveness through "the accumulation of horizontal social capital."[21] Based on their study of conflict situations in Cambodia, Rwanda, Guatemala, and Somalia, Colletta and Cullen have discussed how conflicts, violence and lack of peace have resulted in the loss of social cohesiveness and depletion of social capital depriving the nation of socio-economic growth and its people of their well-being.[22] Their study outlines "how societal cohesiveness can be strengthened through the accumulation of

19 Francis Fukuyama, *Trust: The Social Virtues and the Creation of Prosperity* (London: Penguin, 1995).

20 Corwin E Smidt, ed., *Religion as Social Capital: Producing the Common Good* (TX: Baylor University Press, 2003).

21 Colletta, Nat J., and Michelle L. Cullen, *Violent conflict and the transformation of social capital: Lessons from Cambodia, Rwanda, Guatemala, and Somalia*. Vol. 795 (New York: World Bank Publications, 2000). 110.

22 Ibid.

horizontal social capital (the nurturing of trust and civic engagement among like and divergent groups) and vertical social capital (relations between the state, market, and civil society) and how social capital can be critical means for combating social fragmentation and violent conflict."[23] In this connection, they have highlighted three important transformative actions, namely, "connecting, empowering and integrating people and organizations"[24] that facilitate accumulation of social capital thereby promoting social cohesion and preventing internal conflicts.

These three transformative actions are also to be seen in the three peace Movements we have discussed, though the way they have translated them on the ground in Chennai is different. By collabourating with various religious leaders and organizations and bringing together people of different faiths and castes from civil society, all three organisations make positive *connections* between religious /social groups who may otherwise turn adverse to one another during the time of communal conflict. Thus, they make conscious efforts to explore the potentiality of religious resources to bridge religious and caste divides which in turn would generate new social capital. This has transformed and broadened local social relationships among the Muslims (through IFT), the adolescents and the youth in the colleges (through IDCR and Blink) and a section of Hindus (through VMF).

The works of these organisations have also *empowered* women and the youth. According to Susan Hayward,[25] in the project of religious peace-building at the global level, one of the biggest lacunae is that women and the youth are neither involved in nor empowered to deal with the situations of conflict. There is no proper recognition of their role as peace makers. The peace initiatives of the religion-based organisations in Chennai highlight the role of women in effecting peace and harmony. The VMF's activities to promote peace are drawn upon the teachings of its woman founder, Sri Sathguru Swami Gnandanda Saraswathi. It is her message that formed the backbone of VMF's mission for peace. Similarly the involvement of the adolescents and the youth of Chennai in the promotion of peace and harmony is clearly evidenced in the activities of the Blink. In particular, the proactive and creative role of young women as peace-rangers is IDCR's programms and as change agents in Blink's activities are very obvious. Quick glance of video-clips, posters and pictures seen in official websites of these two organization would capture the eyes of

23 Colletta, Nat J., and Michelle L. Cullen, *Violent conflict and the transformation of social capital: Lessons from Cambodia, Rwanda, Guatemala, and Somalia*. Vol. 795 (New York: World Bank Publications, 2000). 113.

24 Ibid.

25 Susan Hayward "Religion and Peace Building: Reflections on Current Challenges and Future Prospects," *Special Report* 313, (August 2012), United States Institute of Peace, accessed May 4, 2018, www.usip.org.

any viewers who cannot but appreciate transformative role this young girls and boys play for the societal peace in the city of Chennai. IFT in some ways provide platform for Muslim women in Chennai to articulate their views on various issues through its sister organisation called 'Federation of Tamilnadu Muslim women.'

Thirdly, all the organisations, in their own way, work for *integration* of various groups in the city of Chennai across caste and religious lines. When we analyse the vision and the activities of all three peace Movements, it is rather clear that they seek to overcome social differences that polarise the civil society on the basis of inherited inequality which weakens social cohesiveness. Thus, they strengthen societal cohesiveness through the accumulation of horizontal social capital. While all three seek to fight against Indian view of social difference on a vertical axis, they seem to build upon Indian notion of acceptance of religious differences on horizontal axis too as in the Indian saying. 'religions are different rivers flowing into the same ocean. They are different paths leading to the same destination.' These groups also seek to nurture social capital in collabouration with governmental agencies (ICPR, state universities) and bureaucrats (diplomats, IAS officers) and international actors thereby strengthening social cohesion through multiple strategies and thus promoting peace and harmony.

Viewing the initiatives of the religion-based organisations through social capital describes what religious actors do to promote peace and harmony but it does not explain why they do what they do. In other words it does not unpack the motive and the purpose behind such acts and does not explain the religious rationale for their actions. To do so I want to employ the idea of religious/spiritual capital to capture their motivation and purpose. Following Baker and Skinner, I prefer to describe spiritual capital found in each of the religious tradition as "value system, moral vision and a basis of faith. Spiritual capital is often embedded locally within faith groups but also expressed in the lives of individuals,"[26] and religious capital as "the practical contribution to local and national life made by faith groups."[27] They further expand the idea of spiritual capital and religious capital "as ways of describing faith-based engagement within the public domain."[28] According to them, these notions not only unfold distinctive ways in which faith communities engage with mainly secular

26 Chris Baker and Hannah Skinner, *Faith in Action: The Dynamic Connection between Spiritual and Religious Capital* (Final Report of The William Temple Foundation's Research Project, 2006), 4., Also see: https://williamtemplefoundation.org.uk/wp-content/uploads/2014/03/Faith-In-Action-William-Temple-Foundation-2014.pdf, accessed, October 7, 2018.

27 Ibid.

28 Ibid.

understandings of civil society but also some of "religious and spiritual capital naturally overlap with the practices and values of secular civil society."[29]

When probed, the interlocutors on the ground state that they are inspired by each of their religious tradition's teachings and mandate to bring about peace. Religious organisations do draw upon their own respective tradition's teachings to work for peace. For instance, IFT takes its inspiration from Quran and seeks to advance the teachings of prophet Muhammad to bring about peace. Its efforts are aimed not only to overcome external religious conflict with external religious other but also to deal with the internal religious other . They deliberately distance themselves such versions of Islam that polarise people on the basis of religion as Muslims, Christians and Hindus. Such attempts towards deliberate distancing from Hindu fundamentalism is less pronounced in the Hindu organisation of VMF. In the interview Swamiji held that Jnana Marga, which they subscribe to, will bring about right knowledge in human beings and make them embrace the whole world as one and with love. Thus they seem to have adopted an indirect method to prune fast-spreading religious bigotry in the nation. Admission of Christian resources is also present in IDCR's and its offshoot Blink's works. Strong influence of Kingdom values of equality, fraternity, universalism on the activities of both are very palpable. In a personal interview, the founder of Blink said, "Jesus is a prince of peace. He asked his followers to work for peace in the Sermon of Mount. He accepted the people as they are. Unlike other rabbis of his time, he interacted with the so called outcastes of his time. It means he accepted differences and believed in the equality of all."[30] Similarly, Blink's mission of celebrating differences is seen as very much a Christian idea as its young founder articulated it as follows: "Christians see and worship their Trinitarian God as plural. God is not one but three different persons. So, acceptance of differences in religions should come naturally to Christians. Recognition and celebration of differences are so important in multi-religious country like India especially in our present context fast spreading fundamentalism all over the world including India."[31] Inspired by the core values provided by the spiritual capitals of each of these traditions, the above said Movements have evolved their own goals and missions. Though each of the organisations have their own specific goals to pursue, they all converge on one point, namely, promotion of religious harmony and societal well-being, thereby making practical contribution to

29 Chris Baker and Hannah Skinner, *Faith in Action: The Dynamic Connection between Spiritual and Religious Capital* (Final Report of The William Temple Foundation's Research Project, 2006), 4., Also see: https://williamtemplefoundation.org.uk/wp-content/uploads/2014/03/Faith-In-Action-William-Temple-Foundation-2014.pdf, accessed, October 7, 2018, 5.

30 Interview with the founder of *Blink*, April 27, 2018.

31 Ibid.

local civil society. Thus, the initiatives undertaken by these three institutions confirm Appleby's observation that "religious actors build peace when they act religiously, that is, when they draw on the deep wells of their traditions, and extract from those depths the spiritual instincts and moral imperatives for recognizing and embracing the humanity of the other; and, when they employ the distinctive ritual and symbolic and psychological resources of religion for transforming the dream of a common humanity into a tangible, felt reality."[32] It also ratifies Cynthia Sampson's observation that "many religiously motivated peacemakers have a natural predisposition to working on reconciliation—the restoration of relationships—as well as personal and social transformation,"[33] and that "conflict resolution is natural terrain for religious peace—builders."[34]

Conclusion

To sum up, the paper points to a new direction in which inter-religious interactions in the city of Chennai has been advancing. Moving beyond the idea of cultivating religious tolerance through formal inter-religious dialogue, interfaith peace Movements in Urban Chennai focus on celebrating religious differences that are already present and deeply rooted in Indian societies. Faced with the growing campaigns of religious bigotry in the age of religious fundamentalism, these leaders and their groups make conscious efforts to avert the influx of biases and prejudices about the religious other propagated by such campaigns. These Movements, through their various programmes, reach out to different groups in civil society in multiple ways aiming at not only removing biases but cultivating open attitude towards others. Thus they promote informed understanding of the religious other. They make people accept others as they are and help them appreciate and celebrate religious differences. In the process, they have explored new sites of engagement not only between people of different faith traditions but also with socially marginalized/disabled groups, such as Muslim women and children with HIV. By enlisting the support of various social stake holders such as writers, college students, lawyers, children and the common people, these peace organisations have created new interlocutors of religious and social harmony in urban Chennai. In doing so, they have not only explored new ways of faith-based engagement within the public domain and have also made the religious and spiritual capitals of each of their traditions become coterminous with the practices and values of secular civil society.

32 Susan Hayward "Religion and Peace Building," 5.

33 Cynthia Sampson, "Religion and Peace-building," 207.

34 Ibid.

19

The Pro-Life Movement: A Transformative Movement of Society

Fr Jose Pennaparambil
St John's Church, Vadakara

Abstract: Pro-life stands for, whatever is opposed to life itself, whatever violates the integrity of the human person, whatever insults human dignity and also where people are treated as mere instruments of gain rather than as free and responsible persons. Early church teachings, Bible, all the Councils of the Church, Popes and Bishops' Conferences condemned all actions and Movements against life. There is a dichotomy and constant fight between the "culture of life" and the "culture of death." The promoters of life use all possible means to protect and sustain lifewhereas, promoters of death destroylife by all possible means. The primary objectives of promoters of death are to paralyze effective actions against the "Culture of Death" by sowing confusion and discord among its members. Pro-abortionists do notrely on democracy.Hence, they force their agenda on the nation by gaining control of society's organs of power and influence through a tacticcalled "infiltration and subversion." There is a "*conspiracy against life*" and this conspiracy involves not only individuals in their personal, family or group relationships, but also goes far beyond, to the point of damaging and distorting, at the international level, relations between peoples and States. Human beingis no longer able to see himself as "mysteriously different" from other earthly creatures; but reduced to a thing to be used and the values of *being* are replaced by those of *having*. The so-called "quality of life" is interpreted primarily or exclusively as economic efficiency, inordinate consumerism, physical beauty and pleasure, to the neglect of the more profound dimensions of interpersonal, spiritual and religious existence of human beings.

Keywords: Pro-Life Movement, Culture of Death, Culure of Life, Pro-Choice,

Introduction

In the history of the world, we cannot see a person. other than Jesus Christ, who has transformed the world in all realms of the society. His teachings and life influenced and motivated millions of people all around the world and as an outcome thousands of spiritual, social, political, revival Movements have emerged. Pro-life movement is one among them, which has transformed the minds of millions of people and equipped them to fight and stand for the protection and abundance of life. Pro-life or pro-birth Movements have drawn energy from the words of Jesus. Jesus the Son of true living God came to this world to "have life and have it in abundance" (Jn.10:10). But, in this fast growing world we do see the proliferation of death, like abortion, suicide, homicide, killing, war, capital punishment, euthanasia etc., than the abundance of life. Or in other words, a "culture of death" has got prominence over "culture of life." As Pope John Paul II says, "there is a kind of conspiracy against life"[1] all over the world. Therefore, it is the duty of every human being who is created in the image and likeness of God (Gen.1:26) to stand for and protect life in all possible means. Hence, there is the relevance of pro-life Movements in the present day scenario. Pro-life stands for all kinds of Movements and actions against life viz., against, abortion, contraception, sterilization, euthanasia, suicide, death penalty or capital punishment, drugs and all kinds of atrocities against women and children, as well as the promotion of life. In this study, chiefly I would like to present the philosophical analysis of the pro-life movement in the present day society basing on the Catholic teachings.

1. Pro-Life Movement-A Brief History

At first Pro-life movement started as anti-abortion movement (or right-to-life movement) contains elements opposing elective or therapeutic abortion on both moral and sectarian grounds and supports its legal prohibition or restriction. But, in a broader scenario as *Second Vatican Council* described, pro-life is a stance against:

> "whatever is opposed to life itself, such as any type of murder, genocide, abortion, euthanasia, or willful self-destruction, whatever violates the integrity of the human person, such as mutilation, torments inflicted on body or mind, attempts to coerce the will itself; whatever insults human dignity, such as subhuman living conditions, arbitrary imprisonment, deportation,

1 John Paul II, *Evagelium Vitae*, 12 (March 25, 1995), accessed June 1, 2019, http://w2.vatican.va/content/john-paul-ii/en/encyclicals/documents/hf_jp-ii_enc_25031995_evangelium-vitae.html.

> slavery, prostitution, the selling of women and children; as well as disgraceful working conditions, where people are treated as mere instruments of gain rather than as free and responsible persons; all these things and others like them are infamies indeed.[2]

The anti-abortion movement includes a variety of organizations, with no single centralized decision-making body.[3] There are diverse arguments and rationales for the anti-abortion stance. Some anti-abortion activists concede arguments for permissible abortions, including therapeutic abortions, in exceptional circumstances such as incest, rape, severe fetal defects or when the woman's health is at risk.[4]

Anti-abortion Movements actually started in United States and before the Supreme Court 1973 decisions in *Roe v. Wade* and *Doe v. Bolton*, anti-abortion views predominated and found expression in state laws which prohibited or restricted abortions in a variety of ways.[5] There is also a smaller consistent life ethic movement, favoring a philosophy which opposes all forms of killing, including abortion, war, euthanasia, and capital punishment.

2. Pro-Life Teachings in the Church

For the Jewish people, as for many peoples of antiquity, blood is the source of life. Indeed "the blood is the life" (Deuteronomy 12:23), and life, especially human life, belongs only to God: for this reason *whoever attacks human life, in some way attacks God himself.*[6] From its first contacts with the Greco-Roman world, where abortion and infanticide were widely practiced, the first Christian community, by its teaching and practice, radically opposed the customs rampant in that society, as is clearly shown by the *Didache* "You shall not murder a child by abortion nor kill that which is born."[7] Among the Greek ecclesiastical writers, Athenagorasand among the Latin authors, Tertullian affirms: "It is anticipated murder to prevent someone from being born."[8]

---

2 See: "Gaudium et Spes: Pastoral Constitution on the Church in the Modern World," in *Vatican Council II - The Conciliar and Post Conciliar Documents*, ed., Austin Flannery (Bombay: St Paul's Press Training School, 1995), 27.

3 Mohr James C., *Abortion in America: The Origins and Evolution of National Policy* (Oxford: Oxford University Press, 1978), 35–36.

4 Ibid.

5 Ibid., 110.

6 John Paul II, *Evagelium Vitae*, 9.

7 *The Didache* ("The Lord's Instruction to the Gentiles through the Twelve Apostles"). II, 2, translated by J.A. Kleist, *Ancient Christian Writers*, Volume 6. Westminster, 1948, 16.

8 Tertullian, *Apology*, trans., S. Thelwall, ANF 3 (Edinburgh: T&T Clark, 1993) IX, 8: CSEL 69, 24.

Throughout Christianity's two thousand years history, even scientific and philosophical discussions about the precise moment of the infusion of the spiritual soul have never given rise to any hesitation about the moral condemnation of abortion.

Pius XI in particular, in his Encyclical *CastiConnubii,* rejected the specious justifications of abortion.[9]Pius XII excluded all direct abortion, i.e., every act tending directly to destroy human life in the womb "whether such destruction is intended as an end or only as a means to an end."[10] John XXIII reaffirmed that human life is sacred because "from its very beginning it directly involves God's creative activity."[11] The Second Vatican Council, as mentioned earlier, sternly condemned abortion: "From the moment of its conception life must be guarded with the greatest care, while abortion and infanticide are unspeakable crimes."[12]

The *Church's canonical discipline,* from the earliest centuries, has inflicted penal sanctions on those guilty of abortion. This practice, with more or less severe penalties, has been confirmed in various periods of history. The 1917 *Code of Canon Law* punished abortion with excommunication.[13] In the Church the purpose of the penalty of excommunication is to make an individual fully aware of the gravity of a certain sin and then to foster genuine conversion and repentance.

Given such unanimity in the doctrinal and disciplinary tradition of the Church, Pope Paul VI was able to declare that this tradition is unchanged and unchangeable.[14] Therefore, by the authority which Christ conferred upon Peter and his Successors, in communion with the Bishops *I declare that direct abortion, that is, abortion willed as an end or as a means, always constitutes a grave moral disorder*, since it is the deliberate killing of an innocent human being. This doctrine is based upon the natural law and upon the written Word of God, is transmitted by the Church's Tradition and taught by the ordinary and universal Magisterium.[15]

9 Pius XI, *Casti Connubii* 1: *AAS* 22 (December 31,1930), 562-592.

10 Address to the Biomedical Association "San Luca" (12 November 1944): *Discorsi e Radiomessaggi*, VI (1944-1945), 191; cf. Address to the Italian Catholic Union of Midwives (29 October 1951), No. 2: *AAS* 43 (1951), 838.

11 John XXII, *Mater et Magistra*, 3: *AAS* 53 (May 15, 1961), 447.

12 "Gaudium et Spes," 51.

13 Code of Canon Law, canon 1398; cf. *Code of Canons of the Eastern Churches,* canon Canon 2350, # 1.

14 Paul VI, *Humanae Vitae* (July 25, 1968), 14: *AAS* 60 (1968), 490. Address to the National Congress of Italian Jurists (December 9, 1972).

15 "Lumen Gentium," in *Vatican Council II: Constitutions, Decrees, Declarations*, ed., Austin Flannery (Northport: Costello, 1996), 25.

After having discussed the ecclesial teaching about the life culture let us discuss the biblical basis of the same.

3. Biblical Basis of Pro-Life Teachings

The advocates of Pro-abortion argue that the Bible does not say anything about abortion. The answer is as follows. If Bible condemns the killing of the innocents, if pre-born children are innocent, and human life is present from fertilization, then the Bible also condemns the killing of pre-born children.[16] There are more than a dozen Biblical references to God opening and shutting thc womb.

The Bible repeatedly and forcefully condemns other sexual sins such as homosexuality, divorce, fornication and adultery, yet pro-abortionists tolerate and even embrace all of these as "basic human rights. In spite of more than fifty Biblical passages denouncing these sins, Frances Kisling[17] casually stated that" I really think God cares very little about the sexual rules, about who is sleeping with whom, other than to wish that we treat each other with well and respect."[18]

In order to be balanced and fair, we must ask the advocates of pro-abortion a simple question: If they insist upon talking about the Bible, where does it justify abortion? There is no phrase in the Bible remotely approaching the phrase "freedom of choice", "woman's body", woman's choice, "plan your family", use your conscience," or any of the popular pro-abortion slogans. There is however, the phrase, "*choose life*, therefore that you and your descendants may live." (Deut: 30:19).

Now, on the basis of these thoughts let us move to the two great Movements of the world pertaining to life viz., "pro-life" and "pro-choice."

4. "Pro-life" Versus "Pro-Choice"

In line with "pro-life" advocates, all the Popes and Bishop's Conferences have condemned all actions or Movements against life as immoral and sin. On the contrary the advocates of "pro-choice" argue for the termination of pregnancy on the basis of human freedom. But, we can see that their arguments are baseless and against the plan of God who is the sole source and owner of life. Now let's see for what the advocates of "pro-choice" stands.

According to *Encyclopedia of Associations*, Catholics For a Free Choice (CFFC) is an association of "Catholics within the Roman Catholic Church who supports the right to legal reproductive health care, especially to family

16 "Lumen Gentium," 25.

17 One of the founding figures of the Catholics For Free Choice

18 Frances Kissling, "Abortion: Taking on the Hard Questions," *Conscience*, (Autumn 1999), 56-57.

planning and abortion,"[19] and itsgoal is to "preserve the right of women's choices in childbearing and child rearing, social and economic programmess for women, families and children" by engaging in "public education on being Catholics and pre-choice"[20] CFFC is a Washington, D.C. based organization whose objective is to convince lawmakers, the popular media and Catholics that there can be an authentic "Catholic pro-choice" philosophy.[21] The group has clearly stated its ultimate" goal: CFFC recommends a change in the policies held by the Holy See to support the use of condoms to prevent AIDS and other diseases; to approve the use of modern methods of contraception, including emergency contraception, to prevent unwanted pregnancy; and to support non-coercive, safe and legal abortion.[22]

But, as per the United States National Council of Catholic Bishops "Because of its opposition to the human rights of some of the most defenseless members of human race, and because its purposes and activities deliberately contradict essential teachings of the Catholic faith.... Catholics for a Free Choice merits no recognition or support as a Catholic organization.[23]

Some people try to justify abortion by claiming that the result of conception, at least up to a certain number of days, cannot yet be considered a personal human life. But the position of the Catholic Church is that, "from the time that the ovum is fertilized, a life is begun which is neither that of the father nor the mother; it is rather the life of a new human being with his own growth. It would never be made human if it were not human already.[24]

---

19 *Encyclopedia of Associations,* s.v. Catholic for a Free Choice.

20 Ibid.

21 Magaly Llaguno, "Catholics for a Free Choice:' A Dossier." *Vida Humana Internacional*, (December 1994), 2. CFFC was founded in 1970 by three members of a pro-abortion group called the National Organization for Women (NOW). Its first public act was to ridicule the Catholic Church by crowning one of these women "Pope Joan I" on the steps of St Patrick's Cathedral in New York City. CFFC defined its identity as "a national educational organization that supports the right to legal reproductive health care, especially family planning and abortion.

22 Statement submitted to the United Nations Commission on Population and Development. *Friday Fax*, April 5, 2002 (New York: Catholic Family & Human Rights Institute).

23 "Catholics for a Free Choice Not a Catholic Group," November 4, 1993, Statement of the National Conference of Catholic Bishops (now the United States Conference of Catholic Bishops), Washington, D.C.

24 Congregation For The Doctrine Of The Faith, *Declaration on Procured Abortion* (18 November 1974), NOS. 12-13: *AAS* 66 (1974), 738.

A step further CFFC:

> denies the authority of the Catholic Church to teach in God's name, worships pagan gods and goddesses, even he bloody Old Testament Ba'al. It even glorifies Satan.[25]

No thinking person can possibly believe that Catholics for a Free Choice even remotely resembles anything Christian or Catholic, despite all of its protestations to the contrary.

On the basis of the above discussions let's move to the philosophical implications of this culture of life and the opposite culture of death.

5. A Philosophical Analysis: "Culture of Life" Versus "Culture of Death"

Philosophically speaking pro-life movement is a movement against all kinds of killings, attacks, actions or Movements or even the very existence human life. All creatures have the right to live, right to grow and multiply, hence any attempt against this right is an aggression or belligerence over life. Man's life comes from God; it is his gift, his image and imprint, a sharing in his breath of life. *God* therefore *is the sole Lord of this life*: man cannot do with it as he wills.[26] Hence, every life vegetative or non-vegetate comes from God and he is the giver and source of every life[27] and devil or the powers of darkness doesn't like life and he tries to destroy every kind of life.

Henceforth, in this world there is a dichotomy and constant fight or in other words there is an unending animosity between the "culture of life" and "culture of death." The promoters of life use all possible means to protect and sustain life by health care facilities; advance medicines and treatments etc. whereas, promoters of death destroys life by using treachery or tricks in the label or in the pretext as promoters of life. At first instance we will not be able to recognize the promoters of death because they are camouflaging and work with the promoters of life. It can be well explained in the words of Cicero. He said before the Roman Senate:

> A nation can survive its fools and even ambitious. But, it cannot survive treason from within. An enemy at the gate is less formidable,

25 Brian Clowes, *Catholics For A Free Choice* (Virginia USA: Human Life International, 2001), 32.

26 Ibid., 39.

27 See the Biblical references-Human life and death are thus in the hands of God, in his power: "In his hand is the life of every living thing and the breath of all mankind", exclaims Job (12:10). "The Lord brings to death and brings to life; he brings down to Sheol and rises up" (1 Samuel 2:6). He alone can say: "It is I who bring both death and life" (Deuteronomy 32:39).

> for he is known and he carries his banners openly against the city. But the traitor moves among those within the gates freely, his sly whispers rustling through all the alleys, heard in the very halls of government itself. For the traitor appears no traitor: he speaks in the accents familiar to his victims, and he wears their face and their garments and he appeals to the baseness that lies deep in the hearts of all men.[28]

In connection with the words of Cicero, Brian Clowes, in his book *Catholics For A Free Choice* says about the promoters of death:

> They are (promoters of death) the traitors whose sly whispers are couched in terms familiar to real Catholics. They actively work and look and sound like real Catholics. And they most certainly appeal to the fallen nature-the weakness and baseness that lies deep in hearts of all men and women. CFFC occupies a vital niche in the worldwide pro-abortion movement. The Catholic Church has always been most powerful opponent of abortions in the world. The primary objectives of CFFC are to paralyze effective action by Catholic Church against the "Culture of Death" by sowing confusion and discord among its members.[29]

The advocates of "Pro-choice" are like double headed chameleons. This we can see from their strategies given below.

Pro-abortionists know full well that their agenda is repugnant to the majority of thinking individuals. They don't rely on democracy. Hence, they force their agenda on the nation by gaining control of society's organs of power and influence through a tactic called "infiltration and subversion." Their strategy is to place talented people in the leadership positions of the sources of influence in society, which are;[30]

* The executive branches of national governments, regions and states
* The courts, particularly national court system
* The legislators at the national, regional and state levels
* The leaders and boards of associations with relevant missions, including organized medical and legal professionals, foundations, non-governmental organizations (NGOs) and public interest groups
* The media particularly the entertainment industry (motion pictures, television, radio) the print and news media (newspapers magazines,

28 Cicero, quoted in "Worth Repeating," *The New American*, (May 12, 1997), 30.

29 Clowes, *Catholics For A Free Choice,* 3.

30 Ibid., 1.

book authors etc.) and arts.[31] School leaders, from grade school board members to the policy makers at medical and legal colleges

* The leadership of churches, particularly catholic church[32]

Once they accomplish these objectives, the new leaders can introduce their agendas, stonewall pro-life initiatives, and subvert the organization so that its voice is added to the ranks of those prestigious groups loudly chorusing for "progress" and "change."[33]

This culture is actively fostered by powerful cultural, economic and political currents which encourage an idea of society excessively concerned with efficiency. The Malthusian theory of population explosion is being advocated by the rich countries on the basis of this efficiency and quality of the person. The fact is that in this modern technologically advanced world there is no population explosion or poverty or starvation, because geographically some of the states of America can contain the total world population and even United States or Canada can produce food for the sustenance of the whole world. The reality is that less developed countries are thickly populated and developed countries are thinly populated. Now the developed countries realized that "population is not curse but strength and wealth" (Former Prime Minister Manmohan Singh). So, the rich countries fear that populated countries such as India, China etc. will rule the modern world. Hence, in order the curb this danger the rich countries are advocating abortion or pro-choice Movements and funding the pro-abortion Movements.

In order to facilitate the spread of *abortion*, the promoters of "culture of death" especially CFFC have received enormous sums of money as donation from various pro-abortion organizations and institutions.[34] These resources were continued to be invested in the production of pharmaceutical products which make it possible to kill the foetus, in the mother's womb without recourse to medical assistance. On this point, scientific research itself seems to be almost exclusively preoccupied with developing products, which are ever

---

31 Clowes, *Catholics For A Free Choice,* 3.

32 Ibid., 3.

33 Ibid., 2.

34 See the donations of various Pro-abortion organizations-*FGI*: *Foundation Grants Index*, published by The Foundation Center, 79 Fifth Avenue, New York, New York 10003-3076, telephone (212) 620-4230. Total donations to Catholics for a Free Choice by the Mary Reynolds Babcock Foundation: $60,000. [*FGI*, 1983, page 343]. Total donations to Catholics for a Free Choice by the Brush Foundation: $164,853. [*The Brush Foundation: 1928-1980*, page 21]. Total donations to Catholics for a Free Choice by the Buffett Foundation: $675,000. [*FGI*, 1996, page 217]. Total donations to Catholics for a Free Choice by the Robert Sterling Clark Foundation: $457,000. [*FGI*, 1986, page 329]. Total donations to Catholics for a Free Choice by the Educational Foundation of America: $887,900. [CFFC's 1981 Federal income tax return].

more simple and effective in suppressing life and which at the same time are capable of removing abortion from any kind of control or social responsibility.

As mentioned earlier a kind of "*conspiracy against life*" is unleashed. This conspiracy involves not only individuals in their personal, family or group relationships, but goes far beyond, to the point of damaging and distorting, at the international level, relations between peoples and States.[35]

In seeking the deepest roots of the struggle between the "culture of life" and the "culture of death", we cannot restrict ourselves to the perverse idea of freedom alone. We have to go to the heart of the tragedy being experienced by modern man: *the eclipse of the sense of God and of man*, typical of a social and cultural climate dominated by secularism, which, with its ubiquitous tentacles, succeeds at times in putting Christian communities themselves to the test. Those who allow themselves to be influenced by this climate easily fall into a sad vicious circle: *when the sense of God is lost, there is also a tendency to lose the sense of man*, of his dignity and his life; in turn, the systematic violation of the moral law, especially in the serious matter of respect for human life and its dignity, produces a kind of progressive darkening of the capacity to discern God's living and saving presence.[36]

Material and consumerist mentality of the modern world is very well depicted by Pope John Paul II twenty three years earlier. Man reduces himself to a "thing." Pope says in his Encyclical *Evagelium Vitae*:

> Man is no longer able to see himself as "mysteriously different" from other earthly creatures; he regards himself merely as one more living being, as an organism which, at most, has reached a very high stage of perfection. Enclosed in the narrow horizon of his physical nature, he is somehow reduced to being "a thing", and no longer grasps the "transcendent" character of his "existence as man". He no longer considers life as a splendid gift of God, something "sacred" entrusted to his responsibility and thus also to his loving care and "veneration". Life itself becomes a mere "thing", which man claims as his exclusive property, completely subject to his control and manipulation.[37]

Yet another thing to be noted is that, the values of *being* are replaced by those of *having*. The only goal which counts is the pursuit of one's own material well-being. The so-called "quality of life" is interpreted primarily or exclusively as economic efficiency, inordinate consumerism, physical beauty

---

35 Clowes, *Catholics For A Free Choice*, 2.

36 John Paul II, *Evangelium Vitae*, 23.

37 Ibid.

and pleasure, to the neglect of the more profound dimensions interpersonal, spiritual and religious existence.[38]

It is at the heart of the moral conscience that the eclipse of the sense of God and of man, with all its various and deadly consequences of life is taking place. It is a question, above all, of the *individual* conscience, as it stands before God in its singleness and uniqueness.[39] But it is also a question, in a certain sense, of the "moral conscience"*of society*: in a way it too is responsible, not only because it tolerates or fosters behavior contrary to life, but also because it encourages the "culture of death", creating and consolidating actual "structures of sin" which go against lifc. Thc moral conscience, both individual and social, is today subjected, also as a result of the penetrating influence of the media, to an *extremely serious and mortal danger*: that of *confusion between good and evil,* precisely in relation to the fundamental right to life.[40]

6. Indian Context of Pro-life Movements

Since the pro-life Movements start from United States, in India we cannot find much roots of this movement. Besides, in India Catholics are a meager minority. However in Kerala one of the states of India, where Catholics have a decisive share in the population, we can find pro-life Movements have much roots. But, India is a democratic and Hindu majority country and the government policies are designed in such a way that everyone has a say of his own in this regard. One must acknowledge, at the outset, that the polarized nature of the pro-life/pro-choice debate ends up ignoring the fact that there need not necessarily be an unalloyed 'pro-life' or 'pro-choice' position. Someone may consider abortion to be 'destruction of life' but may still acknowledge that as a matter of policy, the State ought not to interfere in a woman's choice on her pregnancy. Further, in cases of rape and incest, persons who generally oppose abortions may see permissible exceptions. Alternatively, a Pro-choice person may understand the need for certain limitations on abortion. A prime example of other factors being alloyed with a pro-choice position is the issue of sex selective abortions. Indian women's rights activists, who may be decidedly pro-choice, are likely to oppose sex-selective abortion, seeing it as an insidious form of gender based violence. In the Indian context, feminists, policy-makers and activists have had to do a great deal of tightrope-walking to generate public awareness against sex-selective abortions, while avoiding a backlash against women's autonomy and the right to abortions themselves.[41]

---

38 John Paul II, *Evangelium Vitae*, 21.

39 "Gaudium et Spes," 16.

40 John Paul II, *Evagelium Vitae*, 24.

41 Srishti Agnihotri, "Abortion Rights in India," *feminismindia.com*, accessed April 11, 2016, https://feminisminindia.com/.

The issue of abortion in India is governed by the Medical Termination of Pregnancy Act, 1971. This Act allows pregnancies of up to 20 weeks to be terminated (with the consent of the woman). In the termination of a pregnancy of up to 12 weeks the presence of one registered medical practitioner is required, while in a pregnancy of 12 weeks to 20 weeks, the presence of two medical practitioners is required. These practitioners need to form an opinion in good faith that:[42]

1. The continuance of the pregnancy would pose a risk to the mental or physical health of the pregnant woman,
2. Or that the child, if born, will 'suffer from such physical or mental abnormalities as to be seriously handicapped'.

A pregnancy alleged to be caused by rape will be presumed to constitute a grave injury to the mental health of the woman, under the Act. Also when there is a failure of contraceptives used by a married woman or her husband, the 'anguish caused' by the resulting pregnancy will be presumed to be a grave injury to the mental health of the woman. This presumption allows the failure of contraceptives exemption only to married women. Though discriminatory towards unmarried women, it does reflect that the State's policy endorses the right of married women to make reproductive choices. It is only fair to point out that the language of the MTP Act has been criticized as being 'liberal seeming' but open to becoming restrictive without a single word in it being altered.[43]

There are other social movements in the world such as anti-Consumerism Movement, Civil Rights Movement, Children's Right Movement, Right to Life Movement etc., which all are fighting for the promotion and protection of life. All these Movements have their own goals and principles and they work for the betterment and protection of life. Hence, it is the duty of the pro-life workers to join hand in hand with other social transformative Movements and work for the fundamental right to life, thereby building a better world, where the value and rights of life are held high. We are not against the quality of life. Quality should be upheld of course but, in this process, value and rights of every innocent and voiceless should not be at risk. All types of exploitation, against life and consumerist mentality of life should be stopped. Human being is to be respected and treated not as a thing but as a person, from the moment of conception till the natural end.

42 Srishti Agnihotri, "Abortion Rights in India," *feminismindia.com*, accessed April 11, 2016, https://feminisminindia.com/.

43 "Anti-Abortion Movements," *Wikipedia.org*, accessed October 20, 2018, https://en.wikipedia.org/wiki/Anti-abortion_Movements.

Conclusion

From the philosophical analysis we understood that in the materialist world, the human being is reduced merely to a "thing" rather than a "being". Disregarding his personhood man is counted on the basis of quality. Man's procreative capacity is reduced to a pleasure making activity rather than partaking in the creative act of God, who is the source and giver of all life. Catholic Church has always taught and continues to teach that the result of human procreation, from the first moment of its existence, must be guaranteed that unconditional respect which is morally due to the human being in his or her totality and unity as body and spirit: "*The human being is to be respected and treated as a person from the moment of conception*; and therefore, from that same moment his rights as a person must be recognized, among which in the first place is the inviolable right of every innocent human being to life."[44]

This situation, with its lights and shadows, ought to make us all fully aware that we are facing an enormous and dramatic clash between good and evil, death and life, the "culture of death" and the "culture of life". We find ourselves not only "faced with" but necessarily "in the midst of" this conflict: we are all involved and we all share in it, with the inescapable responsibility of *choosing to be unconditionally pro-life*.[45]

For us too, Moses' invitation rings out loud and clear: "See, I have set before you this day life and good, death and evil.... I have set before you life and death, blessing and curse; *therefore, choose life, that you and your descendants may live*" (Deuteronomy 30:15,19). This invitation is very appropriate for us who are called day by day to the duty of choosing between the "culture of life" and the "culture of death". But, the call of Deuteronomy goes even deeper than the philosophical implications, for it urges us to make a choice which is properly religious and moral.

Human life, as a gift of God, is sacred and inviolable. For this reason procured abortion and euthanasia are absolutely unacceptable. Not only must human life not be taken, but it must be protected with loving concern. The meaning of life is found in giving and receiving love, and in this light, human sexuality and procreation reach their true and full significance. Love also gives meaning to suffering and death; despite the mystery which surrounds them, they can become saving events.[46] Respect for life requires that science and technology should always be at the service of human beings and his integral development. Society, as a whole must respect, defend and promote the dignity of every human person, at every moment and in every condition of that person's life. Protect life and stand for life.

44 Congregation For The Doctrine Of The Faith, "Declaration on Procured Abortion," (18 November 1974), NOS. 12-13: *AAS* 66 (1974), 738.

45 John Paul II, *Evagelium Vitae*, 28.

46 Ibid., 81.

20

Science-Religion Dialogue as a Movement: The Need of the Hour to Transform Society

Prof. Dr S. Stephen Jayard
Jnana-Deepa Vidyapeeth, Pune

Abstract: Science and Religion are two powerful enterprises of humanity. Both, in their rudimentary forms, have been there for millennia and they have witnessed steady growth over the centuries. In our modern times, whether or not one is a religious follower, one is affected by religions as one finds them to be powerful in the society; similarly, whether or not one is scientific-minded, one is constantly affected by science in everyday life, not only at the level of comforts but also at the level of one's attitude. Due to the misuses and abuses of religions, people get dissatisfied with religions; on the other hand, people get disillusioned with modern science as it creates ethical and ecological issues. When we bring them together for healthy interaction and integration, not only science and religion can get enriched but also humanity grows to be holistic. For instance, more discoveries and insights from the world of science can purify religions and similarly, with the refined understanding of religions, science can be helped to have a human face.

It is in this scenario that the science-religion dialogue gains more and more importance in the modern times. However, it is not enough to have this dialogue only at the academic or institutional levels, but it needs to evolve as a social movement so that it gains more momentum even at the public arena. This paper, thus, analyses some basic ideas of a social movement in general and sees some advantages of having this dialogue as a movement. Among several common platforms between science and religion, this paper focuses on just one important notion of "life". Finally the paper ends with some practical suggestions to make it a "movement" in the Church and seminaries in particular and in society at large, so that we can move towards constructive and holistic humanity.

Keywords: Science-Religion Dialogue, Social Movements, Challenges to Religion, Notion of Life, Benefits of Interfacing Science and Religion.

Introduction

All really want to better the world in all possible ways. Bringing science and religion, I believe, is one of the most powerful ways to better the world. For, those who are dissatisfied and discouraged with religions, because religions are misused and abused, they can look towards science to get some realistic picture of religion. More discoveries and insights from the world of science can purify religions and they can become more acceptable. Similarly, those who are disillusioned with science, as it gets more and more materialistic and mechanistic, can look towards the refined understanding of religions so that science can be helped to have a human face. I suggest that the efforts towards science-religion dialogue [*henceforth, SRD*] must not be seen as a mere academic exercise, nor as the concerns only of the believers to make themselves relevant in the world of science. The whole effort should evolve into a movement.

In part I, we discuss some basic features of a social movement; in part II we highlight the need and the relevance of SRD. Among the several possible common platforms of bringing them together we just focus on the notion of life, which could be one of the powerful aspects of interfacing. Then we end up with some suggestions, in Part III, to make this dialogue into a social movement and the steps to be taken in the Church and the seminaries in particular and in the society at large.

PART I

The Notion of a Social Movement – Some Ideas and Clarifications

Social sciences define a social movement as rational attempt "by excluded groups to mobilize sufficient political leverage to advance collective interests through non-institutionalized means."[1] A movement involves lots of people but it is not just a crowd because, unlike in a crowd, there are organizational and motivational mechanisms in a movement and they keep the members going. These members stress upon a change in the society as they are dissatisfied with the present set-up. Social Movements can occur at the levels of some individuals or at the level of society. These Movements can advocate for either

1 D. McAdam, *Political Process and the Development of Black Insurgency, 1930-1970*, 2nd edition, (Chicago: Chicago University Press, 1999), 36.

minor or radical changes. In 1950s and 1960s the demands for civil rights were at their peak. In India, new forms and vigour in social movements began gaining momentum by 1970s. They were identified with different names such as, social movements, people's movement, popular Movements, socio-political Movements etc. Social Movements are becoming increasingly important because they can bring about social changes in political, religious, educational, health, corporate, government, and other institutional arenas. Some examples of social movements in history are: civil rights movement in the United States, environmental movement, green movement, gay rights movement and so on.

Social Movements aim at either establishing or preventing a change in the structure, functions and values of the society. They work to bring changes in politics, to give voice to the voiceless. Sometimes the very coming together itself is the aim of the Movements and to create one voice over an issue, by making the members and the society at large being aware of the need and urgency of the issues at hand. Further, they aim at creation of a new order in the society. As Herbert Blumer puts it: "Social Movements can be viewed as collective enterprises to establish a new order of life. They have their inception in the condition of unrest, and derive their motive power on one hand from dissatisfaction with the current form of life, and on the other hand, from wishes and hopes for a new scheme or system of living."[2]

Earlier social movements were seen only as a threat to the ruling class and as a disturbance to the peace and harmony in the society. Therefore the immediate reaction would be to curtail and supress these Movements. They were associated with mobs, riots, violence and ransacking of the public properties and so on. The members of the Movements, blindly following their leaders, behaved like herds; it was claimed that these disruptive mobs were opposing the rational and constructive developments of the powerful elite.[3] But fortunately, after a few decades the approach toward the Movements was changed. Though some Movements aim at overthrowing the existing social order, several Movements sincerely look for genuine changes in the social system for the betterment.[4] But by the beginning of the 20th century there has been a welcome change in the way these Movements are treated. As Marc Hooghe points out, "in the 1960s especially… social movement participation could be seen as a normal and even necessary element within democratic

---

2 See: http://www.yourarticlelibracry.com/india-2/social-movements-in-india-meaning-features-and-, accessed December 25, 2017.

3 For instance, see the work of Gustav Le Bon, *The Crowd: A Study of the Popular Mind* (New York: Penguin Books, 1977), first published in French, 1895.

4 William Kornhauser, *The Politics of Mass Society* (New Brunswick: Free Press, 2008), first published in 1959.

political systems."[5] By the 20th century, there was an evolution in looking at the movement; they are "seen as a very typical phenomenon related to specific developmental phase of highly industrialized societies."[6]

Types of Social Movements: Basing the target groups or the issues that the Movements try to change and how much change they try to propose, Aberle proposes four types of Movements, based on: redemptive, reformative, revolutionary and alternative Movements: a) ***Redemptive Movements*** aim at creating a more dramatic change in an individual's life. By completely transforming the lives of individuals they hope to change the world. It is typically religious in nature. The movement by Christian missionaries is a good example for this type of movement.[7] b) ***Reformative*** (Reform) ***Movements*** are those Movements that are geared to make gradual change or changes in some aspects of society, rather than aiming at rapid or radical changes. Thus, reform Movements are differentiated from radical social revolutionary Movements. The reform Movements of the 1830s, gave women a chance to get involved in the public arena. Women reformers soon began to agitate not just for temperance and abolition, but also for women's rights. c) ***Revolutionary Movements*** is a specific type of social movement dedicated to carrying out a revolution. Charles Tilly defines it as a social movement advancing exclusive competing claims to control of the state, or some segment of it."[8] d) ***Alternative Movements*** refer to social movements which aim at limited social change. They focus on a small group of people and their particular behaviour and tries to change it in relation to that issue at hand.[9]

Features of Social Movements: Though social movements are studied in Sociology, it touches upon various disciplines, like Philosophy, Political Science, Psychology and Anthropology. In the recent times, philosophers show more interests in analysing social movements in order to enrich the ideas of social justice, democracy etc.[10] They discuss ontological, ethical, political

---

5 Marc Hooghe, "Social Movements", in John Ishiyama, Breuning eds, *21st Century Political Science – A Reference Handbook*, Vol. 1 (Thousands Oaks: Sage Publications, 2011), 225-232, 226.

6 Ibid., 228.

7 See: https://prezi.com/ska_dcjnqglt/redemptive-social-movement/, accessed January 20, 2018.

8 Quoted in: https://prezi.com/ska_dcjnqglt/redemptive-social-movement/, accessed May 17, 2018.

9 For more on this, see: https://www.google.co.in/search?q=basic+features+of+a+social+movement&rlz=1C1CHBD_enIN807IN807&oq=features+of+a+social+move&aqs=chrome.2.69i57j0l5.8255j1j7&sourceid=chrome&ie=UTF-8, accessed July 15, 2018.

10 For elabourate discussion on these issues, see: M. Fricker, *Epistemic Justice* (New York: Oxford University Press, 2009); J. Gainous and K. M. Wagner, *Rebooting American Politics: The Internet Revolution* (Lanham, MD: Rowman & Littlefield, 2011); S. Hampshire, *Justiceis Conflict* (Princeton: Princeton University Press, 2000); C. Barry

and epistemological questions of these Movements. Some of the features of social movements are as follows: i) The sense of belonging and group consciousness is very important for a social movement. Such consciousness can be brought about through active participation of the group members; ii) Social Movements lead to the creation of an entirely new social, economic, and political order; iii) Most of the social movements tend to develop a new set of ideas, which become obligatory for the members of the group to adopt and follow; iv) It is obvious that the social movements involve collective action rather than individual action; v) Social Movements may be organized or unorganized. vi). Social Movements may be peaceful in nature or they may also turn violent; vii) The aim of a social movement is to bring about or resist social change in the society; viii) The life of the social movement is not certain. This is because it may continue for a long period or it may die out soon. In my opinion, a movement of science and religion dialogue in order to be effective, will have to include the features of the social movements. Let us now focus on one important common platform upon which they can come together.

PART II

The Notion of Life – A Possible Common Platform for Science-Religion Dialogue

What is life or living or what makes something living?- Dictionaries understand life as "the condition that distinguishes insects, animals and plants from inorganic matter, including the capacity for growth, reproduction, functional activity, and continual change preceding death" or it may also refer to "the existence of an individual human being or animal."[11] The question of life can be a strong and insightful platform for the integration of science and religion. As T. D. Singh puts it: "A sincere attempt to have a clear understanding of life... is of foundational importance and it will have important relevance in deciding the relation between science and religion."[12] Discussion of life touches upon diverse disciplines – biosciences, molecular physics, organic chemistry, history, anthropology, sociology – all

---

and K. MacDonals, "How Should We Think about Individual Consumer Responsibility to Address Labour Injustices?," in *Global Justice and International Labour Rights*, eds, Yossie Dahan, Hanna Lemer, and Faina Milman-Sivan, (New York: Cambridge University Press, 2016).

11 https://www.google.ca/webhp?sourceid=chrome-instant&ion=1&espv=2&ie=UTF-8#q=what%20is%20life%3F, accessed June 15, 2018.

12 T. D. Singh, *Essays on Science and Religion* (Kolkotta: The Bhaktivedanta Institute, 2005), 66.

are interested in it. Even quantum physicists are interested in understanding life from philosophical perspectives; for instance, E. Schrodinger, a famous physicist, wondered about life from philosophical perspectives and the main focus was to discuss "how can the events in space and time which take place within the spatial boundary of a living organism be accounted for by physics and chemistry?"[13]

Science can separate all biochemicals like nucleic acids (RNA, DNA), carbohydrates, lipids, enzymes and all the basic building blocks of organic bodies but will they ever discover what is that which gives life to them? We have more than fifty chemical salts and minerals in our body that are found in nature. All these don't have life in themselves but they are essentially required in the right ratio to make life possible. For instance, if sodium is more in our body, it accumulates in the fluid between cells and thus the volume of the blood increases; it means more work for the heart and more pressure on blood vessels. On the other hand, deficit of sodium will reduce blood pressure and damages the activity of nerve cells and the muscles of the heart and digestive systems.[14]

Going a step further, another intriguing question: 'When does human life begin?' – At the very conception? After a few weeks? At the birth? Many scientists do agree that the human life starts at the very moment of fertilization. The embryology by and large affirms that human person begins right at the time of fertilization, where the male and female cells, sperm and egg, come together: "fertilization marks the beginning of the life of the new individual human being."[15] Several religions also assert that human life begins at the very moment of conception; for instance, Christian bioethics affirms that at the moment of fusion of these two cells, we have the beginning of the human being. "Therefore, the embryo as well as the handicapped and patients in the coma state are all persons with dignity and any intervention on their body is to be in accordance with and respecting the dignity of the human person."[16] Human life gets all the more complicated because the *"questioner" and the "questioned" are one and the same here.*

---

13 Erwin Schrodinger, *What is Life?* (UK: Cambridge University Press, 1944). Also see: https://en.wikipedia.org/wiki/What_Is_Life%3F#cite_note-Margulis-1, accessed October 10, 2018.

14 For more details, see: https://www.verywellfit.com/what-happens-if-i-dont-consume-enough-sodium-2507757; https://www.health.harvard.edu/heart-health/take-it-with-a-grain-of-salt, accessed September 19, 2018.

15 S. Gilbert, *Developmental Biology*, 5th edition, (Sunderland: Mass Sinnaure Associates, 1997), 60.

16 Francis Chittuparambil, *The Human Body in Bioethics; Christian and Upanishadic Perspective* (Bangalore: Asian Trading Corporation, 2011), 492.

Our understanding of life is still far from complete; for example, the living status of virus. Science is not certain about whether or not virus is alive. Some consider it to be life, a missing link between life and non-life, while others disagree with this because they are dead matter if it is left outside a living cell. These viruses are able to live only in another living organism; since virus is not able to convert energy it is considered as not living. Therefore, 'what is alive' is not just a scientific question, but a philosophical one as well. Philosophically speaking, life must have some agency. For instance, amoebas and bacteria manifest actions and choice for their survival, say, in reaching out to food. But in the case of viruses there is no such agency, nor any metabolism. Traditionally, a certain set of conditions are given for something to be considered as living: ability to grow and reproduce, capacity to use and convert energy, having at least one cell and possessing some degree of organization. Viruses may suit some of these conditions but not all; for instance, they don't grab nutrients for their survival; their actions are mostly mechanical, though they respond to stimuli. They don't reproduce on their own, but they need a host for this purpose. Thus the life-status of virus is still debatable.[17]

Scientists, thus, are baffled about their actual status of living. For instance, Werner Arber confesses, "Although a biologist, I must confess that I don't understand how life came about. Of course, it depends on the definition of life. To me auto replication does not yet represent life. Even a viral particle is not a life organism, it only can participate in the life processes when it succeeds in becoming part of a living host cell... The most primitive cell may require at least several hundred different specific biological micromolecules. How such already quite complex structure may have come together, remains a mystery to me. The possibility of the existence of a creator, of God, represents to me a satisfactory solution to this problem."[18]

When we don't understand what makes something living how *can we hope to artificially create life in a lab?* In fact, it was claimed that life was 'created' in the lab in 2010. After about 15 years of such toiling in his labs in Rockville, MD, J. Craig Venter, co-mapper of the human genome, and his team have pieced together the entire genome of a bacterium and then inserted those genetic instructions into another bacterium; but it is NOT the creation of new life but the creation of artificial, synthetic genome. This is only 1 % of the cellular machinery of the recipient cell; they have created a new species.

---

17 For more discussion on this issue, see: https://www.reddit.com/r/askscience/comments/to543/why_cant_we_create_life_in_a_labourator/ and http://www.biology-direct.com/content/1/1/29, accessed May 29, 2018.

18 Henry Margenau and Roy Varghese, eds, *Cosmos, Bios, Theos* (USA: Illionis, 1992), 142., quoted by T. D. Singh, *Essays on Science and Religion* (Kolkotta: The Bhaktivedanta Institute, 2005), 75-76.

We can never create life anew, say, out of nothing, as God can do. We can only manipulate what is already present and manifest life in it. It is just realizing the potentialities with which they have already been created.[19]

The holistic concept of life involves more than the combination of materials, but also mind and intelligence, spiritual elements of consciousness (*atman*). Without clarifying consciousness, life cannot be understood but consciousness is still an enigma, not only for philosophers but also for scientists.[20] That is why, Niels Bohr confesses: "We can admittedly find nothing in physics or chemistry that has even remote bearing on consciousness. Yet all of us know that there is such a thing as consciousness, simply because we have it ourselves. Hence consciousness must be part of nature, or more generally, of reality, which means that, quite apart from the laws of physics and chemistry, as laid down in quantum theory, we must also consider laws of quite a different nature."[21]

Charles Darwin, projected to be an atheist as he claimed that the whole evolution is due to natural selection, is actually wonderstruck about the notion of life: "(There is) the extreme difficulty or rather the impossibility of conceiving this immense and wonderful universe, including man, with his capacity for looking backwards, and far into futurity, as the result of blind chance or necessity. When thus reflecting I feel compelled to look to a First Cause having an intelligent mind in some degree analogous to that of man, as *I desire to be called a theist.*"[22] About the mystery of life, Einstein declared: "It is enough for me to contemplate the mystery of conscious life perpetuating itself through all eternity, to reflect upon the marvellous structure of the universe which we can dimly perceive, and to try humbly to comprehend even an infinitesimal part of the intelligence manifested in nature."[23] Thus the notion of life, and conscious life at that, is still (and ever will be?) an enigma for every discipline.

---

19 For more on this, see: Alice Park, "Scientist Creates Life. That's a Good Thing, Right?," *time.com*, accessed March 25, 2018, http://www.time.com/time/health/article/0,8599,1990836,00.html.

20 For more on the relationship between body and mind (consciousness) see my paper: S. Stephen Jayard, "Towards Enlightened and Enriched Humanity: Rays of Hope from Critical Interactions with the Contemporary Science," in *Committed to the Church and the Country*, eds. Kuruvilla Pandikattu SJ, James Ponnaiah and Thomas Kuriacose SJ (Delhi: ISPCK, and Pune: Jnana-Deepa Vidyapeeth, 2013), 56-76.

21 Quoted by T. D. Singh and L. Thompson, *Consciousness: The Missing Link*, back cover (Kolkotta: Bhaktivedanta Book Trust, 2013).

22 Francis Darwin, ed., *Life and Letter of Charles Darwin* (New York: D. Appleton, 1887), 1:274, 275. Emphasis mine.

23 Quoted by Nancy K. Frankenberry, edited with commentary, *The Faith of Scientists – In Their Own Words* (Princeton & Oxford: Princeton University Press, 2008), 154.

PART III

The Need for Science-Religion Dialogue as a Movement

Deeper questions which cannot be avoided by any thinking person stare at our face – the meaning and purpose of our very existence, the missing links in the process of evolution etc. cannot be meaningfully grappled with by science alone. Even some scientists, who are basically agnostic regarding the existence of God, seem to be ready to recognize the need for the role of non-scientific disciplines in dealing with profound questions of our existence. For instance, Professor Brian Cox, an eminent physicist, in an interview with the Telegraph in 2014, acknowledged: "There is naivety in just saying there's no God… [and the questions about the existence about cosmology and human existence] have not been discussed widely; they need novelists and artists and philosophers and theologians and physicists to discuss them."[24]

The coming together of Science and Religion is neither a recent phenomenon, nor an artificial marriage; it is actually a long-lasting and spontaneous one. Right from the dawn of the Western history of human thoughts, philosophy and science have gone hand in hand. The Socratic philosophers whose philosophical credentials are beyond doubt were also scientists. Socrates, Plato, and Aristotle contributed to various fields of science in their own way. St Thomas Aquinas, a great philosopher and theologian, was also deeply involved with the areas of science; he has written commentaries on Aristotelian scientific treatises. Descartes, the father of modern philosophy, was also one the founders of modern science along with Copernicus and Galileo. Descartes' Cartesian Geometry was dominant till Newton's days. Newton who is known as a great scientist was also a philosopher. He was very much influenced by Arianism and found fault with the doctrine of Trinity. Immanuel Kant, known as one of the great philosophers of the modern times, began his career as a student of science and his doctoral defence was on thermodynamics. Albert Einstein, the man of the millennium, was convinced of the cosmic religion and divinity. The sense of mystery, according to him, is not something alien to any of the thinking mind. Many other quantum physicists, like David Bohm and Werner Heisenberg, were deeply religious-minded and philosophically-oriented.[25]

---

24 Quoted by Sr **Clare Condon SGS, see:** https://www.goodsams.org.au/article/engaging-in-science-religion-dialogue/, accessed March 4, 2018.

25 I have elsewhere elabourated the mystical inclinations and religious convictions of many of the leading quantum physicists. Please see my paper: S. Stephen Jayard, "Mysticism and Quantum Physicists – Friends or Foes?" *Omega – Indian Journal of Science and Religion* 3, no. 2 (2004), 89-106.

The Catholic Church in general and seminaries, Catholic universities and educational institutes in particular, have much more to contribute to the task of making people aware of the need and the relevance of science-religion dialogue. Of course, it has done quite much in the past and continues to do now also, but given the resources available at the disposal of the Catholic Church and the influential position that it enjoys, much more is expected from it. The Catholic Church has been instrumental in encouraging studies in Astronomy and Cosmology, for the past few centuries. J. L. Heilbron observes: "The Roman Catholic Church gave more financial aid and support to the study of astronomy for over six centuries, from the recovery of ancient learning during the late Middle Ages into the Enlightenment, than any other, and, probably, all other, institutions."[26] Even today, the Holy See supports the Vatican Observatory (*Specola Vaticana*) at the summer residence of the Pope in Castel Gandolfo, Italy, and another observatory at the Mount Graham International Observatory in the Unites States of America.

A social movement is formed when an important issue affects large sections of the people. In my opinion the one-sided stress upon science or religion alone has created enough and more harm to individuals, societies and humanity at large. We can give umpteen number of incidents and events where religious fanaticism, down the centuries, has destroyed societies and killed millions. When the emotions and blind dogmatism sweep over the religious followers, then reason bids good bye to them. In such a situation science must step in to bring in some rational touch to the religions, so that the mere emotional outbursts and irrational justification of the superstitious practices may be kept under control. Similarly, when only scientific or rational dimensions are stressed upon there is a likelihood that 'human face' may be totally lost in all our human endeavours; the production of weapons of mass destruction, deadly war technologies, unimaginably serious damages to the environment, steady increase of the global warming and the pollution levels in air, water and land – are just some examples of the unbridled growth of science that is oblivious to values and morals. Too much stress on religion or science alone, without the openness to learn from each other, will result in a distorted picture of science and religion. Too much of a rationalistic approach is not good for science, nor for human society. Being too rationalistic, science runs the risk of becoming value-neutral and similarly religion, being devoid of rational consideration, runs the risk of becoming superstitious or fanatic. Both these distorted forms will damage holistic humanity. Therefore, the need to integrate science and religion is very serious and urgent, more than ever before. We need to bring both to the dialoguing table so that one can learn

26 J. L. Heilbron, *The Sun in the Church: Cathedrals as Solar Observatories* (Cambridge: Harvard University Press, 1999), 3.

and correct from each other; both stand to gain from each other's interaction; both will be enriched with coming together. People should feel the need of bringing science and religion together, for their mutual enrichment and that in turn would lead to holistic humanity.

Suggestions to Make Science-Religion Dialogue as a Movement:

At the Society Level

- Private companies, non-governmental organizations, corporate establishments, Information Technology sectors, etc. can think of organizing seminars and workshops for the experts and the general public.
- Social media, both electronic and social, can focus on such themes in their regular debates, talk-shows, documentaries, editorials, special columns and so on. The need and advantages of bringing them together will have to reach the general public and it should become an issue of their everyday discussion.

At the Educational Level

- The Departments of education at all levels need to think of making new syllabi with courses on the interfacing of science and religion, history & philosophy of science. When students learn about the philosophical issues of science, they will overcome the traditional picture of science as a mere rationalistic and objective enterprise. They need to be informed of the revised understanding of science, which involves several non-rational, social and ethical factors in the very make up of science.
- Various types of competitions can be held for the students, on relevant themes to encourage them and to percolate such thinking among them.

At the Religious / Church Level

- In the religious worship places efforts can be had to have discourses by the experts, about the need of interfacing science and religion.
- The Church at large, and every diocese in particular, need to encourage priests to go in for some science studies. They can be given special sabbatical breaks to update their knowledge about science disciplines.
- As the Church gives importance to the inter-religious and ecumenical dialogues it can give importance to science-religion dialogue as well. Thus, commissions can be established at the diocesan level,

as we have commissions for youth, family, Bible and so on. Special liturgies can be prepared to be circulated among all the parishes.

- At the parish/diocesan levels seminars can be conducted on SRD, may be at a non-technical level. Special Sunday-liturgies can be conducted on this theme. Libraries can be established and the literatures on science-religion interaction can be made available.

At the Level of Seminary-training

- Seminarians need to be encouraged to take up science disciplines at least at the pre-university and graduation levels; in the modern times, basic science is basic, because science is basic; yes, as it affects every aspect of our modern lives.
- They need to be exposed to the seminars or symposia on the related themes of science-religion integration; they need to visit science parks, planetariums, science-museums and so on to create interests in science.
- Retreats and spiritual inputs can be imparted to show how contemporary science can help us deepen our spirituality.[27]

Conclusion

Science is so powerful that it cannot be left in the hands of just a few individuals like some experts, business people, politicians or a group of influential nations; they are sure to manipulate to suit their own vested interests and to exploit it to their own benefits. Science is by humans and for humans. So, it cannot be hijacked by certain people to enhance their own resources. If science stops caricaturing religion and religion ceases to alienate science, if science is open to inter-disciplinary approaches, including religion and philosophy, and if religions are keen to learn from sciences, then both can get mutually enriched by the interaction. SRD is not an option, but an obligation; it is urgent and necessary. The collabouration between science and religion is not an encroachment into one another's turf, but a great mutual help to enrich humanity and cosmos.

Job Kozhamthadam, a pioneer in this field in India, is very optimistic: "Thanks to the different recent developments in religious and scientific circles, they seem to be willing to talk to each other, respectfully and creatively. In some ways, the dialogue has already started. Let us hope that it will not be too long before they come together to forge a more dynamic partnership to work

---

27 More on this, Contributions of the Church, Papal Documents and Christian-Scientists, please see my paper: S. Stephen Jayard, "Seminary, Science and Signs of the Times: An Invitation to Be Wise, not Otherwise," *Vidyajyoti Journal of Theological Reflection* 80, no. 9, (2016), 706-717.

for the betterment and enrichment of our world."[28] In this task philosophy has a major role. As J. Wentzel van Huyssteen affirms: "The question how theology and science should relate to one another is, of course, neither a theological nor a scientific issue. It is rather, an epistemological issue, that is, an issue about how two very different claims in knowledge are to be related."[29]

These days, social movements are fortunately taken seriously. From ordinary people to political powers; it is no more than a mere academic phenomenon. There are now journals dedicated to the study of social movements; for instance, *Mobilization – An International Journal* (established in 1996) and *Social Movement Studies* (established in 2002). I am hopeful that as the mature social movements will slowly and steadily bring about the positive changes in society, if SRD also evolves into a movement, it will also bring in substantial changes that the modern world is in need of, in both the realms of science and religion, paving the path towards holistic humanity. The need for SRD is so urgent and essential that I tend to believe, as N. Whitehead prophesized: "***When we consider what religion is for mankind, and what science is, it is no exaggeration to say that the future course of history depends upon this generation as to the relations between them.***"[30]

---

28 Job Kozhamthadam, ed., "The Changing Face of Science-Christianity Dialogue," in *Science, Technology and Values – Science-Religion Dialogue in a Multi-Religious World* (Pune: ASSR Publications, Jnana-Deepa Vidyapeeth, 2003), 3-34, 30.

29 J. Wentzel van Huyssteen, *Essays in Postfoundationality Theology* (Cambridge: William B. Erdmann Publishing Company, 1997), 221.

30 https://books.google.co.in/books?isbn=0739130803, accessed November 21, 2015.

21

Agapocracy: A New Response to the Ideological Foundation of the RSS Movement

Dr George Panthanmackel, M.S.F.S.
St Francis de Sales, Guwahati

Abstract: *Rashtriya Swayam Sevak Sangh* (RSS), gained respectability during Jayaprakash Narayan's movement and has been growing steadily. The RSS ideology is centred around the vital force of nationalism, which binds societies. According to it, 'Hindutva' is the 'quality of being a Hindu' in ethnic, cultural and political terms. A Hindu is one who considers India to be his motherland (*mathrubhumi*), the land of his ancestors (*pitrbhumi*), and his holy land (*punyabhumi*). India is the land of the Hindus since their ethnicity is Indian and their faith as Hindu originated in India. Other faiths born in India are qualified as variants of Hinduism. RSS ideologues also believed that Hinduism is a national identity rather than a communal one. Some others advocated an ideology of integral humanism. There are two strands of Hindutva seen in the ideology of RSS, one aggressive, and the other, liberal.

Keywords: Rashtriya Swayam Sevak Sangh (RSS), Hindu MahaSabha, nationalism, *Akhand Bharat*, *Agapocracy,* Nationalism, patriotism, *mathrubhumi*, *pitrbhumi*, *punyabhumi*

Introduction

Rashtriya Swayam Sevak Sangh (RSS) was formed in September 1925, on the day of Vijayadeshami, at Nagpur by Dr Kesav Baliram Hedgewar.[1] Thanks to the respectability which the Jan Sangh gained during Jayaprakash Narayan's movement and in the Janata Party government, the RSS gained considerably. Between 1977 and 1982 the RSS growth was phenomenal. The total number of *shakhas*[2] increased from 6,000 to 19,000. The only organization which has consistently geared itself to micro-level politics is the RSS. The RSS claims to be a cultural body committed to democracy and secularism. It is accused of bigoted communalism, addiction to violence and practice of deceit to capture political power. The RSS was accused even by Sardar Patel of spreading communal poison. Patel wrote to Golwalkar on September 11, 1948: "As a final result of the poison, the country had to suffer the sacrifice of the invaluable life of Gandhiji. Even an iota of the sympathy of the Government or of the people no more remained for the RSS. In fact opposition grew. Opposition turned more severe, when the RSS men expressed joy and distributed sweets after Gandhiji's death."[3]

The history of its formative period comprises three important stages: from 1925 to 1940 when the founder of the RSS himself has been guiding it; from 1940 to 1973 when M.S. Golwalkar, known as Guruji, has been the Sarsanghachalak; and the period from 1973 to 1994, the time of Bala Saheb Deoras.[4]

1. RSS Movement

First Period from 1925 to 1940: Dr Hedgewar had the belief that the building of a nation was a task beyond the capacity of political parties. So, he decided to build up a cadre of young people who did not belong to the political field. Within a short period, he succeeded in forming a group of strong patriots who travelled far and wide and established *shakhas* or branches of the RSS. In the first six years Dr Hedgewar concentrated his attention in areas around Nagpur, but later sent workers to other areas. Though RSS was a non-political organization, its main aim was the independence of the country, the freedom of the Hindu people. The RSS always welcomed Congress efforts for independence. For example, when the Indian National Congress adopted

1 K. Jayaprasad, *RSS and Hindu Nationalism* (New Delhi: Deep and Deep Publications, 1991), 58.

2 As per the RSS Annual Report of 2018, there were a total of 58,967 shakhas within India (in 2017, 57165 shakhas and 56,569 in 2016).

3 A.G. Noorani, *The RSS and the BJP: A Division of Labour* (New Delhi: Left Word Books, 2000), 29.

4 K. Jayaprasad, *RSS and Hindu Nationalism*, 62-63.

complete independence as its goal in 1929, the RSS decided to observe 26th January 1930 as Independence Day by sending circulars to all its branches. Hedgewar himself participated in the satyagraha of Gandhiji in 1930. He was arrested and imprisoned for nine months, also several other members of the RSS.[5]

The RSS grew fast in all the Provinces of the country from 1932 to 1940. Hedgewar was assisted by a band of dedicated companions, including Baba Saheb Apte, M.S. Golwalker, Vasant Rao Oak and Digambar Paturkar. The Hindu MahaSabha and AryaSamaj, who were ideologically close to Dr Hedgewar's thinking, proved to be of invaluable help to RSS in its formative years. In 1934, Gandhiji visited the annual Wardha District Winter Camp of RSS and was wonderstruck how RSS made different castes live together. At that time, the British wanted to stop the expansion of the RSS. On December 15, 1932, the Governor – in – Council of the Central Province issued orders, prohibiting Government servants from attending RSS branches. The growth of the RSS can be judged from the fact that the number of Swayamsevaks was only 99 in 1928. From 1932 to 1940, branches of the RSS were established in all the Provinces of the country. Of course, it had its strong footing only in the Central Province and it was fast growing in other Provinces.[6]

Second Period from 1940 to 1973: The founder of the RSS, Dr Hedgewar, expired on June 21, 1940. He was succeeded by M.S. Golwalkar, the second Sarsanghachalak. He was only 34 years when he took the office in 1940. The progress of the RSS under Golwalkar was multi-dimensional. During his time, the RSS moved out into various social, cultural, economic, educational and political areas of activities. About a dozen large organizations were established along with some hundred small ones. In 1947, the RSS claimed the support of 50,00,000 Hindus, and there were 5,000 Shakhas. Golwalkar frequently visited the main centres of Sangh activity. The British, apprehensive of the nation-wide spread of the RSS, imposed restrictions on the activities of the organization. On January 30, 1948, Mahatma Gandhi was assassinated by a fanatic Hindu, who was a member of Hindu MahaSabha and a former member of the RSS. On February 4, 1948, the Government of India placed the RSS under a ban and about 1700 prominent workers were arrested, including Golwalkar. Later, the restrictions on Golwalkar's movement were lifted on October 13, 1948, and the ban on the RSS was lifted on July 12, 1949. The Government accepted the constitution of the RSS before lifting the ban on it. Meanwhile, the judgment in the Gandhiji murder trial delivered on June

5 K. Jayaprasad, *RSS and Hindu Nationalism,* 63-64.

6 Ibid., 64.

21, 1949, did not contain any remark against the RSS, nor did it imply any involvement of the Sangh in the murder.[7]

Third Period from 1973 to 1994: After Golwalkar's death in 1973, the march of the RSS continued under the leadership of Bala Saheb Deoras, the third Sarsanghachalak. Having been in the Sangh since his boyhood, he is truly a child of the organization. He gave a social orientation to the work of RSS, despite many challenges that he had to face. The RSS participated in the movement led by Jaya Prakash Narayan in 1973-1974, followed by the National Emergency declared by the Government headed by Indira Gandhi on June 25, 1975. The RSS was banned for the second time after independence. More than 25,000 RSS members, including Deoras, the Sarsanghachalak, were arrested under DIR or MISA. Many leaders of the RSS went underground and actively participated in Lok Sangharsha Samithi formed by non-Communist opposition parties. It also organized a country-wide satyagraha in protest against emergency on November 14, 1975. Following the defeat of Congress in 1977 elections, the outgoing Government of Indira Gandhi lifted the ban on RSS. In a surprise move, the RSS decided to open its door to non-Hindus in November 1977. The number of Shakahas went up from 10,000 during the pre-ban period to 13,000 in 1978. The growth of the RSS was visible in the states of Kerala, Karnataka, Uttar Pradesh, Rajasthan and Bihar. In 1987, there were more than 20,000 Shakhas in the whole country with 10,00,000 young members.[8]

2. RSS Ideology and its Architects

The RSS believes in the ideology[9] of nationalism which binds societies. Nationalism and patriotism are parallel factors. Rousing of national consciousness and building up of national solidarity guarantee national survival. The RSS has no objection to any person's religion or system of worship, but it is insistent on a sense of community about motherland. It is not for a nationalism based on geographical considerations, but on cultural heritage. The preamble of the RSS Constitution says, "Whereas in the disintegrated conditions of the country it was considered necessary to have an organization – (a) to eradicate the fissiparous tendencies arising from diversities of sect, faith, caste and creed and from political, economic, linguistic and provincial differences amongst Hindus, (b) to make them realize the greatness of their past, (c) to inculcate in them a spirit of service, sacrifice and selfless devotion

7 K. Jayaprasad, *RSS and Hindu Nationalism,* 65-66.

8 K. Jayaprasad, *RSS and Hindu Nationalism,* 68-70.

9 Ideology divides, whereas philosophy unites; ideology limits reality to a particular 'idol,' of practice or of idea, whereas philosophy tries to comprehend the incomprehensible and infinite reality.

to Hindu Samaj (society) as a whole, (d) to build up an organized and well disciplined corporate life, and (e) to bring about an all-round regeneration of Hindu Samaj (society)."[10]

Article 3 of the same Constitution states, "The aims and objects of the Sangh are to weld together the diverse groups within the Hindu Samaj (society), and to revitalize and rejuvenate the same on the basis of Dharma and Sanskriti (religion and culture) that it may achieve an all-sided development of the Bharatavarsha[11] (India)." The main moulders of RSS ideology are Vinayak Damodar Savarkar, M.S. Golwalkar, Shyama Prasad Mukherjee and Pandit Deen Dayal Upadhyaya.

2.1. Vinayak Damodar Savarkar (1883-1966)

For Savarkar,[12] 'Hindutva' is the 'quality of being a Hindu' in ethnic, cultural and political terms. A Hindu is one who considers India to be his motherland (*mathrubhumi*), the land of his ancestors (*pitrbhumi*), and his holy land (*punyabhumi*). India is the land of the Hindus since their ethnicity is Indian and since their faith as Hindu originated in India. Other faiths born in India – of Sikhism, Buddhism and Jainism – are qualified as variants of Hinduism since they fulfilled the essential criteria; whereas Islam and Christianity, born outside India, are not qualified to be Hindu. Thus, a Hindu is someone born of Hindu parents, who regards India as his motherland as well as his holy land. 'Hindutva' is an indefinable quality inherent in Hindu race. Hindutva, in Savarkar's view, is 'so varied and so rich, so powerful and so subtle, so elusive and yet so vivid.' Of course, the concept would have made no sense unless it was explained in relation to the religion of Hinduism. So Hinduism is only a derivative, a fraction, a part of Hindutva. The religion of Hinduism is only a subset of the political idea of Hindutva, rather than synonymous with it.

10 Taken from K. Jayaprasad, *RSS and Hindu Nationalism,* 351. This book reproduces the entire text of the RSS Constitution as Appendix I, 351-361.

11 Varsha can be translated as, a division of the earth as separated off by certain mountain ranges. Bharatvarsha is one of the nine such divisions enumerated in the *shastras.* (Some mention only seven.) It is said in Vishnu Purana: The country (varṣam) that lies north of the ocean and south of the snowy mountains is called Bhāratam; there dwell the descendants of Bharata." Starting from Himalayas and extending upto the Indian Ocean is the nation built by Gods, Hindusthan. Thus it fits the description of a varsha perfectly as it is a massive piece of earth separated from rest of the world by a mountain range.

12 Vinayak Damodar Savarkar was born on May 28, 1883. On October 7, 1905, during Dusshera, he set up a bonfire (holi) and burnt all his foreign clothes and goods. He was arrested in 1909. He tried to escape by diving in the water but was arrested as he reached the shore. On July 1911, Savarkar was sentenced to two life sentences i.e., 50 years in the cellular jail of Andamans, also known as Kala Pani. In 1964, Savarkar felt his goal of Independence of India was achieved. So he declared his wish to attain Samadhi and started hunger-strike on February 1, 1966 and passed away on February 26, 1966.

Hence, we know well from Savarkar's teaching, that Hindutva is not identical with Hinduism. Hindutva is more than the Hindu religion. The Hindus constituted the Indian nation. Hindutva is the animating principle of the Hindu nation (Hindu Rashtra), that extended across the entire Indian subcontinent and was rooted in an undivided India (Akhand Bharat). Hinduness is synonymous with Indianness. Hindutva embraces all the departments of thought and activity of the Hindu race, which is inextricably bound to the idea of the nation. The Muslims and Christians form 'a sort of second-class citizenship in which they could live in India only on sufferance.'[13] (=unwilling permission).

2.2. M.S. Golwalkar (1906-1973)

Madhav Sadhashiv Golwalkar,[14] in his book *We, or Our Nationhood Defined,*[15] makes it clear that India is the holy land of the Hindus. For him, India was a pristine Hindu country in ancient times, a place of unparalleled glory destroyed in successive assaults by foreign invaders. Hence, a national regeneration is necessary, which is possible only through a revival of its Hinduness. For him, a territory is not a nation, but people, the Hindu people in the case of India. He is a passionate advocate of cultural nationalism, which is opposed to the civic nationalism enshrined in the Constitution of India. India's independence from colonial rule in 1947 did not constitute real freedom because the new leaders held on to the perverted concept of nationalism in terms of territory, which is an unnatural, unscientific, lifeless and hybrid concept. In his another work *Bunch of Thoughts,* he argues that territorial nationalism is a barbarism since it is deprived of national culture, of ancient and sublime Hindu culture. He also writes approvingly of Manu as a 'great soul' held in high regard by the people of the world. For Golwalkar, in the words of Manu S. Pillai and Tharoor, salvation lies not in Indian democracy, but in embracing 'dharmocracy'. Golwalkar

---

13 Shashi Tharoor, *Why I am a Hindu* (New Delhi: Aleph, 2018), 143-145.

14 Madhav Sadashiv Golwalkar was born on February 19, 1906 to a Marathi Karhade Brahmin family. In 1922, Golwalkar enrolled in Hislop College. In 1924, Golwalkar left Hislop College for Benaras Hindu University (BHU) in Varanasi, receiving a Bachelor of Science degree in 1925 and a master's degree in biology in 1927. Golwalkar returned to Nagpur, and obtained a law degree by 1935. In October 1936, Golwalkar abandoned his law practice and RSS work for the Sargachi Ramakrishna Mission ashram in West Bengal to renounce the world and become a sanyasi. He returned to Nagpur in a state of depression and indecision to seek Hedgewar's advice after his guru died in 1937, and Hedgewar convinced him that his obligation to society could best be fulfilled by working for the RSS. He died on June 5, 1973.

15 For a full text of the book, see *Golwalkar's 'We or Our Nationhood Defined',* A critique by Shamsul Islam with the full text of the book (New Delhi: Pharos Media, 2017), Total Pages-216.

intends that traditional Hindu practices, including caste discrimination,[16] should prevail in Hindu Rashtra. "We know as a matter of history that our north-Western and north-eastern areas, where the influence of Buddhism had disrupted the caste system, fell an easy prey to the onslaught of Muslims.... But the areas of Delhi and Uttar Pradesh, which were considered to be very orthodox and rigid in caste restrictions, remained predominantly Hindu even after remaining the very citadels of Muslim power and fanaticism." So, for Golwalkar, the more caste-ridden society was, the more robustly it was able to resist the encroachments of foreign faiths. For Golwalkar, "the so-called 'caste-ridden' Hindu society has remained undying and inconquerable...while casteless societies crumbled to dust."[17]

2.3. Syama Prasad Mookerjee (1901-1953)

Syama Prasad Mookerjee[18] was the founder of Bharatiya Jana Sangh. To Mookerjee and his followers, Hinduism was a national identity rather than a communal one. The Bharatiya Jana Sangh claimed the national mantle for its Hindutva agenda.[19] It was after he finished his term as Vice Chancellor of Kolkata University, that he entered into active politics, joining the Congress party, and entering the Legislative Council in Bengal. However, with Congress boycotting the legislatures, he also quit, and later stood for elections as an Independent candidate, and won. As an opposition leader, he firmly believed in individual liberty and freedom of expression. He opposed the amendment to the Indian Constitution, putting restrictions on Freedom of Expression and also detention without trial. The main ideological points of BJS which were laid down by Shyama Prasad Mukherjee were Uniform Civil Code[20] for everyone,

16 Parvathy Appaiah, *Hindutva Ideology and Politics* (New Delhi: Deep & Deep Publications, 2003), 92-93.

17 Shashi Tharoor, *Why I am a Hindu*, 146-149.

18 Born on July 6, 1901 in a famous family and graduated from Calcutta University, he became a fellow of the Senate in 1923. At the age of 33, he became the world's youngest Vice-Chancellor of the Calcutta University and held the office till 1938. Pandit Nehru inducted him in the Interim Central Government as a Minister for Industry and supply. On issue of Delhi pact with Likayat Ali Khan, Mookerjee resigned from the Cabinet on April 6, 1950. Mookerjee founded Bharatiya Jana Sangh on October 21, 1951. He went to visit Kashmir in 1953 and was arrested on 11th May while crossing border. He died as detenu on June 23, 1953.

19 Ratnakar Sadasyula, "History: What is the role of Shyama Prasad Mukherjee in India's freedom and politics thereafter?," *Ask New Question.com*, accessed July 17, 2018, https://www.quora.com.

20 Is Uniform Civil Code necessary for India? Let us look at the opinion of the Law Commission appointed to study the possibility of introducing Uniform Civil Code in the country: "The Law Commission has suggested certain changes in marriage and divorce laws that should be uniformly accepted in the personal laws of all religions, while holding

including Muslims and Hindus, scrapping Article 370 and full integration of Jammu and Kashmir with Indian Union and a ban on Cow Slaughter.[21]

2.4. Pandit Deen Dayal Upadhyaya (1916-1968)

Pandit Deen Dayal Upadhyaya advocated a philosophy of integral humanism.[22] Upadhyaya, who couched his ideas in moderate language, enjoyed broader acceptability. His philosophy was the animating spirit of a life of practical reason. He saw himself as a thinker whose role was to project genuine nationalistic thought in the political sphere, well beyond the limited and short-term aim of the attainment of political office. He saw his political party as merely a vehicle to build a nation. The Indian nation failed to become strong and unified because of political corruption, looked at from the perspective of the general public's lack of any urge to make India strong and prosperous, a degeneration of society and the fading away of the idealism that had inspired the struggle for freedom. Indians equated freedom with mere overthrow of foreign rule. This negative view overlooked the need for a genuine and patriotic love for the motherland.[23] Since love for the motherland had never been inculcated in its inhabitants, their lives in independent India are now centred on money and greed. Dazzled by the material advances of the West, India has taken to aping the foreigners in matters of development projects. Our democracy and Constitution is imitative of the West, divorced from any real connection to our mode of life rooted in Indian culture. The Constitution is deficient for not incorporating teachings from *Manusmriti.*[24] Hence, there should be a Hindu political philosophy based on a positive concept of patriotism and a

---

that the uniform civil code is neither necessary nor desirable at this stage in the country. The Commission, headed by former Supreme Court judge Justice B.S. Chauhan has come out with a 185-page consultation paper on Family Law Reforms' said **a unified nation does not necessarily need to have uniformity.** It is said the best way forward was to preserve diversity of personal laws even while ensuring they did not contradict fundamental rights guaranteed under the Constitution. Also Cfr. Krishnadas Rajagopal, "No need for uniform civil code now, says law panel," *The Hindu*, September 1, 2018, accessed September 3, 2018, https://www.thehindu.com/todays...uniform-civil-code...law.../article24837046.ece.

21 Ratnakar Sadasyula, "History: What is the role of Shyama Prasad Mukherjee in India's freedom and politics thereafter?" *Ask New Question.Com*, accessed July 17, 2018, https://www.quora.com.

22 An integral understanding of reality was believed by Sri Aurobindo. For Aurobindo, the nation becomes an entity and will enter into a plural world confederation. It means that the nation cannot be thought of in isolation, but as part of a world family.

23 Shashi Tharoor, *Why I am a Hindu*, 157-160.

24 *Manusmriti* literally means reflections of Manu. birth. Of the nearly 2,500 verses, more than a thousand are for brahmins, the next thousand for kings, statecraft and governance, only eight for vaishyas and two for shudras.

comprehensive vision of the nation based on its inherent character, culture, spiritual underpinnings and permanent values that have stood the test of time.[25]

3. *Agapocracy* as a Response to RSS Suspicion of Indian Democracy

Democracy is a system of government[26] of the people, by the people, and for the people in which the supreme power is vested with the people who exercise their power directly or through their elected representatives.[27] Democratic countries have been more successful in living peacefully with their neighbours, educating their citizens, liberating human energy and initiative for constructive purposes and economic growth.[28] In spite of its enormous contribution to an all-round development of society, there are many instances of failure of its noble objectives. The RSS' view that modern Indian democracy is a copy of Western democracy cannot be justified since Indian ethos and culture are deeply rooted in democracy.

For instance, the early Greek and Roman accounts of India, mostly histories of India during and just after Alexander the Great's invasion of India in 327-324 B.C., spoke of numerous cities and even larger areas being governed as democracies, but they were not always believed by scholars. Yet, research into the Buddhist Pali Canon during the nineteenth century confirmed this picture of widespread republican form of administration. The Pali Canon is the earliest version of the Buddhist scriptures, and reached its final form between 400-300 B.C. It contains the story of Buddha's life and teaching and his rules for monastic communities. Thus the Pali Canon provides us with many details of life in ancient India, and specifically of democratic institutions permeated with democratic spirit.[29] The Constitution of India remains faithful to this perennial and unbroken democratic spirit and culture of our people.

The Constitution of India with its fundamental rights is the foundation of contemporary Indian democracy.[30] All important words of the Constitution can be sifted and reduced to the one all-encompassing word that permeates the whole of the Constitution: **justice**. The Constitution understands justice as 'the absence of any arbitrary distinction of human and human in social, economic and political sphere.' Justice is the source of all fundamental rights, of liberty, equality and fraternity. Hence, justice is the foundation of Indian democracy.

25 Shashi Tharoor, *Why I am a Hindu*, 160-162.

26 John Pike, *Political Philosophy A-Z* (Edinburg: Edinburg University, 2007), 40-43.

27 www.merriam-webster.com/dictionary/democracy, accessed June 16, 2011.

28 www.icpd.org/democracy/index.html, accessed July 23, 2011.

29 Steve Muhlberger, "Democracy in Ancient India," accessed August 28, 2011, www.nipissingu.ca/department/**history**/muhlberger/.../**india**dem.htm*l*.

30 Valerian Rodrigues, "Introduction: Engaging with the Constitution," in *The Constitution of India: A Philosophical Review*, ed., George Panthanmackel (Delhi: Media House, 2003), 14.

It provokes another question: what is the foundation of justice. Justice, as we already mentioned, is giving that to which one has a right. The best of all giving is self-giving, which is love par-excellence.

In classical Greek, especially in Plato's *Symposium,*[31] there are two terms for love. These are *eros* and *philia. Eros* is based on strong feelings toward another. It usually occurs in the first stages of a man-woman relationship. It is based more on physical traits. *Philia* is love based on friendship between two persons. Undoubtedly, friendship is the foundation of a successful relationship. This is true whether it is marriage, relationship between family members, relationship with co-workers, employer, etc. With *eros*, one sees only each other's strengths/good side, everything is rosy. *Philia* is based on "give-and-take," where two people benefit each other in a mutual relationship. There is also a third Greek term '*agape*', which occurs rather infrequently in Greek usage [of course, the verb *agapao*='to love' was common in classical Greek[32]], occurred in the Septuagint (LXX) borrowed from the popular Egyptian dialect.[33] It is love above *philia* and *eros*. It is a love that is totally selfless, where a person gives out love to another person even if this act does not benefit her/him in any way. That is the way Jesus Christ loved humanity, and responded to violence. That is the core message of the Vedas and the Upanishads, of all religions. That is the foundation of true justice. That is the core principle of *agapocracy*.

Agapocracy should not be an alternative to democracy, but transcendence of democracy in an inclusive way. Inclusive transcendence[34] means to possess in an eminent way the same values that the inferior or lower beings possess only partially and imperfectly. Transcendental experience is the experience of Being which by being present in every human experience goes beyond the particular. For, Being is both the absolute condition of the possibility of every being and experience as well as that which is present in all human experience. By being present in all human experiences, it goes beyond every particular experience.

---

31 Plato, *Symposium,* Trs., Alexander Nehamas & Paul Woodruff (Indianapolis and Cambridge: Hackett Publishing Company, 1989), xiii; in *Symposium,* the distinction and co-existence of *eros*and *philia* become obvious in Phaedrus' discussion of the example of Alcestis who alone was willing to die in her husband's place: "Because of her love (*eros*), she went so far beyond her parents in family feeling (*philia*) that she made them look like outsiders" (179C).

32 C. Bernas, "Love," *New Catholic Encyclopedia,* Vol. 1 (Washington D. C.: The Catholic University of America, 1967, Reprint:1981), 193.

33 *Ibid.*

34 The idea of "inclusive transcendence" is also implied in the teaching of the Second Vatican Council when it speaks of the acts of religion which transcend the earthly and temporal order of things; see DH, 3.

Being, which is essentially love, is the cause of all beings.[35] There are beings because Being gives itself, allows itself to be limited in the finite being through the principle of essence. Being is love because it always gives itself. To be is to give. This self-giving or *agape* of Being is a transcendental condition without being exclusively restricted to any one being and without which no being is possible. It is also a transcendental experience because it is present in all human experience; and by being present in all human experiences it goes beyond every particular experience.

Applying to democracy, it means we should not do away with democracy, but we ought to transform democracy by taking an *agapeic* approach to governance. What democracy lacks today is agape; by incorporating agape in its core structure, we will be both transforming and transcending democracy. Democracy will become *agapocracy* through inclusive transcendence.

In other words, the fundamental rights of the Indian constitution have their foundation in justice. Justice is giving that to which one has a right. Love is the perfection of justice. In love, one not only gives something to which another has a right, but also gives one's own self. Genuine love is self-giving. Self-giving is expressed in the joy and commitment with which one gives oneself to another. For long, democracy everywhere worked on the principle of justice. Now, it is time it should work on another basis, going beyond justice, transcending the principle of justice and embracing the principle of love which would consequently include the principles of justice and fundamental rights.

Conclusion

Rashtriya Swayam Sevak Sangh (RSS) was founded by Dr Kesav Baliram Hedgewar. The RSS ideology is centred around the vital force of nationalism, which binds societies. Nationalism and patriotism are parallel factors. For Savarkar, 'Hindutva' is the 'quality of being a Hindu' in ethnic, cultural and political terms. A Hindu is one who considers India to be his motherland (*mathrubhumi*), the land of his ancestors (*pitrbhumi*), and his holy land (*punyabhumi*). Golwalkar makes it clear that India is the holy land of the Hindus, a place of unparalleled glory destroyed in successive assaults by foreign invaders. To Syama Prasad Mookerjee and his followers, Hinduism is a national identity rather than a communal one. Pandit Deen Dayal Upadhyaya advocated an ideology of integral humanism.

The RSS speaks about two types of Hindutva: aggressive and liberal. M.S. Golwalkar stuck to the former but his successors appear to move towards the latter. But all remain unable to spell out clearly how social, political, economic and defensive set up has to be based on their fundamentals.

---

35 St Thomas Aquinas, *Commentary on the Metaphysics of Aristotle,* Vol. I, Translated by John P. Rowan (Chicago: Henry Regnery Company, 1961), 42.

22

Communist Movement in India: Democracy Implications

Sujan Amurutham
Pontifical Institute, Aluva

Abstract: Left Political parties, as a movement, have got not a trivial influence in the political arena. Left parties, though worked more as a social movement in its formative period before Independence, became very much like any other political party after independence. This paper evaluates, how the left parties, being a cadre party getting clear orders from the Soviet Union, struggled to cope up with leading their governments within the framework of a democratic country, as well as how it still lags behind in meeting new challenges put forward by new social and cultural Movements in the country, with progressive approach as it should have been; we make a critique of its errors in praxis, going through a historical analysis as well as in its theories, in brief, making use of analysis of Amartya Sen.

Keywords: Indian Model Communism, Democratic Centrism, New Social Movements, Democratic Values, People's Democracy.

Introduction

Sidney Tarrow's widely cited definition of social movements as "collective challenges, based on common purposes and social solidarities, in sustained interaction with elites, opponents, and authorities,"[1] is very much appealing.

1 Tarrow Sidney G., "Power in Movement: Social Movements and Contentious Politics," updated 3rd edition, in *Cambridge Studies in Comparative Politics*, (New York: Cambridge

This definition encompasses four empirical properties of social movements—collective challenge, common purpose, social solidarity, and sustained interaction—that, taken together, distinguish them from protests and other forms of contentious action.[2]

As for this definition, the Communist Movement in India (hereafter referred as CPM) suits to be a social movement. By CPM, we mean the movement of the Left Political Parties. The 'Communist Party of India' (CPI), which was started as a Left Party in 1920, will be later split in 1964, into CPI and CPI (M) [CPI (Marxist)]. The Left parties, entered into the political arena, by participating in the Indian way of democratic parliamentarism, though constantly changing their tactics and strategy, engaging themselves, compromisingly, both with agitation, as well as, parliamentarianism, or say, activism as well as power politics, on a trial and error basis. We will restrict our study to the CPM's institutional influences, that is, in political arena, as well as non-institutional influences, that is, in people's culture and beliefs.

1. Communist Movement: Beginning and Nature

a. General Outline of the CPM: The CPI at the national level, officially commenced at the time of Lenin at Tashkant (in Uzbekistan, formerly part of Soviet Union) in 1920, and in Kerala in 1939. The CPI was elected to rule the State of Kerala in 1957, after winning the first Assembly elections. Since then, Left Democratic Front in Kerala, which is headed by CPI (M) along with CPI and others, wins every alternate election to the Assembly. In West Bengal, CPI (M) was first elected to power in 1977, and then in Tripura in 1986.

b. Violent Path to socialism: E.M.S. admits that, more than Leninism, M. N. Roy's political and ideological vision ('Royism'), an antagonist approach towards Gandhi, laid the basis of the Indian CPI, in its formative period.[3] As the CPI was clandestinely working with INC, the CPI's co-operation or non-cooperation towards INC's independence Movement depended on Royism, and later as an Independent Party, on the political gain of Stalin's changing pro-British or contra-British policy, always for his own country Russia's gain. CPI was therefore, against 'Quit India movement' of 1942 due to Soviet Union's Pro-British War Policy, and had, in its dark periods of history, formulated its

---

University Press, 2011), 9.

2 Yelena Margaret Bidé, *Social Movements and Processes of Political Change: The Political Outcomes of the Chilean Student Movement,* A Thesis submitted to the Brown University, in partial fulfilment for the Degree of Bachelor of Arts with Honors in International Relations, 2015, 4.

3 E.M.S. Namboodiripad, *Indian Communist Prasthaanam 1920-1998,* 2nd edition, (Trivandrum: Chintha Publications, 2005), 17.

Culcutta Thesis of 1948-49, of promoting armed revolutions in different parts of India with a wishful thinking that time is up for bloody socialist insurrection in Russian model, for establishing 'People's Democracy' – a democracy combined with socialism, and also due to Telengana Thesis of 1950-51 of reviving the line of violence, aiming at Mao Model village insurrections in India. They considered Independence of 1947 as fake, on account of their 'Culcutta Thesis' of 1948-49, and supported Muslim League's call for the formation of Pakistan, due to their blind anti-INC stand only. The 'Culcutta Thesis' was withdrawn by them in 1949 and 'Telengana Struggle' withdrawn in 1951, and were admitted by them to be a failure; In Kerala, during the Culcutta Thesis period, CPM unleashed forcible seizure of paddies in many places, causing deaths of many peasants. Later, the Maoists or the Naxalites, who made a split from the CPI (M), followed Mao's ideals to forcefully obliterate of landlordism, and to overthrow constitutionalism, elected governments and courts. But, CPM was not in favour of Naxalites. E.M.S. himself attributed errors of CPI, in following Stalinism, with regard to the wrong views about the party dictatorship model governance, about intent of literature for art-for-life's sake only, and above all, about inconsistent political decisions with regard to Freedom movement, separation of Pakistan, Nehru's government policies, peasants violent Movements etc. Thus, most of approaches followed by CPM, during its formative period, in the Stalinist era, were admitted as errors.

c. Peaceful Transition to socialism: After having admitted as a failure the Party Programme of violence implemented before 1951, due to falling in numbers in party membership and in public opinion, the Party Programme of 1951 evaluated that the Indian situation is not ripe for workers and peasants for a violent insurrection; and it paved the way for an experiment of 'peaceful transition to socialism' over the course of time, though the violent revolution is still the essence of proletarian revolution for Marxism-Leninism. 'Peaceful transition to socialism' in principle meant participating temporarily in the parliamentary democracy or 'bourgeois democracy', as a means or with a long-term objective to overthrow the Indian State by means of revolution and substitute it with a 'People's Democratic State' ruled by the proletariat.

d. Communist Government: The communists were much better organised as a disciplined party from the early 1950s, by working along, with new communist priorities, within India's democracy,[4] even to the extent of holding on to Stalinist 'democratic centrism'. It meant, on the one hand,

4 John Harriss and Olle Törnquist, "Comparative Notes on Indian Experiences of Social Democracy: Kerala and West Bengal" in *Simons Papers in Security and Development*,

avoiding the deviation of being dictatorial or bureaucratic, rather being with the oppressed masses, and on the other hand, avoiding the deviation of not following class ideal of socialism or collective consciousness of the working class people. The 'principles of democratic centralism' indicate that the Party leadership be constantly vigilant against two deviations, either of the becoming dictatorial with people, rather than being with them, or the opposite feeling to keep off the ideals of socialism. In other words, CPM should avoid falling either into the errors of "trailing behind the backward sections of the masses, or the party descending to the level of the consciousness of the masses rather than raising them to higher level of consciousness."[5]

Arundhati Roy sums up the administrative nature of that first Elected Communist Government in 1957-59, saying "suddenly the communists found themselves in the extraordinary – critics said absurd – position of having to *govern a people and foment revolution simultaneously* (italics added). Comrade E.M.S. Namboodiripad (E.M.S. in short) evolved his own theory about how he would do this. (He tried to implement) *The Peaceful Transition to Communism* with an adolescent's obsessive diligence and an ardent fan's unquestioning approval. It set out in detail how Comrade E.M.S.'s government intended to enforce land reforms, neutralize the police, subvert the judiciary and 'Restrain the Hand of the Reactionary Anti-People's Congress Government at the Centre."[6] This first Government introduced Kerala Land Reform Bill to end landlordism, which ended up in the CPM's disputes with higher castes. Police was used by the government to favor workers and peasants in labour disputes. And, E.M.S. admitted to the instances of CPM cell courts at villages having decided on matters relating to cases such as boundary disputes, inter-caste marriages, dispute on eviction and other petty cases, and having functioned as parallel institutions of interference. The Comrades' understanding at that time that party members shall teach a lesson to the capitalists, by meddling in police cases, disputes, etc. was not corrected by the party leaders. The Education Bill presented in the Assembly with the intention that Aided school managers' power be reduced, to appoint only from the list of teachers issued from government, that teachers' salary be directly given to teachers, that government take over the schools for five years if warranted, and that local and the state advisory education board shall be constituted, to advise management in school matters. This interference in police cases by political *netas* still continues in Kerala.

---

published by The School for International Studies, Simon Fraser University, No. 39/2015, January 2015, 13.

5 E.M.S. Namboodiripad, *World Capitalist Crisis and Revolutionary Perspectives* (Trivandrum: Chintha Publishers, March 1982), 16-18.

6 Arundhati Roy, *The God of Small things*, 2nd edition, (New Delhi: Penguin Books, 2002), 67.

The 1957-59 government was ousted by the President of India, due to mass protests against Agrarian Bill and Education Bill, and failure of law and order situation.

e. Communist Movement after its first government: CPI's government of 1957-59, having found in a 'position of having to *govern a people and foment revolution simultaneously'*, and its consequent ousting in 1959, led the Party to concentrate on winning elections, only to struggle itself to work within constitution; and eventually the Party would degenerate itself on concentrating on Party politics rather than on people's rights as before, or on internal conflicts that led to split in 1964, and eventually leading to a further faction of Naxalites in 1968, or on its supporting Emergency in 1975, which would be evaluated as faulty later, and would also accept having committed similar other errors on its strategy and tactics laid down in Party's programme and action on varied aspects. The party would also concentrate on vindicating its actions when in government, and on winning elections in Kerala, West Bengal since 1977, and in Tripura since 1986, besides making occasional acts of violence of political vendetta in Malabar, to keep up the party spirit among the youth, and supporting factionalism. The party also fell prey to corruption and blind opposition through violent mass protests to developmental policies of the government of the opposition party. All these led the CPM to reduce itself in stature and operation, to just like any other political party and lose the revolutionary character of its old cadre for a continued movement for the cause of the poor, with an exception perhaps of firebrand communist A. K. Gopalan in 1960's, in and outside Parliament.

f. Changes effected in the Party's view of People's Democracy**:** The Indian State's constitution, in its preamble, lays down that India is a 'socialist' secular democratic Republic'. John Harris, who made a comparative study between West Bengal and Kerala, claims that what both States were experimenting was social democracy. The social democracy is defined as "a politics based on political equality and that strives to realise social justice, by democratic means, and in such a way that the realization of social justice and democratic deepening serve each other."[7] But the Party Programme lays down that the CPM has a 'strategy', the goal of instituting people's democratic nation, which combines democracy, with socialism. The updated Party Programme of 2000, advocated to retain the Party Programme of 1964, after the split, of following the stage of the revolution, the strategy, class character of the Indian state and the government and the

7 John Harriss and Olle Törnquist, "Comparative Notes on Indian Experiences of Social Democracy: Kerala and West Bengal," 5.

class alliance to achieve the people's democratic revolution. It has its roots in the 1951 Party Programme.

The *Paragraph 88(9)* of the old Programme stated that "the people's democratic state shall strive to infuse the *spirit of democracy* into all our social and political institutions. Trade unions peasant and agricultural workers organizations will play decisive role in this". But, it was *silent on providing space for any other parties* other than the CPM and *frontal organizations* of workers and peasants.[8]

But in the new framework of thinking, plurality is emphasized, the updated Programme, in as many words: "the people's democratic state shall strive to infuse in all our social and political institutions *the spirit of democracy*. It extends *democratic forms of initiative* and control over *every aspect of national life*. A key role in this will be played by *the political parties*, trade union, peasant and agricultural workers associations, and other class and mass organisations of the working people."[9] However, it forgets the simple factor that it had to apply the democratic principle today to create a base for the proposed culture of plurality in future. This element is completely missing.

In the agrarian field, a new paragraph was added in the context of the paradigm shift in the economy that, apart from 'ensuring long term and cheap credit for the peasants, artisans and agricultural workers and fair prices for agricultural produce' (*Paragraph 89 of the old programme),* the updated programme added that the State should also develop a State-led marketing system to protect the peasantry from big traders and Multi National Companies and from sharp fluctuation in prices (*Paragraph 6.4).* Another significant change was with regard to the party's attitude to foreign capital. The earlier position was that 'all foreign capital in plantation, mines, oil refineries, shipping and trade will be taken over'. While the updated programme committed the party to 'take steps to eliminate Indian and foreign monopolies in different sectors of industry, finance, trade and services, through suitable measures including state takeover of their assets'.

2. A Critical Appraisal of CPM's Democracy Implications

To better evaluate Democracy implications of the CPM, we shall, first of all, have a critical look at its economic approaches, and secondly, into how it viewed social movements, such as capitalist movement, LGBT, caste movement, and Media.

---

8 E.K. Santha, *Marxist Praxis: Communist Experience in Kerala: 1957-2011*, A Dissertation submitted to the Department of History, Sikkhim University, in partial fulfilment of the requirements for the Degree of Doctor of Philosophy, 2016, 333.

9 CPI (M)'s Updated Programme, 2000, 6.3 (vii), as referred in E.K. Santha, *Marxist Praxis*, 327.

3. Economic Appraisal of CPM

Kerala, though a backward state economically, is high in social growth, which is, however, the goal of any economic growth. This is called the 'Kerala Experiment' hailed as a model for the world by Amartya Sen to prove his concept of development as expansion of freedom through capabilities, in his book '*Development as Freedom*'. For Amartya Sen, the old view that economic growth is the source and basis for any social growth has no base, as the Kerala experiment shows. Instead, though economic income contributes substantially to the capability improvement of a person or a State, there are other influences also that contribute to the economic growth, such as that of the social growth. Hence Kerala Experiment is shown as an instance for disproving Marxian principle of economic growth as base, and other developmental aspects as its superstructure.

Kerala's retarded industrial development is a case to be studied. CRISIL research on the performance of states, conducted in 2018, rates Kerala one among the three States which had the lowest GDP growth in this period – Kerala, Punjab, Uttar Pradesh are among them. The CPI had to be blamed for the terror of trade unionism in all areas of labour. They neutralized the police in the disputes of labour in industries, in favour of workers, and so much so the protests of the labourers for hike in the salary and for other rights, under trade unions, forced the industrialists not only to close down their industries but also to turn down requests from government for starting new ones, resulting in the loss of employment. An anti-industrialist culture was created in this way among party cadres, primarily due to the CPM's declared approach of the nationalization of all private businesses, embedded in the mind of the ordinary Party workers, though clarified otherwise by its leaders in writing and in speech, and due to preference of the labour class in labour disputes. Thus, more and more complicated and stringent procedures and rules were legislated against capitalists, from a labourers' point of view. Trade unionism ruled the industry so much so that the *nokkuooli* (the pay without work), exacted from people by labourers, was silently nodded to, by trade unions, with neutralization of police. Traditional industries also suffered very badly, due to volatility of prices in the world market.

3.1. Social Movements and Communist Movement

3.1.1. Capitalist Movement Supports New Social Movements

Karl Marx speaks of economic inequality in society, and consequently, cherishes a dream of a perfect world of equality, which is eventually possible in a Stateless society called Communism. Economic equality is the goal of Marxian view of development. The economic equality between bourgeois and labourers classes lie around single-handed management of production, exchange, distribution of commodities by the former. Noam Chomsky, a critic of capitalism, says "Polls show that almost half the population believe that the U.S. Constitution—a sacred document—is the source of Marx's phrase 'from each according to his ability, to each according to his need'. So obviously right does the sentiment seem."[10] In this sense, what he wants to say is that even the capitalist countries seek to follow the dream of Karl Marx, in principle.

However, Capitalist movement supports New Social Movements: Curiously though, it is in the democratic and not socialism-experimented nations that the social movements sprouted and let sprout more. Students' protest at Tianmen square in Beijing was suppressed by Chinese dictatorship without any scope for dialogue in 1989. "Capitalist dynamics alternately inhibit or facilitate the formation of new *collective identities and solidarities*, including both class and non-class identities. In this way, capitalism shapes the very conditions of existence of many social movements. The balance of class forces in a society powerfully shapes the way Movements evolve over time and what they can win for their constituents...ideologies and cultural idioms closely linked to capitalist institutions and practices may also strongly influence movement strategies and goals."[11] "Unlike 'old' social movements – pre-eminently the labour movement – in which issues of material deprivation and inequality are considered central, new social movements are typically seen as revolving around 'non-material' or 'post-materialist' issues, including lifestyles, identities, and 'recognition.'"[12]

3.1.2. LGBT Movement and Communist Movement

We shall take up the new LGBT movement, as an instance to evaluate Marxist view towards social movements. This includes social movements such as gender and other rights protection Movements. Taylor and Van Dyke observes that, 'The core thesis [of New Social Movement theory] is that that new social movements, such as the women's, peace, gay and lesbian, environmental, animal rights, disability rights, mental health, anti-globalization Movements, and even the New Christian Right and contemporary hate Movements, are unique in that they are less concerned with economic redistribution and policy changes than with issues of the quality of life, personal growth and autonomy,

10 FAIR, Press Release, July 19, 1988. "Poll on Constitution,"*Boston Globe Magazine*, September 13, 1987, cited in Julius Lobel, ed., *A Less than Perfect Union* (Monthly Review), (1988): 3, as quoted in Noam Chomsky, *Necessary Illusions: Though control in Democratic Societies*, (London: Pluto Press, 1989), 13.

11 Colin Barker and et. al, *Marxism and Social Movements*, ed., (Boston: Koninklijke Brill NV, 2013), 86.

12 Colin Barker, *Marxism and Social Movements*, 94.

and identity and self-affirmation.'"[13] Colin Barker et. al, observes that "The LGBT movement, which we use as a shorthand expression for the family of Movements focused on issues of sexual orientation, is thus a paradigmatic example of a new social movement."[14] Such Movements are the result of capitalist economy in such a way that "In a sense, these Movements thereby completed earlier democratic or 'bourgeois' revolutions of the eighteenth and nineteenth centuries that only partially extended the civil, political, and social rights that we associate with full citizenship."[15] "It seems likely the support for LGBT rights in strongly social-democratic countries may have something to do with the levels of social solidarity in these countries. Göran Therborn suggests as much, in citing the 'secular pluralism' prevalent in northern Europe, as a chief factor favoring the greater acceptance of same-sex marriage in the region. A second factor worth considering is the inclusive nature of the state in social-democratic nations."[16] "A final factor worth examining relates to the transition from industrial to post-industrial politics. According to Therborn, this shift – from a class-based politics focused on necessity to a post-class-based politics focused on choice – accounts for the emergence of sexuality and other 'choice'-based issues in Swedish politics from the 1980s onwards. Rayside's examination of how 'shifts in the balance of union membership away from the industrial working class have opened up unions to social causes', prompting a greater willingness on the part of Dutch unions to embrace LGBT issues, provides further support for this view."[17] This possibility is supported by Rayside's analysis of the way in which the Dutch state – which, he argues, 'reflects a general pattern of interest-group inclusion in elabourate consultative exercises designed to arrive at consensus'50 – helped to promote LGBT rights, by (eventually) incorporating rather than repressing the country's main gay and lesbian organisation, the *Cultur en Ontspannings Centrum* (COC)."[18] "According to Valocchi, the actions of these reformers, along with the 'reform minded capitalists' with whom they collabourated, must be understood within the context of the shift from 'competitive' to 'reform' capitalism in the early decades of the twentieth century – reinforcing the importance of situating the LGBT movement within its larger political-economic context. Valocchi writes that 'as market relations drastically altered the landscape of virtually every social institution, they created a host of social problems; at least that is

13 Taylor and Van Dyke, "The Targets of Social Movements: Beyond a Focus on the State," *Research in Social Movements, Conflicts and Change* 25, no. 2 (2005), 27.

14 Colin Baker, *Marxism and Social Movements*, 92.

15 Ibid., 93.

16 Ibid., 96.

17 Ibid.

18 Ibid.

how a reform minded middle-class came to see issues of immigration, race, crime, labour conflict, and sexual difference."[19] Thus capitalist countries, with its capitalist relations of productions rather than that of socialist relations of production carried out by the so-called socialist nations, gave a new impetus to the person-oriented new social movements, which respect the person. However, the CPM in Kerala supports the LGBT issue.

3.1.3. Class and Caste

They don't recognize caste but only class. Some say, as long as there is capitalism, Marxism will be relevant. Capitalism is based on division between capitalist and labour classes. Class is differently understood. Class is understood by Marx on the economic terms, whether one is in the possession of or in the capability of possessing of the means of production or not, such as land, capital, buying of labour power, and machine. While castes, which include also Dalits who are still in the poor strata of the society due to their social exclusion for many centuries, are not accepted as a class by the communists in India, they still are against the present caste-wise reservation, rather they are for reservation based on economic backwardness. Therefore, they are for reservation of the economically low among the higher castes. But, it is here we shall better understand class in the sense, E.P. Thompson expanded our understanding of class formation and that classes are emergent. "If we stop history at a given point, then there are no classes but simply a multitude of individuals with a multitude of experiences. But if' we watch these men over an adequate period of social change, we observe patterns in their relationships, their ideas, and their Institutions. Class is defined by men as they live their own history, and, in the end, this is its only definition."[20] A class, in Thompson's view, is "very loosely defined body of people who share the same categories of interests, social experiences, traditions and value-systems, who have a *disposition to behave* as a class, to define themselves in their consciousness In relation to other groups of people in class ways."[21] Class is defined in cultural terms, and in opposition to other social groups. People must see and describe themselves as different. In this sense, caste could be very well incorporated as a class, and that reductionist view of class could be avoided to better understand caste reservation rather than economic reservation.

---

19 Colin Baker, *Marxism and Social Movements*, 100.

20 E.P. Thompson, *The Making of the English Working Class* (New York: Vintage, 1963), 11.

21 E.P. Thompson, *The Poverty of Theory* (New York: Monthly Review Press, 1978), 295, as quoted in Scott G. McNall, "Class Analysis and Social Movement Theory: Towards A Synthesis," *Mid-American Review of Sociology* XI, nos. 23-28, (1986), 4.

3.1.4. Media and Capitalism

For Chomsky, democracy is no better than People's Democracy, which is advocated by Communism. For Chomsky condemns violence sponsored not only by communists, but also by Democracy people, especially the US when they attacked Nicaraguans. He also holds that state sponsored news through all types of media, that cover up the hidden intention of making an action or law by a State, is a sort of violence towards the people.

4. Observations

CPM lost power in Tripura and West Bengal, during the recently held elections to the state legislatures. The only exception was in the case of Kerala, where it has gone so far, as to embrace the ideals of capitalism. On the one hand, the old cadre and the old programme is unattractive, and on the other, the CPM has no response to the new challenges such as Gender inclusive approach, Environmental issues. This is due to its developmental perspective being defective.

First of all, as regards Environmental issue and Development, CPM's response is confused, due to the fact that its developmental concept is based on economic needs. But, commenting on the Sustainable Development, as meeting "needs of the present without compromising the ability of future generations to meet their own *needs*", Amartya Sen says, such a concept has done much good, but, he asks whether "understanding of sustainability takes an adequately capacious view of humanity," and tells, "certainly, people do have needs, but they also have values, and, in particular, cherish their ability to reason, appraise, choose, participate and act."[22] Hence, evaluating people and their development only in terms of their needs may give us rather meager view of humanity. Therefore, discussion on environment cannot be divorced from the lives of existing creatures. Environment is not only a matter of passive preservation, but one of active pursuit. For instance, construction of schools is necessary, for development is fundamentally an empowering process. Human intervention, say for example, purification of water through technology is a part of improving environment. Our reasons for valuing particular opportunities need not always lie in their contribution to our living standards or more generally to our own interests. We attach importance to preservation of species, not exclusively because it would enhance our own living standards; and so, we do not desire destruction of owls because they have nothing to do with our human living standards, either. Hence definition of sustainable freedom can be broadened as "to encompass the preservation, and (when possible) expansion of substantive freedom and capabilities of people today,

22 Amartya Sen, *Idea of Justice* (New Delhi: Penguin books, 2010), 250.

'without compromising capabilities of future generations' to have similar or more freedom."[23]

Secondly, CPM also was much more confused about gender inclusive approach than the bourgeois parties. "When it comes to providing seats for women in the Legislatures and the Parliament, the CPM's performance was sometimes far worse than the bourgeois parties. Gender representation of CPI (M) in Lok Sabha from 1967 to 2014 shows that except in 2004 and 2014, the women representation is well below 10 per cent or just 10 per cent."[24]

Thirdly, CPM in India, just like any CPM wherever sprouted, first began as an underground movement, say in Cuba, China, Russia, before 1917. M. N. Roy, started this movement from abroad in 1920, through pamphlets, money, underground work, and had violence embedded in it. Marxism also used 'tactics' as short-term plan for change, and 'strategy' for is long term plan. For Indian Marxists, Parliamentarianism is a 'strategy' for eventually attaining goals of socialism and communism, while its political alliance with non-communist parties, which may change from time to time, is a tactics. Thus going underground and Parliamentarianism, were justified as tactic and strategy respectively, once its ultimate goals of socialism and communism, are aimed at.

Fourthly, the author in his study of Chilean Student Movement, 2011-2015, indicated about the non-institutional outcomes from the movement, such as changes in attitudes, beliefs or values, other than institutional outcomes such as political change in structures, development, etc. He also observes it brought about non-institutional changes such as increase in political consciousness. Likewise, CPM brought about the non-institutional change called the increase of political consciousness among people, which is a collective consciousness, to discuss and challenge the unpopular policies of governments, in unison. So, much so, there increased trade unions in all types of labour.

Fifthly, Amartya Sen sees the value of debating, discussing, deliberating, in creating and recreating values and beliefs, especially the value of deciding on better acts of justice. CPM nurturing a cadre party concept respects principle of subsidiarity. Unlike the Congress Party, where its President is elected not through from bottom-up election process, CPI (M)'s General Secretary and Politburo members are elected from the Central committee, which consists of elected members, from the bottom-up election process. Though factions or inner party politics play a vital role in elections to such offices of the Party, there is however, a space for interaction and debate on the issues, like the voting for the approval of Party document, democratic process of election

23 Amartya Sen, *Idea of Justice*, 252; See also, Sujan Amurutham, "Virtuous Development: An overview of Amartya Sen's views," *The Living Word* 124, nos. 1-2, (2018), 88.

24 E. K. Santha, *Marxist Praxis*, 371.

for the Party offices within the party, etc. As a movement, we can see some special features in Movement, such as a) having grass root level positive interventions by party workers, say for example, among the peasants and workers, b) having an ideal of creating classless consciousness as well as its praxis, and its constant re-interpretations by admitting errors on its previous interpretations on the same, following trial and error method, and c) making more and more cadre party organization. However, though as a movement, it no longer pursues liberation perspectives for peasants or marginalized people, Mmarxist ideals still continue to influence and inspire people at large such as students, literary men and others.

Statement of the ACPI Annual Research Seminar on "Philosophies of Transformative Practice: Social Movements in India"

We, the Association of Christian Philosophers of India (ACPI), met at the Socio-Religious Centre (SRC), Kozhikode, for the 43rd Annual Research Seminar from 20th to 23rd October 2018. There were 89 participants in attendance.

- India has a rich history of social movements that have brought about revolutionary and life transforming changes at different levels of Indian society. These social movements have contributed to improving the life of citizens, especially more vulnerable ones like the displaced and migrants, people in bonded labour and also those combating climate change and improving tribal welfare. These Movements have also contributed to the education of girls, fighting against caste and gender discrimination, workers Movements, environmental Movements and other salutary causes.
- Many Indian social movements aim to realize the transformative potential of the essential values, rights and duties enshrined in the Preamble of the Indian Constitution.
- Social Movements make change happen because of the courage, zeal, vision, sacrifice and commitment of their participants. No social movement that is truly just and equitable can be sustained without a firm conviction of the truth and the courage to proclaim it whatever be the cost.
- Every social movement must strive to create a culture where people are empowered to believe in their own potential to be agents of change. All true development must aim at integral development, otherwise it is detrimental to every human interest. Genuine human

development becomes a function and fruit of the harmonious activation of human potential and freedom.

- Any attempt at transformative social action must include wisdom, power and care in a healthy tension.

We, as Indian Christian philosophers, by our philosophical reflections, can facilitate the dynamics of social movements by helping to make them liberative, humanizing and constructive. It is imperative that our philosophizing is not confined only to the ideal, but is related to the real and existential situations of life.

We support socio-political Movements that align with the Constitution and which employ democratic and rational approaches along with constructive activism. We encourage social movements which promote sustainable development and aim for integral and holistic growth.

Contributors

Anthony Dias (xisr.mb80@gmail.com) is presently the Director of Xavier Institute of Social Research (XISR) based in Nasik. He has a doctorate from the National Law School of India University. His PhD work was on development-induced displacement and his book, 'Development and Its Human Cost' deals with this subject and that of eminent domain. His action-research on the Nomadic and De-notified tribes has resulted in a publication known as 'Aakrosh Pardyancha' in Marathi. He has participated in national and international conferences on the subject and is consulted by NGOs, colleges and specialized institutions. He has also been associated with some social movements. His other areas of research include Distress Migration, Climate Change, Human Rights and Corporate Social Responsibility.

Ashley Miranda (ashsdb@gmail.com) is a Salesian of Don Bosco. He teaches Ethics, History of Philosophy and Philosophy of History, among other subjects, at *Divyadaan, Salesian Institute of Philosophy,* Nashik. He is at present Rector of Don Bosco Parish and School in Nashik.

Biju Pallippadan (rockpallippadan@gmail.com) belongs to St Thomas Province of Vincentian Congregation, New Delhi. He got ordained in 2016 on 2nd January at Potta-Divine. He holds four Masters (MA English-Bhopal University, MA Philosophy- IGNOU, MSc Psychology from Madras University, MPh from JDV, Pune. He defended his Doctoral Thesis on 9th Dec. in 2016, at JDV, on the topic: "Does Faith heal anxiety? The Inter-Relation among, Anxiety, Freedom and Faith in the Philosophical Writings of Søren Kierkegaard." He worked in minor seminary as Vice Rector and Bursar before pursuing his higher studies. He is actively involved in teaching career for the last five years. He serves as visiting faculty in different institutes such as De Paul Institute Bangalore, CRI Bangalore, and Holy Spirit Seminary Eluru. He was appointed as Staff and Librarian at Morning Star College, Kolkata on June 15th on 2017.

Francis Abraham Aykaraparampil (fraycmi@gmail.com) born at Adivaram in Kottayam District in Kerala, India, is a Catholic priest of the Congregation of the Carmelites of Mary Immaculate, belonging to its Bhavnagar Mission. He holds a Licentiate and Doctorate in Philosophy from Dharmaram Vidya Kshetram, Bangalore, India. At present, he is an Associate Professor of Western Philosophy at Darsana Institute of Philosophy-Wardha; and a visiting faculty at Dharmaram Vidya Kshetram-Bangalore; Mater Dei Academy-Goa; etc. There is couple of books and articles to his credit.

Francis Arackal Thummy (farackal@gmail.com) did his PG Diploma in Media studies from Griffith College, Dublin, Ireland, and Licence and Doctorate in Social Sciences, specializing in media, from Gregorian and St. Thomas Universities in Rome. He has a Master's Degree in Philosophy from Nagpur University and Licence in Philosophy from St. Thomas University, Rome. He has taught Media, and Philosophy for 22 years at many Institutes and colleges; was the Director of *Gyandhara*, Institute of Philosophy, in Orlim, Goa. From 2012-15 he taught the Under Graduate and Post Graduate Programme in the Mass Communication Department, St. Joseph's College (Autonomous) Bangalore. He was also the Head of the Department (HOD). He has published five books, presented papers in national and international conferences and seminars. He has published scientific papers in reputed journals, written numerous articles in religious and secular magazines and filed press reports and letters to the Editor in secular magazines and newspapers. He has a significant presence in online media with a personal website, blogs, and social networking pages offering comments on economic, political, religious, and social issues concerning the nation and the world. At present he is a Professor of Journalism & Mass Communication at Amity University, Gurgaon, Haryana, India.

George Panthanmackel, msfs (gpanthanmackel@gmail.com/panthanmackel@gmail.com) is Provincial of Northeast India Province of the Missionaries of St Francis de Sales, Guwahati. He has been a visiting Professor to several Institutes, including to Symbiosis University, Pune. He holds three doctorates: two in Philosophy and one in Theology. He is author of several books and articles. In 2009-2010, he worked at Indira Gandhi National Open University (IGNOU) as Senior Consultant of Philosophy in the formation of its Philosophy Syllabus and edited the entire BA Instruction Material of Philosophy. He is the Associate Editor of ACPI Encyclopedia of Philosophy. He is also currently the President of the Priests' Section of National CRI.

Gregory Mathew Malayil (gm6272@gmail.com) a catholic priest belongs to the Religious Congregation, Carmelites of Mary Immaculate (CMI), is a lecturer in the Faculty of Philosophy, Dharmaram Vidya Kshetram, Bengaluru.

He has two Masters' Degree (Physics and Philosophy) to his credit. He secured a Doctorate in Physics from Cochin University of Science and Technology. His areas of academic interest include Cosmology, Consciousness and Science-Religion Interface.

Ivan D'Souza (ivanmiyar@gmail.com) is a priest of the Diocese of Mangaluru, Karnataka. He has a doctorate in Indian Philosophy for the thesis "*Paramamukhyavṛtti* (Super-Primary Meaning) in *Dvaita Vedānta* of Madhva: A Hermeneutical Probe into its Scriptural Application and Significance" from Jnana-Deepa Vidyapeeth (JDV), Pune, India. He has M.A. in Philosophy from Indira Gandhi National Open University (IGNOU), M.A. in Kannada Literature from University of Kuvempu, Shivamogga (Karnataka), M.Ph from JDV, Pune. His field of interest is Indian Philosophy. He has been teaching in Pune, Ranchi and Mangaluru seminaries. At present, he is a staff at St. Joseph's Inter-diocesan Seminary, Mangaluru.

James Ponnaiah (jamesponniah@gmail.com) is Assistant Professor of the Department of Christian Studies. He was formerly the dean of the Faculty of Philosophy at Jnana Deepa Vidyapeeth, Pontifical Institute of Philosophy and Religion, Pune. He obtained both his M.A. (in Vaishnavism) and doctorate (on Sudalaimadan Cult) from the University of Madras. He was a visiting scholar for a year in the University of California, Berkeley. His areas of teaching and research include Indian religions, folk religions of India, Modern and Contemporary Indian Thinkers, Religion and Globalization, Popular Catholicism and Dalit Christianity. His publications include a monograph *The Dynamics of Folk Religion in Society: Pericentralisation as Deconstruction of Sanskritisation (2011).*He was a co-investigator with Chad Bauman (Butler University, USA) for the Project on '*Christianity, Religious Freedom, and Religious Violence in Contemporary India' funded by* Berkeley Centre for Religion, Peace and World Affairs, Washington. He was awarded Collabourative International Research Grant by American Academy of Religions in 2015. He won the best researcher's award for the year 2018 in the University of Madras.

Johnson J. Puthenpurackal, OFMCap (johnsonjp@rediffmail.com) is a specialist in the philosophy of Heidegger with a Ph.D. from the University of Louvain (Belgium). He is one of the pioneers of the 'Association of Christian Philosophers of India' (ACPI); he has been in its administration for almost twenty years as its President and Secretary. He was editorially responsible for several of its publications, and was the Editor-in-Chief of the two-volume *ACPI Encyclopedia of Philosophy*. He has delivered lectures in many Institutes, and presented Papers at numerous seminars. To his credit there are several studies published. Presently he is the President of 'Indian Capuchin Research Forum,' and Rector of *Brindisi Bhavan* (Capuchin Formation House for the students of Philosophy). He has been the President of *Vijnananilayam*: Institute of Philosophy and Religion (Eluru, A.P.), where he continues to be professor of philosophy for the last twenty-eight years.

Jojo Joseph Varakukalayil (varakoocst@gmail.com) a catholic priest belonging to Little Flower Congregation (CST Fathers), is a resident staff of the Little Flower Institute of Philosophy & Religion, Aluva, Kerala; and he serves as the President of the Institute. He holds MPh from JDV, Pune, MPhil and PhD in Philosophy from Husserl Archives at Katholeike University, Leuven, Belgium. He had his specialization in Phenomenology and Deconstructive philosophy. He is a visiting faculty at different Institutes and Faculties of Philosophy & Religion. He contributes scholarly articles to internationally and nationally peer-reviewed journals, book chapters and presents papers at conferences, seminars and workshops both in the International and national circles. He conducts seminars in the early Greek, Modern and Contemporary Continental Philosophical trends. His area of interests remains wide ranging to Philosophy, Science and Religion. His research domain ranges from modern to post-modern trends in philosophy, namely, post-metaphysical, post-deconstructive and post-secular philosophy starting with E. Husserl, M. Heidegger, E. Levinas, J. Derrida, J. M. Foucault, J. Lacan, H. Arendt, J. L. Marion, M. Henry, V. Jankelevitch, C. Taylor, and R. Kearney. He conducts motivational seminars and guidance programs for the youths and religious.

Jose D. Maliekal SDB, (jose.maleikal@gmail.com) belonging to the Salesian Province of Hyderabad, holds a doctorate in Subaltern Fundamental Theology, from the Department of Christian Studies, School of Philosophy and Religious Studies, University of Madras. He also has authored a book named 'Standstill Utopias? *Dalits Encountering Christianity'*, (ISPCK, Delhi, 2017), which won the James Massey Subaltern Studies Award from ISPCK, Delhi. He has co-edited two volumes, entitled, '*The Struggle for the Past: Historiography Today'*, (Department of Christian Studies, Madras, 2002) and *Hermeneutics truth or/and meaning: Philosophical Compendium* (St John's Regional Seminary, Kondadaba 1993) At present, he is the academic co-ordinator of St John's Regional Seminary (Institute of Philosophy, Religious Studies and Social Sciences), Kondadaba, Vizianagaram District, Andhra Pradesh, where he teaches systematic philosophy and social praxis. He brings to his long career as a teacher of philosophy, a transdisciplinary approach. His areas of research include subaltern perspectives on the production of knowledge, Dalit identities and empowerment, and the impact of religion on socio-economic transformation. He was in the Provincial Animation Team of the Province for nine years. He has presented several research papers from a Subaltern Perspective.

Jose Nandhikkara (nandhikkara@dvk.in) is Professor Philosophy, Dharmaram Vidya Kshetram (DVK), Bangalore, Chief Editor of the *Journal of Dharma*, Regional Director of Globethics.net India, and International Fellow of KAICIID, Vienna. He was formerly Dean of the Faculty of Philosophy at DVK, Director of the Centre for the Study of World Religions. He was a Visiting Fellow at University of Malaya, Kuala Lumpur, and KU University, Leuven, and Adjunct Professor at IIT Dhanbad. He is a Wittgenstinian scholar who contributes in the fields of Philosophical Anthropology, Ethics and Comparative Religion. He holds a Licentiate in Philosophy from Gregorian University, Rome, MA in Philosophy and Theology from Oxford University, and PhD in Philosophy from Warwick University, UK. Fr Jose has authored a book, edited five volumes, contributed over fifty research articles, and organised and presented research papers in the fields of Philosophy, Ethics and Religions in National and International Conferences.

Jose Pennaparambil (frpenjoe@gmail.com) member of the diocese of Thamarassery, at present of vicar of St. John's church Vadakara and the diocesan Director of Marian Pro-Life Movement. He has completed Masters degree in English from Kerala University. After ordination in 2000, he went for higher studies in Rome and secured Licentiate in Philosophy (Theory of Knowledge and Ethics) from Santa Croce University. He secured doctorate in 2015 January from Dharmaram Vidya Kshetram Bangalore, pertaining to Islamic Ethics. *(Terrorism Versus Justice - A philosophical Analysis of Islamic Fundamentalism and Terrorism on the basis of Rawlsian Principles of Justice).*

Keith D'Souza (keith@jesuits.net) is the Rector of St. Xavier's College, Mumbai. He teaches Philosophy and Religious Studies in several institutions. He has degrees in Science (B.Sc. in Physics), Theology (M.Th. in Systematic Theology) and Philosophy. He did his doctoral studies at Marquette University in Wisconsin, USA, with a specialization in philosophical hermeneutics (Hans Georg Gadamer and Paul Ricoeur). He has edited two books and published around forty journal articles in the areas of hermeneutical theory, socio-political philosophy and religious studies. He is a Vice-President of the Bombay Philosophical Society (based at Mumbai University) and the President of the Association of Christian Philosophers of India (ACPI).

Kuruvilla Pandikattu (kuru@jdv.edu.in) (born 1957-) is a professor of Physics, Philosophy and Religion at Jnana-Deepa Vidyapeeth, Pune, India. Currently, he is the Dean, Faculty of Philosophy. He has been actively involved in dialogue between science and religion. Author of more than 36 books and 160 articles, Pandikattu is a Jesuit priest belonging to Dumka-Raiganj Province, India. He has been involved in organising national and international conferences on science-religion dialogue. Main topics of his research are: anthropology, eschatology, life-management and transhumanism.

Lawrence Pius Dorairaj (dharmapuridiocese@gmail.com) is the Bishop of Dharmapuri diocese in Tamil Nadu. He completed M.A. (Philosophy) from Madras Christian College, Tambaram. In 1994 he acquired his Ph.D. in Gandhian Thought, from University of Sorbonne, Paris & Catholic Institute of Paris, France. He was the Dean of Philosophy and Vice Rector at Sacred Heart Seminary, Poonamallee. On 28th December 1998, he was nominated as the Auxiliary Bishop of Archdiocese of Madras-Mylapore. He held various responsibilities in TNBC and CCBI. He continues to be a visiting Professor at St. Peter's Pontifical Seminary, Bangalore and Good Shepherd Seminary, Coimbatore. He has Published two books, including his doctoral thesis on "Gandhi's Critique of Modern civilization" and several articles. He is also a regular contributor to the "New Leader."

Martin Sebastian Kallungal (frmartink@gmail.com) is a Catholic priest belonging to the Archdiocese of Ernakulam-Angamaly, Kerala. He holds a Masters and Doctorate in Philosophy from the Mahatma Gandhi University, Kottayam, Kerala; and, a Masters and Doctorate in Theology from the Catholic University of Leuven, Belgium. He teaches philosophy and theology at Pontifical Institute Alwaye where he also serves as the director of Licentiate Programme in Philosophy.

Nishant Alphonse Irudayadason (nishant@jdv.edu.in) is a professor of Philosophy and Ethics at Jnana-Deepa Vidyapeeth: Pontifical Institute of Philosophy and Religions (JDV), Pune, India. Having obtained two doctoral degrees in Ethics and Philosophy from Université Paris-Est and Insitut catholique de Paris, France, he has been actively pursuing academic life. He is also visiting faculty in many colleges and universities in India. He has presented research papers in many National and International Conferences. He has authored two books, edited two books and published many articles in National and International Journals as well as in edited books. He is a regular contributor to contemporary political analysis in "Light of Truth," a bimonthly published from Kochi, Kerala. He was the founding director of JDV centre for Applied Ethics and formerly chairperson of the Ph.D. programme in Philosophy at JDV from June 2011 to May 2017.

S. Stephen Jayard (sjayard@gmail.com) A Residential Faculty of Philosophy, JDV, Pune, since June 2008; Coordinator of the Masters' Programme and Head of the Dept. of Systematic Philosophy; Obtained Ph.D. in *Philosophy of Science*, at the Central University, Hyderabad, 2009; Undertaken the Postdoctoral research at Lonergan Research Institute, at Washington DC, Boston USA; and University of Toronto, Canada, 2011-12. Qualified

National Educational Testing of the UG, India, 2002 and awarded *Junior Research Fellowship* by the Indian Council for Philosophical Research, 2004. Published 7 books, including *Towards a Theory of Rationality in Science – A Plea for Reasonableness* (2012), *A Book that Cannot Be Titled* (2015) and *Ippadiyum Paarkalame* (Tamil, meaning *Can See This Way Also*), 2018. Obtained an award in the International Essay Competition, conducted by John Carroll University, USA. Published several research papers in the national and international journals and presented papers at the national and international conferences. Has been a visiting faculty at Sogang University, South Korea, International Institute of Information Technology (IIIT), Hyderabad, Symbiosis of School of Liberal Arts, Pune. A visiting faculty at several Institutes of Higher Education in India.

Sujan Amurutham (s.amurutham@yahoo.co.in) belongs to the Archdiocese of Trivandrum (Kerala). He obtained a Doctorate in Philosophy from the Santa Croce University, Rome in 2008, with *Summa Cum Laude*. He has a M.A. in Philosophy from Kerala University, with Second Rank, and UGC-NET in Philosophy. He Joined as a Resident Staff, at St Joseph Pontifical Seminary, Carmelgiri in 2008. He is teaching various subjects in philosophy, such as Political Philosophy, Modern Western Philosophy and Epistemology, at Pontifical Institute of Philosophy and Theology, Alwaye, since 2008. He has published a number of articles and made presentations in the areas of Aristotle's approach to education, Amartya Sen's idea of Development, Indian Communism and Philosophy of Peace and Development. Besides these, he has authored a book, namely, *Experiment of Elected Communist Government in India: E.M.S.*'s *Philosophical Contributions* (Trivandrum: Lourdu Publications, 2017) and edited another, entitled, *Faith and Culture: An Interdisciplinary Analysis* (Aluva: PIA Publications, 2016).

Varghese Chakkalakal (calicut_diocese@yahoo.com) is the Bishop of Calicut. He has an M.Th. from Pontifical Institute, Aluva, and a Masters in History, from Mysore University. He has secured his doctorate in Canon Law from the Urbanian University, Rome. He has authored a book in Malayalam called, *Ulporul* and has written many articles in various magazines in Malayalam, as well as, in English. He is a well-known retreat preacher and a versatile public speaker. He was on the visiting faculty of various seminaries and on the staff of Jeppu Seminary, Mangalore.

Victor Ferrao (victorferrao@yahoo.co.uk) is Dean of Philosophy at Rachol Seminary; coordinator of Special study Centre of IGNOU; columnist in the newspapers. Has Ph.D. in Philosophy of Science, written six books and has several research papers in peer reviewed journals. He has edited books. At present he is co-founder and director of Science Religion Sangam, Goa and actively involved in Science-Religion dialogue.

ACPI Books

Annual Series

1. The Postmodern: A Siege of the Citadel of Reason (2000)
2. Faith, Reason, Science: Philosophical Reflections with Special Referene to Fides et Ratio (2001)
3. The Constitution of India: A Philosophical Review (2002)
4. Truth, Power, Money: A Postmodern Reading (2003)
5. Philosophical Methods: Through the Prevalent to a Relevant (2004)
6. Subaltern Perspectives: Philosophizing in Context (2005)
7. Pluralism of Pluralism: A Pluralistic Probe into Philosophizing (2006)
8. Romancing the Sacred?: Towards an Indian Christian Philosophy of Religion (2007)
9. Culture as Gift and Task: Philosophical Reflections in the Indian Context (2008)
10. Enigma of Indian Tribal Life and Culture: Philosophical Investigations (2009)
11. Violence and Its Victims: A Challenge to Philosophizing in the Indian Context (2010)
12. Tradition and Innovation: Philosophy of Rootedness and Openness (2011)
13. History and Historizing: Philosophical Reflections (2012)
14. Identity, Difference and Conflict: Postcolonial Critique (2013)
15. The Dynamics of Development: Negations and Negotiations (2014)
16. The Symbolic World: Constructions and Re-Constructions (2015)
17. Philosophizing the Body: Physical, Social, Psychosomatic & Spiritual Dimensions (2016)
18. Becoming a Nation: Processes and Prospects (2017)
19. Indian Hermeneutics of Suspicion (2018)
20. Philosophies of Transformative Practice: Social Movements in India (2019)

Special Series

1. ACPI Encyclopedia of Philosophy, 2 Vols (2010)
2. Authentic Existence: A Philosophical Probe (2012)
3. Raimon Panikkar: Becoming Beyond Borders - A Commemorative Volume (2012)
4. Enhancing Our Home: Re-Claiming and Re-Reading Gandhian Thought (2016)

Index